W9-AFT-291

WRITERS:
CHRISTOS GAGE, MARC SUMERAK, CHRIS CLAREMONT, ROGER STERN & DOUG MOENCH WITH **ALEX ZALBEN & JOHN BYRNE**

PENCILERS:
ANDREA DiVITO, SANFORD GREENE, JHEREMY RAAPACK, JOHN BYRNE & WALTER SIMONSON WITH **JOYCE CHIN**

INKERS:
ANDREA DiVITO, VICTOR OLAZABA, LARRY WELCH, BOB LAYTON & ALFREDO ALCALA WITH **VICENTE CIFUENTES**

★ ★ ★

COLORISTS:
LAURA VILLARI, JANICE COHEN, CHRIS SOTOMAYOR & SOTOCOLOR'S CHRIS GARCIA WITH **ANDREW CROSSLEY**

LETTERERS:
ED DUKESHIRE, JIM NOVAK, IRVING WATANABE & VIRTUAL CALLIGRAPHY'S JOE CARAMAGNA

COVER ARTISTS:
ED McGUINNESS, DEXTER VINES & DAVE McCAIG; MICHAEL GOLDEN; DAVID YARDIN & WIL QUINTANA; JOHN BYRNE & BOB LAYTON; AND **KEN BARR**

PRODUCTION:
RICH GINTER & BRAD JOHANSEN WITH **PAUL ACERIOS**

ASSISTANT EDITORS: **WILL PANZO, JORDAN D. WHITE, CHARLIE BECKERMAN & RALPH MACCHIO** WITH **LEN WEIN & ROY THOMAS**

EDITORS: **ANDY SCHMIDT, NICK LOWE, MARK PANICCIA, BOB HALL & JOHN WARNER**

★★

BOOK COVERS: **ED McGUINNESS, DEXTER VINES & DAVE McCAIG**

★★

COLLECTION EDITOR: **MARK D. BEAZLEY** ★ DIGITAL TRAFFIC COORDINATOR: **JOE HOCHSTEIN**
ASSOCIATE MANAGING EDITOR: **ALEX STARBUCK** ★ EDITOR, SPECIAL PROJECTS: **JENNIFER GRÜNWALD**
SENIOR EDITOR, SPECIAL PROJECTS: **JEFF YOUNGQUIST**
RESEARCH & LAYOUT: **JEPH YORK** ★ BOOK DESIGNER: **RODOLFO MURAGUCHI**
SVP PRINT, SALES & MARKETING: **DAVID GABRIEL**

EDITOR IN CHIEF: **AXEL ALONSO** ★ CHIEF CREATIVE OFFICER: **JOE QUESADA**
PUBLISHER: **DAN BUCKLEY** ★ EXECUTIVE PRODUCER: **ALAN FINE**

★ SPECIAL THANKS TO **MIKE HANSEN** ★

X-MEN VS. HULK. Contains material originally published in magazine form as WORLD WAR HULK: X-MEN #1-3, HULK TEAM-UP #1, X-MEN VS. HULK #1, INCREDIBLE HULK ANNUAL #7 and RAMPAGING HULK #2. First printing 2014. ISBN# 978-0-7851-8902-2. Published by MARVEL WORLDWIDE, INC., a subsidiary of MARVEL ENTERTAINMENT, LLC. OFFICE OF PUBLICATION: 135 West 50th Street, New York, NY 10020. Copyright © 1977, 1978, 2007, 2009 and 2014 Marvel Characters, Inc. All rights reserved. All characters featured in this issue and the distinctive names and likenesses thereof, and all related indicia are trademarks of Marvel Characters, Inc. No similarity between any of the names, characters, persons, and/or institutions in this magazine with those of any living or dead person or institution is intended, and any such similarity which may exist is purely coincidental. **Printed in Canada.** ALAN FINE, EVP - Office of the President, Marvel Worldwide, Inc. and EVP & CMO Marvel Characters B.V.; DAN BUCKLEY, Publisher & President - Print, Animation & Digital Divisions; JOE QUESADA, Chief Creative Officer; TOM BREVOORT, SVP of Publishing; DAVID BOGART, SVP of Operations & Procurement, Publishing; C.B. CEBULSKI, SVP of Creator & Content Development; DAVID GABRIEL, SVP Print, Sales & Marketing; JIM O'KEEFE, VP of Operations & Logistics; DAN CARR, Executive Director of Publishing Technology; SUSAN CRESPI, Editorial Operations Manager; ALEX MORALES, Publishing Operations Manager; STAN LEE, Chairman Emeritus. For information regarding advertising in Marvel Comics or on Marvel.com, please contact Niza Disla, Director of Marvel Partnerships, at ndisla@marvel.com. For Marvel subscription inquiries, please call 800-217-9158. **Manufactured between 3/14/2014 and 4/21/2014 by SOLISCO PRINTERS, SCOTT, QC, CANADA.**

10 9 8 7 6 5 4 3 2 1

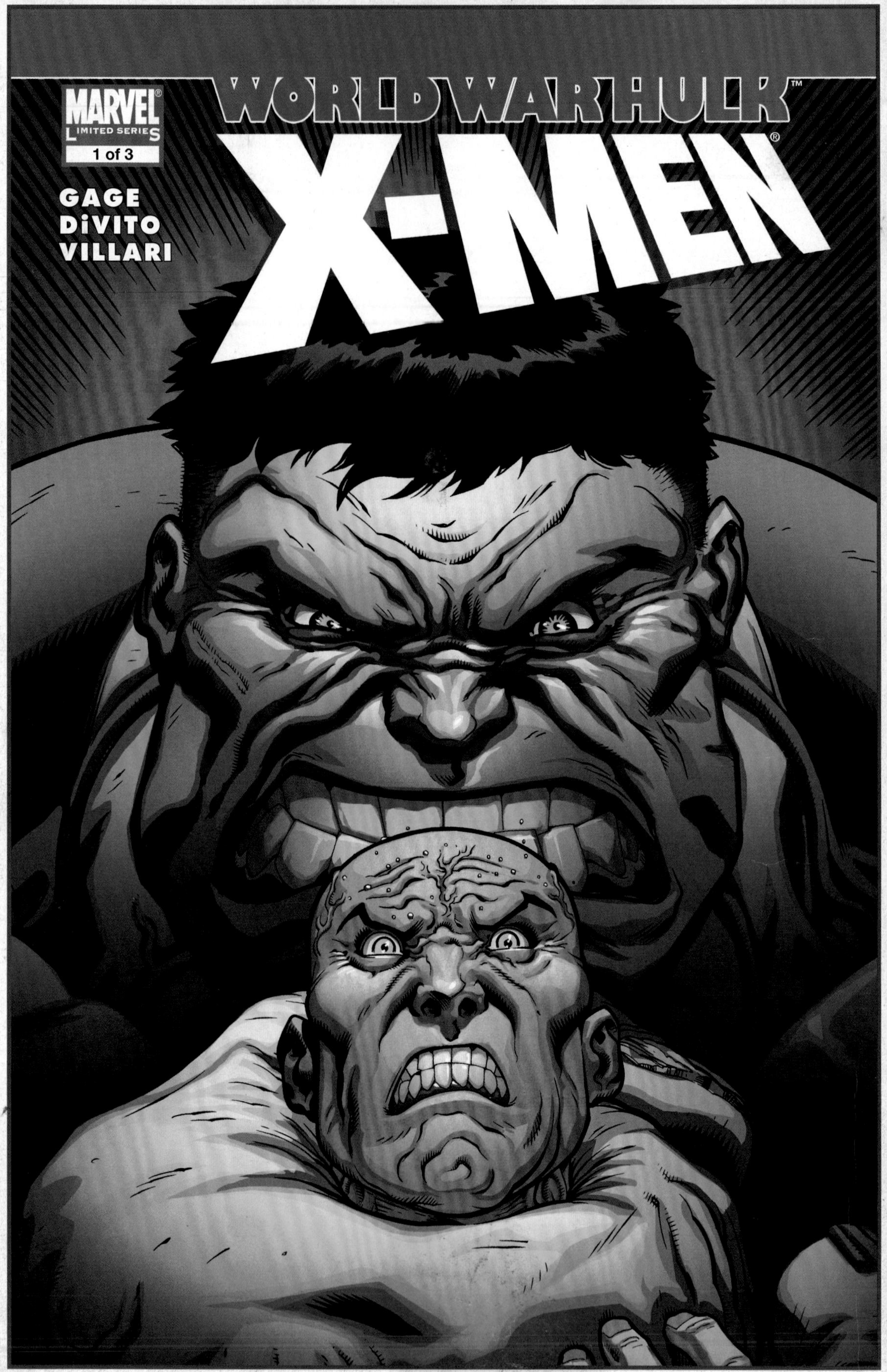
MARVEL
LIMITED SERIES
1 of 3
WORLD WAR HULK
X-MEN
GAGE
DiVITO
VILLARI

★★★ ROUND 1 ★★★

Born with genetic mutations that give them abilities beyond those of normal humans, mutants are the next stage in evolution. As such, they are feared and hated by humanity. But a group of mutants known as the X-MEN fight for peaceful coexistence between mutants and humankind.

While trying to save the life of an innocent, Dr. Bruce Banner was caught in the blast of a Gamma Bomb and became The Incredible Hulk.

WORLD WAR HULK: X-MEN

Recently the Illuminati, comprised of Mr. Fantastic, Iron Man, Dr. Strange, Black Bolt and Namor, sent Hulk to space where, unbeknownst to them, he crashed on the alien world of Sakaar. There, he became emperor and took a queen. Later, his ship exploded and destroyed everyone he cared about. The Hulk blames the Illuminati.

When the Illuminati voted to send the Hulk into space, one of their members -- Professor Charles Xavier, founder of the X-Men -- was not present. But does that absolve him of all guilt?

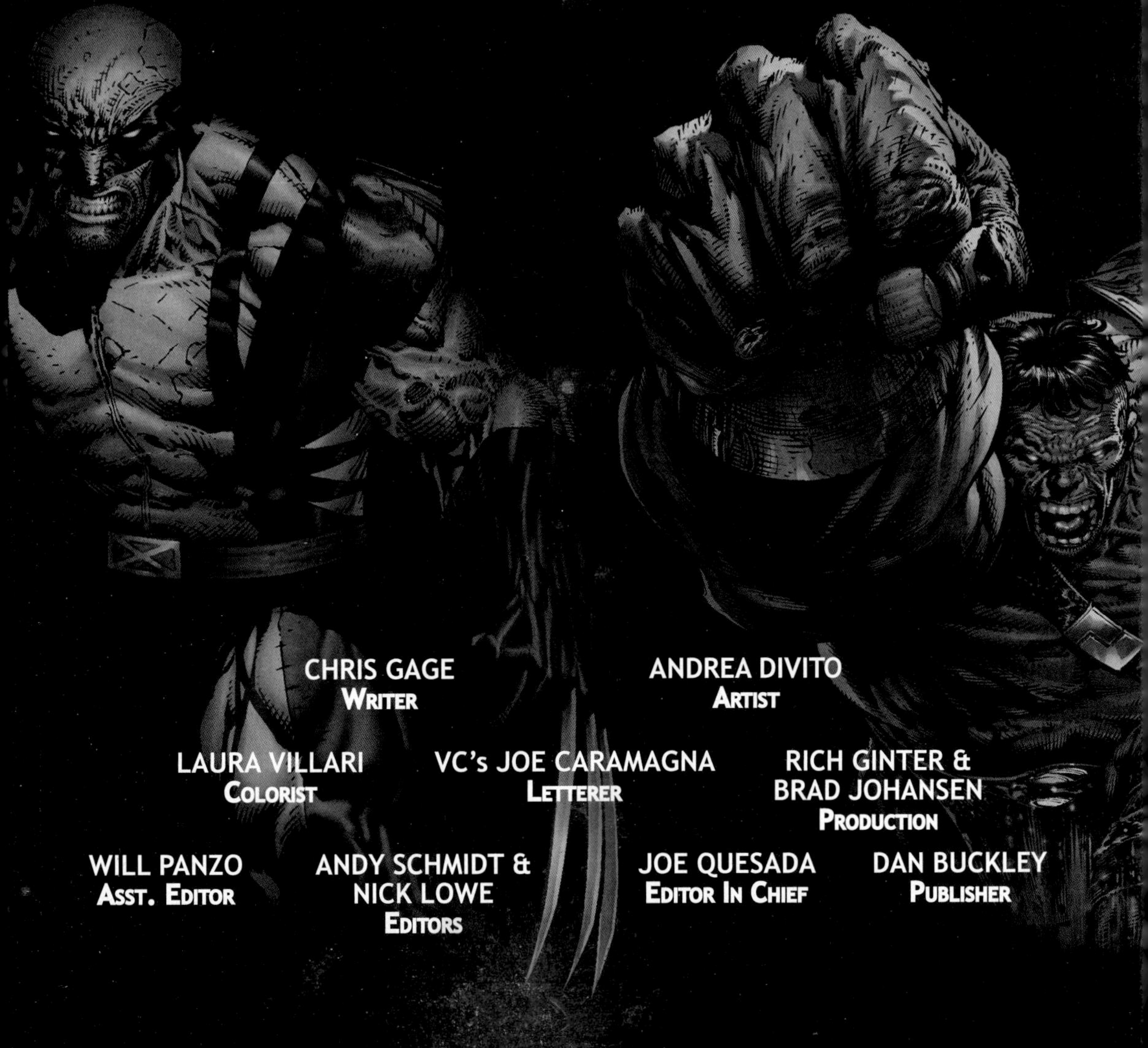

CHRIS GAGE
WRITER

ANDREA DIVITO
ARTIST

LAURA VILLARI
COLORIST

VC's JOE CARAMAGNA
LETTERER

RICH GINTER & BRAD JOHANSEN
PRODUCTION

WILL PANZO
ASST. EDITOR

ANDY SCHMIDT & NICK LOWE
EDITORS

JOE QUESADA
EDITOR IN CHIEF

DAN BUCKLEY
PUBLISHER

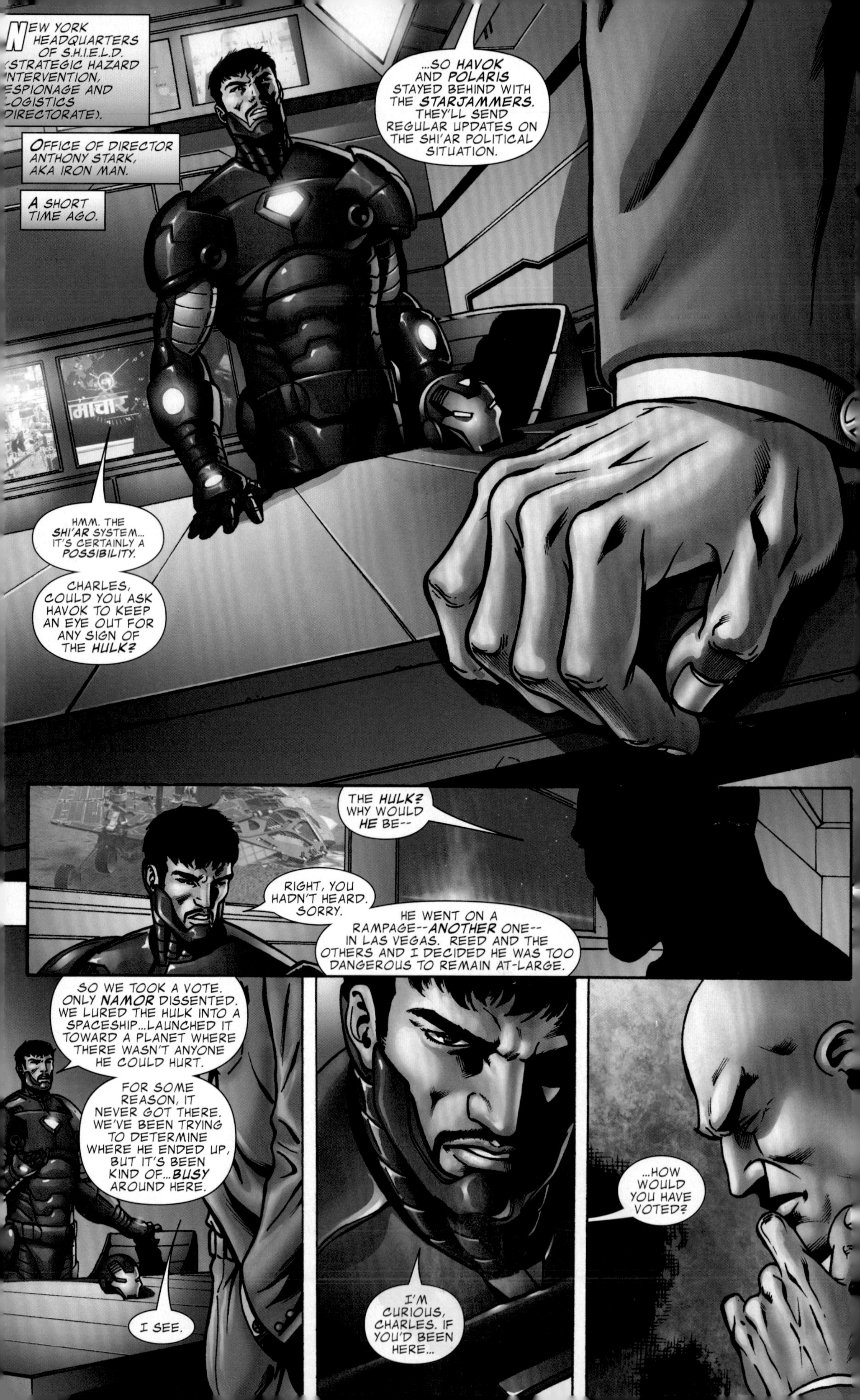
NEW YORK HEADQUARTERS OF S.H.I.E.L.D. (STRATEGIC HAZARD INTERVENTION, ESPIONAGE AND LOGISTICS DIRECTORATE).
OFFICE OF DIRECTOR ANTHONY STARK, AKA IRON MAN.
A SHORT TIME AGO.
...SO HAVOK AND POLARIS STAYED BEHIND WITH THE STARJAMMERS. THEY'LL SEND REGULAR UPDATES ON THE SHI'AR POLITICAL SITUATION.
HMM. THE SHI'AR SYSTEM... IT'S CERTAINLY A POSSIBILITY.
CHARLES, COULD YOU ASK HAVOK TO KEEP AN EYE OUT FOR ANY SIGN OF THE HULK?
THE HULK? WHY WOULD HE BE--
RIGHT, YOU HADN'T HEARD. SORRY.
HE WENT ON A RAMPAGE--ANOTHER ONE--IN LAS VEGAS. REED AND THE OTHERS AND I DECIDED HE WAS TOO DANGEROUS TO REMAIN AT-LARGE.
SO WE TOOK A VOTE. ONLY NAMOR DISSENTED. WE LURED THE HULK INTO A SPACESHIP...LAUNCHED IT TOWARD A PLANET WHERE THERE WASN'T ANYONE HE COULD HURT.
FOR SOME REASON, IT NEVER GOT THERE. WE'VE BEEN TRYING TO DETERMINE WHERE HE ENDED UP, BUT IT'S BEEN KIND OF...BUSY AROUND HERE.
I SEE.
I'M CURIOUS, CHARLES. IF YOU'D BEEN HERE...
...HOW WOULD YOU HAVE VOTED?

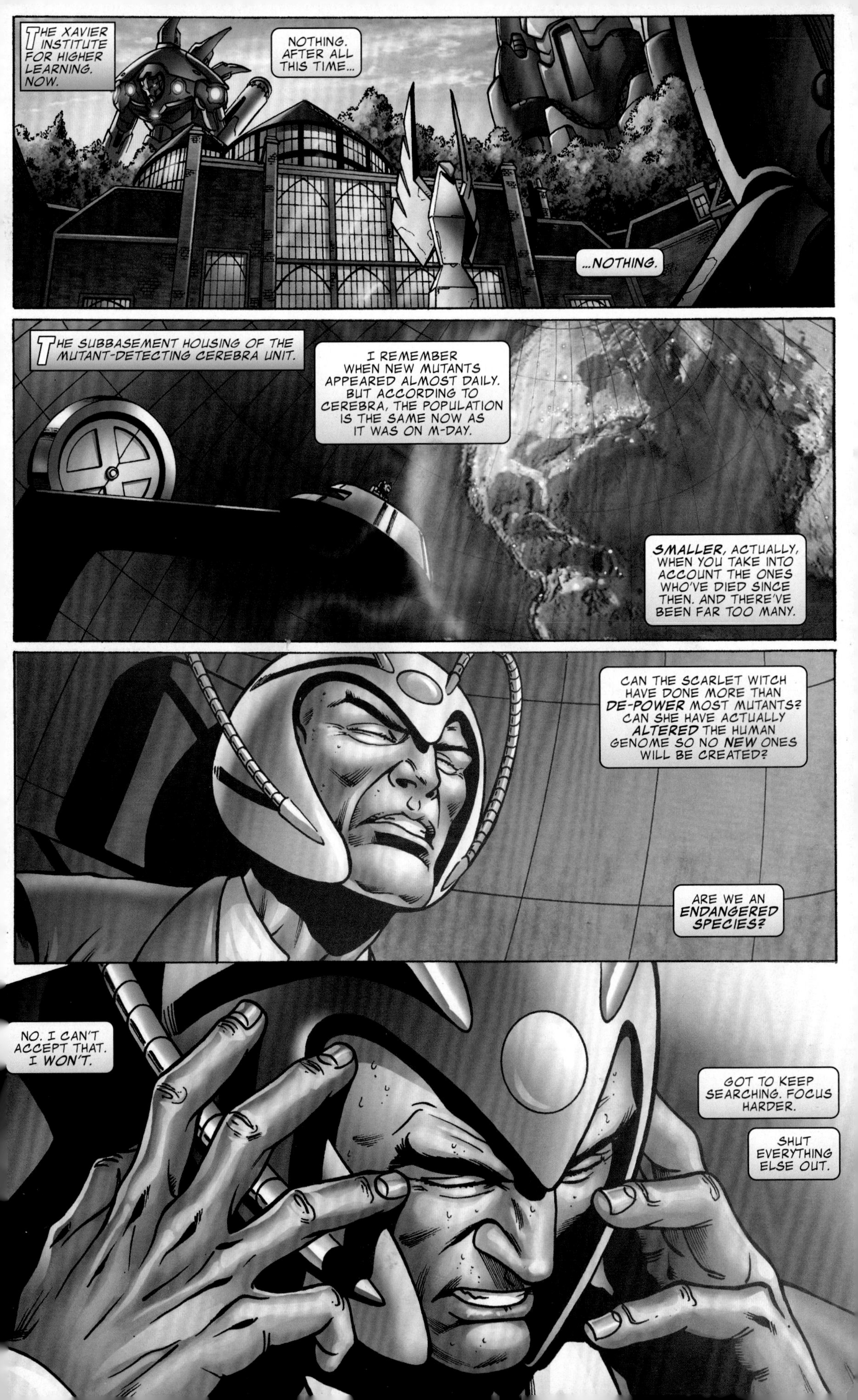
THE XAVIER INSTITUTE FOR HIGHER LEARNING. NOW.
NOTHING. AFTER ALL THIS TIME...
...NOTHING.
THE SUBBASEMENT HOUSING OF THE MUTANT-DETECTING CEREBRA UNIT.
I REMEMBER WHEN NEW MUTANTS APPEARED ALMOST DAILY. BUT ACCORDING TO CEREBRA, THE POPULATION IS THE SAME NOW AS IT WAS ON M-DAY.
SMALLER, ACTUALLY, WHEN YOU TAKE INTO ACCOUNT THE ONES WHO'VE DIED SINCE THEN. AND THERE'VE BEEN FAR TOO MANY.
CAN THE SCARLET WITCH HAVE DONE MORE THAN DE-POWER MOST MUTANTS? CAN SHE HAVE ACTUALLY ALTERED THE HUMAN GENOME SO NO NEW ONES WILL BE CREATED?
ARE WE AN ENDANGERED SPECIES?
NO. I CAN'T ACCEPT THAT. I WON'T.
GOT TO KEEP SEARCHING. FOCUS HARDER.
SHUT EVERYTHING ELSE OUT.

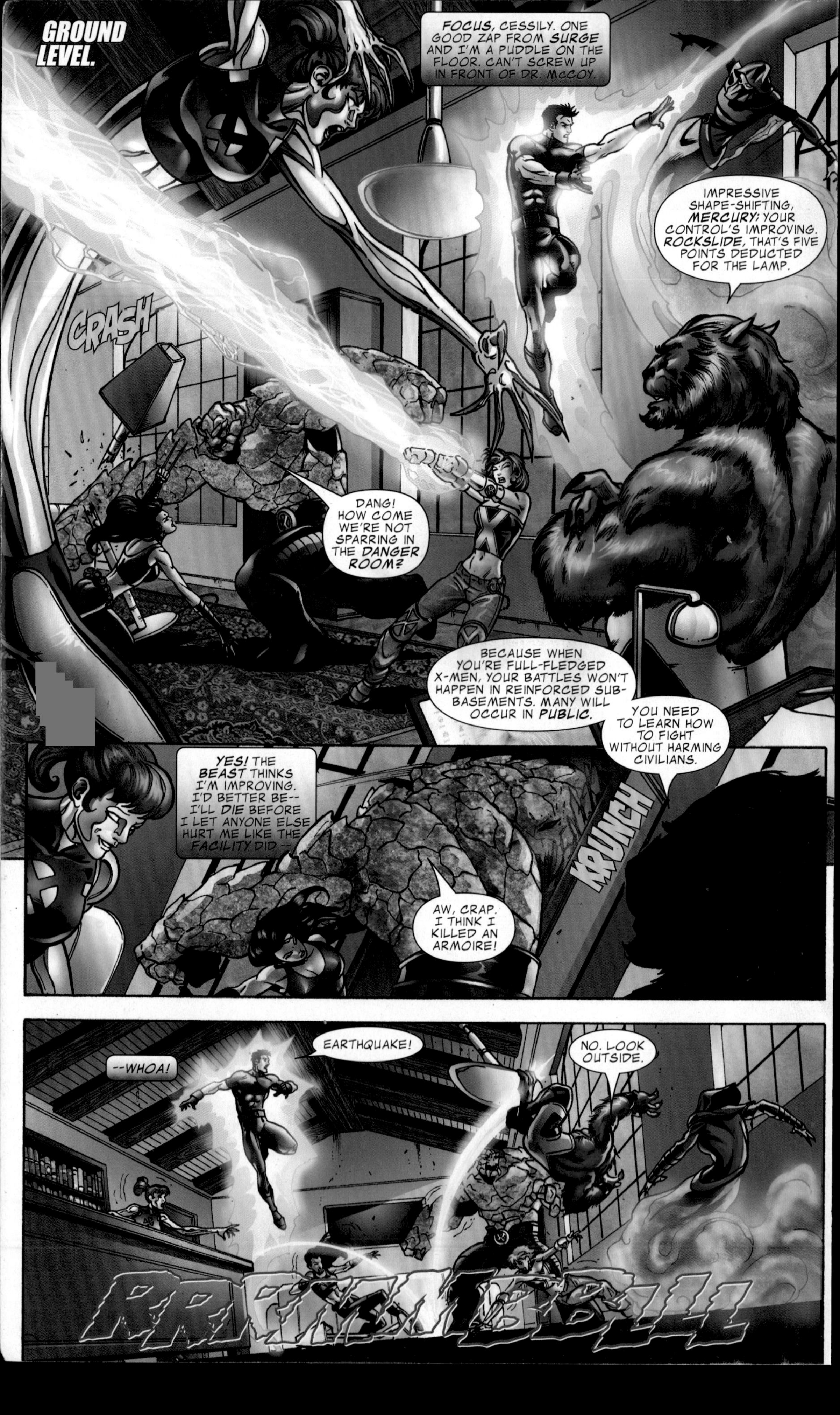
GROUND LEVEL.
FOCUS, CESSILY. ONE GOOD ZAP FROM SURGE AND I'M A PUDDLE ON THE FLOOR. CAN'T SCREW UP IN FRONT OF DR. McCOY.
IMPRESSIVE SHAPE-SHIFTING, MERCURY; YOUR CONTROL'S IMPROVING. ROCKSLIDE, THAT'S FIVE POINTS DEDUCTED FOR THE LAMP.
CRASH
DANG! HOW COME WE'RE NOT SPARRING IN THE DANGER ROOM?
BECAUSE WHEN YOU'RE FULL-FLEDGED X-MEN, YOUR BATTLES WON'T HAPPEN IN REINFORCED SUB-BASEMENTS. MANY WILL OCCUR IN PUBLIC.
YOU NEED TO LEARN HOW TO FIGHT WITHOUT HARMING CIVILIANS.
YES! THE BEAST THINKS I'M IMPROVING. I'D BETTER BE-- I'LL DIE BEFORE I LET ANYONE ELSE HURT ME LIKE THE FACILITY DID--
KRUNCH
AW, CRAP. I THINK I KILLED AN ARMOIRE!
--WHOA!
EARTHQUAKE!
NO. LOOK OUTSIDE.

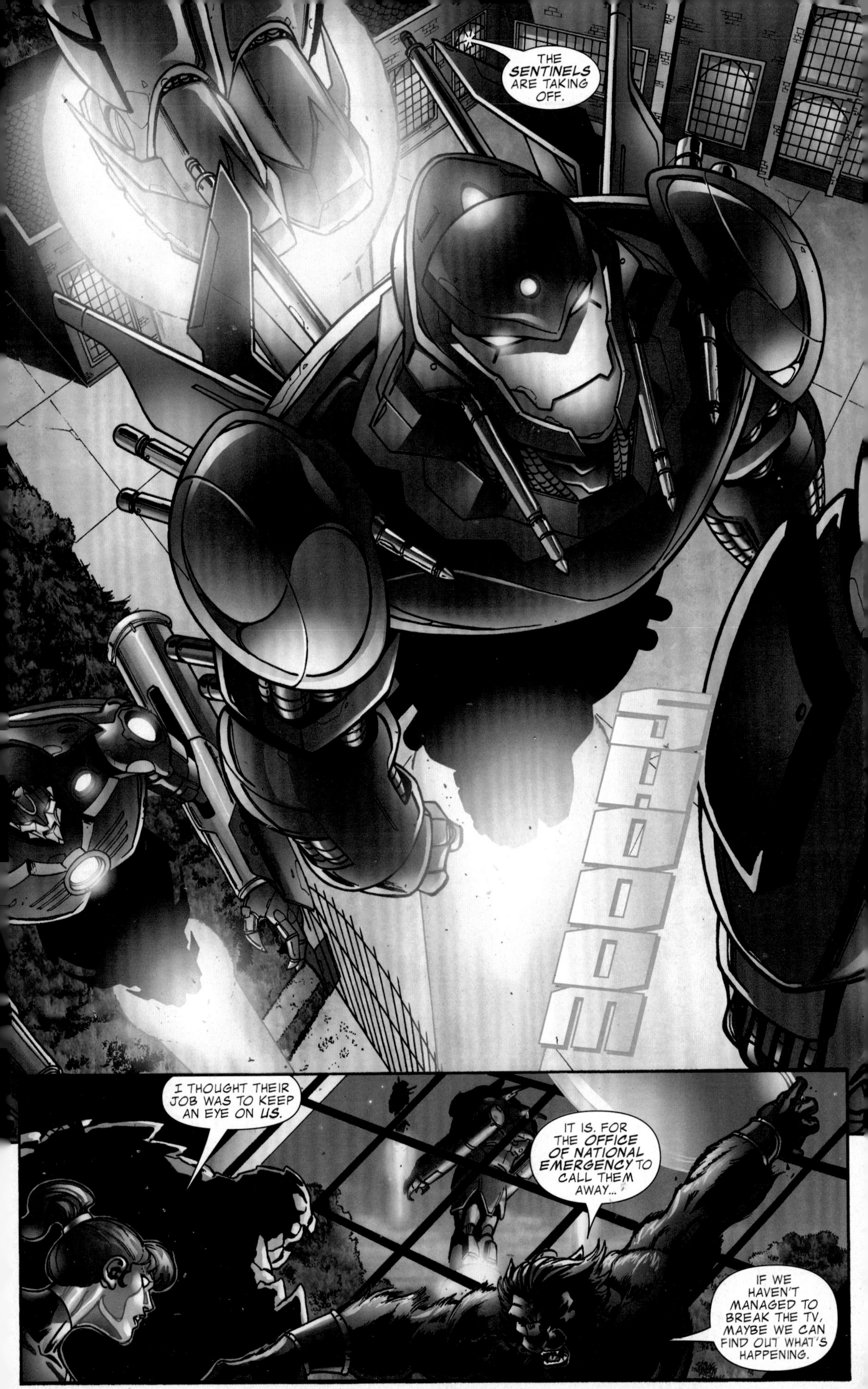
THE SENTINELS ARE TAKING OFF.
I THOUGHT THEIR JOB WAS TO KEEP AN EYE ON US.
IT IS. FOR THE OFFICE OF NATIONAL EMERGENCY TO CALL THEM AWAY...
IF WE HAVEN'T MANAGED TO BREAK THE TV, MAYBE WE CAN FIND OUT WHAT'S HAPPENING.

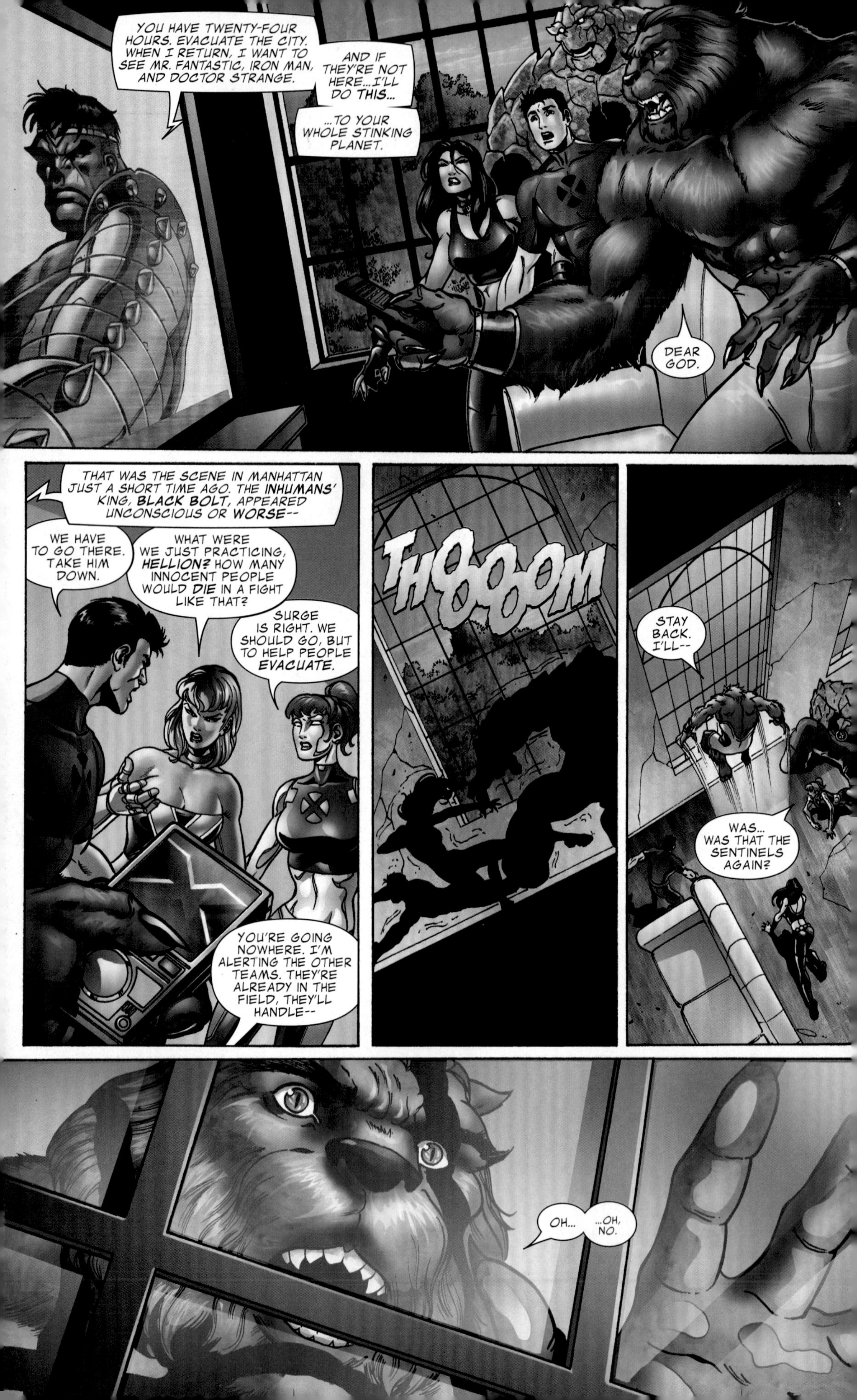
YOU HAVE TWENTY-FOUR HOURS. EVACUATE THE CITY. WHEN I RETURN, I WANT TO SEE MR. FANTASTIC, IRON MAN, AND DOCTOR STRANGE.
AND IF THEY'RE NOT HERE...I'LL DO THIS...
...TO YOUR WHOLE STINKING PLANET.
DEAR GOD.
THAT WAS THE SCENE IN MANHATTAN JUST A SHORT TIME AGO. THE INHUMANS' KING, BLACK BOLT, APPEARED UNCONSCIOUS OR WORSE--
WE HAVE TO GO THERE. TAKE HIM DOWN.
WHAT WERE WE JUST PRACTICING, HELLION? HOW MANY INNOCENT PEOPLE WOULD DIE IN A FIGHT LIKE THAT?
SURGE IS RIGHT. WE SHOULD GO, BUT TO HELP PEOPLE EVACUATE.
YOU'RE GOING NOWHERE. I'M ALERTING THE OTHER TEAMS. THEY'RE ALREADY IN THE FIELD, THEY'LL HANDLE--
THOOOOM
STAY BACK. I'LL--
WAS... WAS THAT THE SENTINELS AGAIN?
OH...
...OH, NO.

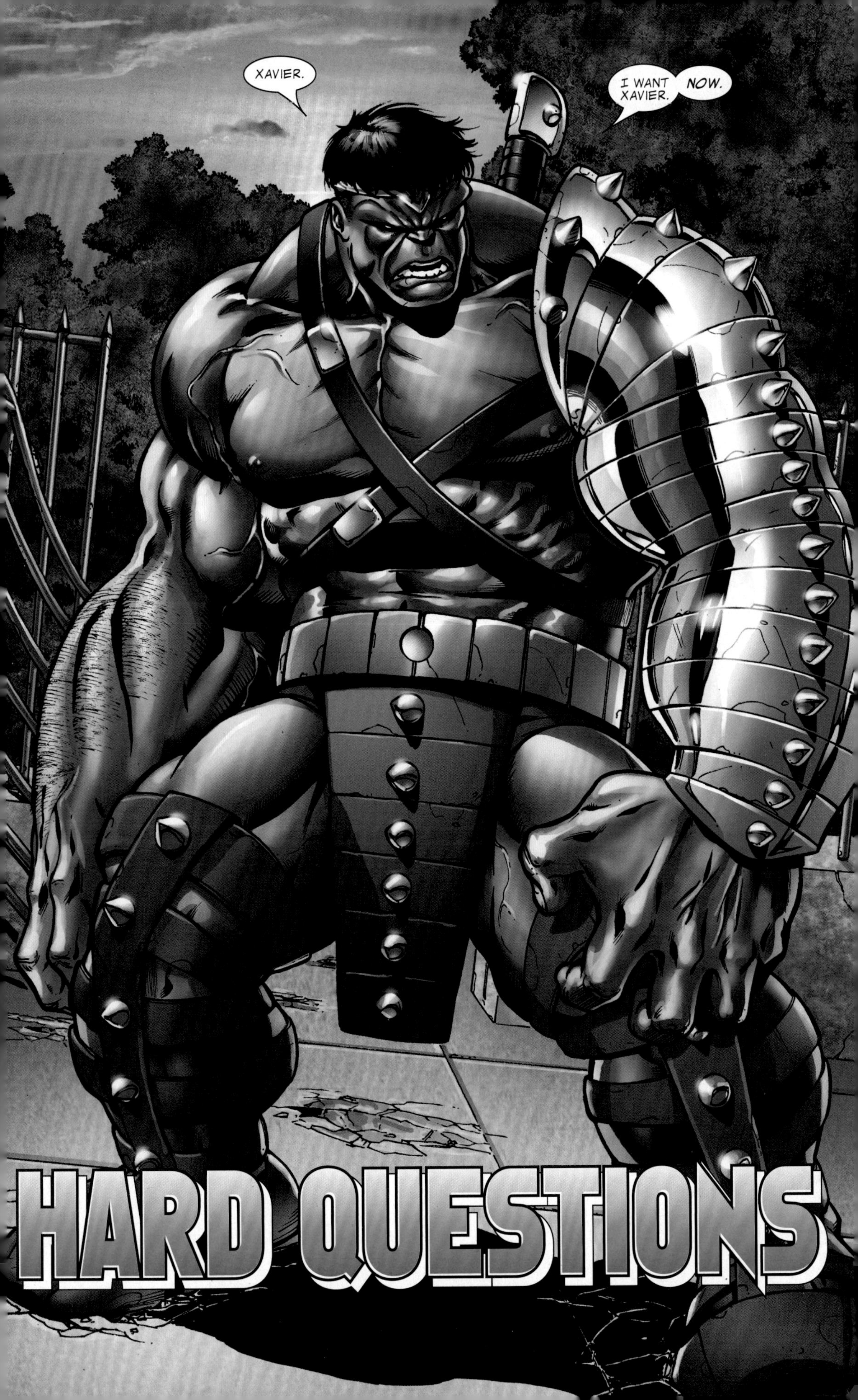
XAVIER.
I WANT XAVIER.
NOW.
HARD QUESTIONS

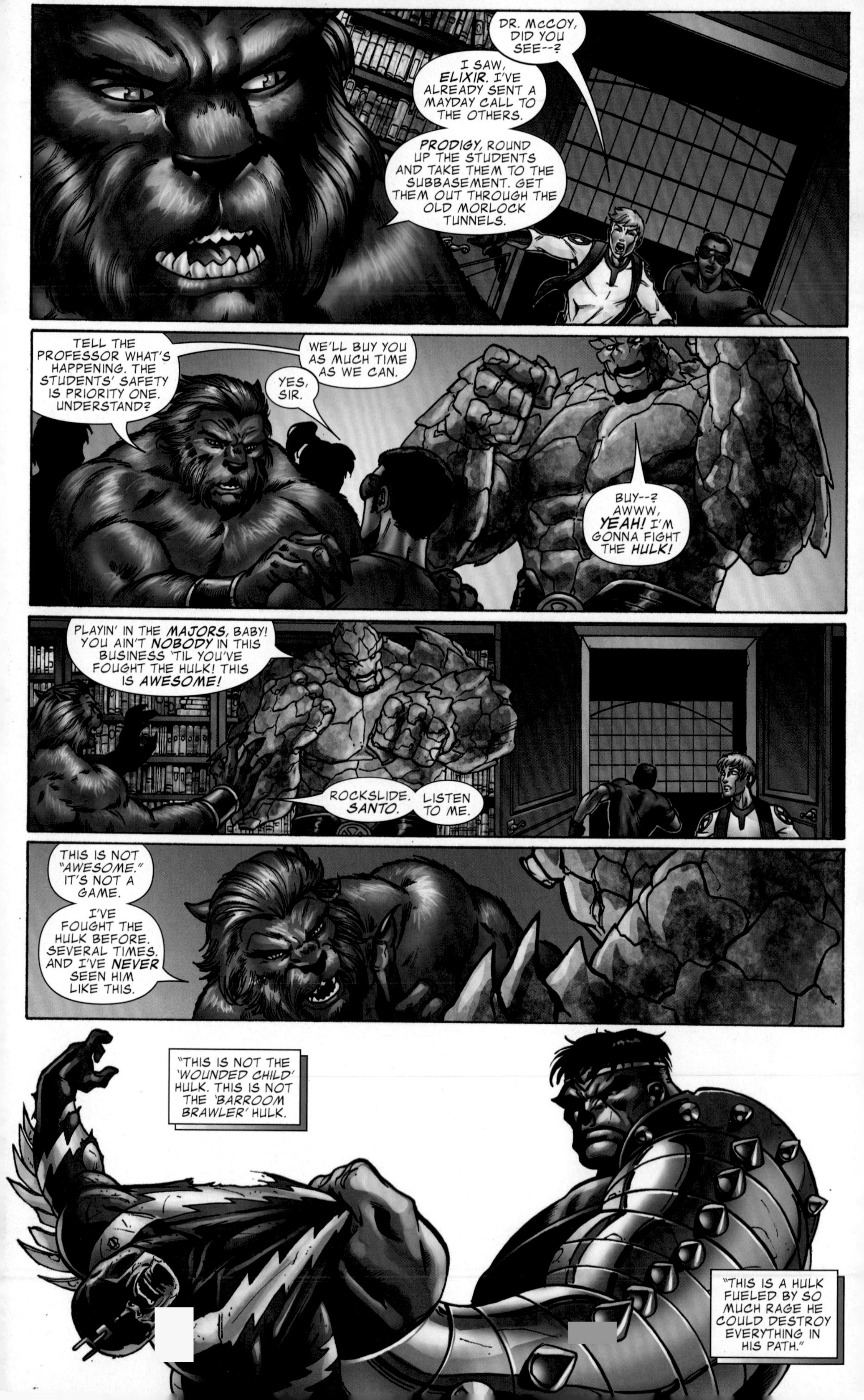
DR. McCOY, DID YOU SEE--?
I SAW, ELIXIR. I'VE ALREADY SENT A MAYDAY CALL TO THE OTHERS.
PRODIGY, ROUND UP THE STUDENTS AND TAKE THEM TO THE SUBBASEMENT. GET THEM OUT THROUGH THE OLD MORLOCK TUNNELS.
TELL THE PROFESSOR WHAT'S HAPPENING. THE STUDENTS' SAFETY IS PRIORITY ONE. UNDERSTAND?
WE'LL BUY YOU AS MUCH TIME AS WE CAN.
YES, SIR.
BUY--? AWWW, YEAH! I'M GONNA FIGHT THE HULK!
PLAYIN' IN THE MAJORS, BABY! YOU AIN'T NOBODY IN THIS BUSINESS 'TIL YOU'VE FOUGHT THE HULK! THIS IS AWESOME!
ROCKSLIDE. SANTO.
LISTEN TO ME.
THIS IS NOT "AWESOME." IT'S NOT A GAME.
I'VE FOUGHT THE HULK BEFORE. SEVERAL TIMES. AND I'VE NEVER SEEN HIM LIKE THIS.
"THIS IS NOT THE 'WOUNDED CHILD' HULK. THIS IS NOT THE 'BARROOM BRAWLER' HULK.
"THIS IS A HULK FUELED BY SO MUCH RAGE HE COULD DESTROY EVERYTHING IN HIS PATH."

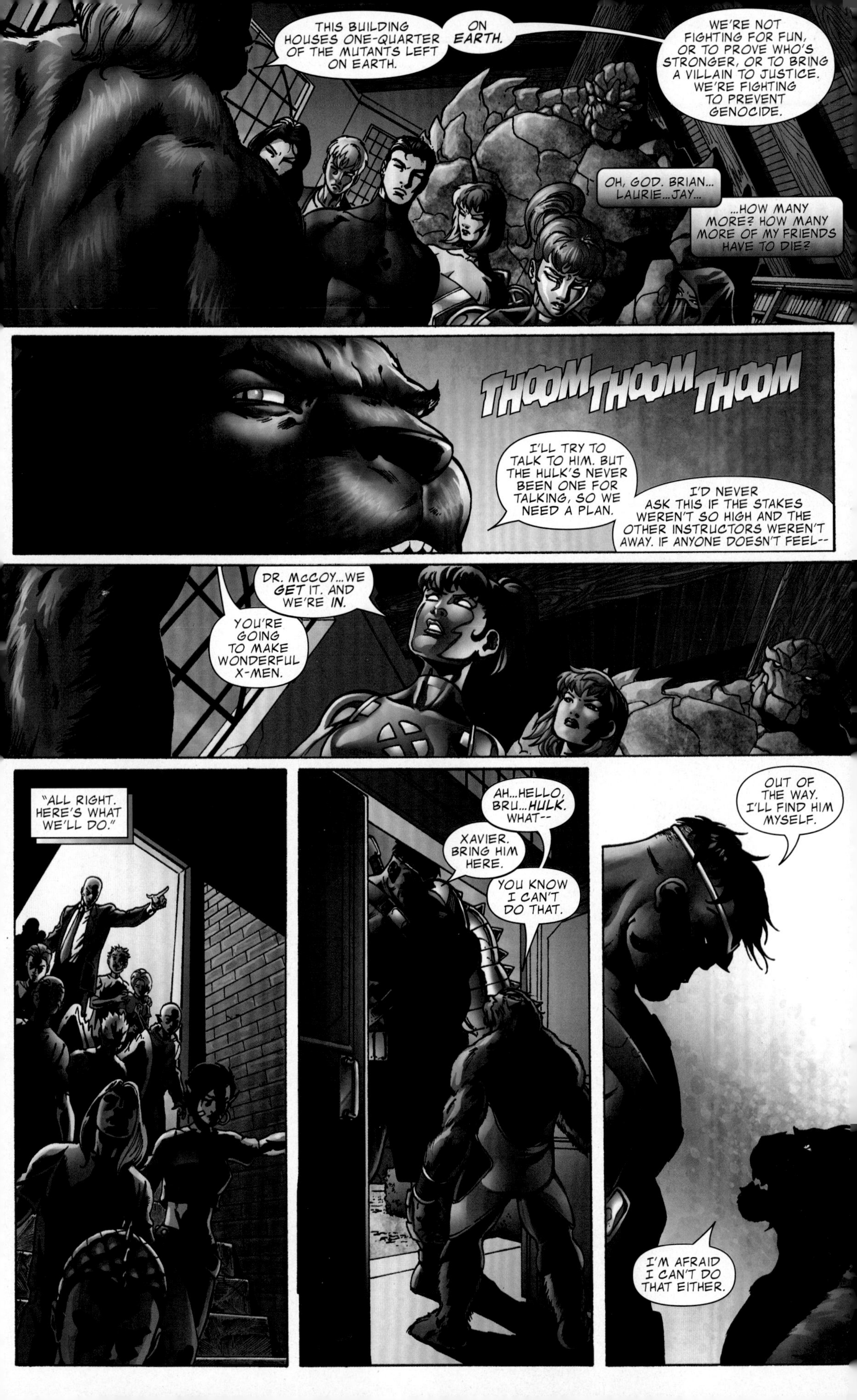
THIS BUILDING HOUSES ONE-QUARTER OF THE MUTANTS LEFT ON EARTH.
ON EARTH.
WE'RE NOT FIGHTING FOR FUN, OR TO PROVE WHO'S STRONGER, OR TO BRING A VILLAIN TO JUSTICE. WE'RE FIGHTING TO PREVENT GENOCIDE.
OH, GOD. BRIAN... LAURIE...JAY...
...HOW MANY MORE? HOW MANY MORE OF MY FRIENDS HAVE TO DIE?
THOOM THOOM THOOM
I'LL TRY TO TALK TO HIM. BUT THE HULK'S NEVER BEEN ONE FOR TALKING, SO WE NEED A PLAN.
I'D NEVER ASK THIS IF THE STAKES WEREN'T SO HIGH AND THE OTHER INSTRUCTORS WEREN'T AWAY. IF ANYONE DOESN'T FEEL--
DR. McCOY...WE GET IT. AND WE'RE IN.
YOU'RE GOING TO MAKE WONDERFUL X-MEN.
"ALL RIGHT. HERE'S WHAT WE'LL DO."
AH...HELLO, BRU...HULK. WHAT--
XAVIER. BRING HIM HERE.
YOU KNOW I CAN'T DO THAT.
OUT OF THE WAY. I'LL FIND HIM MYSELF.
I'M AFRAID I CAN'T DO THAT EITHER.

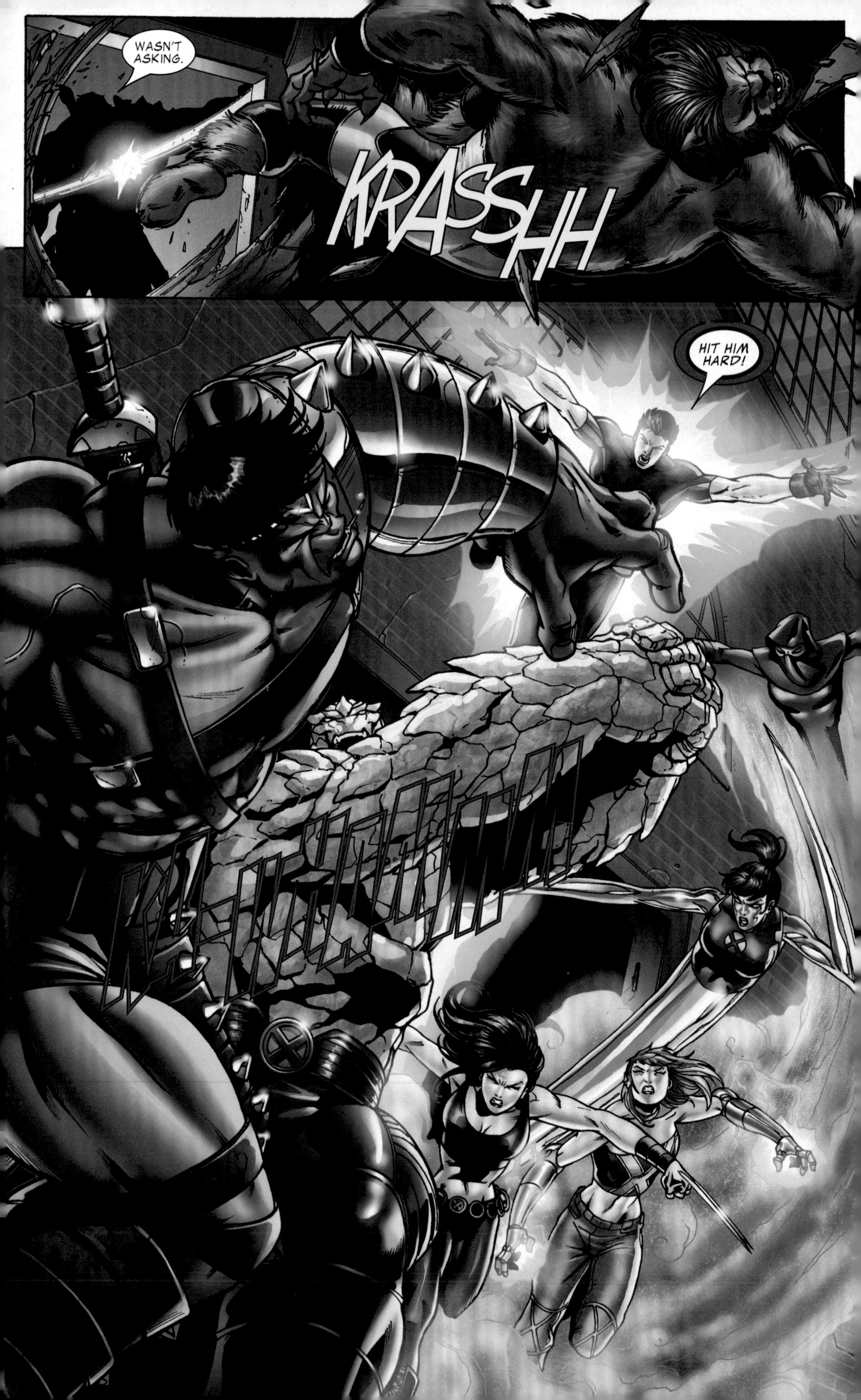
WASN'T ASKING.
KRASSHH
HIT HIM HARD!

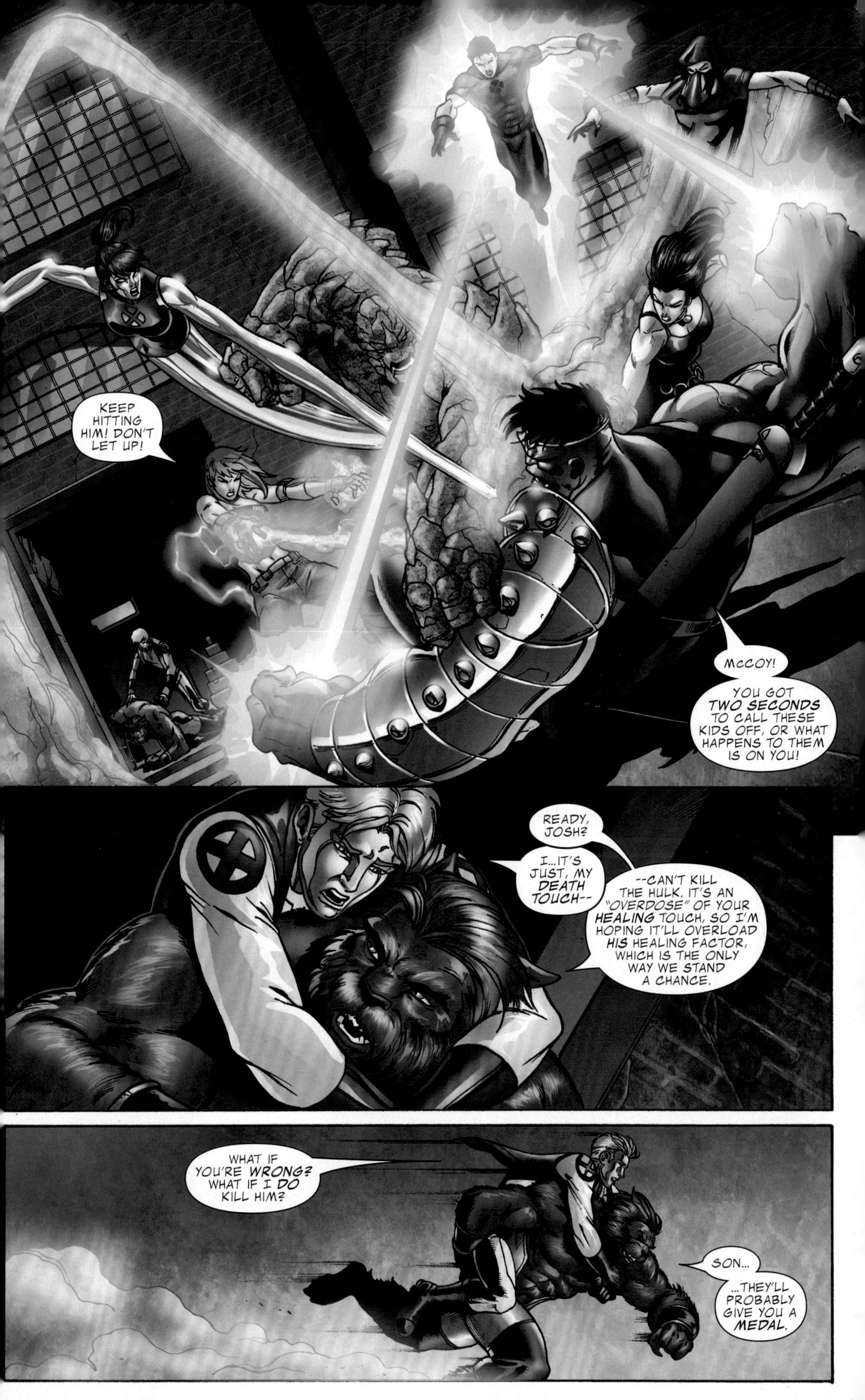
KEEP HITTING HIM! DON'T LET UP!
McCOY!
YOU GOT TWO SECONDS TO CALL THESE KIDS OFF, OR WHAT HAPPENS TO THEM IS ON YOU!
READY, JOSH?
I...IT'S JUST, MY DEATH TOUCH--
--CAN'T KILL THE HULK. IT'S AN "OVERDOSE" OF YOUR HEALING TOUCH, SO I'M HOPING IT'LL OVERLOAD HIS HEALING FACTOR, WHICH IS THE ONLY WAY WE STAND A CHANCE.
WHAT IF YOU'RE WRONG? WHAT IF I DO KILL HIM?
SON...
...THEY'LL PROBABLY GIVE YOU A MEDAL.

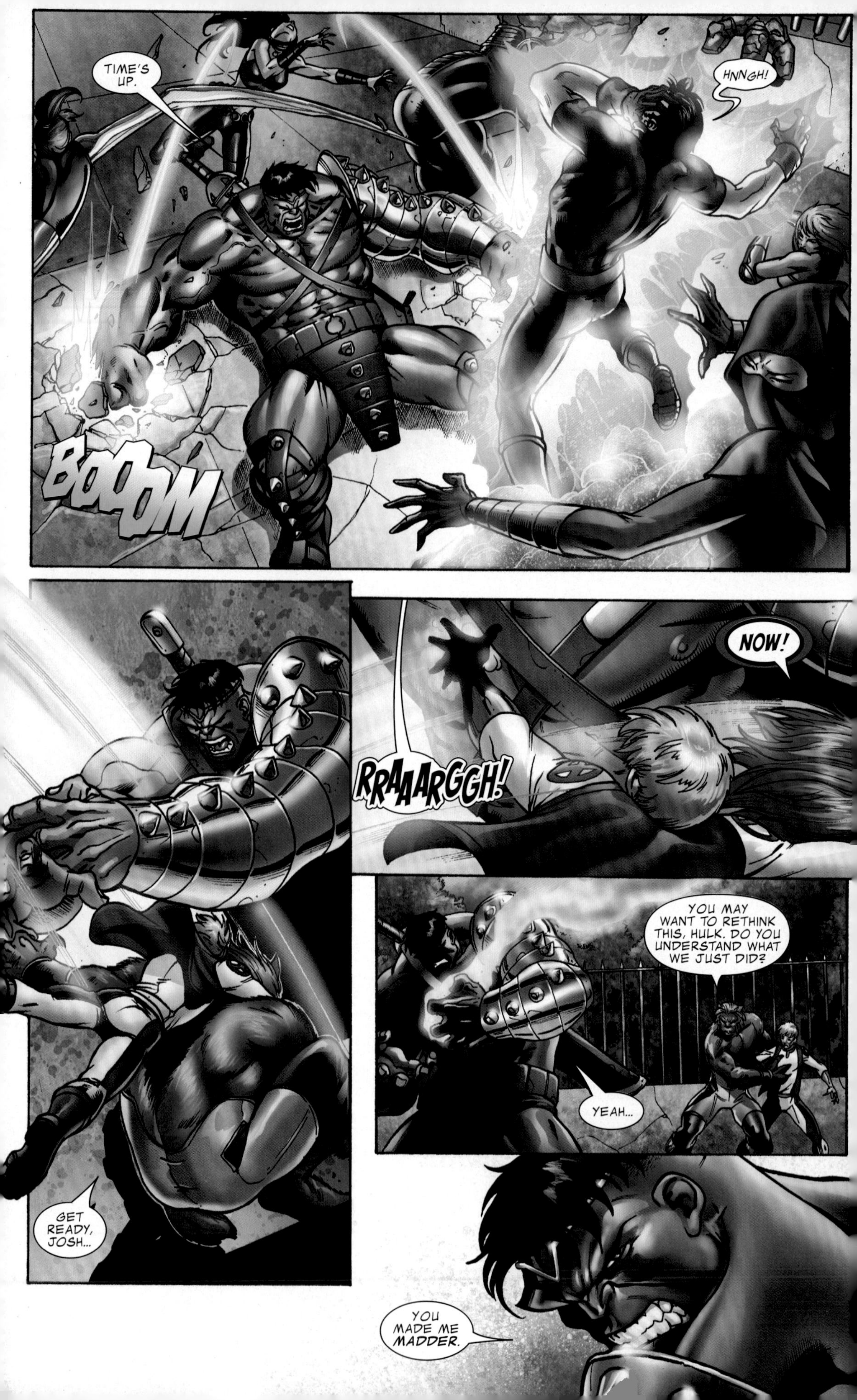
TIME'S UP.
HNNGH!
BOOOOM
GET READY, JOSH...
RRAAARGGH!
NOW!
YOU MAY WANT TO RETHINK THIS, HULK. DO YOU UNDERSTAND WHAT WE JUST DID?
YEAH...
YOU MADE ME MADDER.

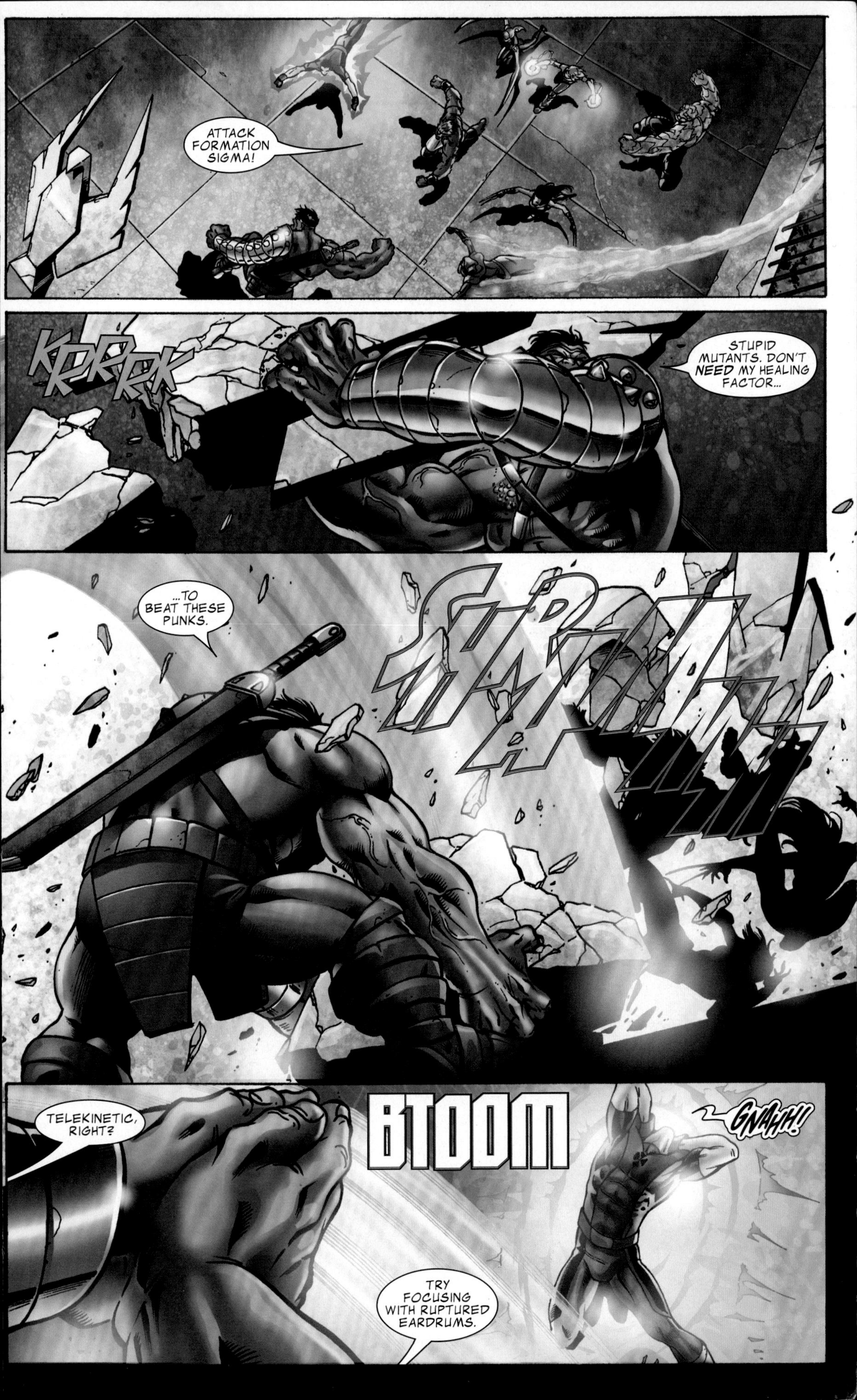
ATTACK FORMATION SIGMA!
KRRRK
STUPID MUTANTS. DON'T NEED MY HEALING FACTOR...
...TO BEAT THESE PUNKS.
TELEKINETIC, RIGHT?
BTOOM
GNAHH!
TRY FOCUSING WITH RUPTURED EARDRUMS.

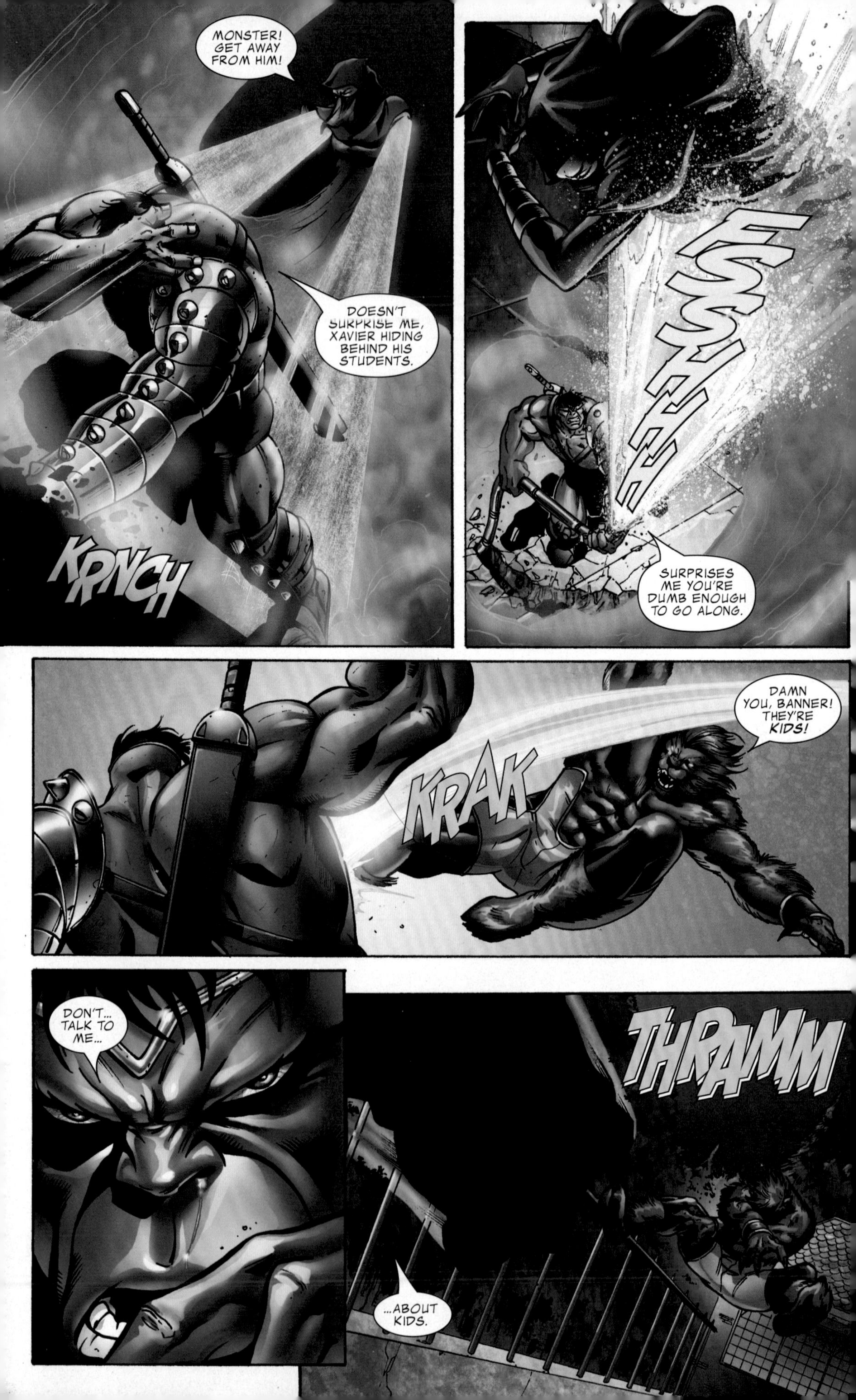
MONSTER! GET AWAY FROM HIM!
DOESN'T SURPRISE ME, XAVIER HIDING BEHIND HIS STUDENTS.
KRNCH
FSSHHHH
SURPRISES ME YOU'RE DUMB ENOUGH TO GO ALONG.
DAMN YOU, BANNER! THEY'RE KIDS!
KRAK
DON'T... TALK TO ME...
THRAMM
...ABOUT KIDS.

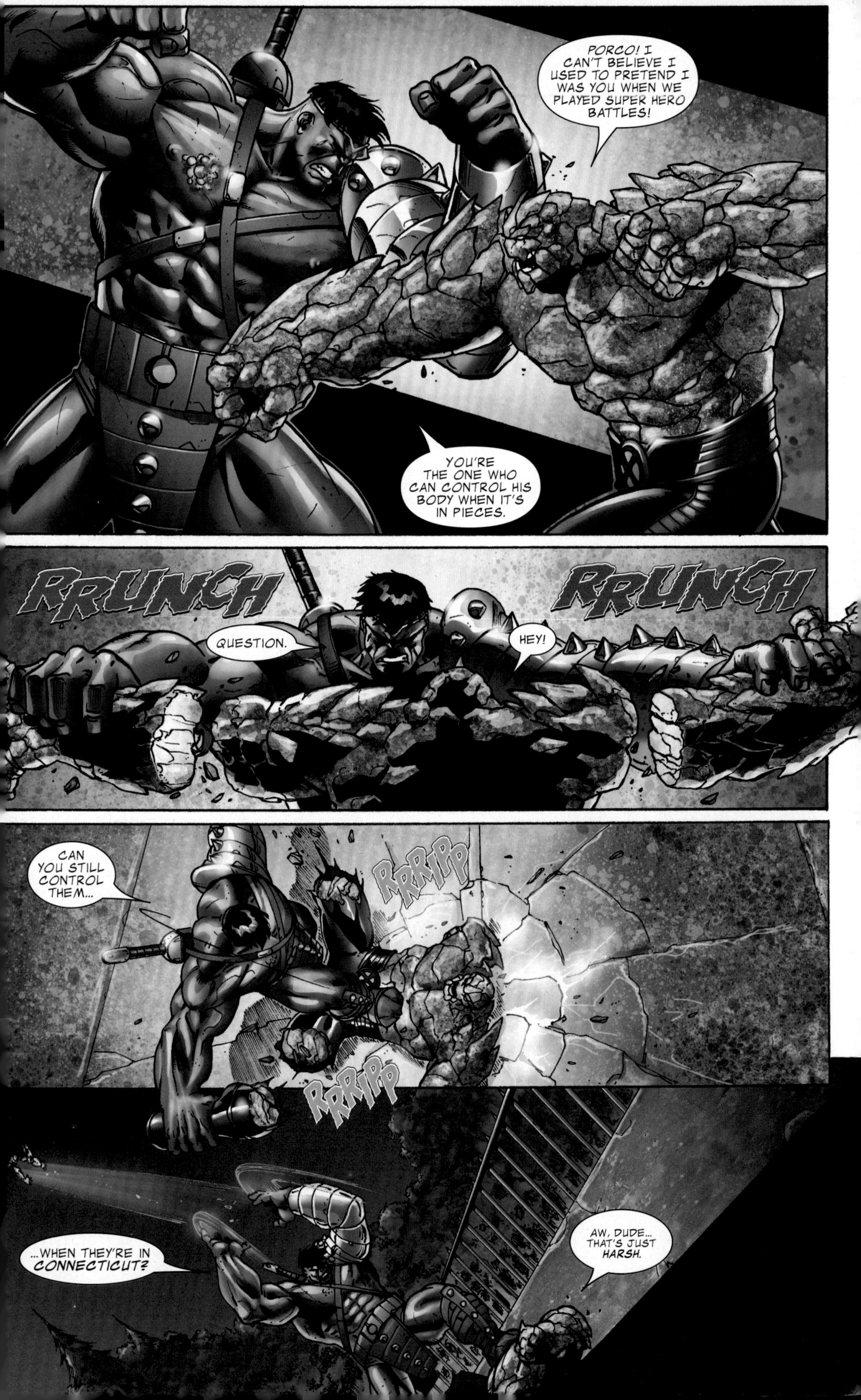
PORCO! I CAN'T BELIEVE I USED TO PRETEND I WAS YOU WHEN WE PLAYED SUPER HERO BATTLES!
YOU'RE THE ONE WHO CAN CONTROL HIS BODY WHEN IT'S IN PIECES.
RRUNCH
RRUNCH
QUESTION.
HEY!
CAN YOU STILL CONTROL THEM...
RRRIPP
RRRIPP
...WHEN THEY'RE IN CONNECTICUT?
AW, DUDE... THAT'S JUST HARSH.

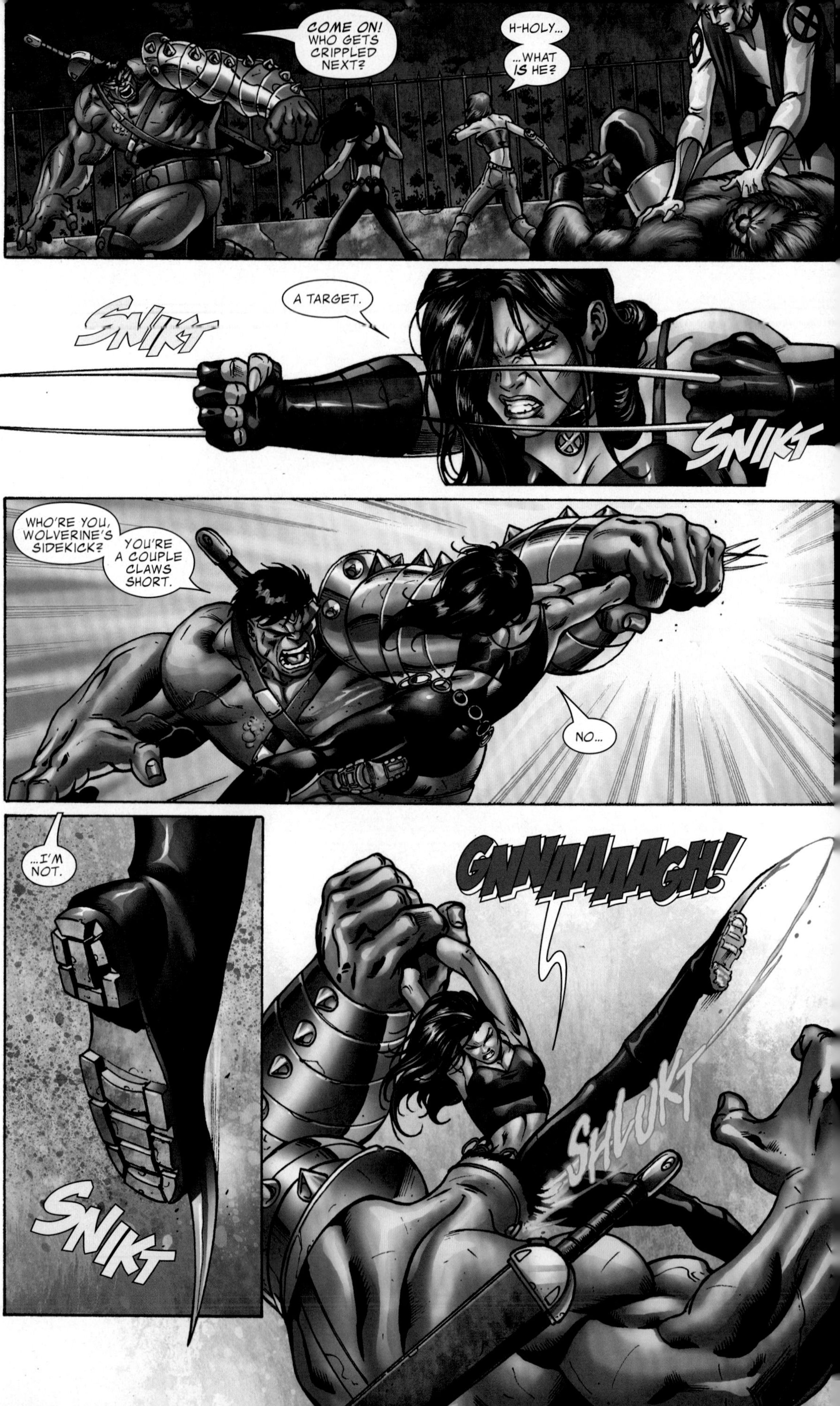
COME ON! WHO GETS CRIPPLED NEXT?
H-HOLY...
...WHAT IS HE?
A TARGET.
SNIKT
SNIKT
WHO'RE YOU, WOLVERINE'S SIDEKICK?
YOU'RE A COUPLE CLAWS SHORT.
NO...
...I'M NOT.
GNNAAAAAGH!
SHLUKT
SNIKT

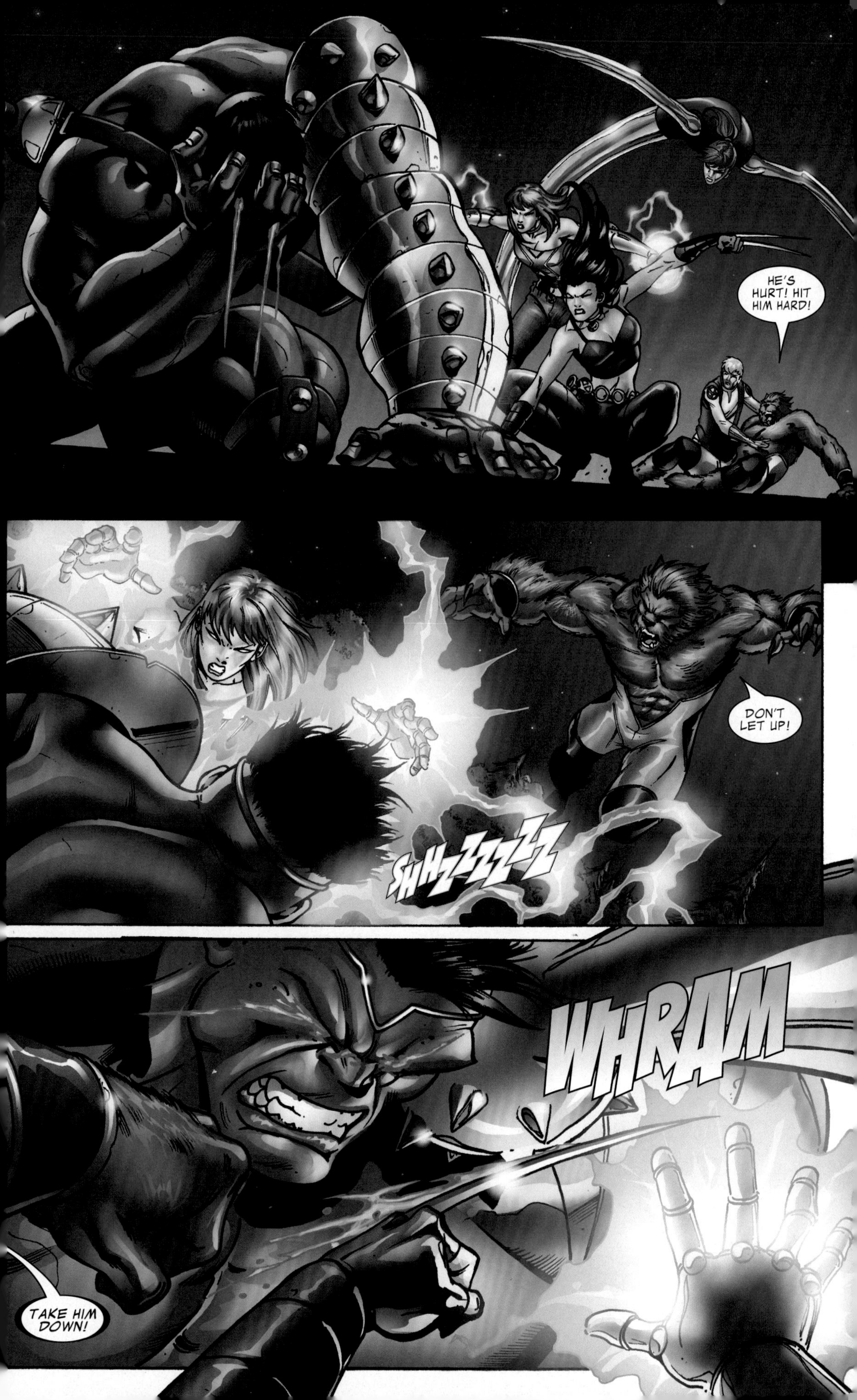
HE'S HURT! HIT HIM HARD!
DON'T LET UP!
SHHZZZZZZZ
WHRAM
TAKE HIM DOWN!

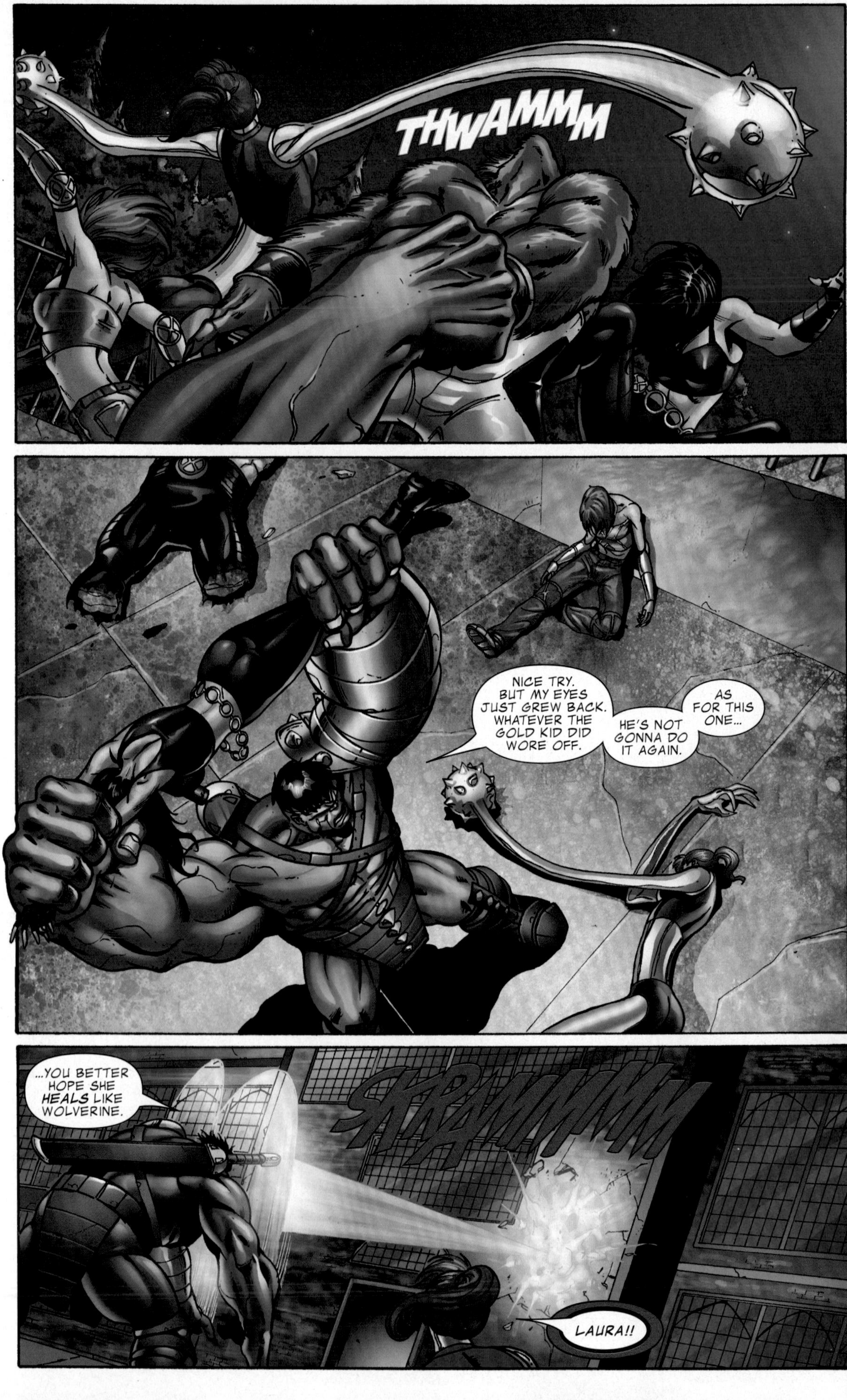
THWAMMM
NICE TRY. BUT MY EYES JUST GREW BACK. WHATEVER THE GOLD KID DID WORE OFF.
HE'S NOT GONNA DO IT AGAIN.
AS FOR THIS ONE...
...YOU BETTER HOPE SHE HEALS LIKE WOLVERINE.
SKRAMMMMM
LAURA!!

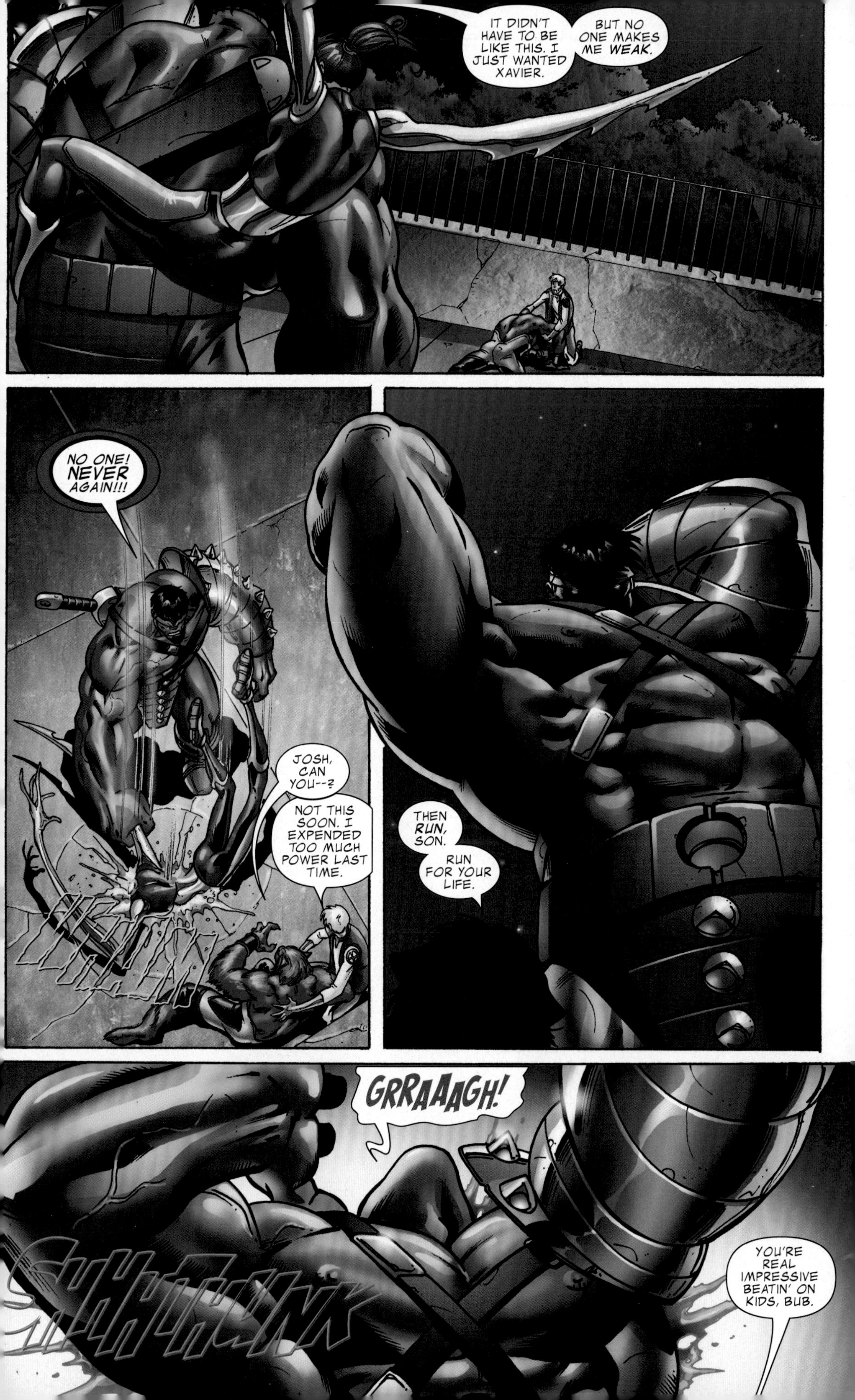
IT DIDN'T HAVE TO BE LIKE THIS. I JUST WANTED XAVIER.
BUT NO ONE MAKES ME *WEAK*.
NO ONE! **NEVER** AGAIN!!!
JOSH, CAN YOU--?
NOT THIS SOON. I EXPENDED TOO MUCH POWER LAST TIME.
THEN *RUN*, SON.
RUN FOR YOUR LIFE.
GRRAAAGH!
YOU'RE REAL IMPRESSIVE BEATIN' ON KIDS, BUB.

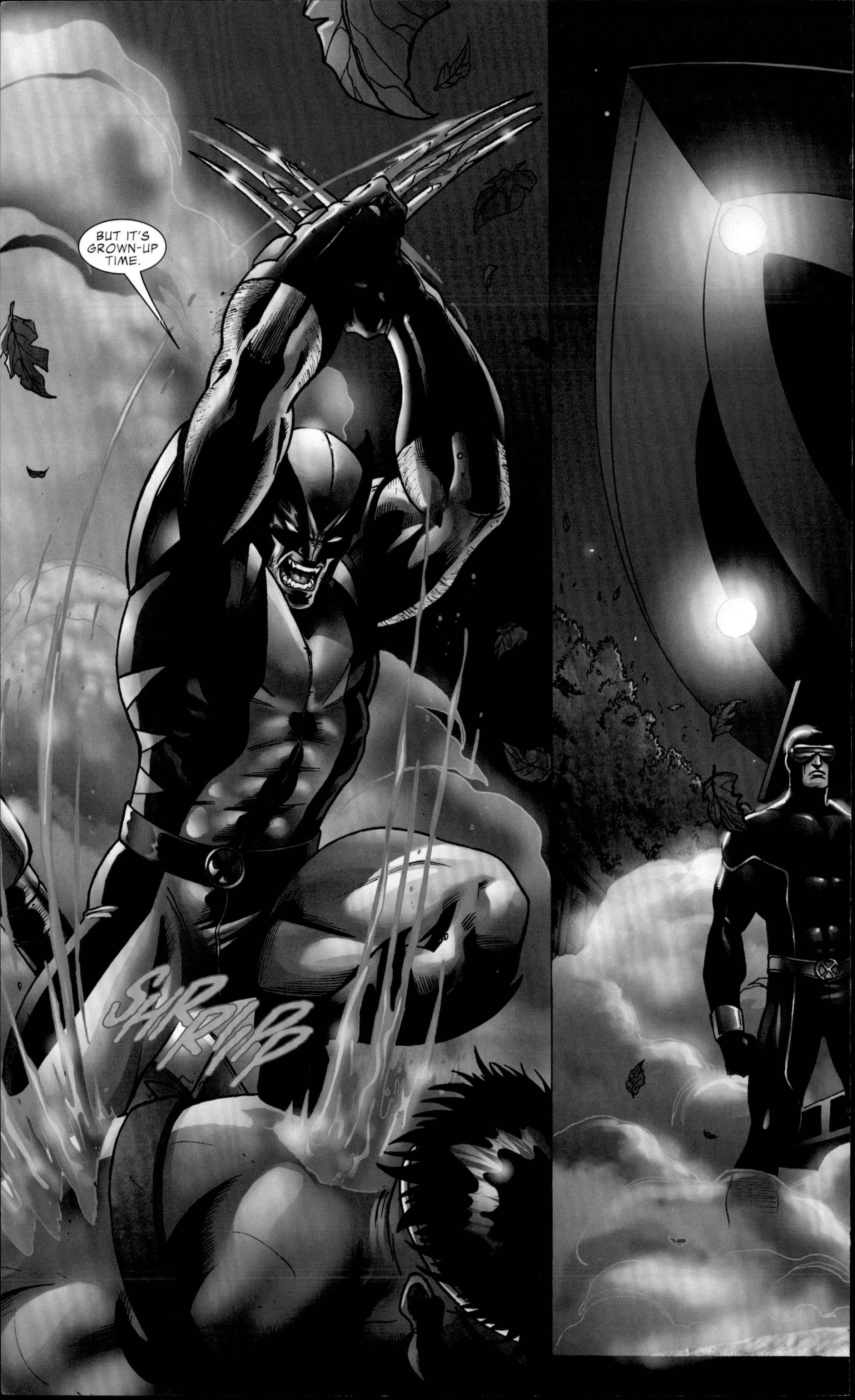
BUT IT'S GROWN-UP TIME.
SHRAKK

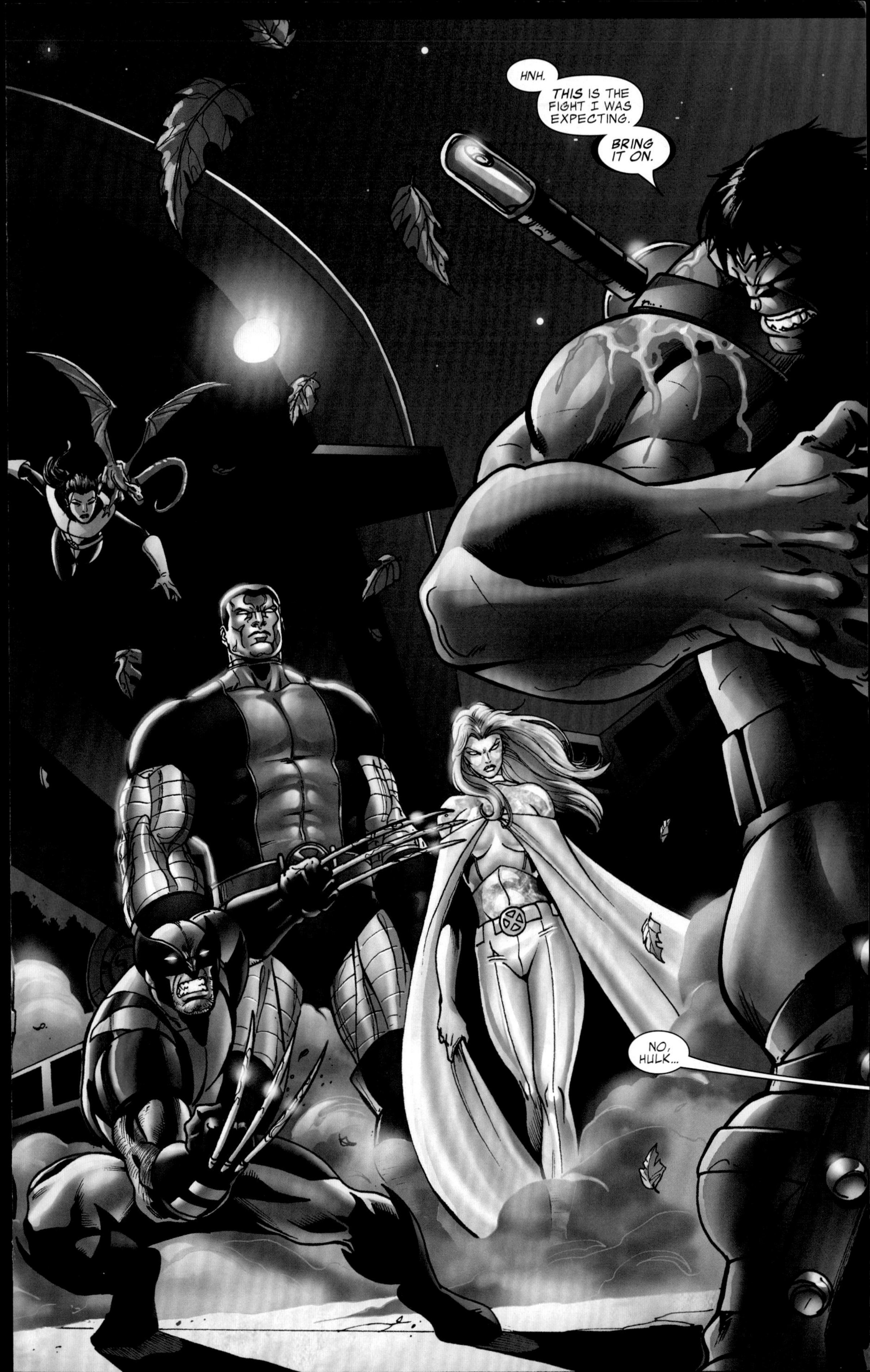
HNH.
THIS IS THE FIGHT I WAS EXPECTING.
BRING IT ON.
NO, HULK...

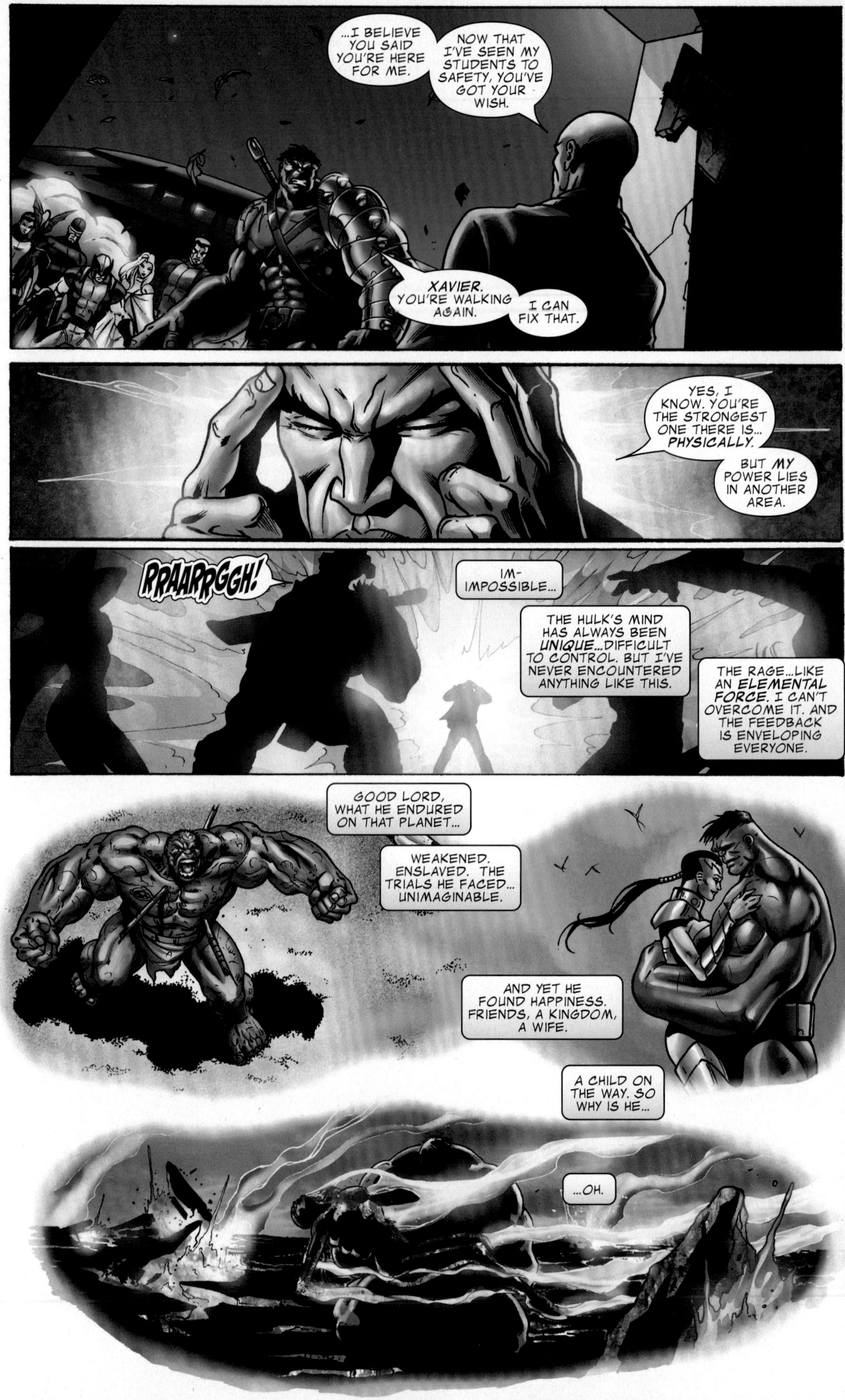
...I BELIEVE YOU SAID YOU'RE HERE FOR ME.
NOW THAT I'VE SEEN MY STUDENTS TO SAFETY, YOU'VE GOT YOUR WISH.
XAVIER. YOU'RE WALKING AGAIN.
I CAN FIX THAT.
YES, I KNOW. YOU'RE THE STRONGEST ONE THERE IS... PHYSICALLY.
BUT MY POWER LIES IN ANOTHER AREA.
RRAARRGGH!
IM- IMPOSSIBLE...
THE HULK'S MIND HAS ALWAYS BEEN UNIQUE...DIFFICULT TO CONTROL. BUT I'VE NEVER ENCOUNTERED ANYTHING LIKE THIS.
THE RAGE...LIKE AN ELEMENTAL FORCE. I CAN'T OVERCOME IT. AND THE FEEDBACK IS ENVELOPING EVERYONE.
GOOD LORD, WHAT HE ENDURED ON THAT PLANET...
WEAKENED. ENSLAVED. THE TRIALS HE FACED... UNIMAGINABLE.
AND YET HE FOUND HAPPINESS. FRIENDS, A KINGDOM, A WIFE.
A CHILD ON THE WAY. SO WHY IS HE...
...OH.

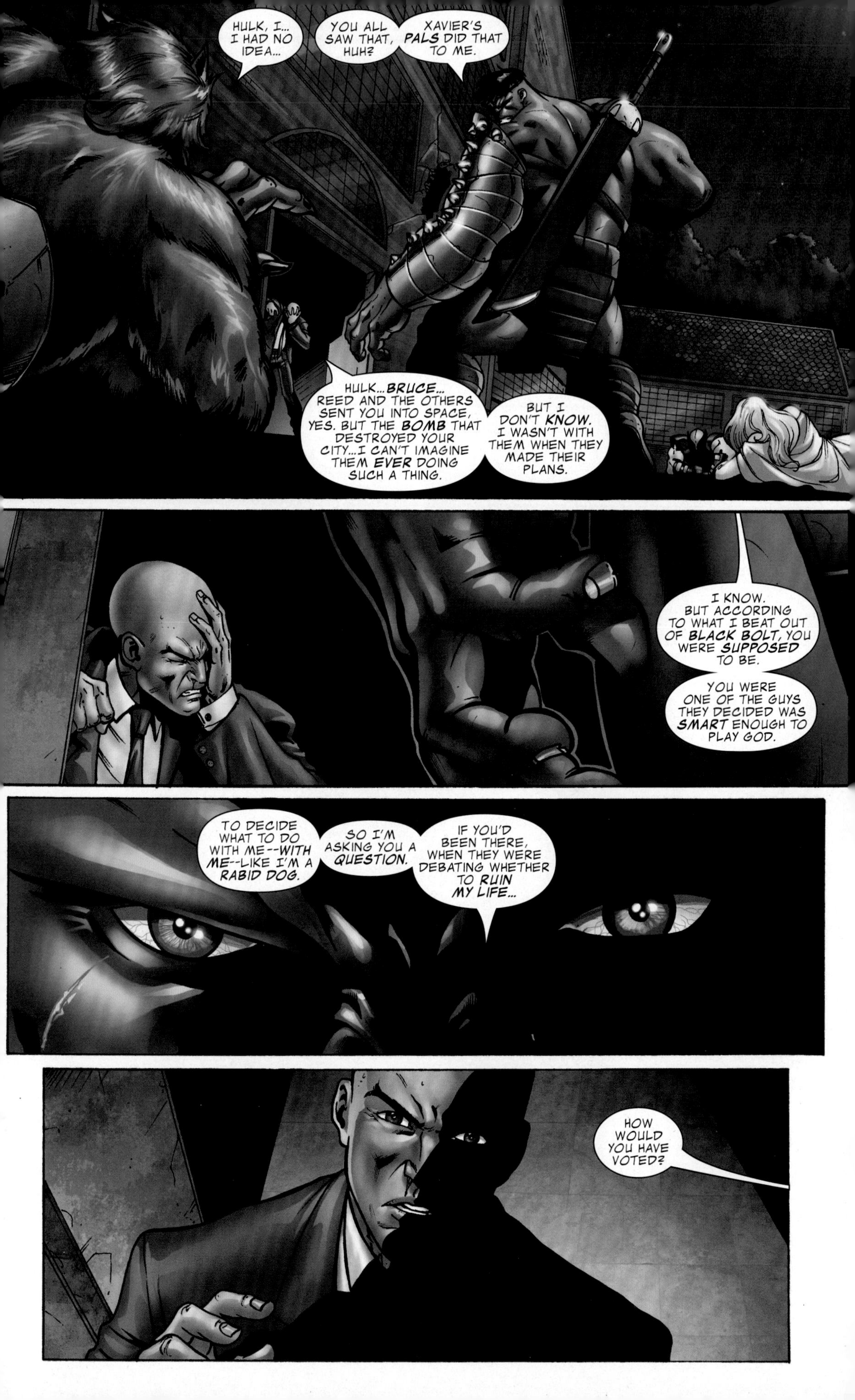
HULK, I... I HAD NO IDEA...
YOU ALL SAW THAT, HUH?
XAVIER'S PALS DID THAT TO ME.
HULK...BRUCE... REED AND THE OTHERS SENT YOU INTO SPACE, YES. BUT THE BOMB THAT DESTROYED YOUR CITY...I CAN'T IMAGINE THEM EVER DOING SUCH A THING.
BUT I DON'T KNOW. I WASN'T WITH THEM WHEN THEY MADE THEIR PLANS.
I KNOW. BUT ACCORDING TO WHAT I BEAT OUT OF BLACK BOLT, YOU WERE SUPPOSED TO BE.
YOU WERE ONE OF THE GUYS THEY DECIDED WAS SMART ENOUGH TO PLAY GOD.
TO DECIDE WHAT TO DO WITH ME--WITH ME--LIKE I'M A RABID DOG.
SO I'M ASKING YOU A QUESTION.
IF YOU'D BEEN THERE, WHEN THEY WERE DEBATING WHETHER TO RUIN MY LIFE...
HOW WOULD YOU HAVE VOTED?

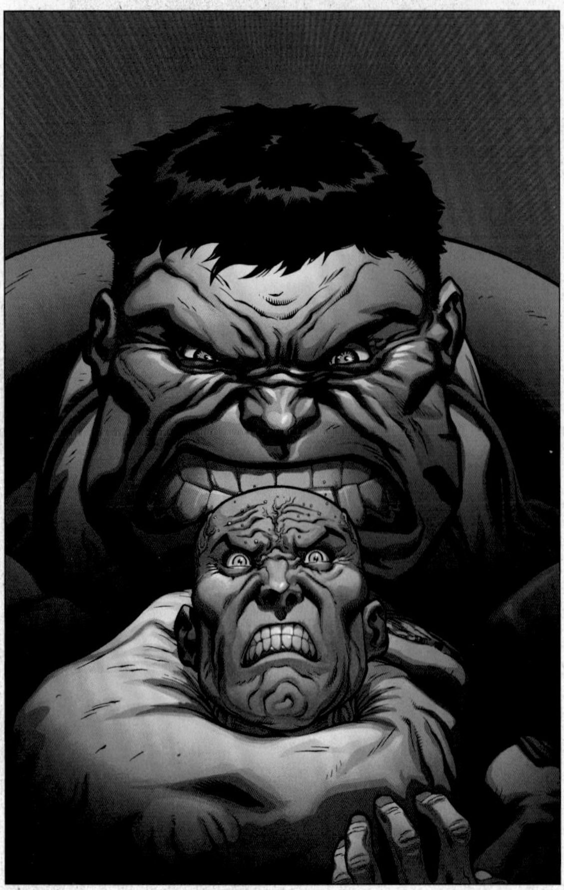

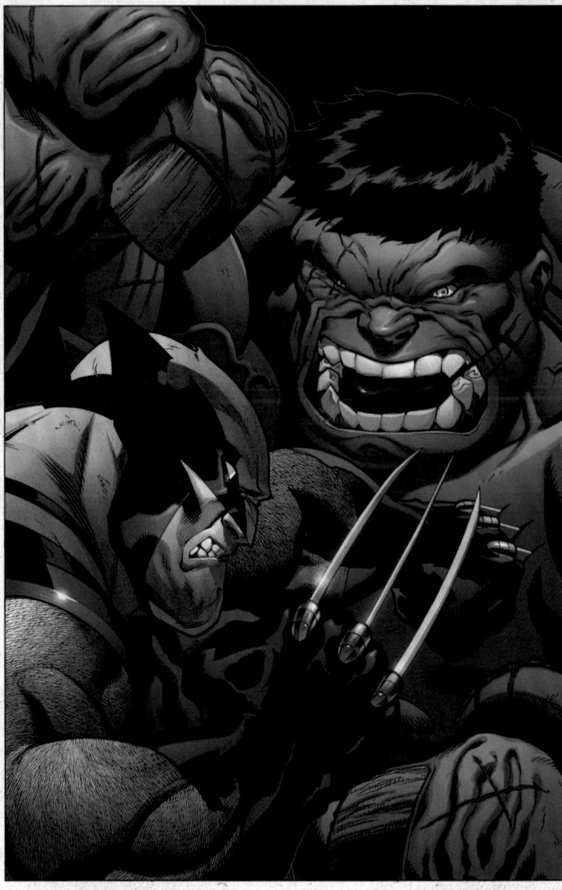

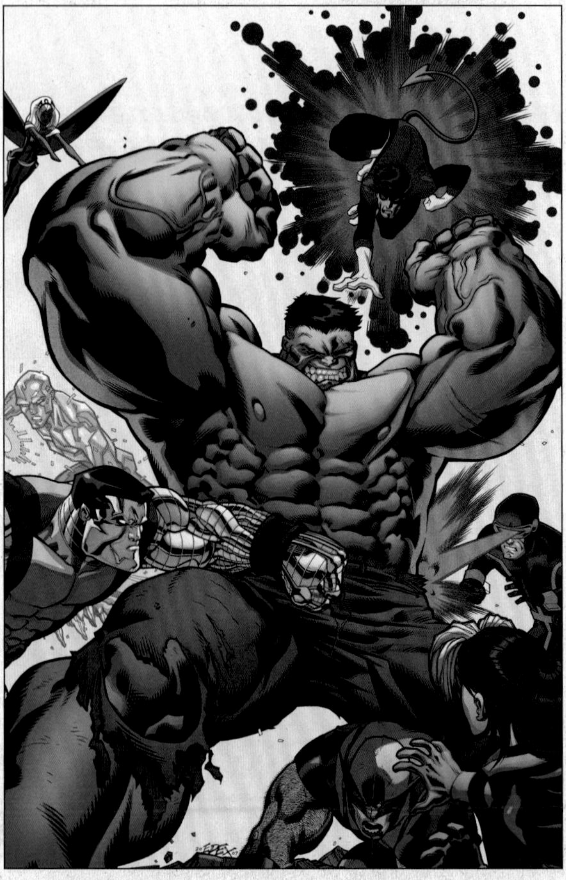

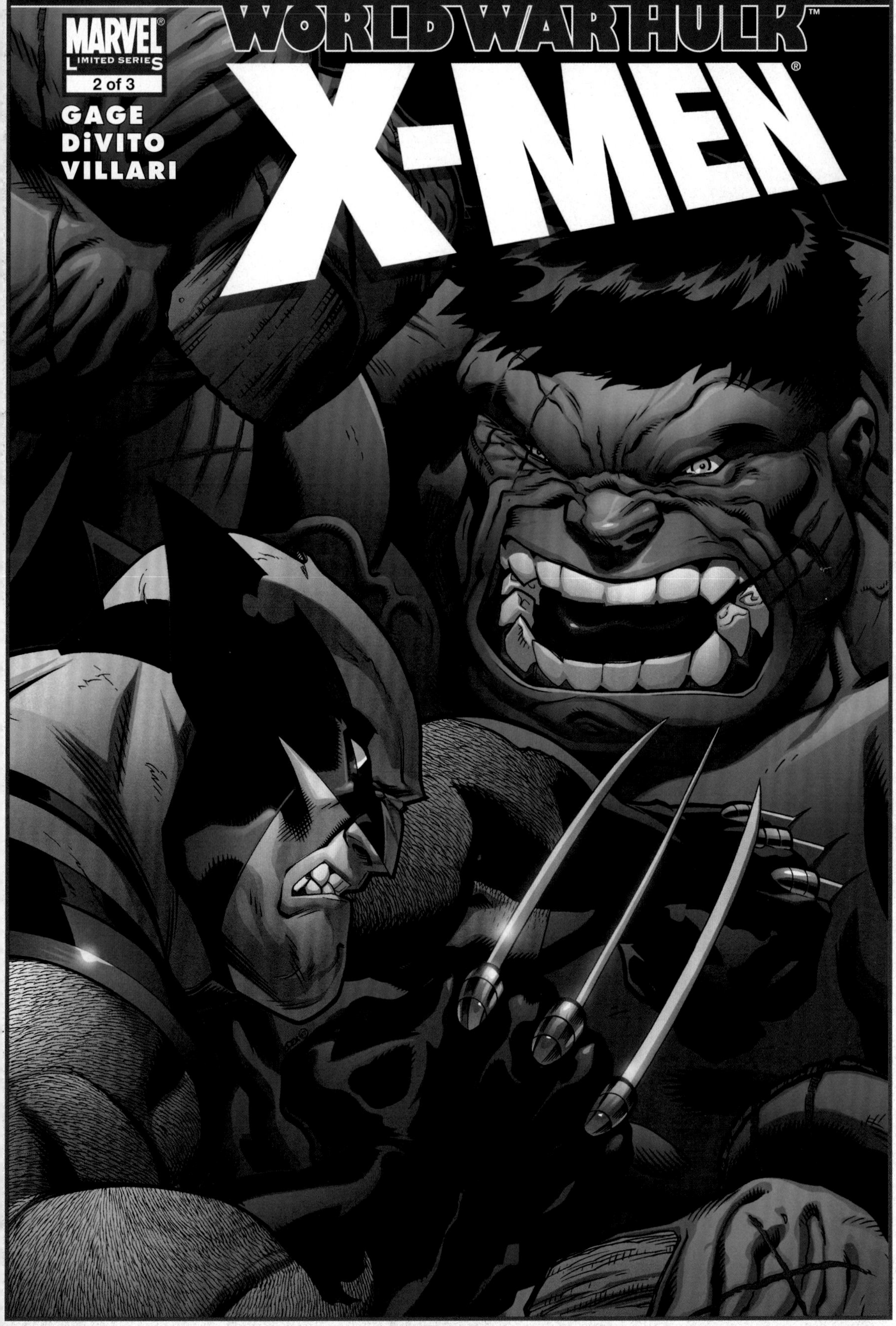
WORLD WAR HULK
X-MEN
MARVEL LIMITED SERIES
2 of 3
GAGE
DiVITO
VILLARI

★★★ ROUND 2: SWORN TO PROTECT ★★★

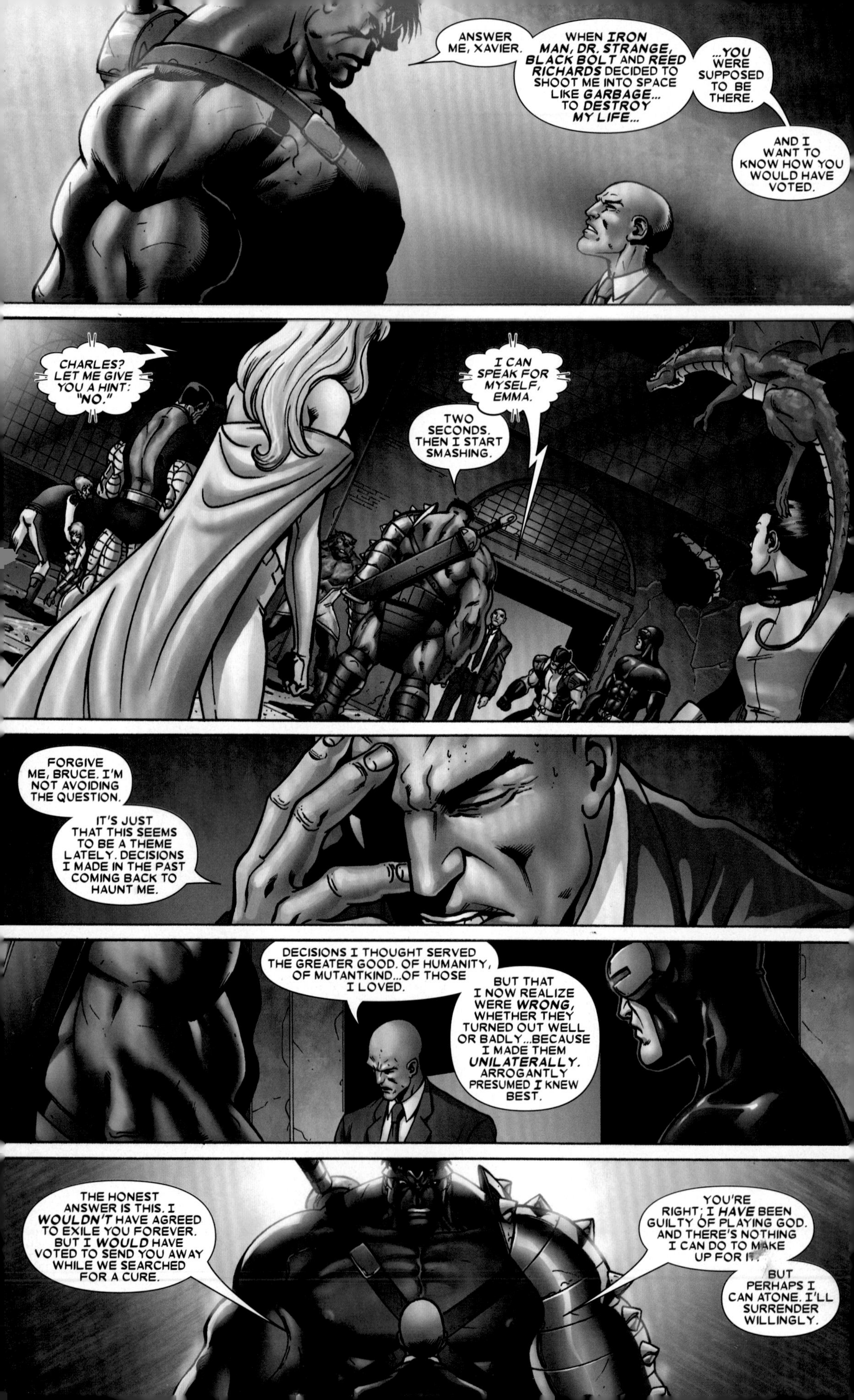
ANSWER ME, XAVIER.
WHEN IRON MAN, DR. STRANGE, BLACK BOLT AND REED RICHARDS DECIDED TO SHOOT ME INTO SPACE LIKE GARBAGE... TO DESTROY MY LIFE...
...YOU WERE SUPPOSED TO BE THERE.
AND I WANT TO KNOW HOW YOU WOULD HAVE VOTED.
CHARLES? LET ME GIVE YOU A HINT: "NO."
I CAN SPEAK FOR MYSELF, EMMA.
TWO SECONDS. THEN I START SMASHING.
FORGIVE ME, BRUCE. I'M NOT AVOIDING THE QUESTION.
IT'S JUST THAT THIS SEEMS TO BE A THEME LATELY. DECISIONS I MADE IN THE PAST COMING BACK TO HAUNT ME.
DECISIONS I THOUGHT SERVED THE GREATER GOOD. OF HUMANITY, OF MUTANTKIND...OF THOSE I LOVED.
BUT THAT I NOW REALIZE WERE WRONG, WHETHER THEY TURNED OUT WELL OR BADLY...BECAUSE I MADE THEM UNILATERALLY. ARROGANTLY PRESUMED I KNEW BEST.
THE HONEST ANSWER IS THIS. I WOULDN'T HAVE AGREED TO EXILE YOU FOREVER. BUT I WOULD HAVE VOTED TO SEND YOU AWAY WHILE WE SEARCHED FOR A CURE.
YOU'RE RIGHT; I HAVE BEEN GUILTY OF PLAYING GOD. AND THERE'S NOTHING I CAN DO TO MAKE UP FOR IT.
BUT PERHAPS I CAN ATONE. I'LL SURRENDER WILLINGLY.

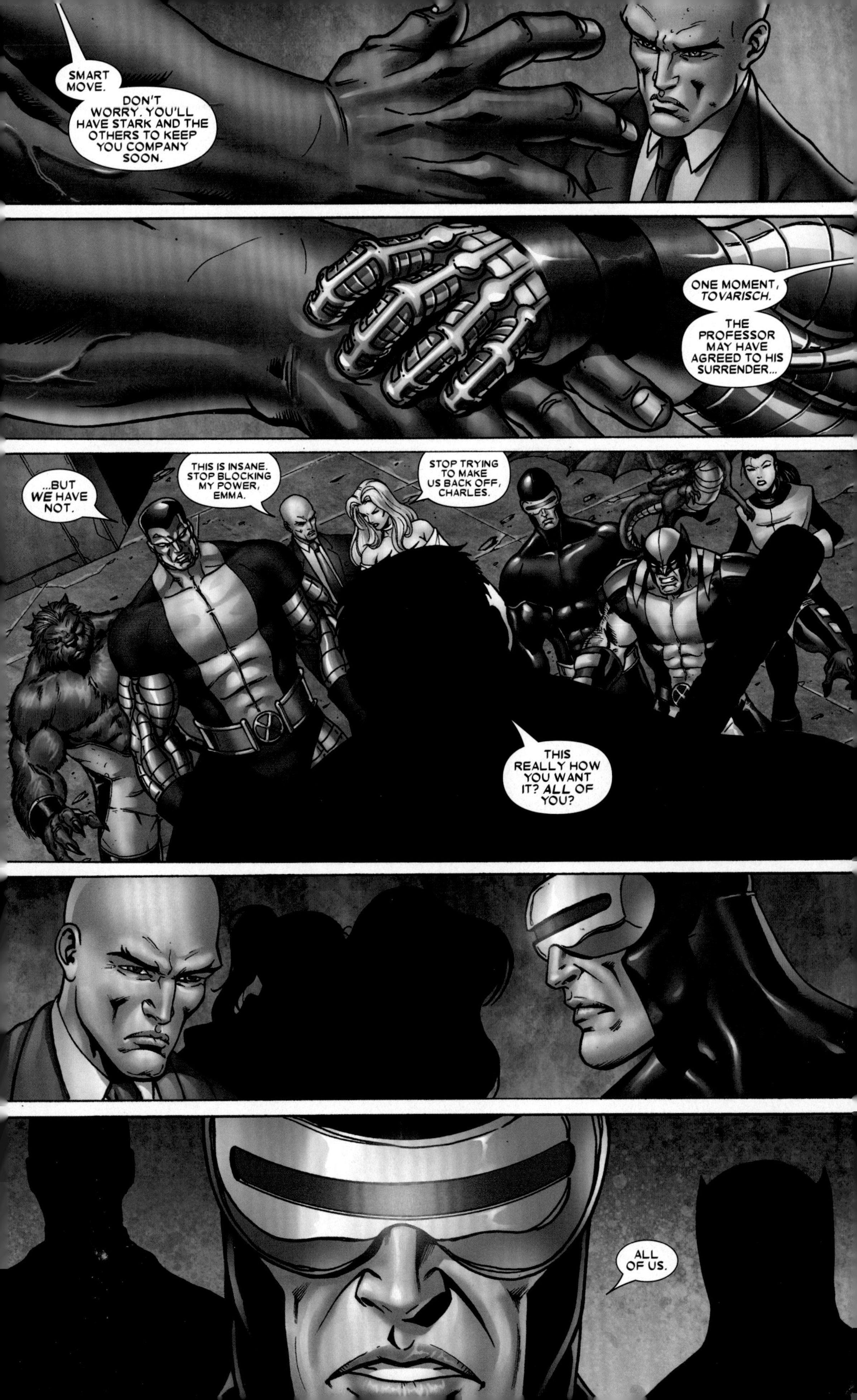
SMART MOVE.
DON'T WORRY. YOU'LL HAVE STARK AND THE OTHERS TO KEEP YOU COMPANY SOON.
ONE MOMENT, *TOVARISCH.*
THE PROFESSOR MAY HAVE AGREED TO HIS SURRENDER...
...BUT *WE* HAVE NOT.
THIS IS INSANE. STOP BLOCKING MY POWER, EMMA.
STOP TRYING TO MAKE US BACK OFF, CHARLES.
THIS REALLY HOW YOU WANT IT? *ALL* OF YOU?
ALL OF US.

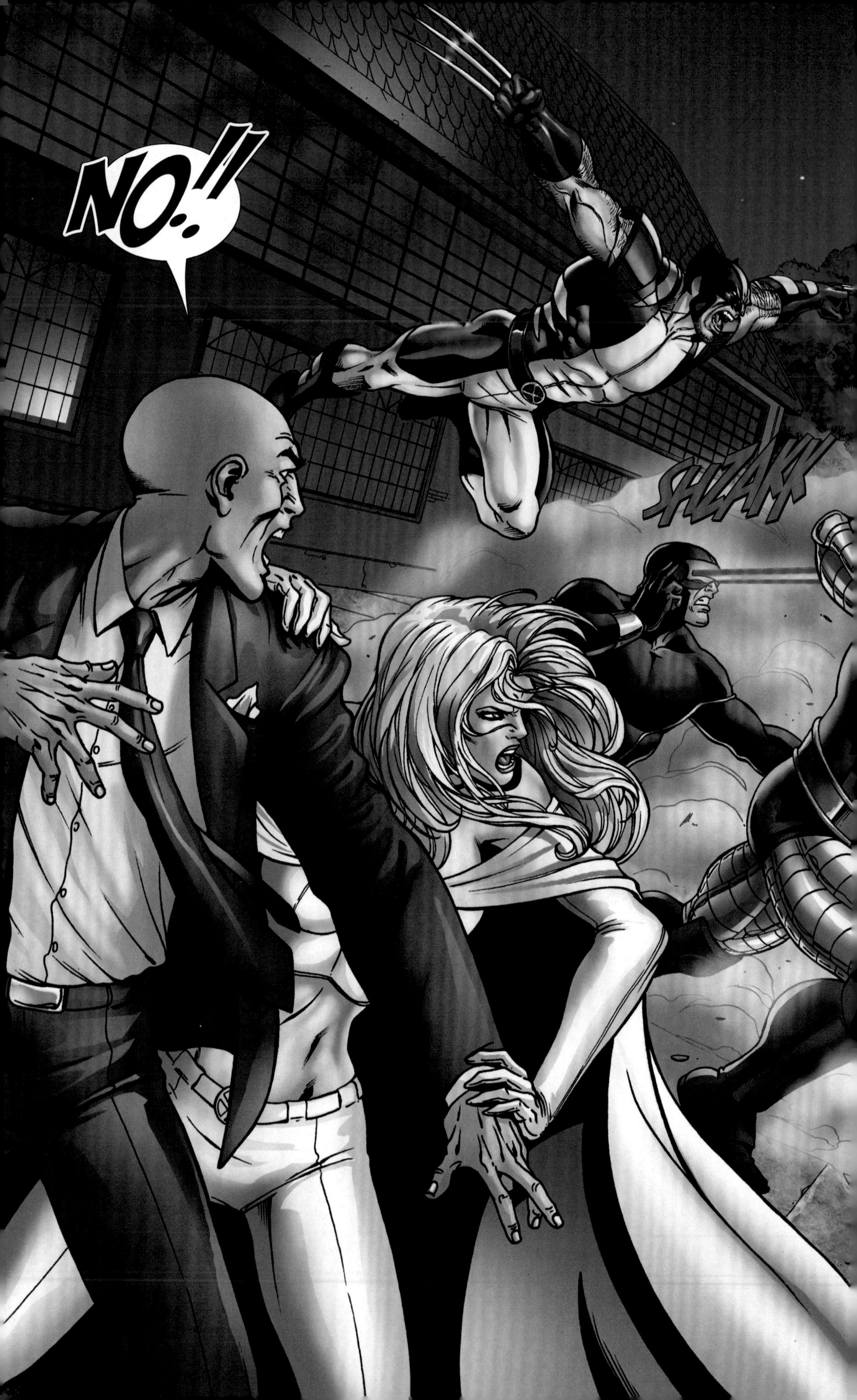
NO..!!
SHZAKK

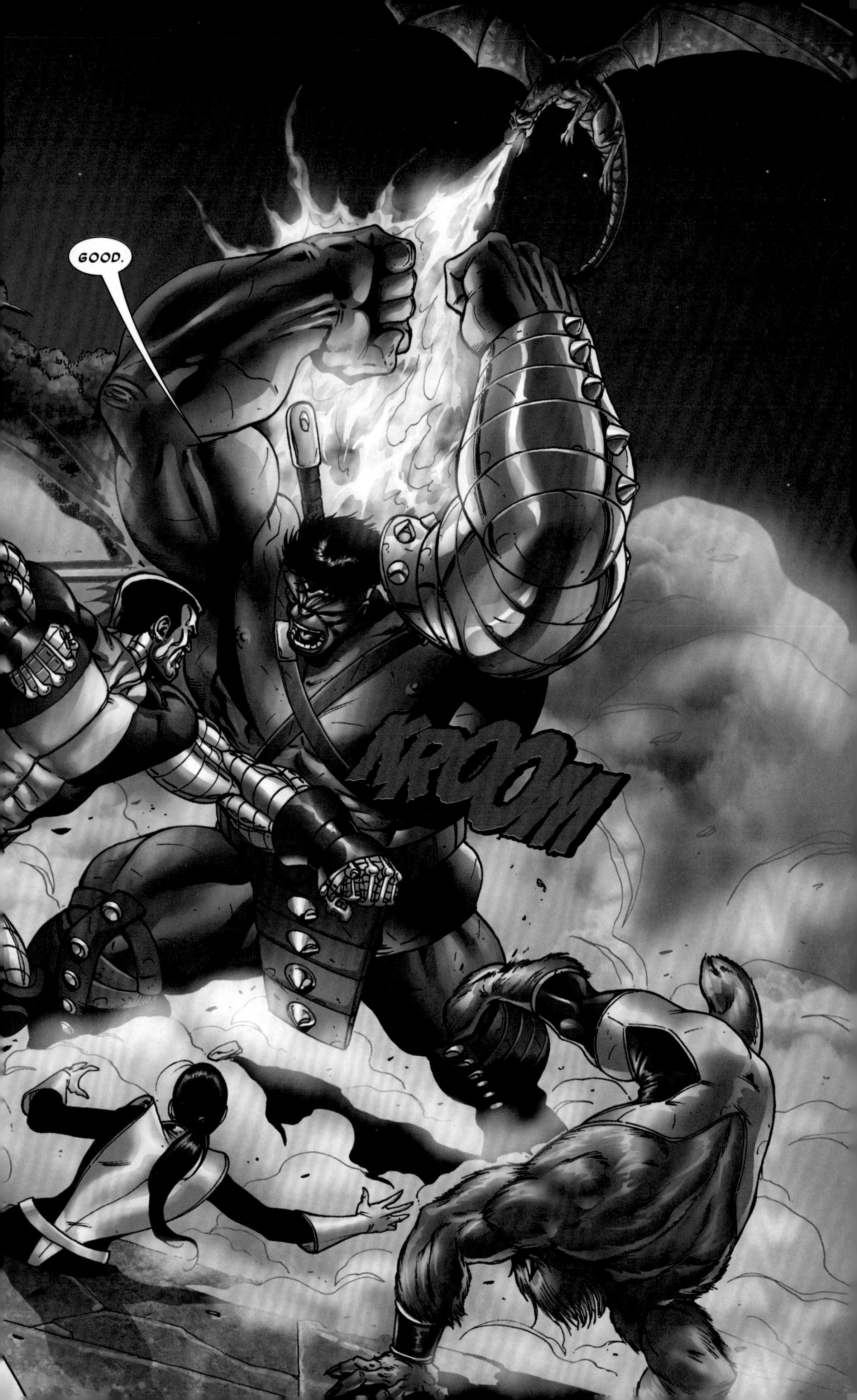
GOOD.
KROOM

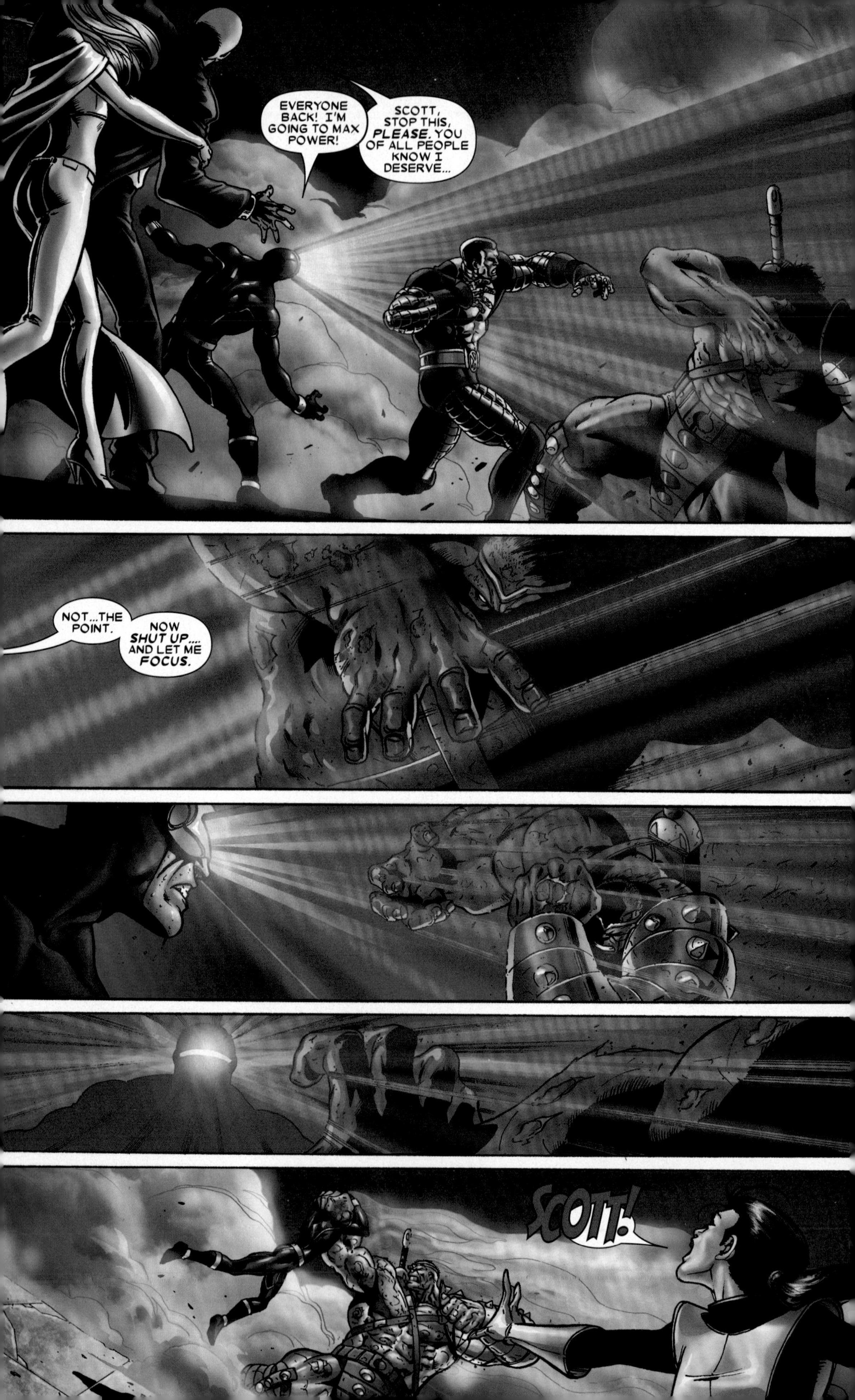
EVERYONE BACK! I'M GOING TO MAX POWER!
SCOTT, STOP THIS, PLEASE. YOU OF ALL PEOPLE KNOW I DESERVE...
NOT...THE POINT.
NOW SHUT UP.... AND LET ME FOCUS.
SCOTT!

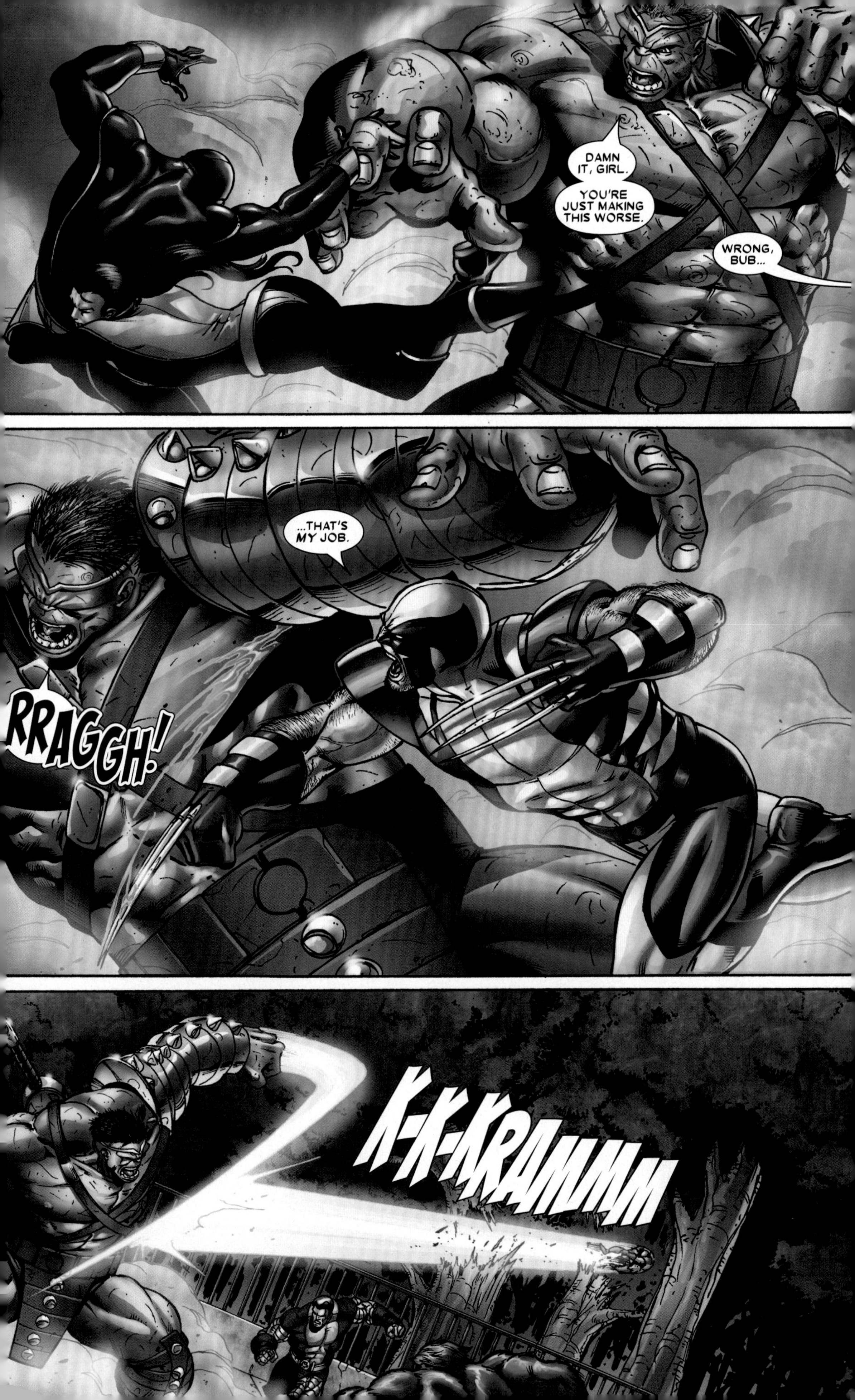
DAMN IT, GIRL.
YOU'RE JUST MAKING THIS WORSE.
WRONG, BUB...
...THAT'S MY JOB.
RRAGGH!
K-K-KRAMMMM

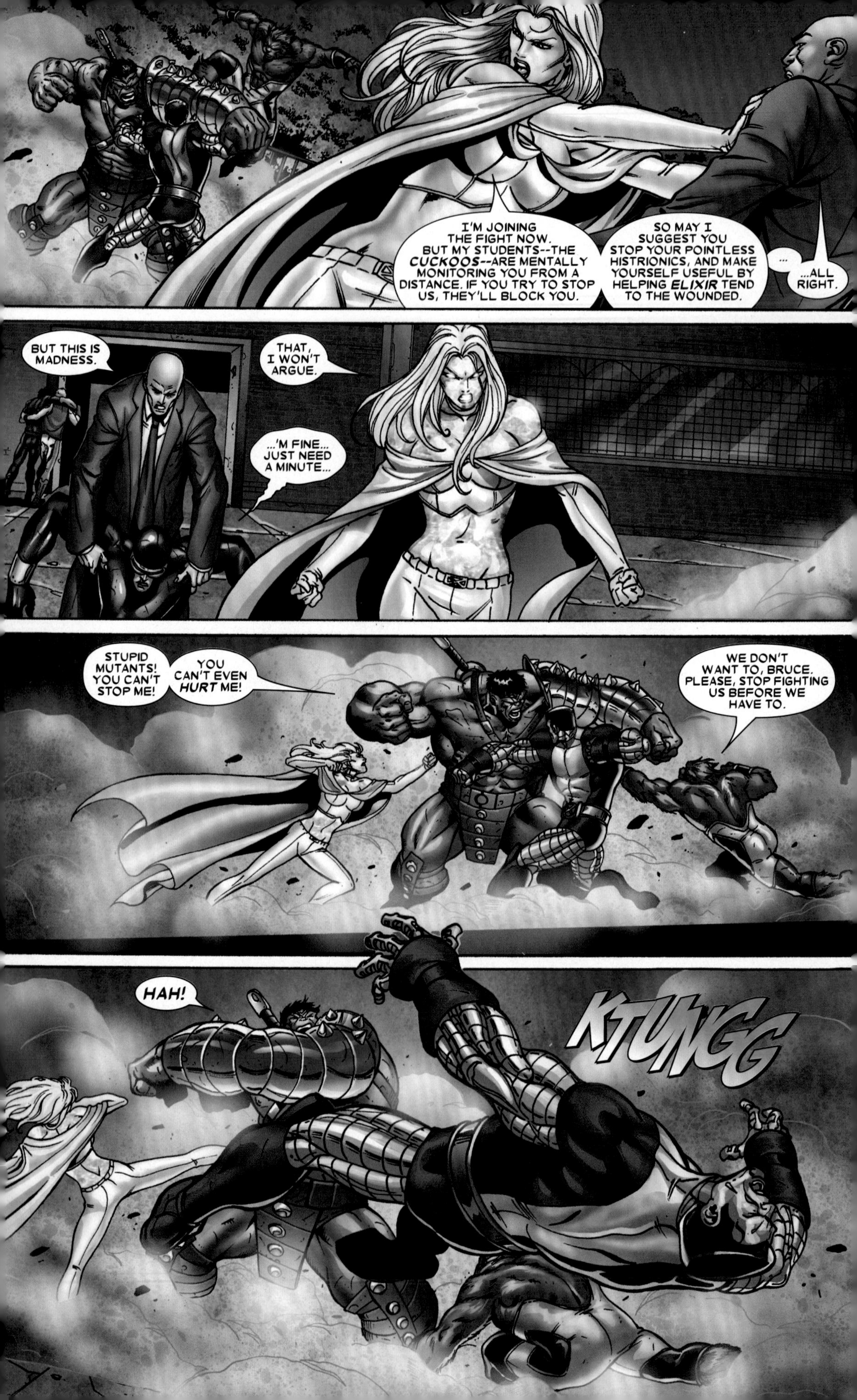

I'M JOINING THE FIGHT NOW. BUT MY STUDENTS--THE CUCKOOS--ARE MENTALLY MONITORING YOU FROM A DISTANCE. IF YOU TRY TO STOP US, THEY'LL BLOCK YOU.
SO MAY I SUGGEST YOU STOP YOUR POINTLESS HISTRIONICS, AND MAKE YOURSELF USEFUL BY HELPING ELIXIR TEND TO THE WOUNDED.
...
...ALL RIGHT.
BUT THIS IS MADNESS.
THAT, I WON'T ARGUE.
...'M FINE... JUST NEED A MINUTE...
STUPID MUTANTS! YOU CAN'T STOP ME!
YOU CAN'T EVEN HURT ME!
WE DON'T WANT TO, BRUCE. PLEASE, STOP FIGHTING US BEFORE WE HAVE TO.
HAH!
KTUNGG

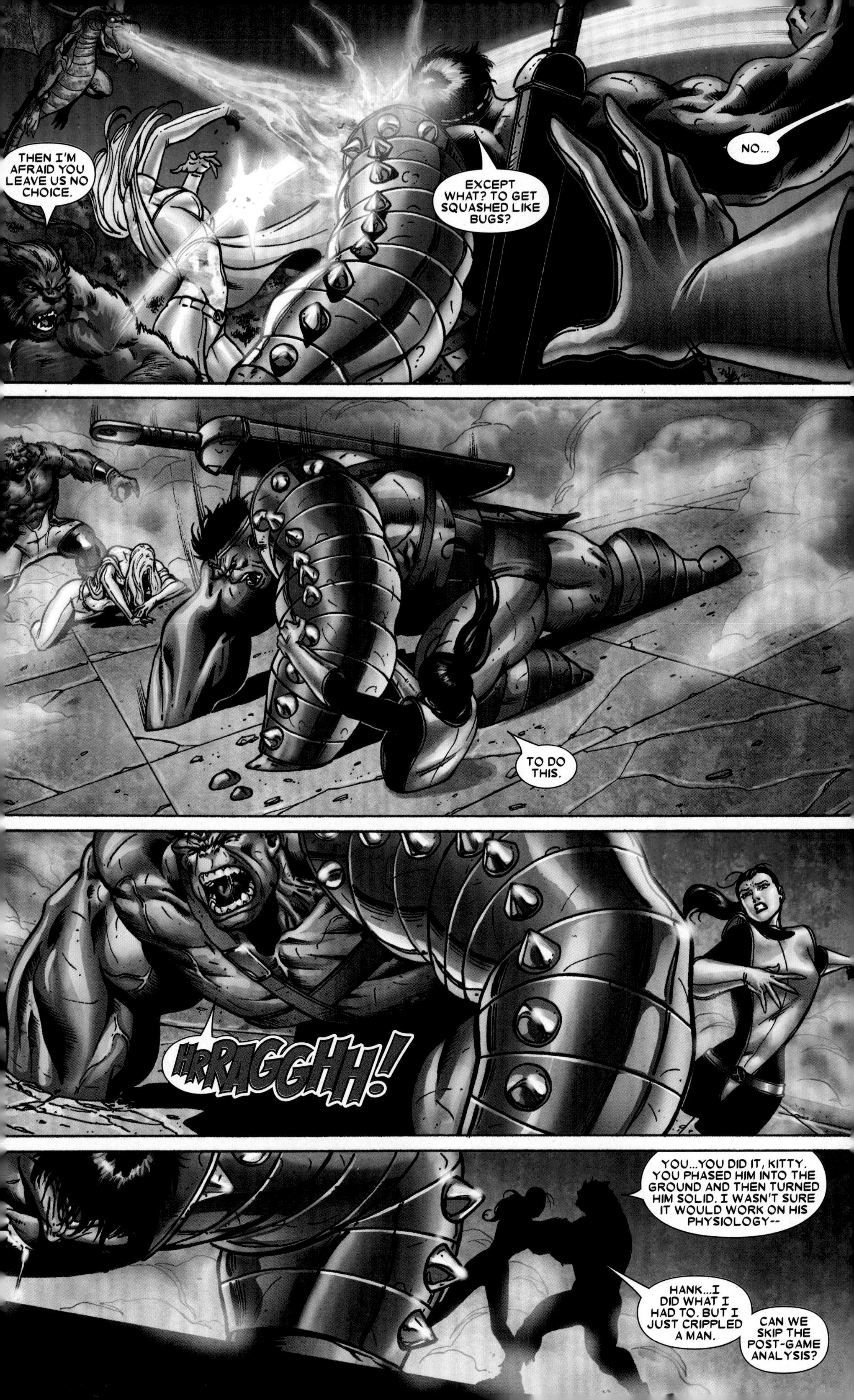
THEN I'M AFRAID YOU LEAVE US NO CHOICE.
EXCEPT WHAT? TO GET SQUASHED LIKE BUGS?
NO...
TO DO THIS.
HRRAGGHH!
YOU...YOU DID IT, KITTY. YOU PHASED HIM INTO THE GROUND AND THEN TURNED HIM SOLID. I WASN'T SURE IT WOULD WORK ON HIS PHYSIOLOGY--
HANK...I DID WHAT I HAD TO. BUT I JUST CRIPPLED A MAN.
CAN WE SKIP THE POST-GAME ANALYSIS?

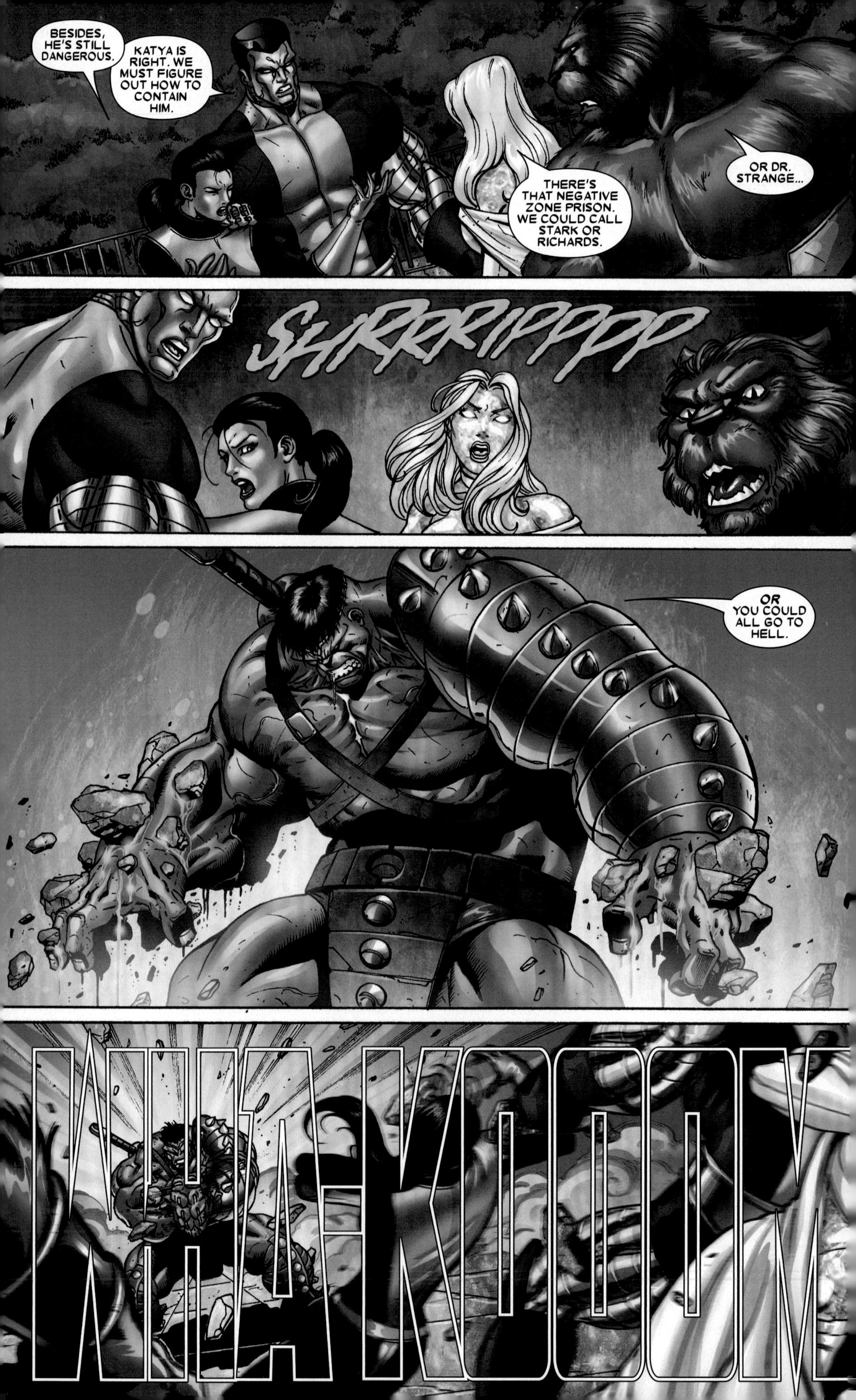
BESIDES, HE'S STILL DANGEROUS.
KATYA IS RIGHT. WE MUST FIGURE OUT HOW TO CONTAIN HIM.
THERE'S THAT NEGATIVE ZONE PRISON. WE COULD CALL STARK OR RICHARDS.
OR DR. STRANGE...
SHRRRIPPPP
OR YOU COULD ALL GO TO HELL.
WHA-KOOOM

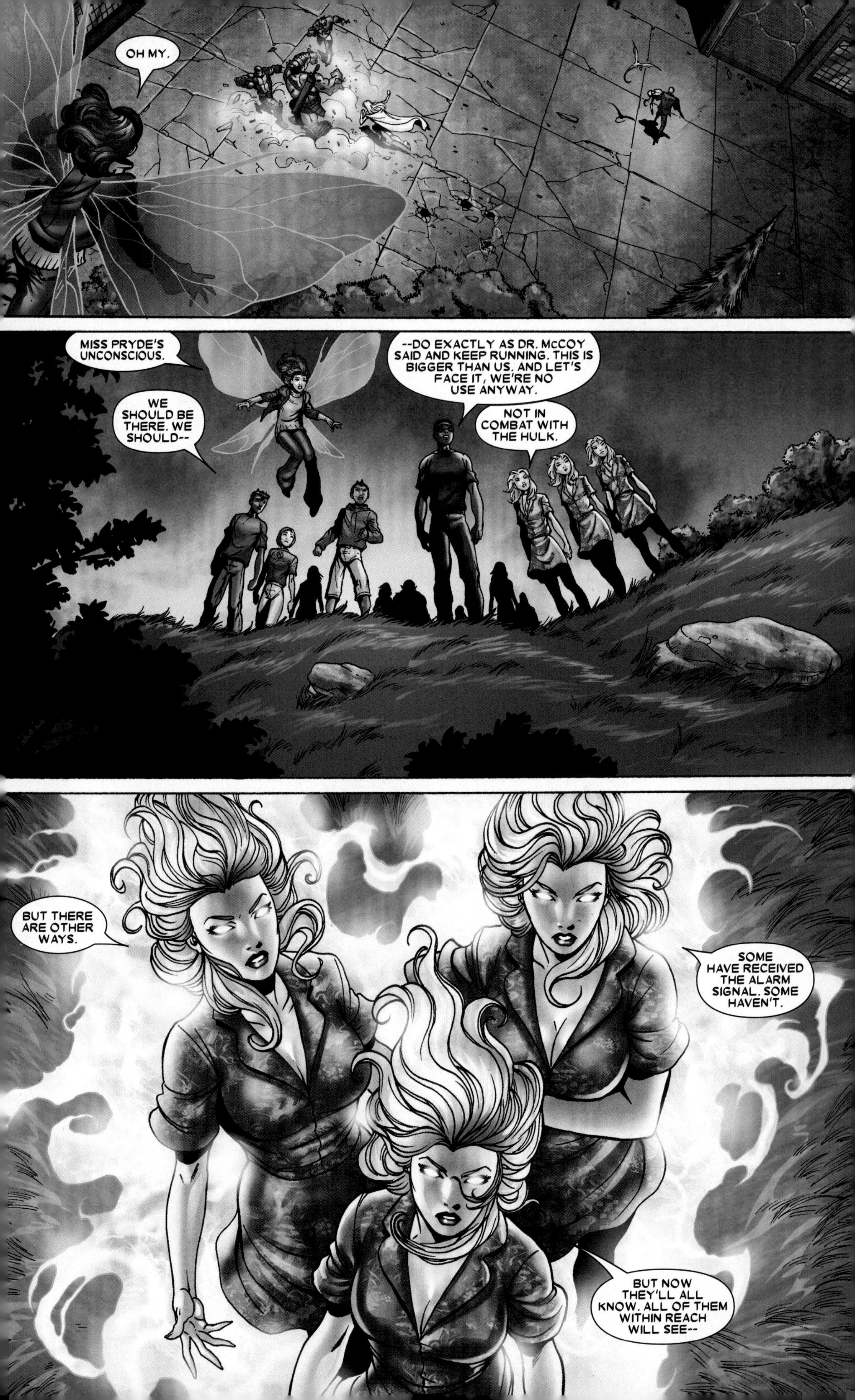
OH MY.
MISS PRYDE'S UNCONSCIOUS.
WE SHOULD BE THERE. WE SHOULD--
--DO EXACTLY AS DR. McCOY SAID AND KEEP RUNNING. THIS IS BIGGER THAN US. AND LET'S FACE IT, WE'RE NO USE ANYWAY.
NOT IN COMBAT WITH THE HULK.
BUT THERE ARE OTHER WAYS.
SOME HAVE RECEIVED THE ALARM SIGNAL. SOME HAVEN'T.
BUT NOW THEY'LL ALL KNOW. ALL OF THEM WITHIN REACH WILL SEE--

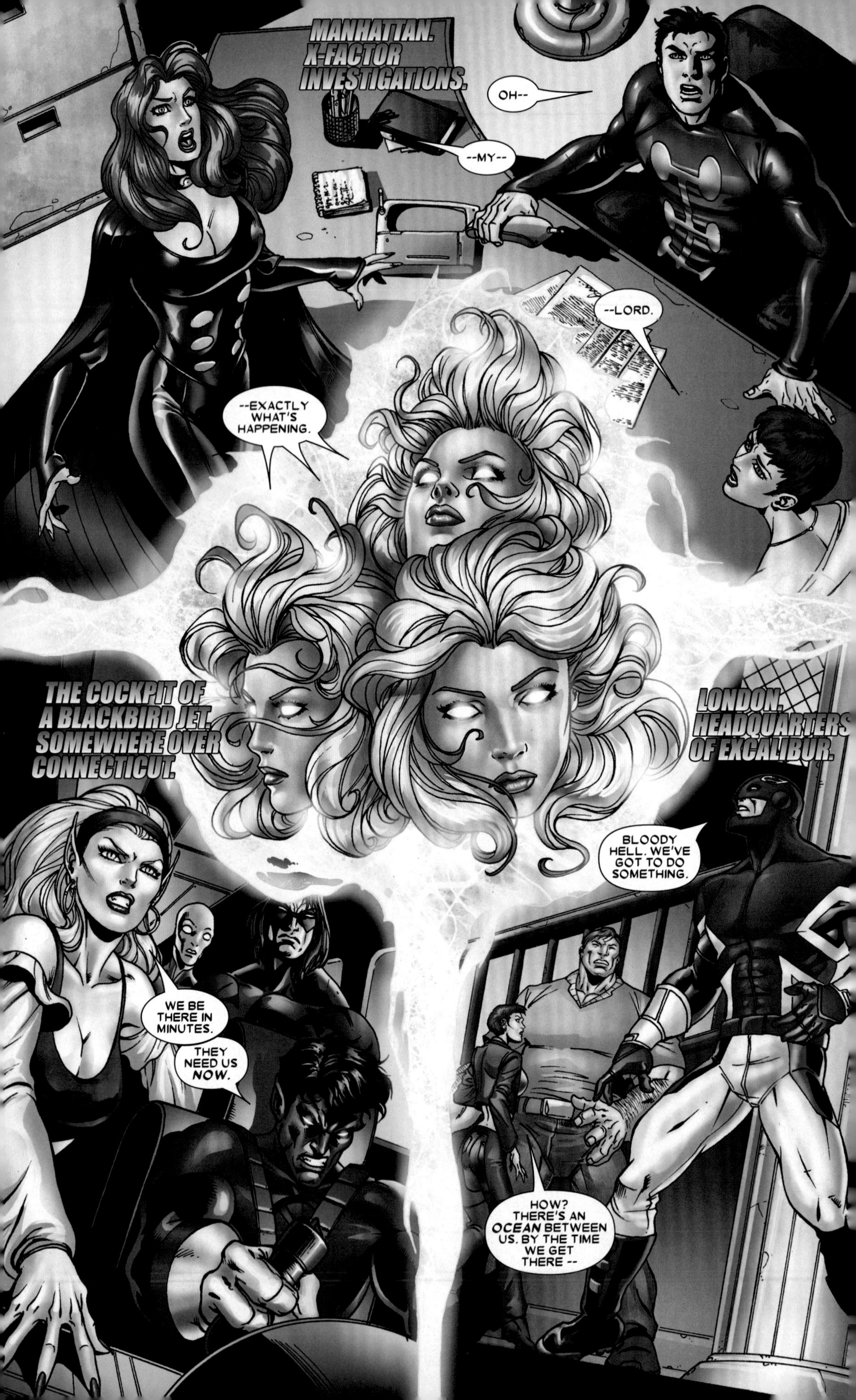

MANHATTAN. X-FACTOR INVESTIGATIONS.
OH--
--MY--
--LORD.
--EXACTLY WHAT'S HAPPENING.
THE COCKPIT OF A BLACKBIRD JET. SOMEWHERE OVER CONNECTICUT.
WE BE THERE IN MINUTES.
THEY NEED US NOW.
LONDON. HEADQUARTERS OF EXCALIBUR.
BLOODY HELL. WE'VE GOT TO DO SOMETHING.
HOW? THERE'S AN OCEAN BETWEEN US. BY THE TIME WE GET THERE --

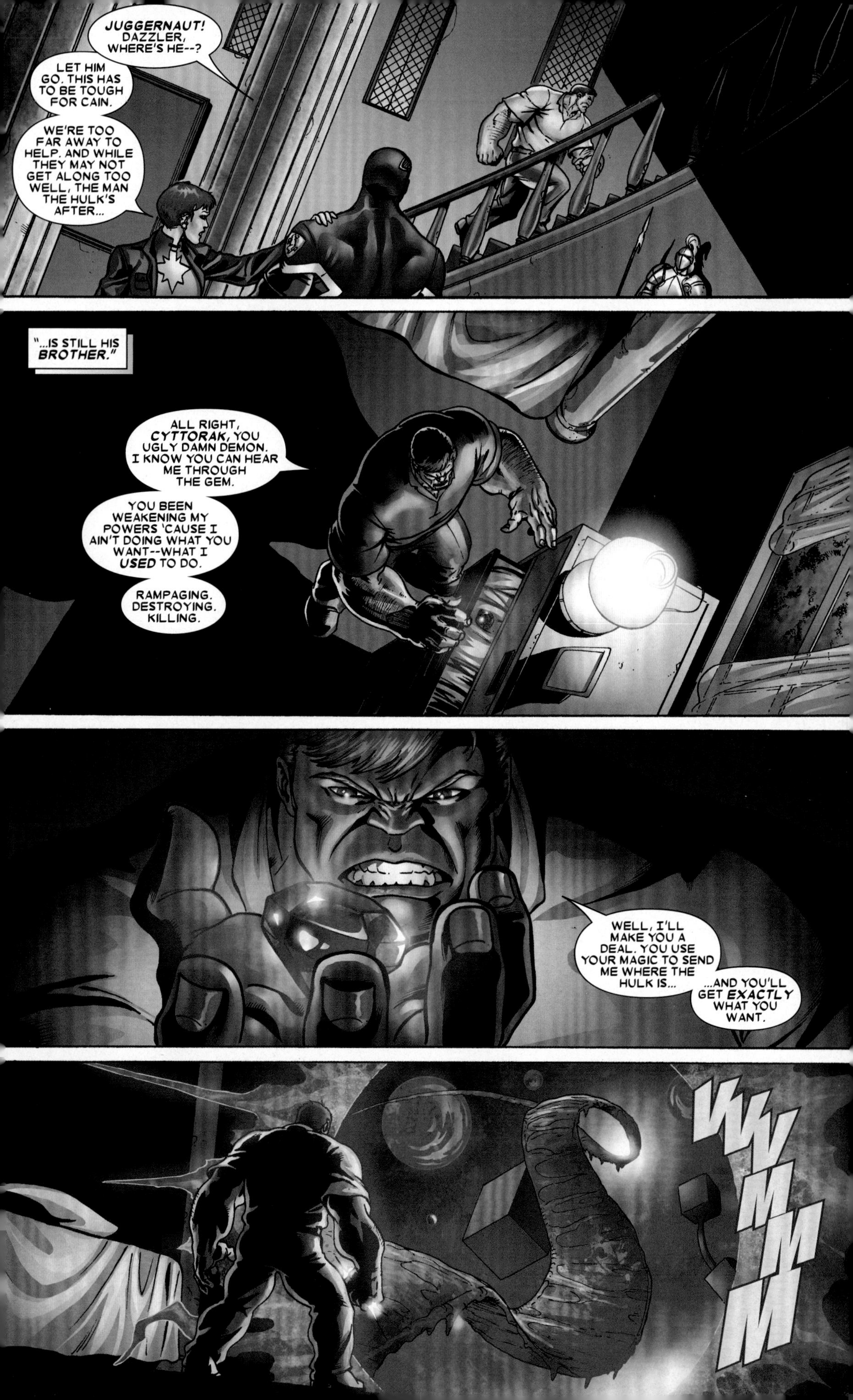
JUGGERNAUT! DAZZLER, WHERE'S HE--?
LET HIM GO. THIS HAS TO BE TOUGH FOR CAIN.
WE'RE TOO FAR AWAY TO HELP. AND WHILE THEY MAY NOT GET ALONG TOO WELL, THE MAN THE HULK'S AFTER...
"...IS STILL HIS BROTHER."
ALL RIGHT, CYTTORAK, YOU UGLY DAMN DEMON. I KNOW YOU CAN HEAR ME THROUGH THE GEM.
YOU BEEN WEAKENING MY POWERS 'CAUSE I AIN'T DOING WHAT YOU WANT--WHAT I USED TO DO.
RAMPAGING. DESTROYING. KILLING.
WELL, I'LL MAKE YOU A DEAL. YOU USE YOUR MAGIC TO SEND ME WHERE THE HULK IS...
...AND YOU'LL GET EXACTLY WHAT YOU WANT.
VVVMMMM

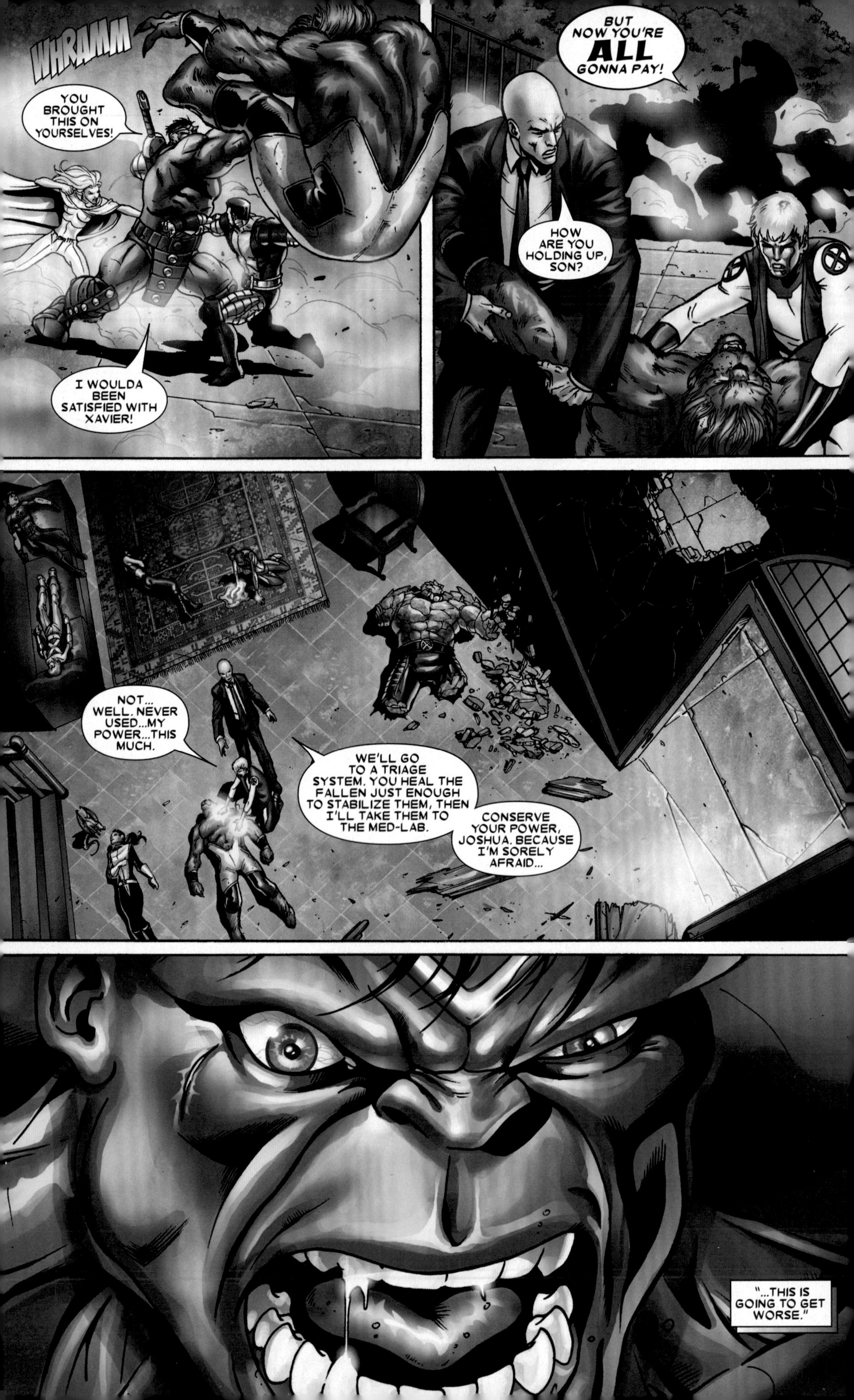
WHRAMM
YOU BROUGHT THIS ON YOURSELVES!
I WOULDA BEEN SATISFIED WITH XAVIER!
BUT NOW YOU'RE ALL GONNA PAY!
HOW ARE YOU HOLDING UP, SON?
NOT... WELL. NEVER USED...MY POWER...THIS MUCH.
WE'LL GO TO A TRIAGE SYSTEM. YOU HEAL THE FALLEN JUST ENOUGH TO STABILIZE THEM, THEN I'LL TAKE THEM TO THE MED-LAB.
CONSERVE YOUR POWER, JOSHUA. BECAUSE I'M SORELY AFRAID...
"...THIS IS GOING TO GET WORSE."

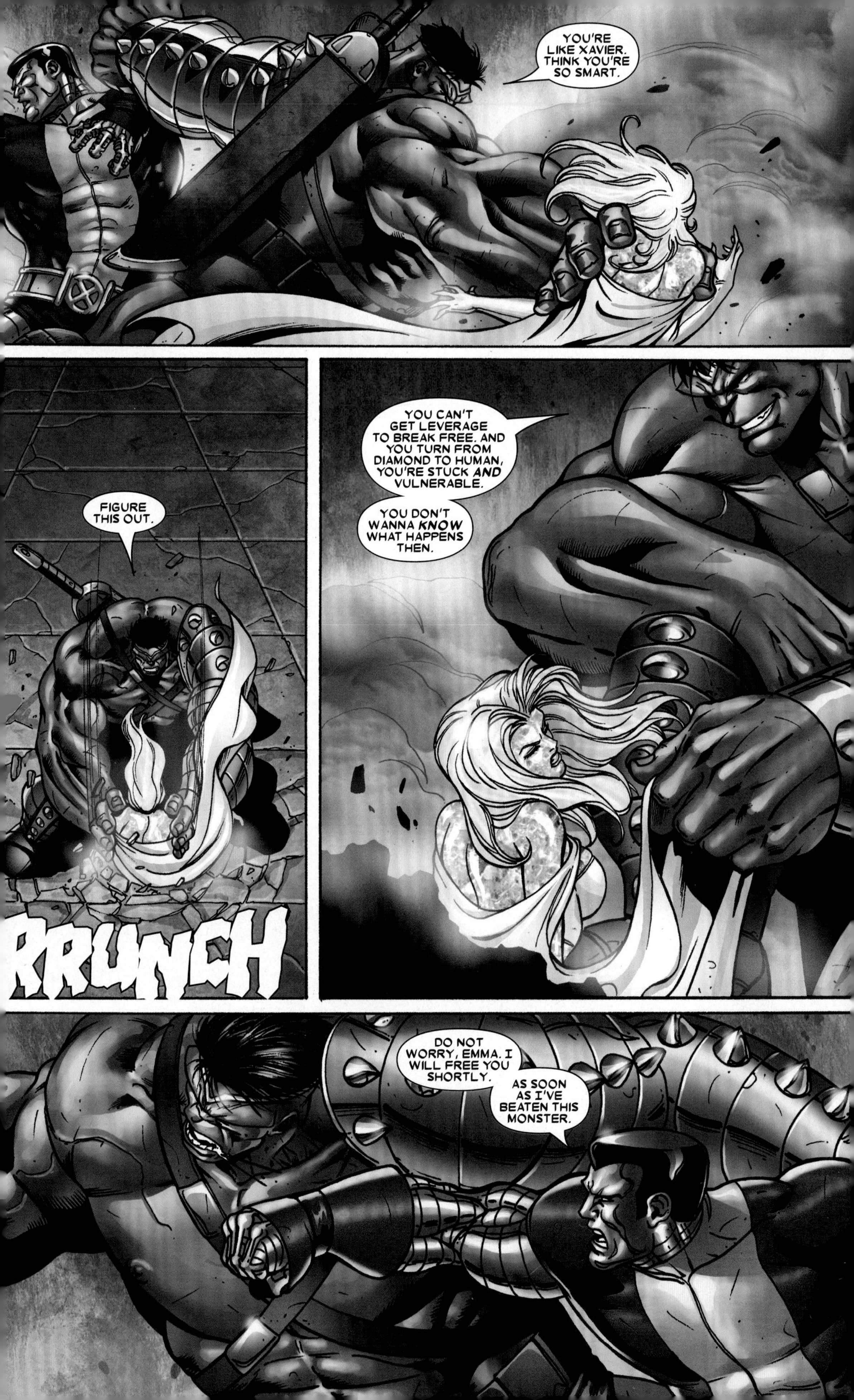

YOU'RE LIKE XAVIER. THINK YOU'RE SO SMART.
FIGURE THIS OUT.
RRUNCH
YOU CAN'T GET LEVERAGE TO BREAK FREE. AND YOU TURN FROM DIAMOND TO HUMAN, YOU'RE STUCK *AND* VULNERABLE.
YOU DON'T WANNA *KNOW* WHAT HAPPENS THEN.
DO NOT WORRY, EMMA. I WILL FREE YOU SHORTLY.
AS SOON AS I'VE BEATEN THIS MONSTER.

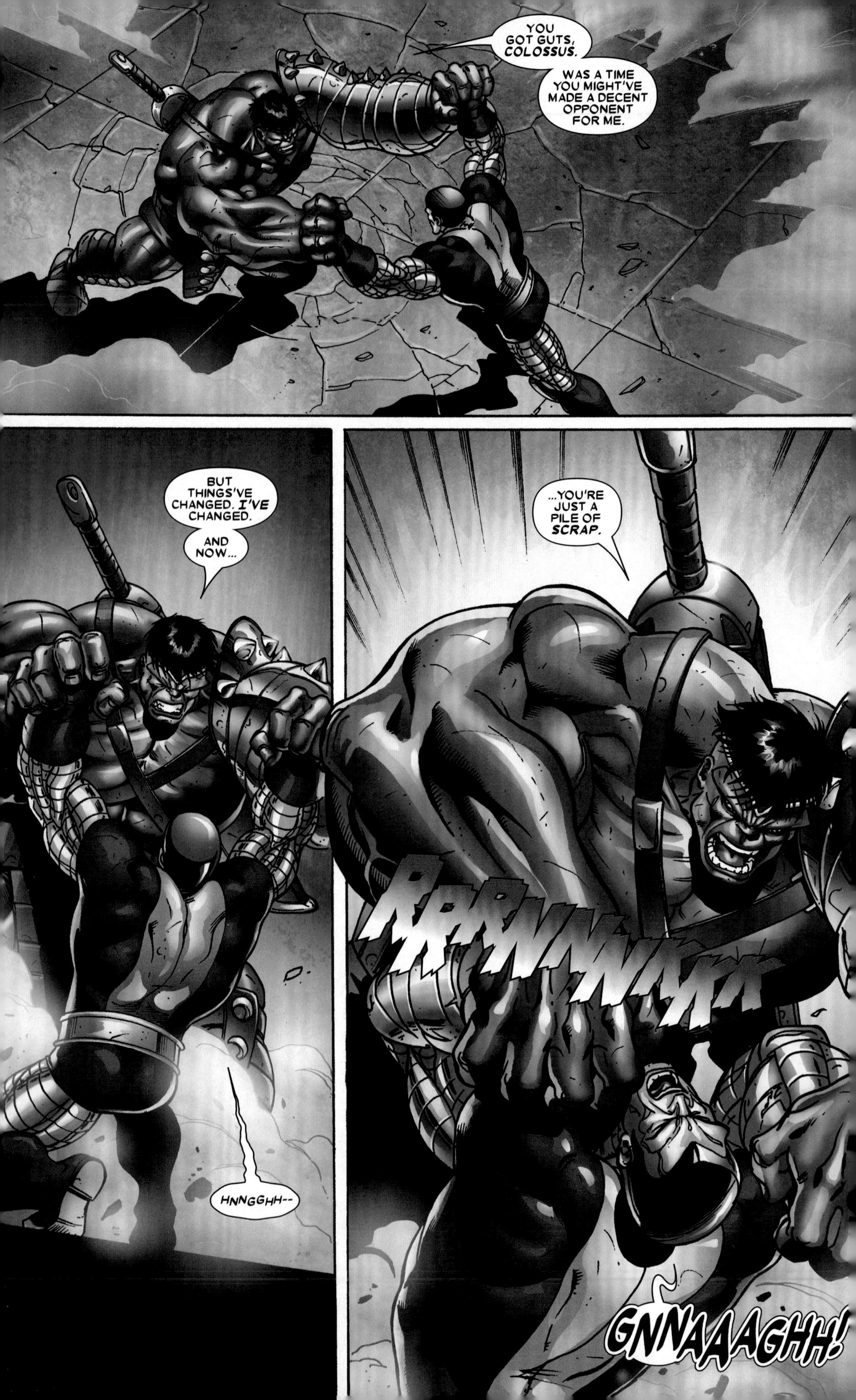
YOU GOT GUTS, *COLOSSUS.*
WAS A TIME YOU MIGHT'VE MADE A DECENT OPPONENT FOR ME.
BUT THINGS'VE CHANGED. *I'VE* CHANGED.
AND NOW...
HNNGGHH--
...YOU'RE JUST A PILE OF *SCRAP.*
RRRNNNNNKK
GNNAAAAGHH!

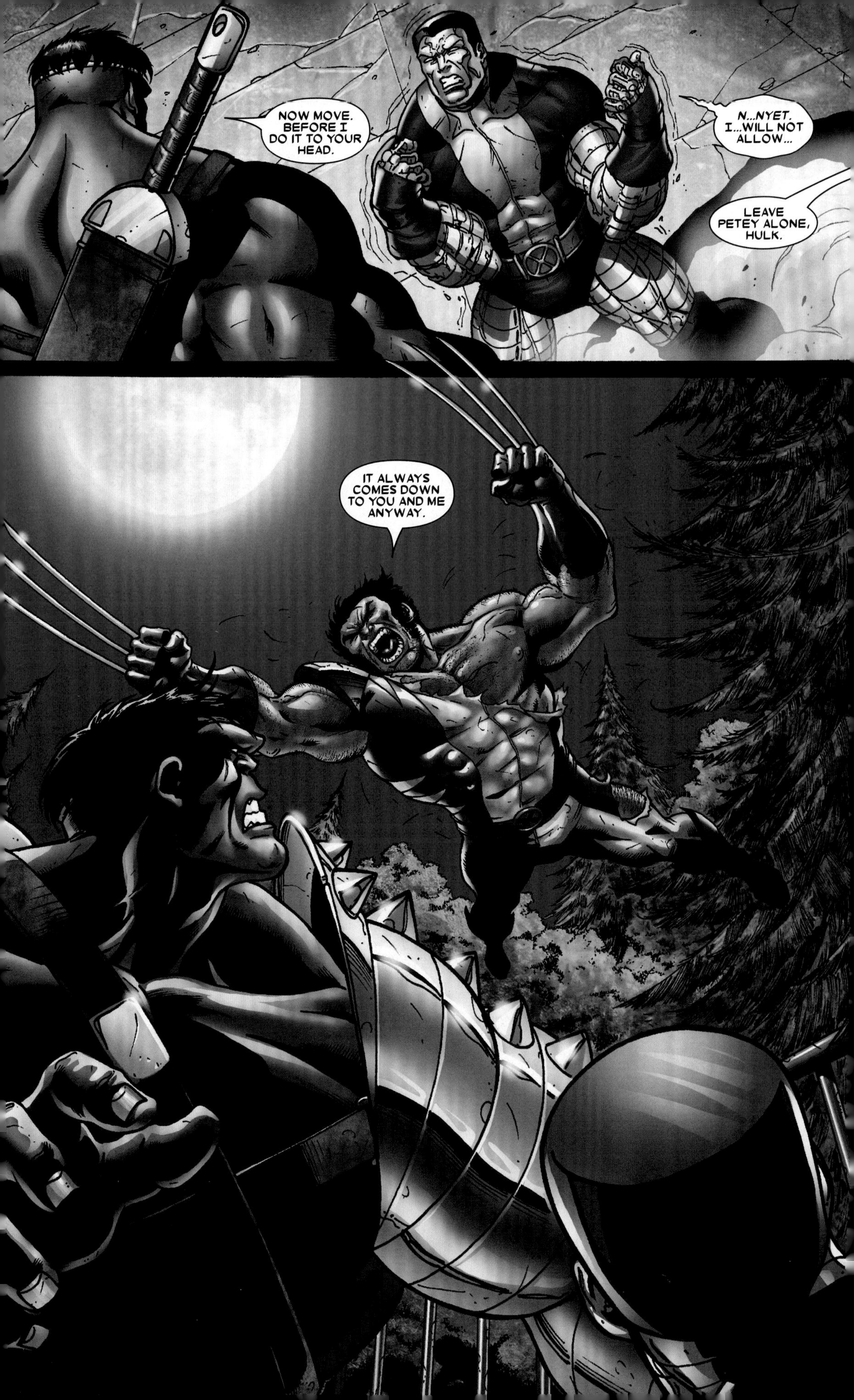
NOW MOVE. BEFORE I DO IT TO YOUR HEAD.
N...NYET. I...WILL NOT ALLOW...
LEAVE PETEY ALONE, HULK.
IT ALWAYS COMES DOWN TO YOU AND ME ANYWAY.

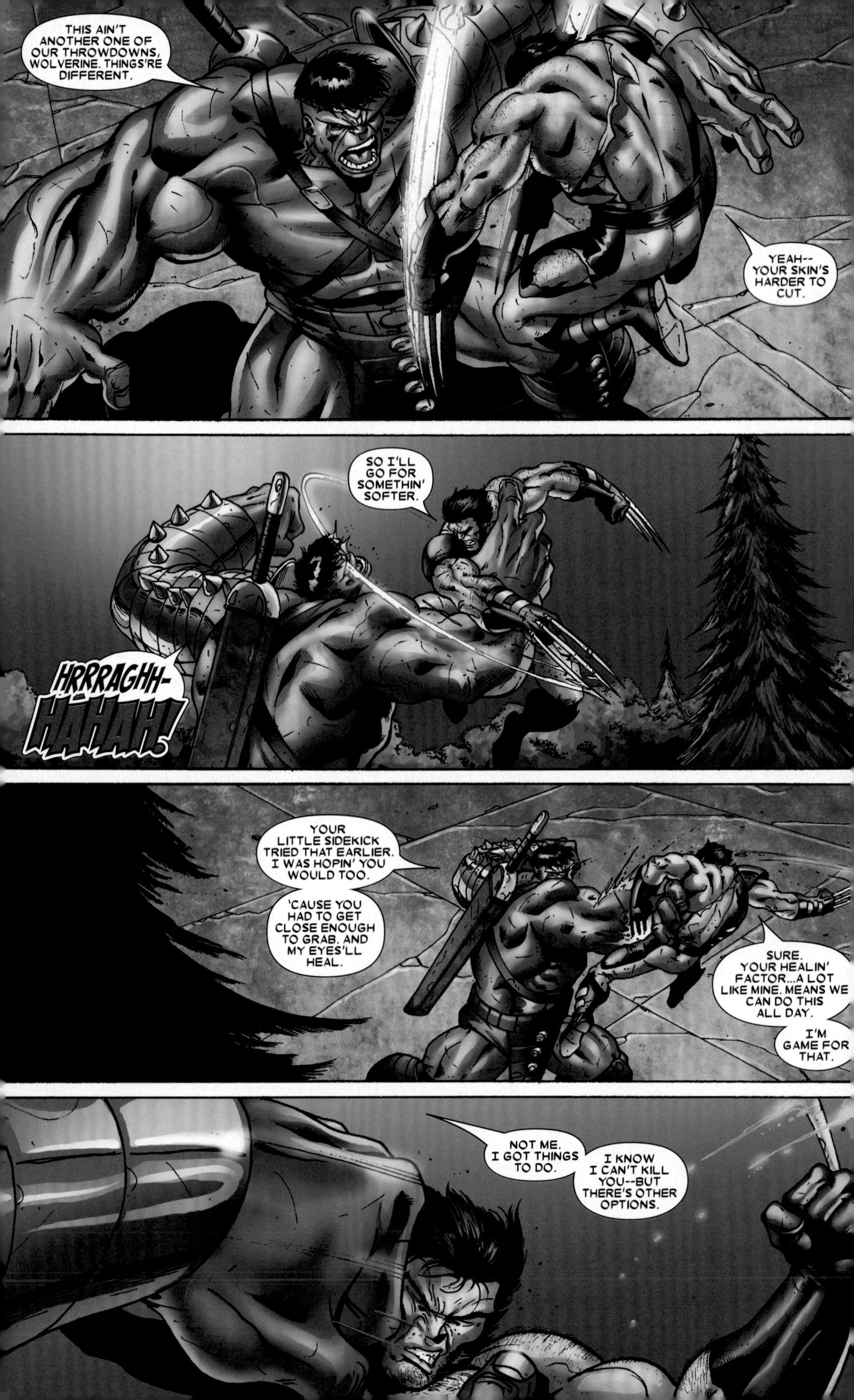
THIS AIN'T ANOTHER ONE OF OUR THROWDOWNS, WOLVERINE. THINGS'RE DIFFERENT.
YEAH-- YOUR SKIN'S HARDER TO CUT.
SO I'LL GO FOR SOMETHIN' SOFTER.
HRRRAGHH-HAHAH!
YOUR LITTLE SIDEKICK TRIED THAT EARLIER. I WAS HOPIN' YOU WOULD TOO.
'CAUSE YOU HAD TO GET CLOSE ENOUGH TO GRAB. AND MY EYES'LL HEAL.
SURE. YOUR HEALIN' FACTOR...A LOT LIKE MINE. MEANS WE CAN DO THIS ALL DAY.
I'M GAME FOR THAT.
NOT ME. I GOT THINGS TO DO.
I KNOW I CAN'T KILL YOU--BUT THERE'S OTHER OPTIONS.

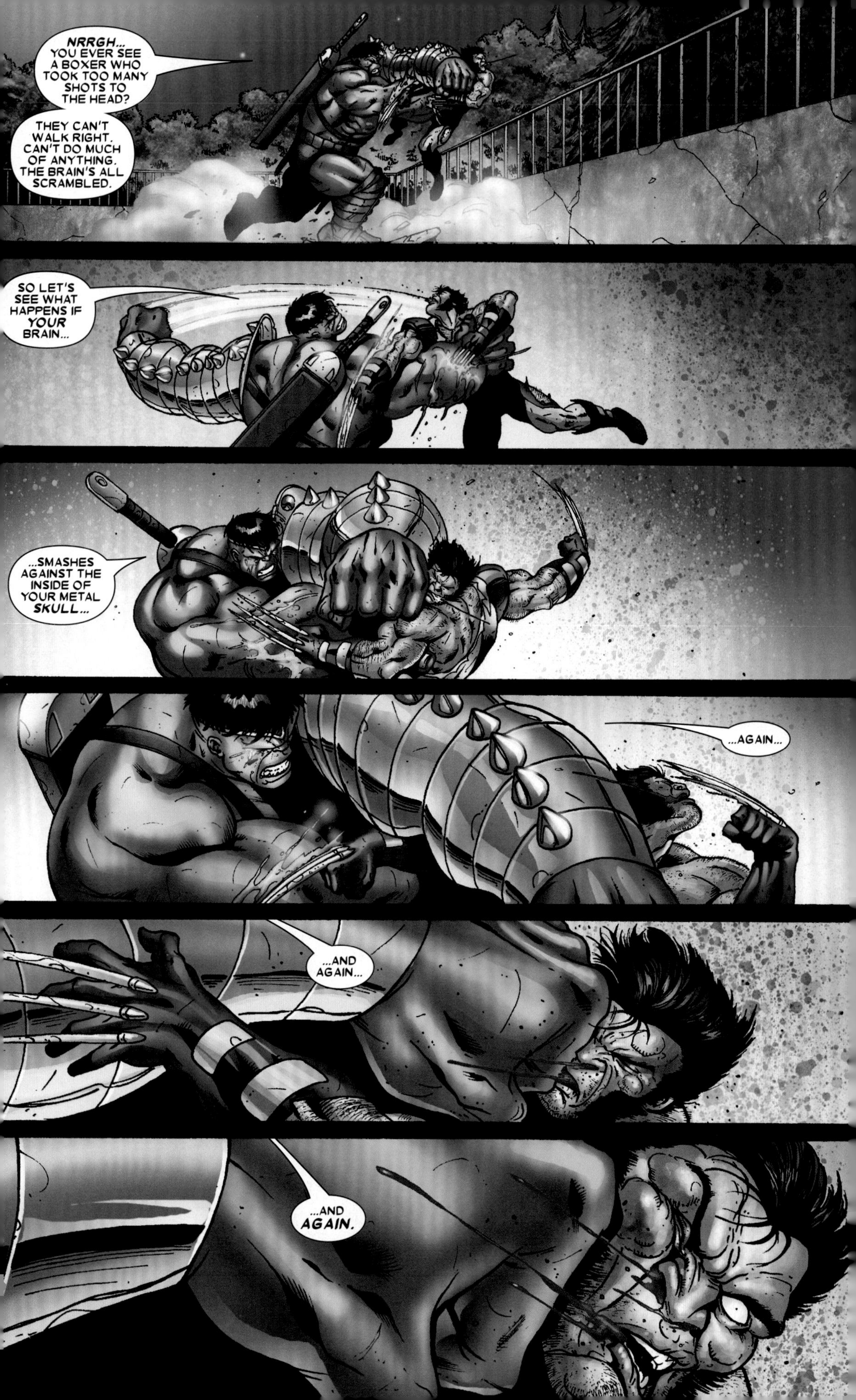
NRRGH... YOU EVER SEE A BOXER WHO TOOK TOO MANY SHOTS TO THE HEAD?
THEY CAN'T WALK RIGHT. CAN'T DO MUCH OF ANYTHING. THE BRAIN'S ALL SCRAMBLED.
SO LET'S SEE WHAT HAPPENS IF YOUR BRAIN...
...SMASHES AGAINST THE INSIDE OF YOUR METAL SKULL...
...AGAIN...
...AND AGAIN...
...AND AGAIN.

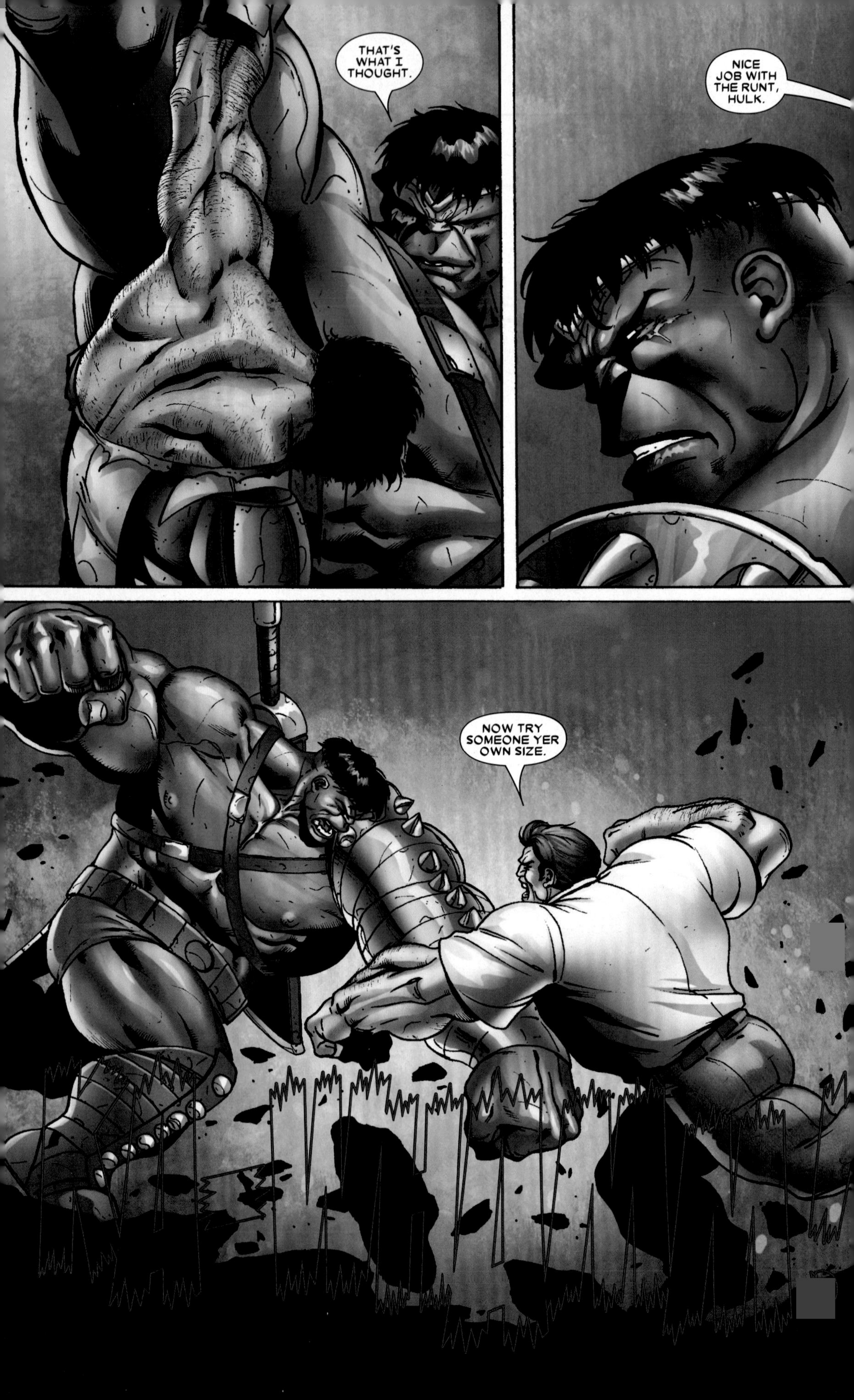
THAT'S WHAT I THOUGHT.
NICE JOB WITH THE RUNT, HULK.
NOW TRY SOMEONE YER OWN SIZE.

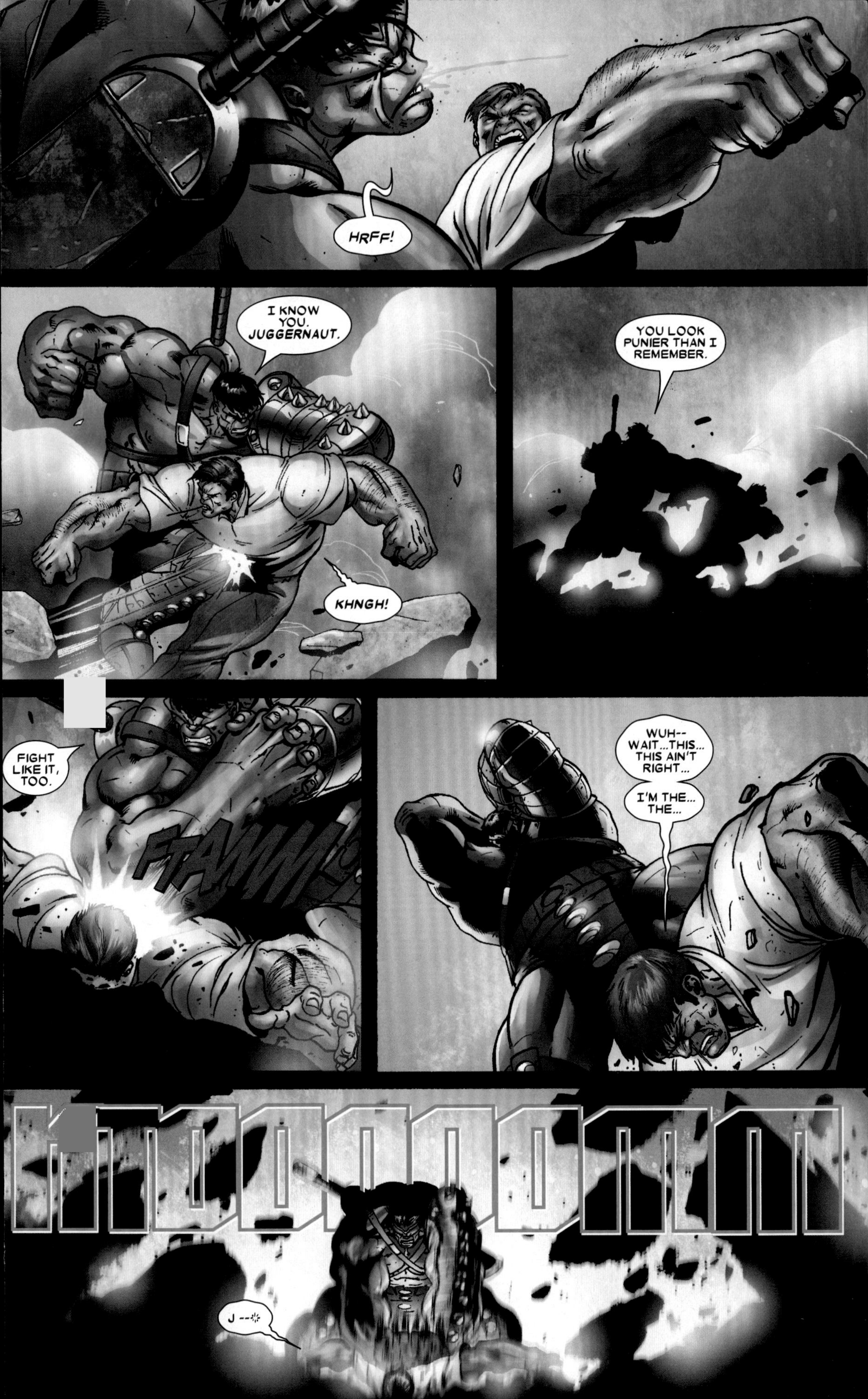
HRFF!
I KNOW YOU. JUGGERNAUT.
KHNGH!
YOU LOOK PUNIER THAN I REMEMBER.
FIGHT LIKE IT, TOO.
WUH-- WAIT...THIS... THIS AIN'T RIGHT...
I'M THE... THE...
J --

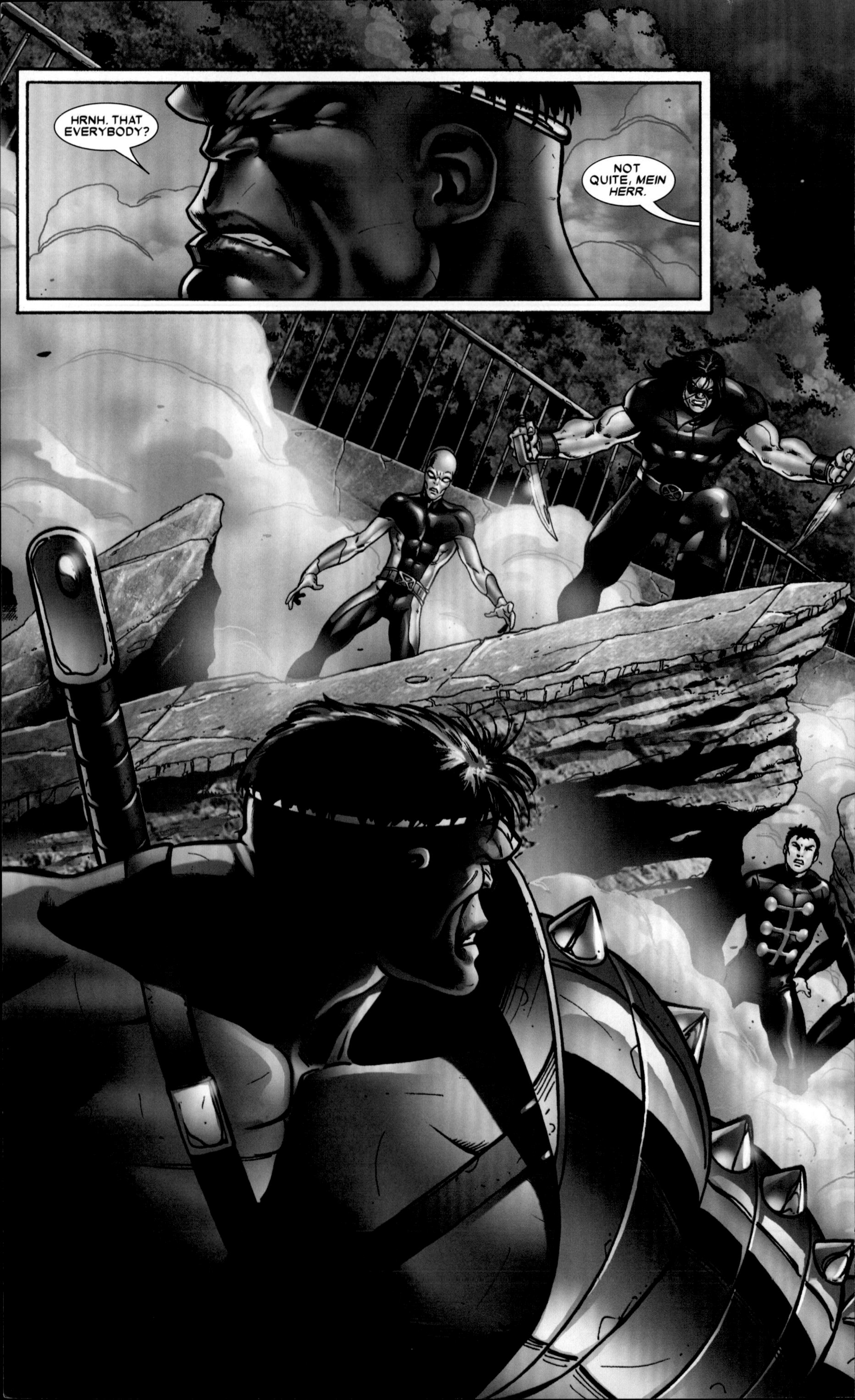
HRNH. THAT EVERYBODY?
NOT QUITE, MEIN HERR.

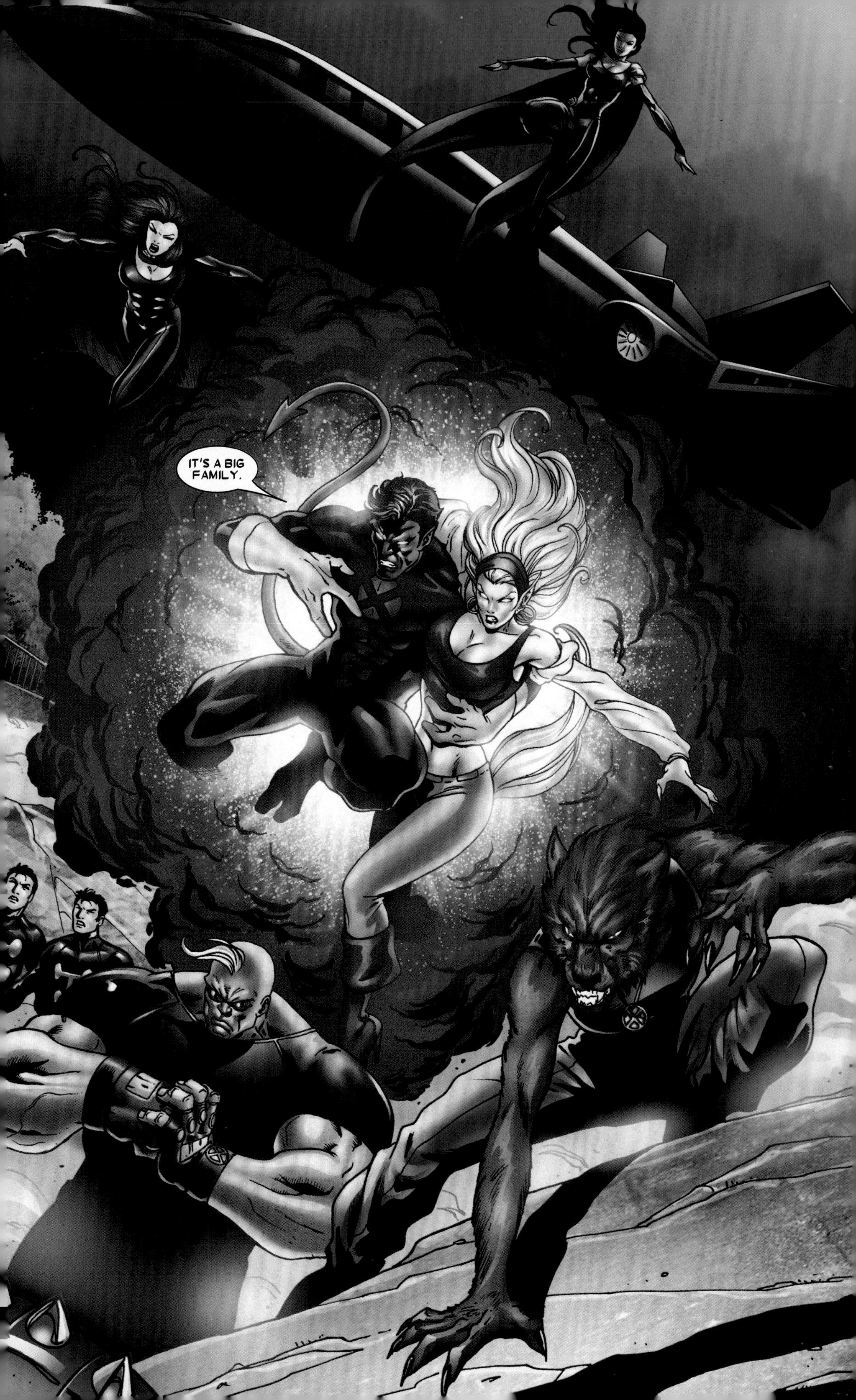
IT'S A BIG FAMILY.

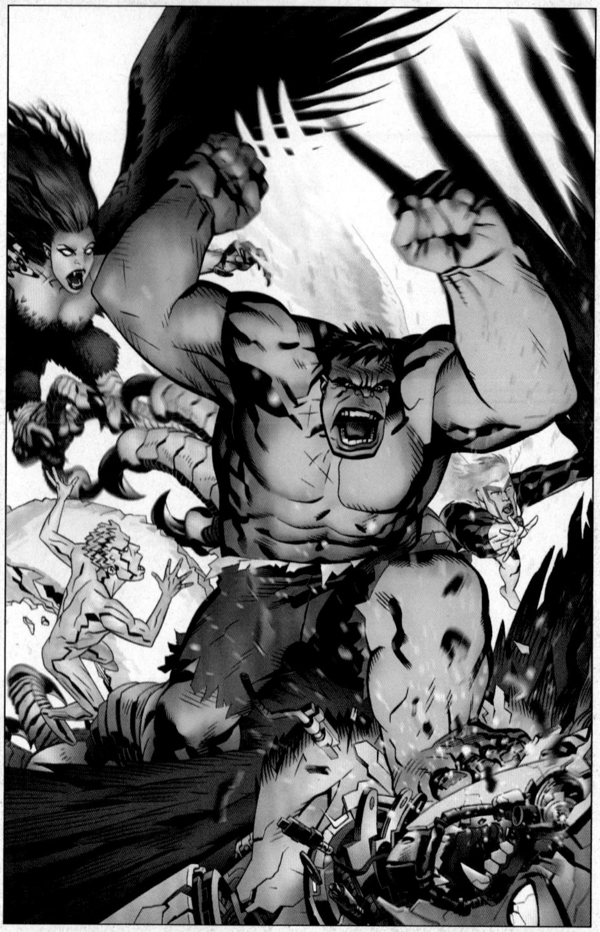

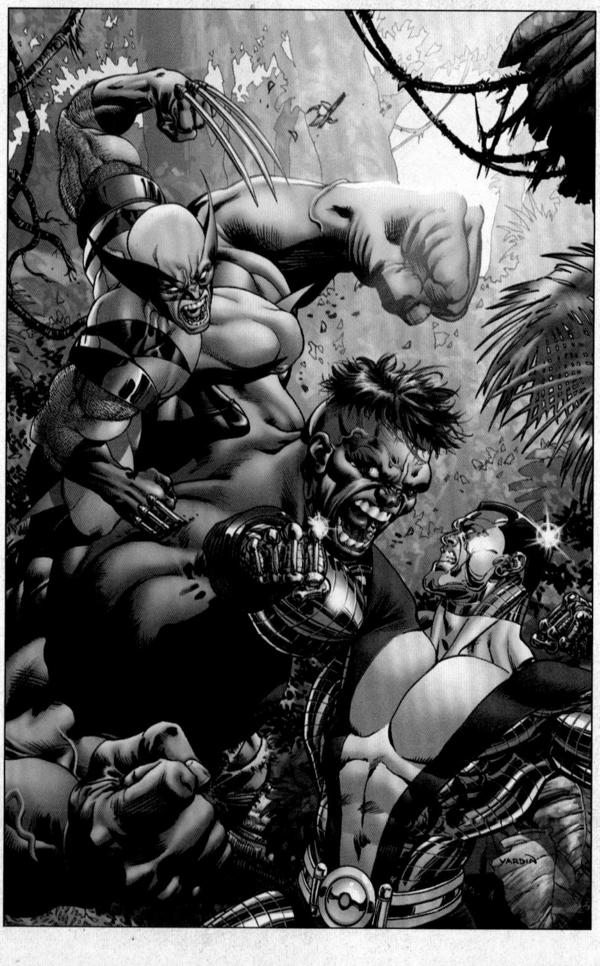
YARDIN

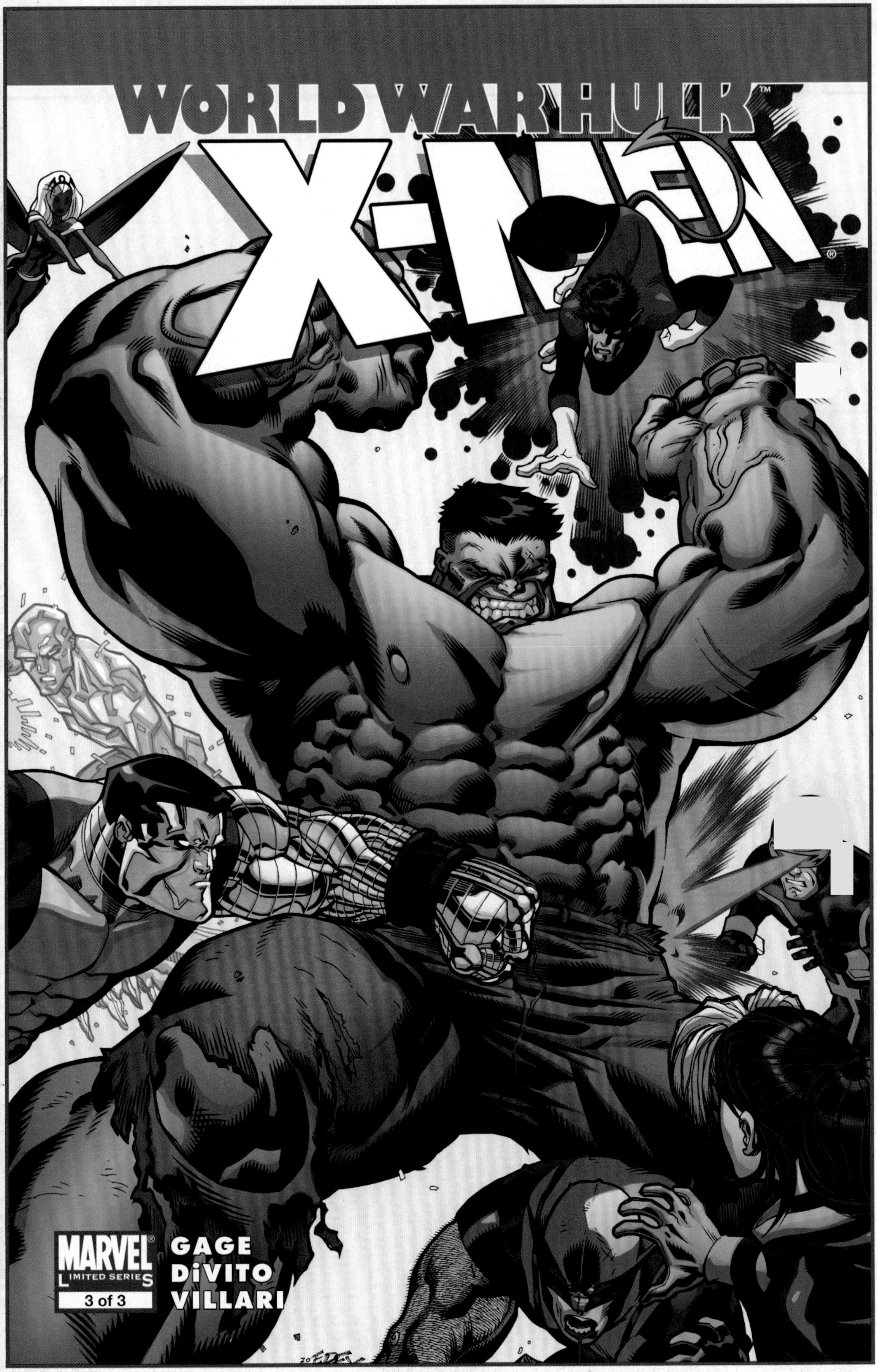
WORLD WAR HULK™
X-MEN®
MARVEL®
LIMITED SERIES
3 of 3
GAGE
DiVITO
VILLARI

★★★ ROUND 3 ★★★

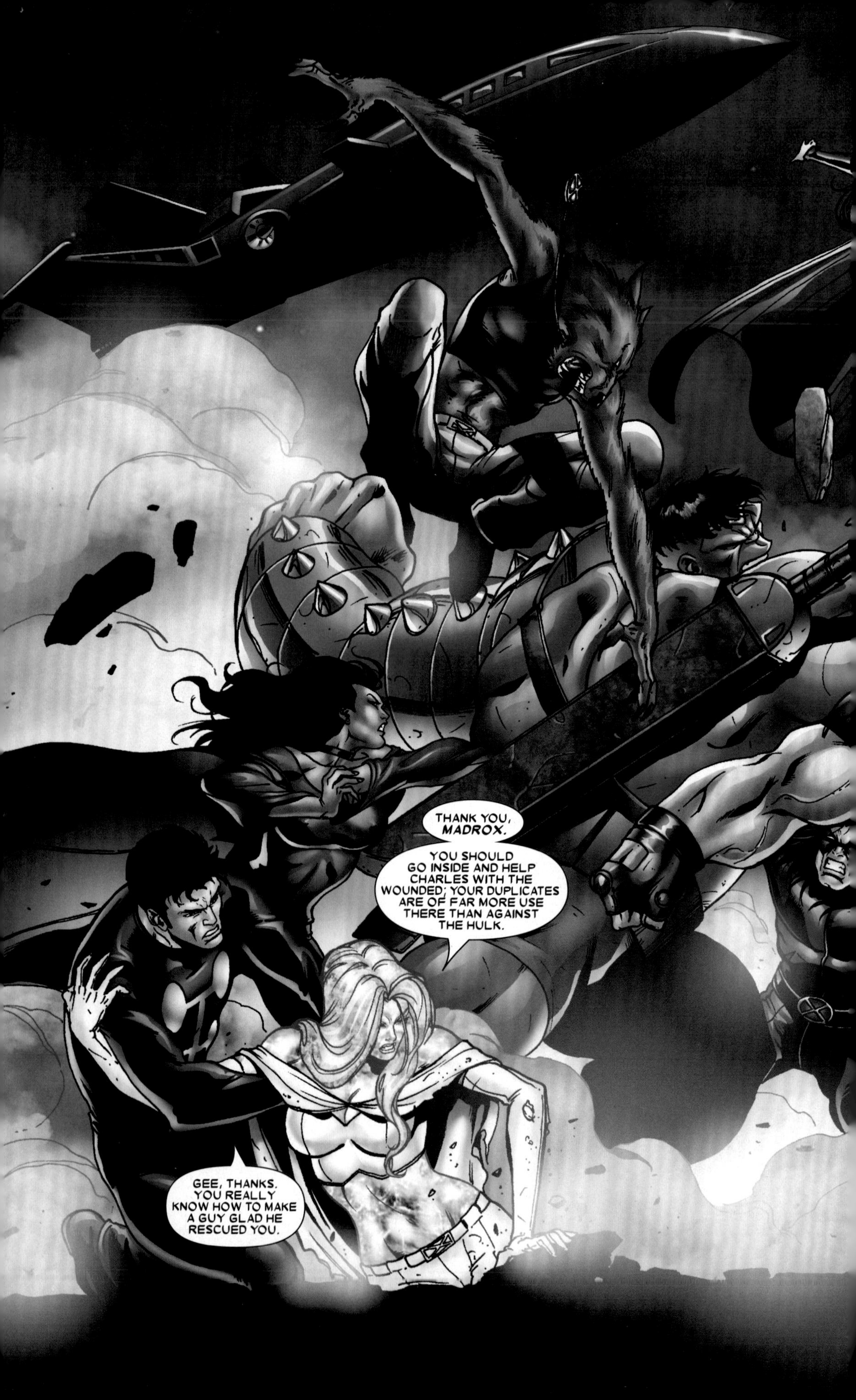
THANK YOU, *MADROX.*
YOU SHOULD GO INSIDE AND HELP CHARLES WITH THE WOUNDED; YOUR DUPLICATES ARE OF FAR MORE USE THERE THAN AGAINST THE HULK.
GEE, THANKS. YOU REALLY KNOW HOW TO MAKE A GUY GLAD HE RESCUED YOU.

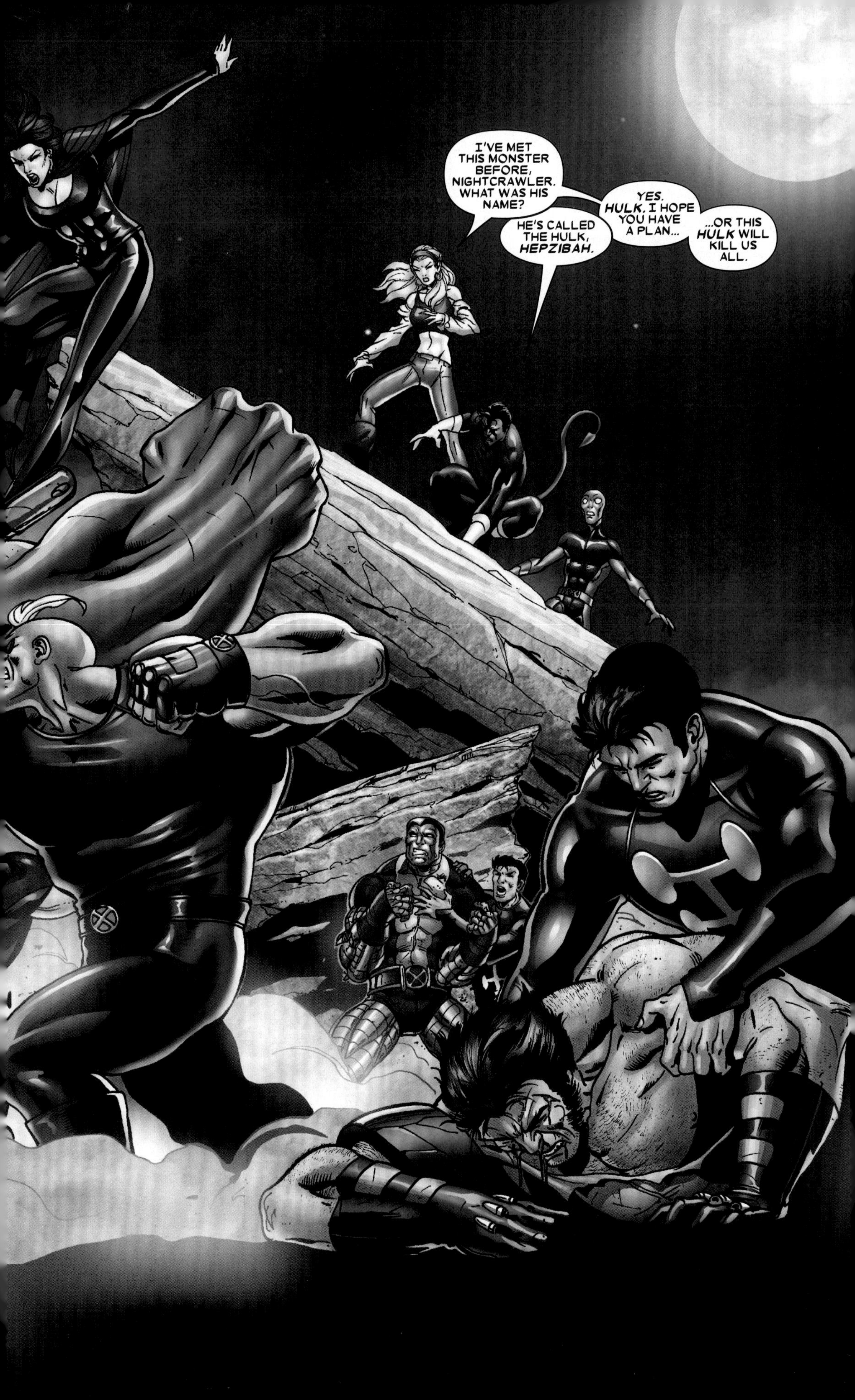
I'VE MET THIS MONSTER BEFORE, NIGHTCRAWLER. WHAT WAS HIS NAME?
HE'S CALLED THE HULK, HEPZIBAH.
YES. HULK. I HOPE YOU HAVE A PLAN...
...OR THIS HULK WILL KILL US ALL.

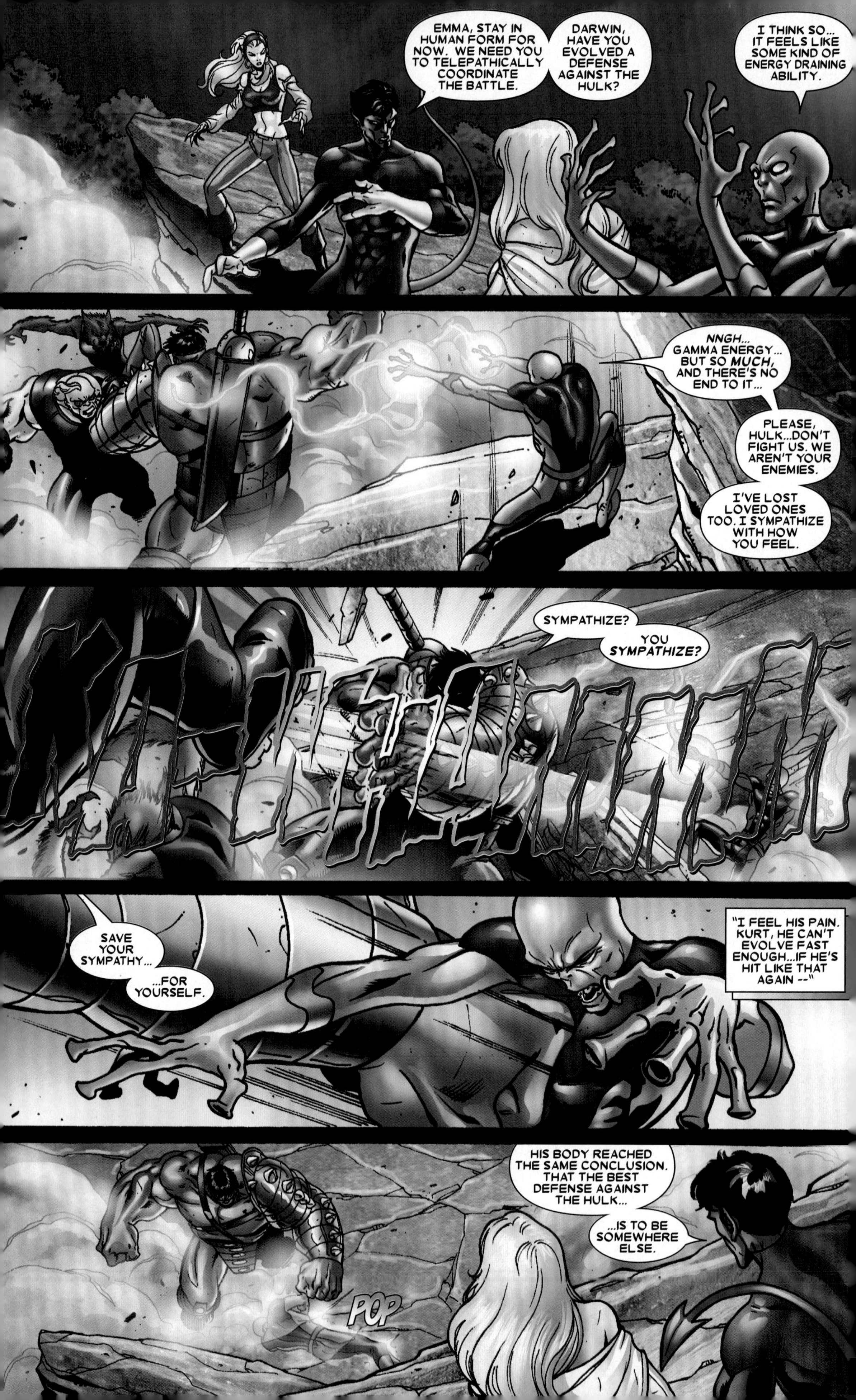
EMMA, STAY IN HUMAN FORM FOR NOW. WE NEED YOU TO TELEPATHICALLY COORDINATE THE BATTLE.
DARWIN, HAVE YOU EVOLVED A DEFENSE AGAINST THE HULK?
I THINK SO... IT FEELS LIKE SOME KIND OF ENERGY DRAINING ABILITY.
NNGH... GAMMA ENERGY... BUT SO MUCH, AND THERE'S NO END TO IT...
PLEASE, HULK...DON'T FIGHT US. WE AREN'T YOUR ENEMIES.
I'VE LOST LOVED ONES TOO. I SYMPATHIZE WITH HOW YOU FEEL.
SYMPATHIZE?
YOU SYMPATHIZE?
SAVE YOUR SYMPATHY...
...FOR YOURSELF.
"I FEEL HIS PAIN. KURT, HE CAN'T EVOLVE FAST ENOUGH...IF HE'S HIT LIKE THAT AGAIN --"
HIS BODY REACHED THE SAME CONCLUSION. THAT THE BEST DEFENSE AGAINST THE HULK...
...IS TO BE SOMEWHERE ELSE.
POP

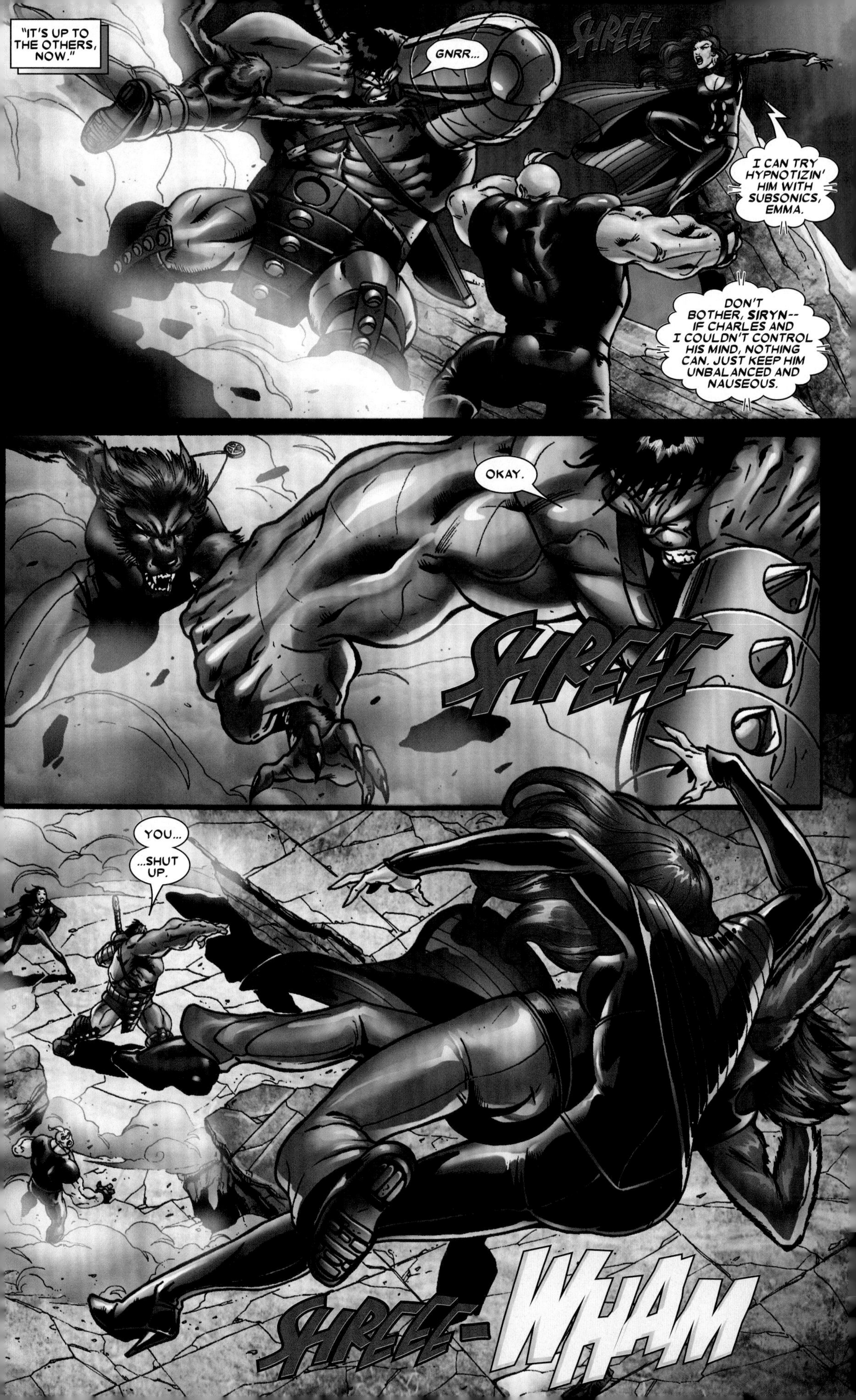
"IT'S UP TO THE OTHERS, NOW."
GNRR...
SHREEE
I CAN TRY HYPNOTIZIN' HIM WITH SUBSONICS, EMMA.
DON'T BOTHER, SIRYN-- IF CHARLES AND I COULDN'T CONTROL HIS MIND, NOTHING CAN. JUST KEEP HIM UNBALANCED AND NAUSEOUS.
OKAY.
SHREEE
YOU...
...SHUT UP.
SHREEE-WHAM

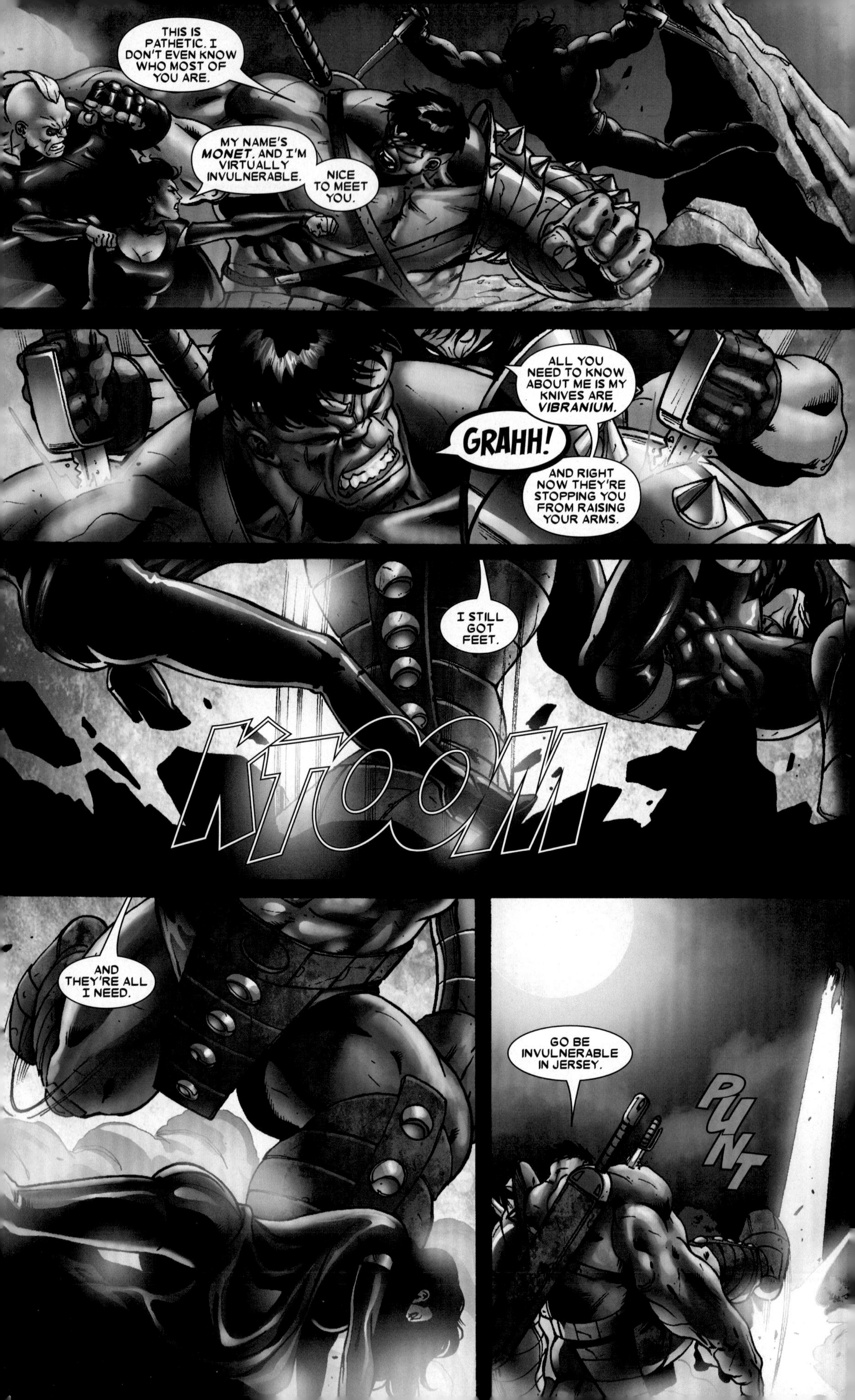
THIS IS PATHETIC. I DON'T EVEN KNOW WHO MOST OF YOU ARE.
MY NAME'S *MONET*, AND I'M VIRTUALLY INVULNERABLE.
NICE TO MEET YOU.
ALL YOU NEED TO KNOW ABOUT ME IS MY KNIVES ARE *VIBRANIUM*.
GRAHH!
AND RIGHT NOW THEY'RE STOPPING YOU FROM RAISING YOUR ARMS.
I STILL GOT FEET.
K'TOOM
AND THEY'RE ALL I NEED.
GO BE INVULNERABLE IN JERSEY.
PUNT

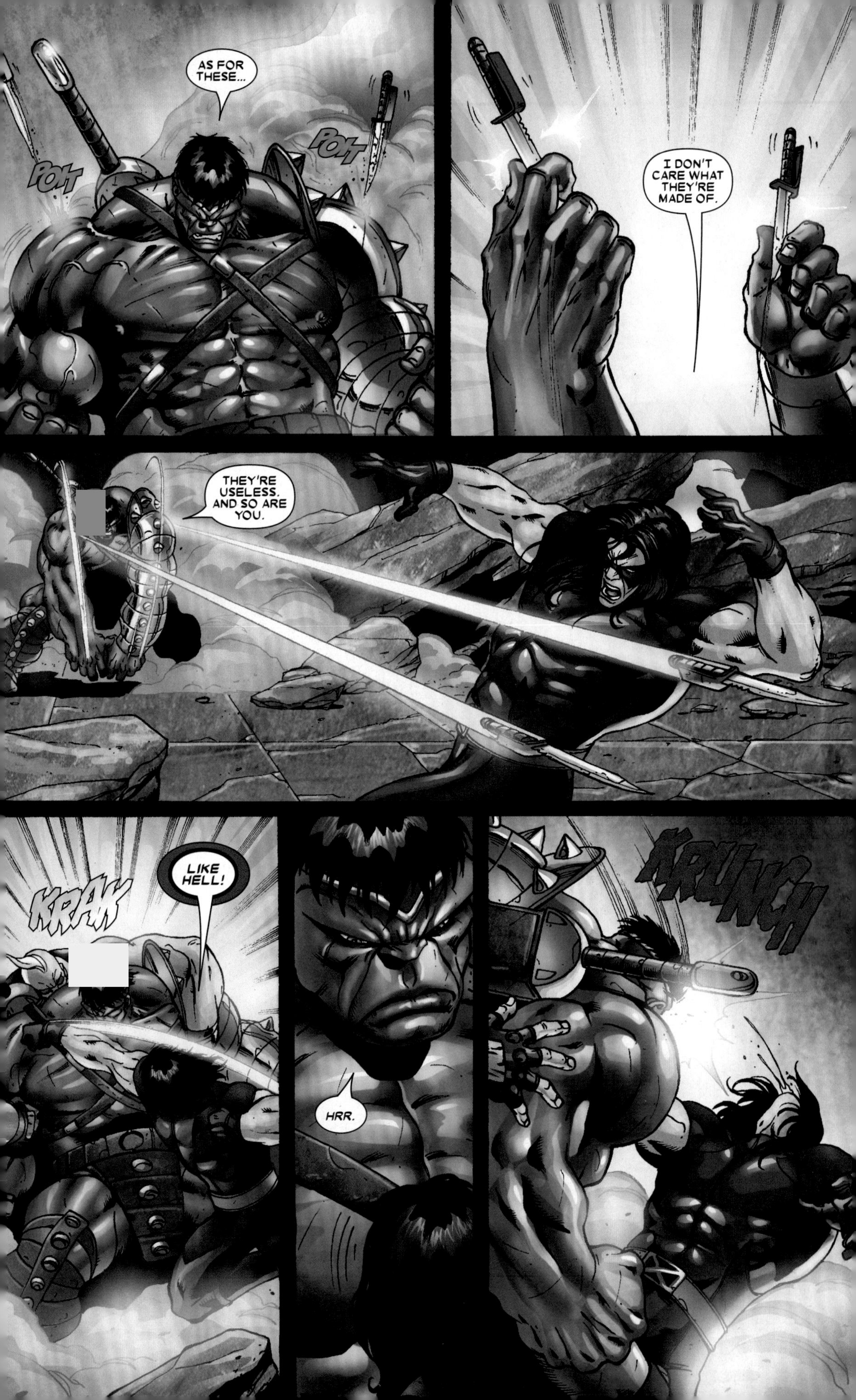
AS FOR THESE...
POIT
POIT
I DON'T CARE WHAT THEY'RE MADE OF.
THEY'RE USELESS. AND SO ARE YOU.
KRAK
LIKE HELL!
HRR.
KRUNCH

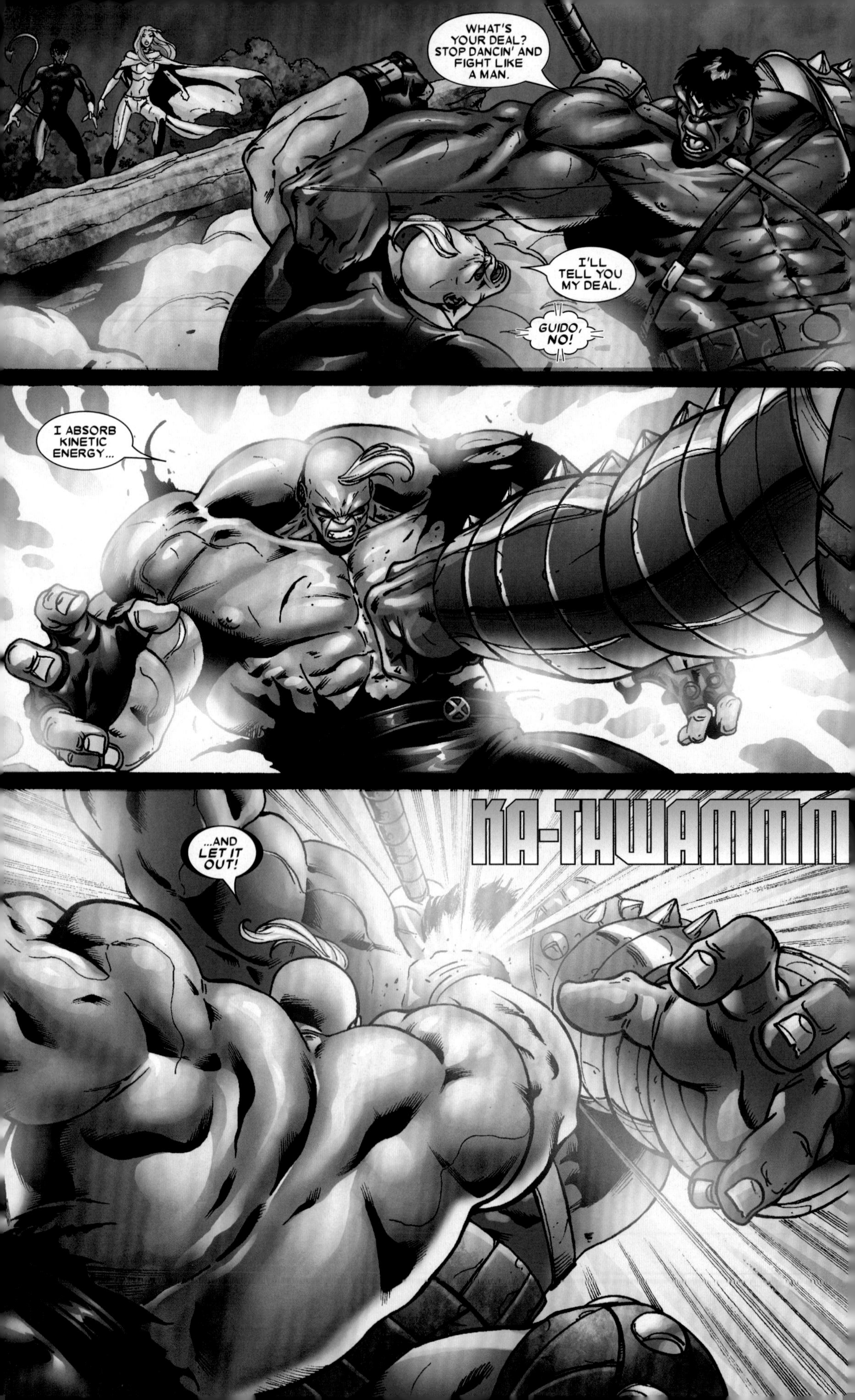
WHAT'S YOUR DEAL? STOP DANCIN' AND FIGHT LIKE A MAN.
I'LL TELL YOU MY DEAL.
GUIDO, NO!
I ABSORB KINETIC ENERGY...
KA-THWAMMM
...AND LET IT OUT!

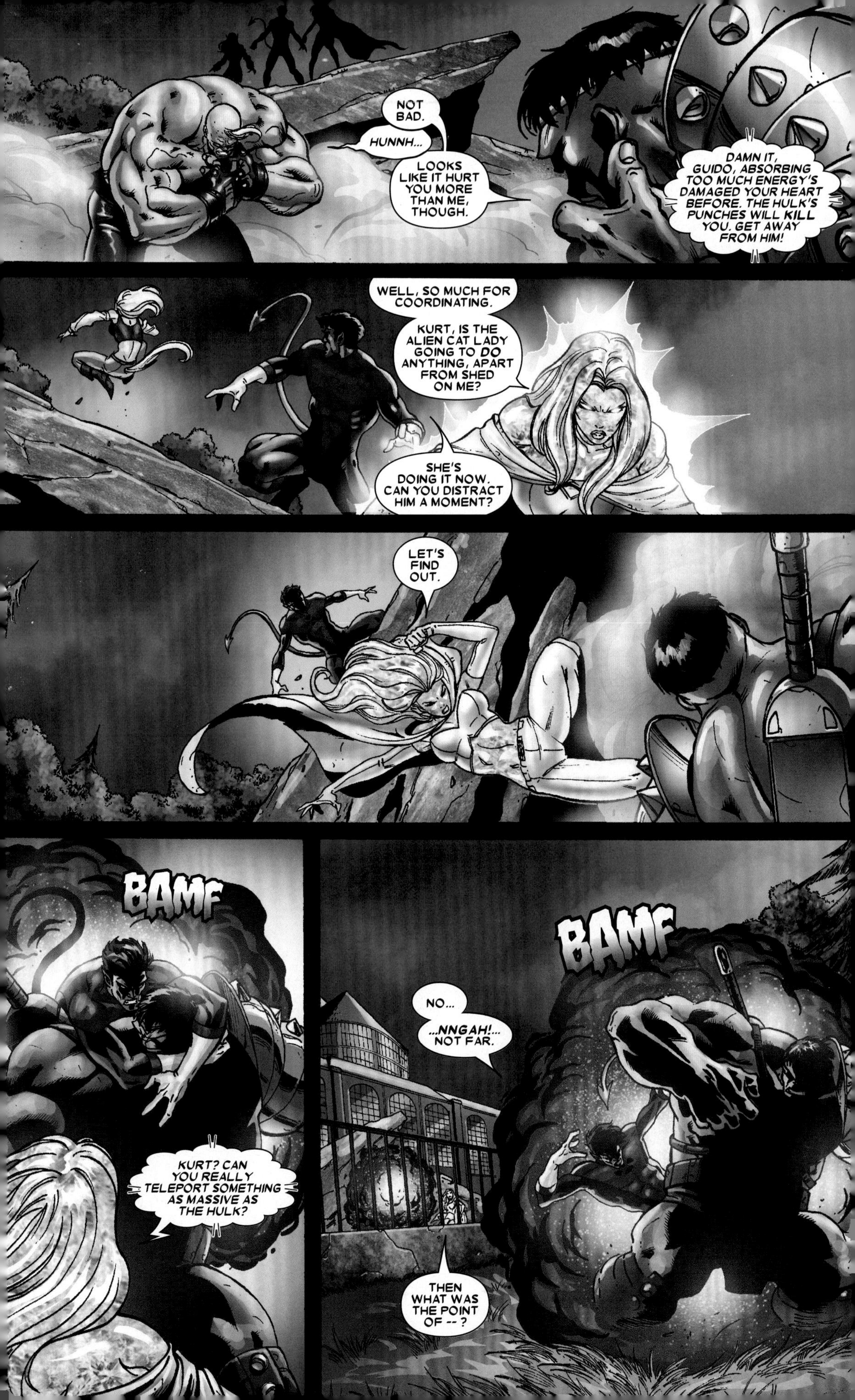
NOT BAD.
HUNNH...
LOOKS LIKE IT HURT YOU MORE THAN ME, THOUGH.
DAMN IT, GUIDO, ABSORBING TOO MUCH ENERGY'S DAMAGED YOUR HEART BEFORE. THE HULK'S PUNCHES WILL KILL YOU. GET AWAY FROM HIM!
WELL, SO MUCH FOR COORDINATING.
KURT, IS THE ALIEN CAT LADY GOING TO DO ANYTHING, APART FROM SHED ON ME?
SHE'S DOING IT NOW. CAN YOU DISTRACT HIM A MOMENT?
LET'S FIND OUT.
BAMF
KURT? CAN YOU REALLY TELEPORT SOMETHING AS MASSIVE AS THE HULK?
BAMF
NO...
...NNGAH!... NOT FAR.
THEN WHAT WAS THE POINT OF -- ?

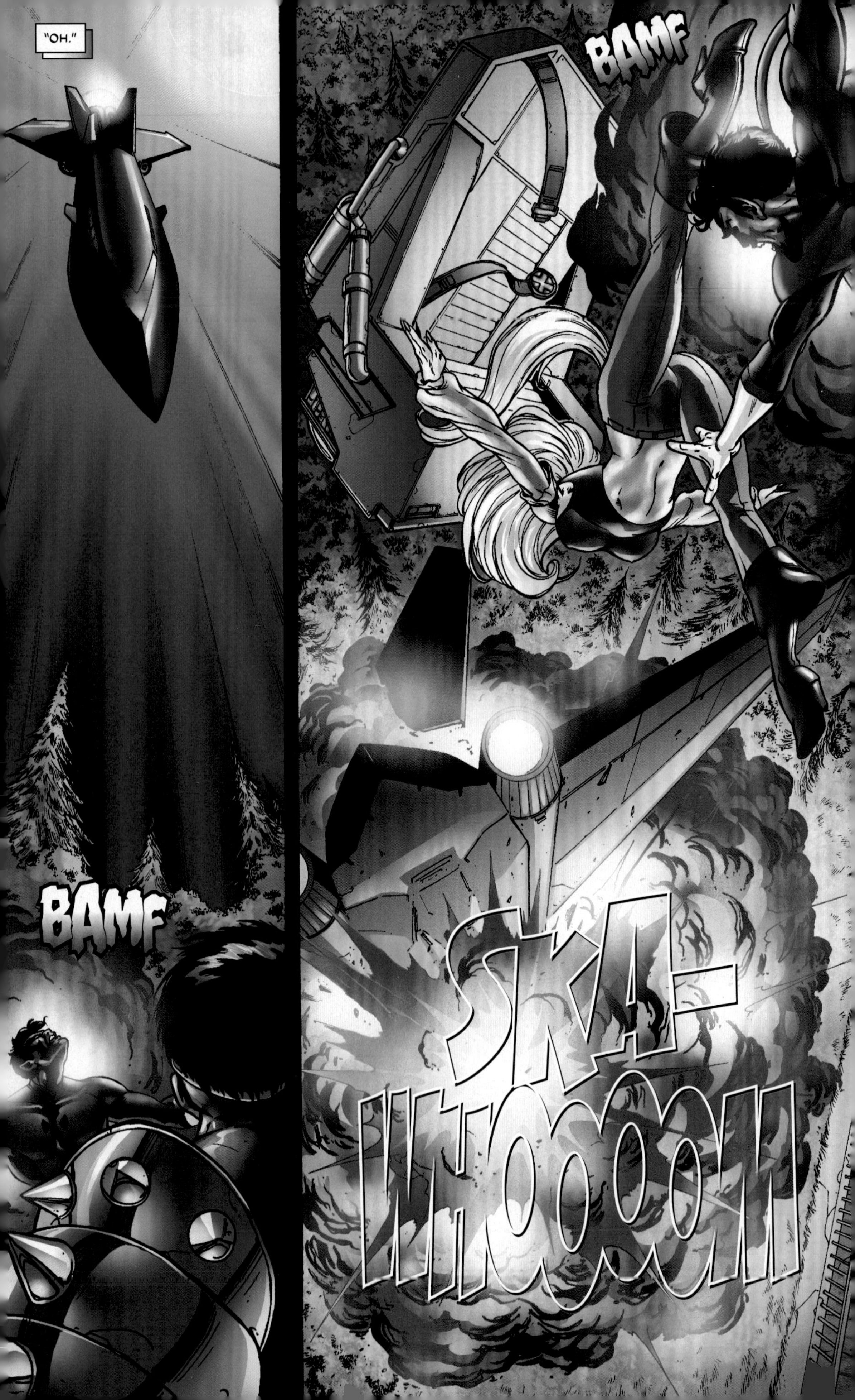
"OH."
BAMF
BAMF
SKA-WHOOOOM

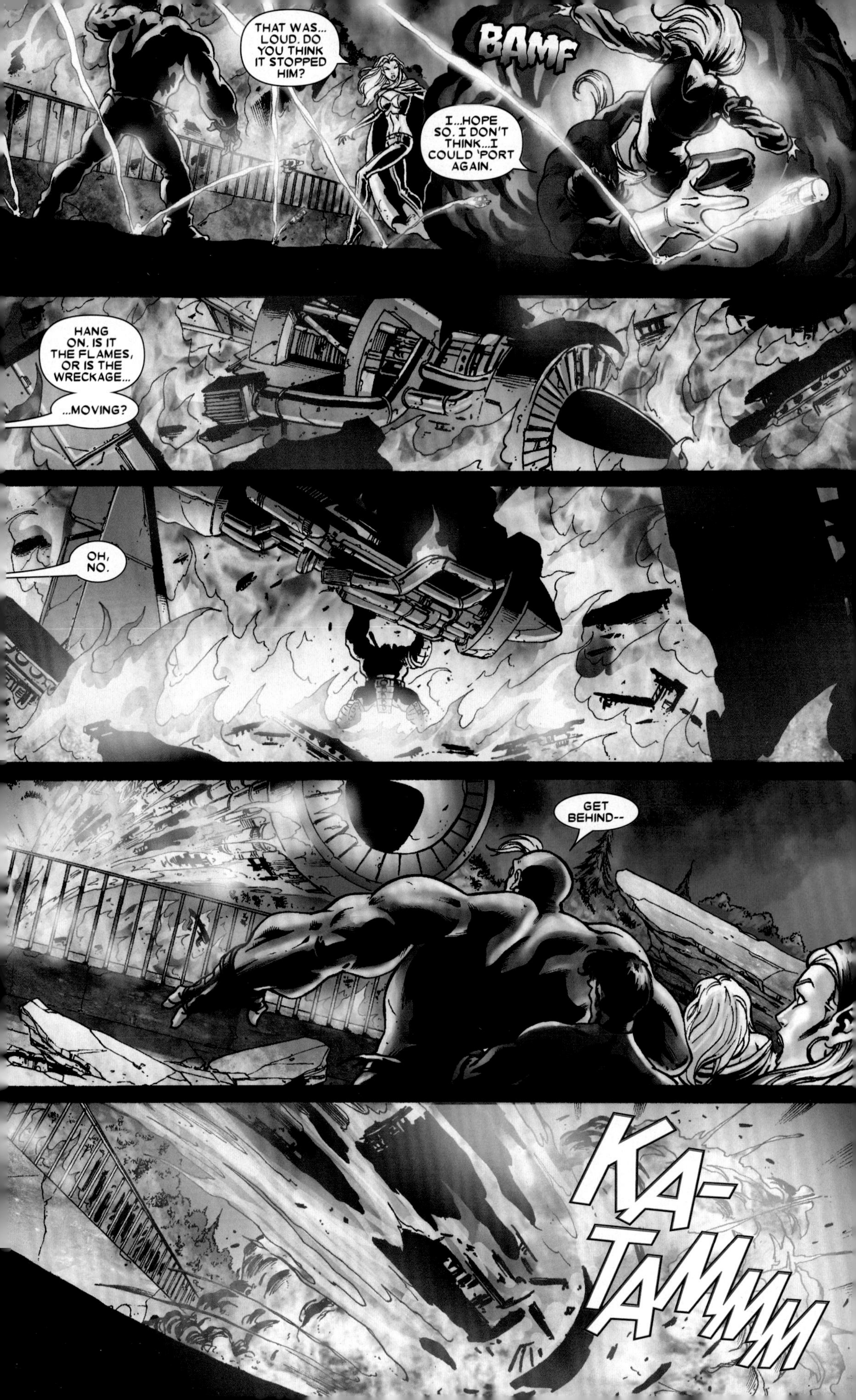
THAT WAS... LOUD. DO YOU THINK IT STOPPED HIM?
BAMF
I...HOPE SO. I DON'T THINK...I COULD 'PORT AGAIN.
HANG ON. IS IT THE FLAMES, OR IS THE WRECKAGE...
...MOVING?
OH, NO.
GET BEHIND--
KA-TAMMMM

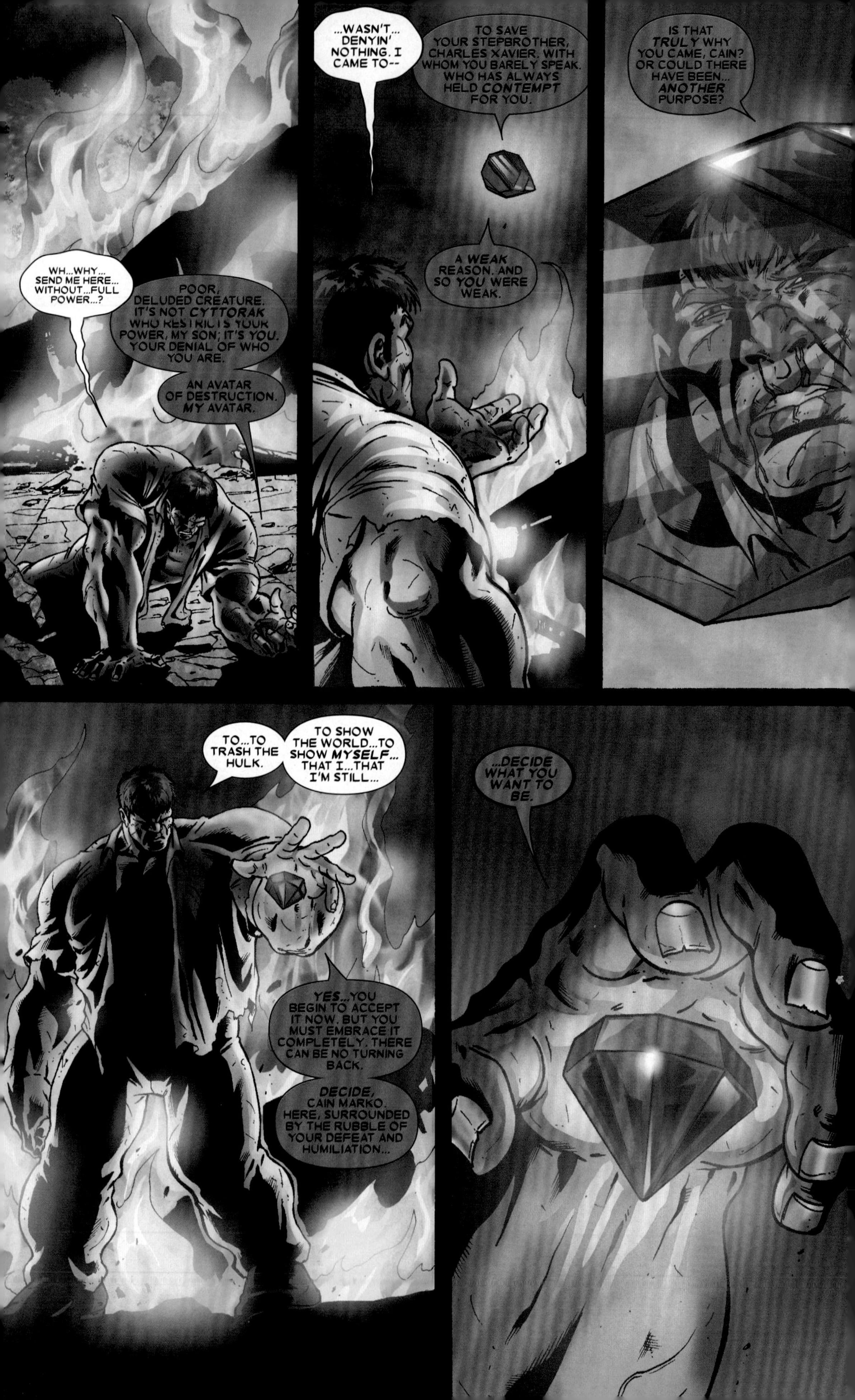
WH...WHY... SEND ME HERE... WITHOUT...FULL POWER...?
POOR, DELUDED CREATURE. IT'S NOT CYTTORAK WHO RESTRICTS YOUR POWER, MY SON; IT'S YOU. YOUR DENIAL OF WHO YOU ARE.
AN AVATAR OF DESTRUCTION. MY AVATAR.
...WASN'T... DENYIN' NOTHING. I CAME TO--
TO SAVE YOUR STEPBROTHER, CHARLES XAVIER, WITH WHOM YOU BARELY SPEAK. WHO HAS ALWAYS HELD CONTEMPT FOR YOU.
A WEAK REASON. AND SO YOU WERE WEAK.
IS THAT TRULY WHY YOU CAME, CAIN? OR COULD THERE HAVE BEEN... ANOTHER PURPOSE?
TO...TO TRASH THE HULK.
TO SHOW THE WORLD...TO SHOW MYSELF... THAT I...THAT I'M STILL...
YES...YOU BEGIN TO ACCEPT IT NOW. BUT YOU MUST EMBRACE IT COMPLETELY. THERE CAN BE NO TURNING BACK.
DECIDE, CAIN MARKO. HERE, SURROUNDED BY THE RUBBLE OF YOUR DEFEAT AND HUMILIATION...
...DECIDE WHAT YOU WANT TO BE.

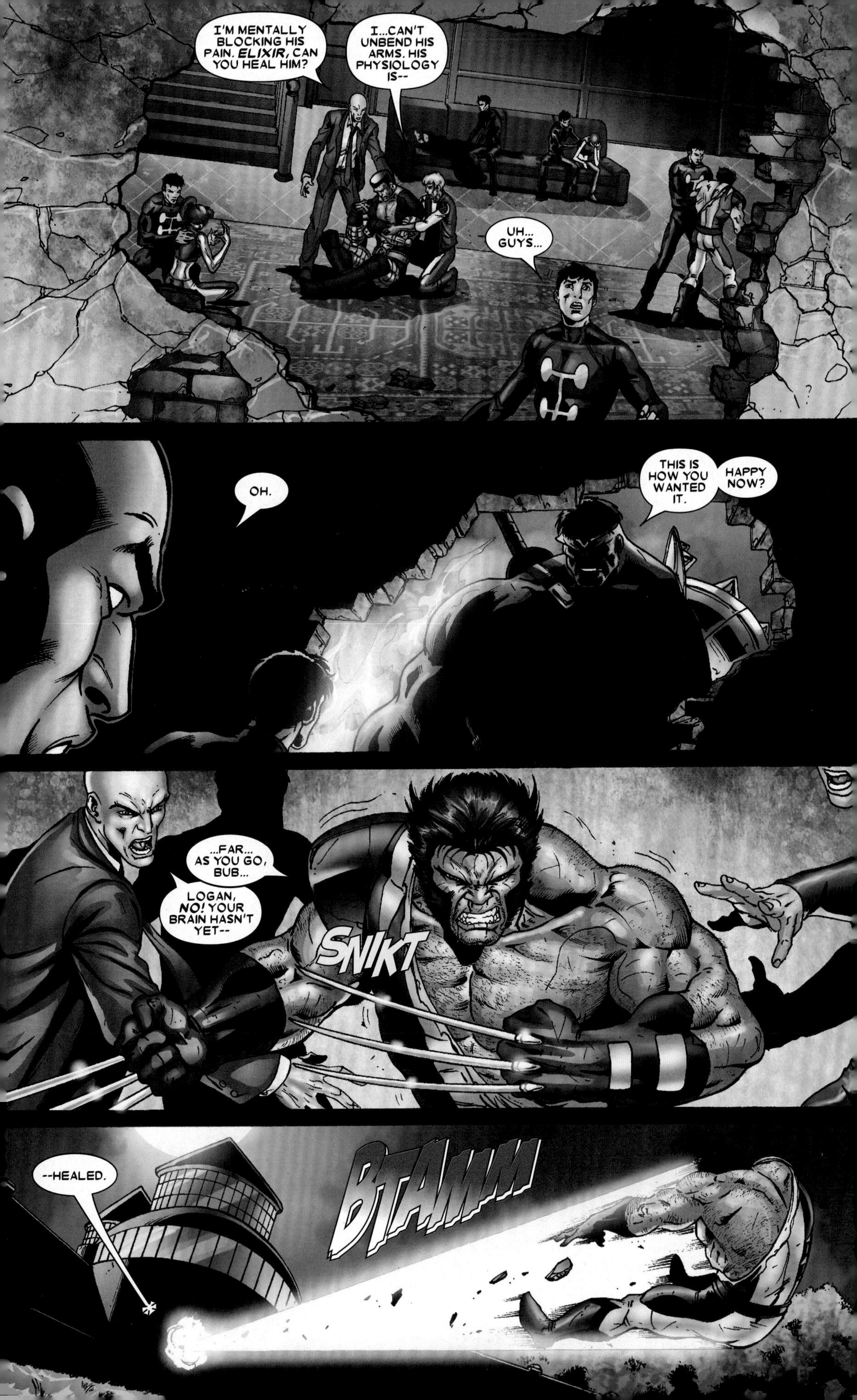
I'M MENTALLY BLOCKING HIS PAIN. ELIXIR, CAN YOU HEAL HIM?
I...CAN'T UNBEND HIS ARMS. HIS PHYSIOLOGY IS--
UH... GUYS...
OH.
THIS IS HOW YOU WANTED IT.
HAPPY NOW?
...FAR... AS YOU GO, BUB...
LOGAN, NO! YOUR BRAIN HASN'T YET--
SNIKT
--HEALED.
BTAMM

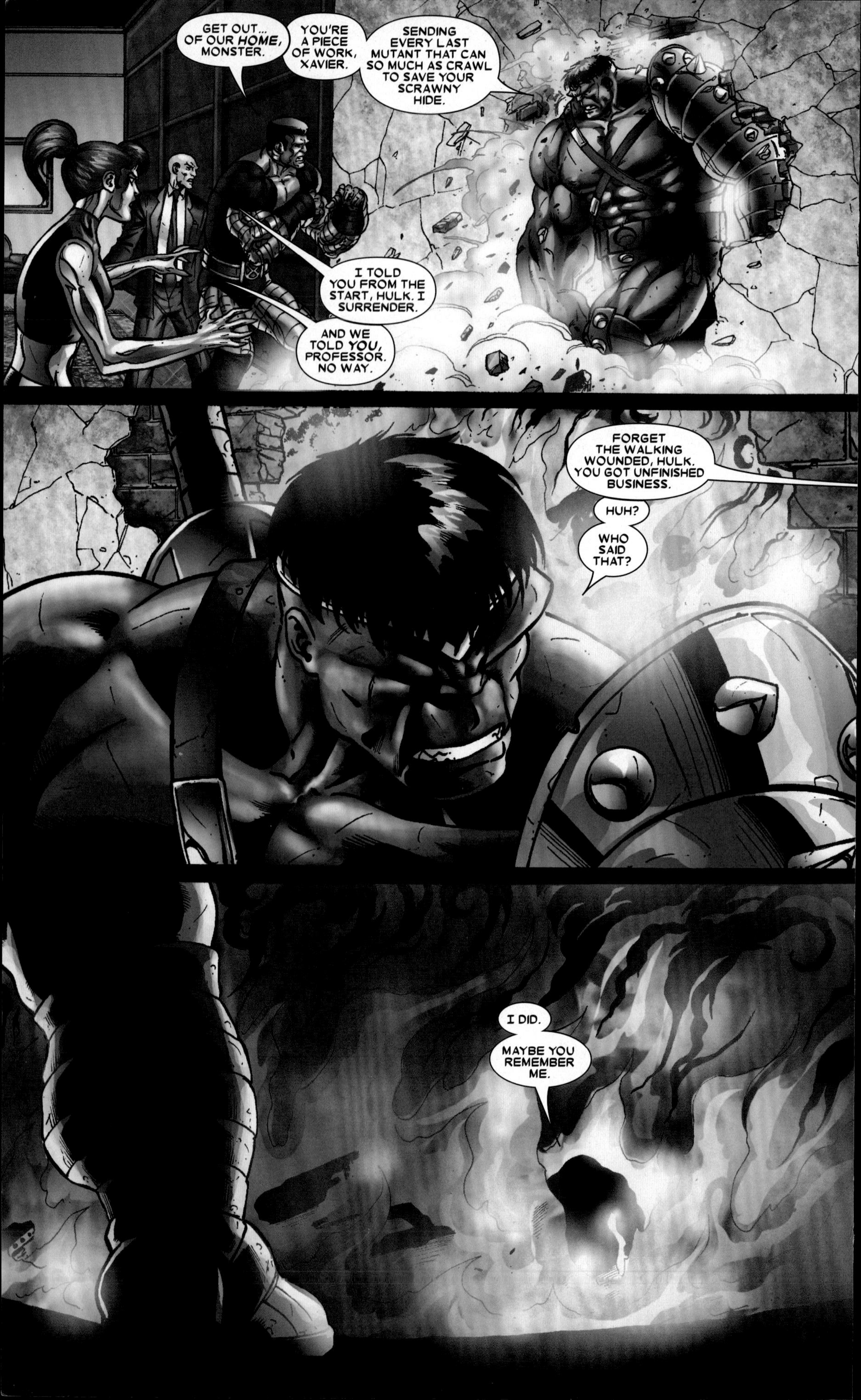

GET OUT... OF OUR *HOME,* MONSTER.
YOU'RE A PIECE OF WORK, XAVIER.
SENDING EVERY LAST MUTANT THAT CAN SO MUCH AS CRAWL TO SAVE YOUR SCRAWNY HIDE.
I TOLD YOU FROM THE START, HULK. I SURRENDER.
AND WE TOLD *YOU,* PROFESSOR. NO WAY.
FORGET THE WALKING WOUNDED, HULK. YOU GOT UNFINISHED BUSINESS.
HUH?
WHO SAID THAT?
I DID.
MAYBE YOU REMEMBER ME.

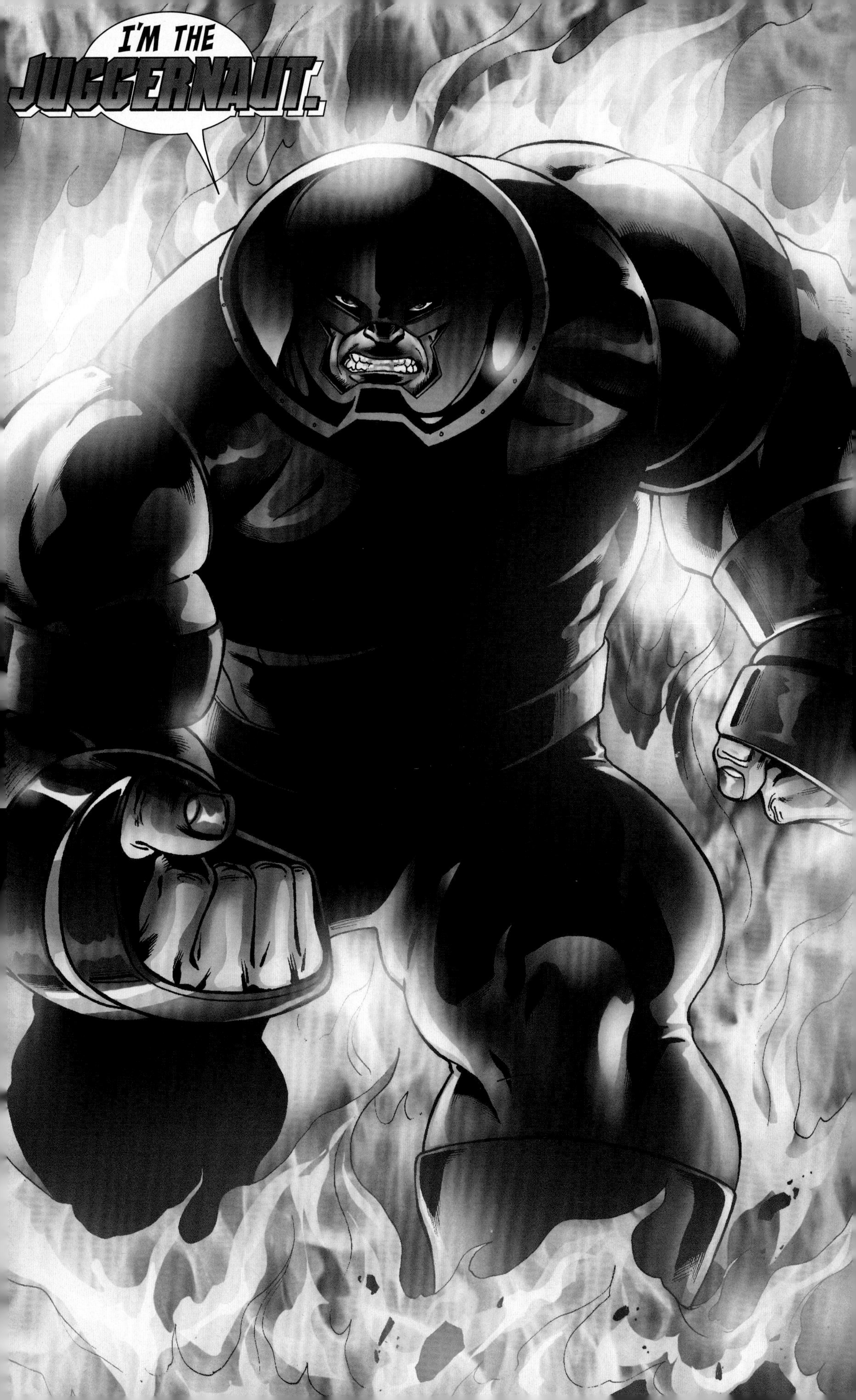
I'M THE JUGGERNAUT.

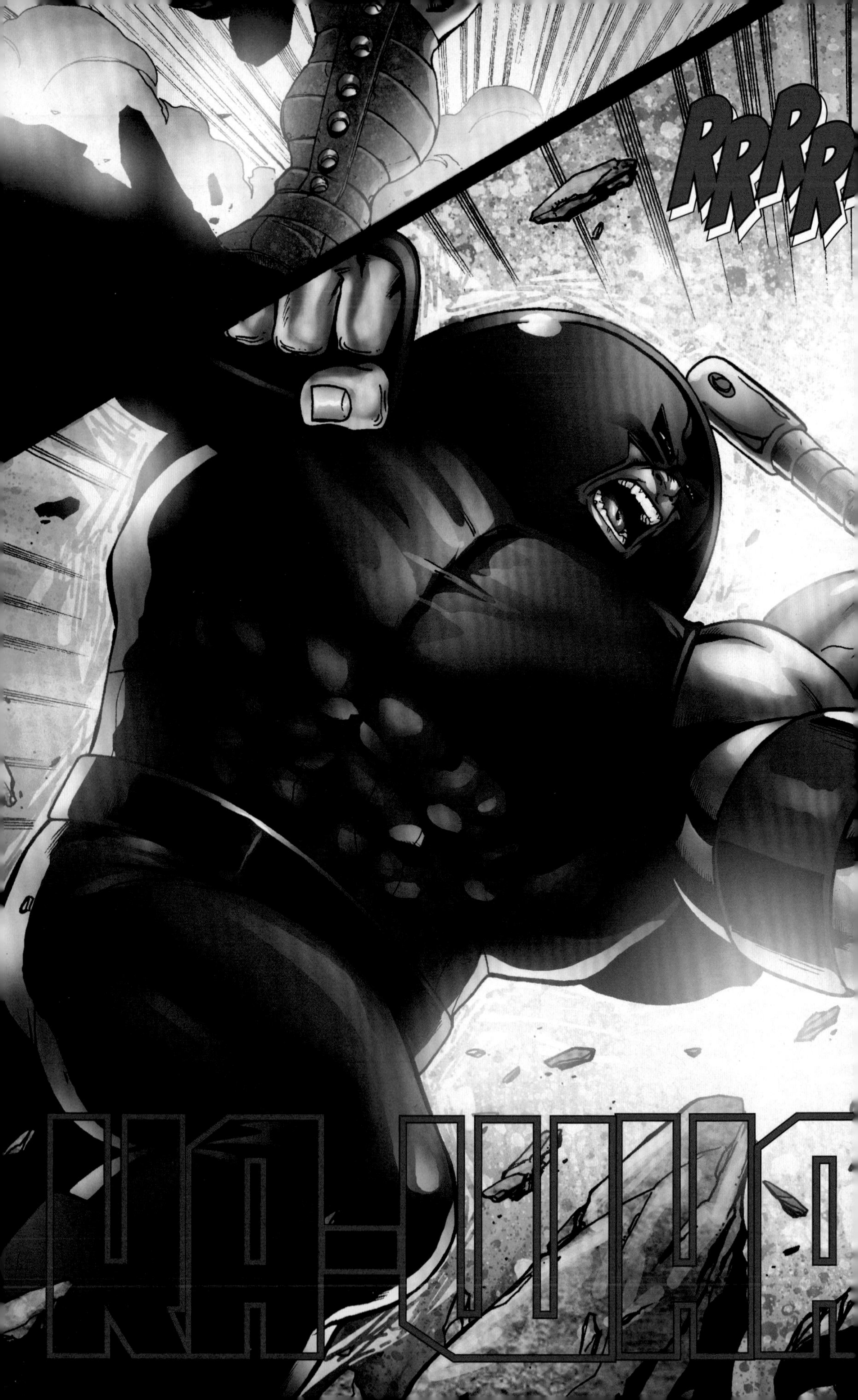
RRRR

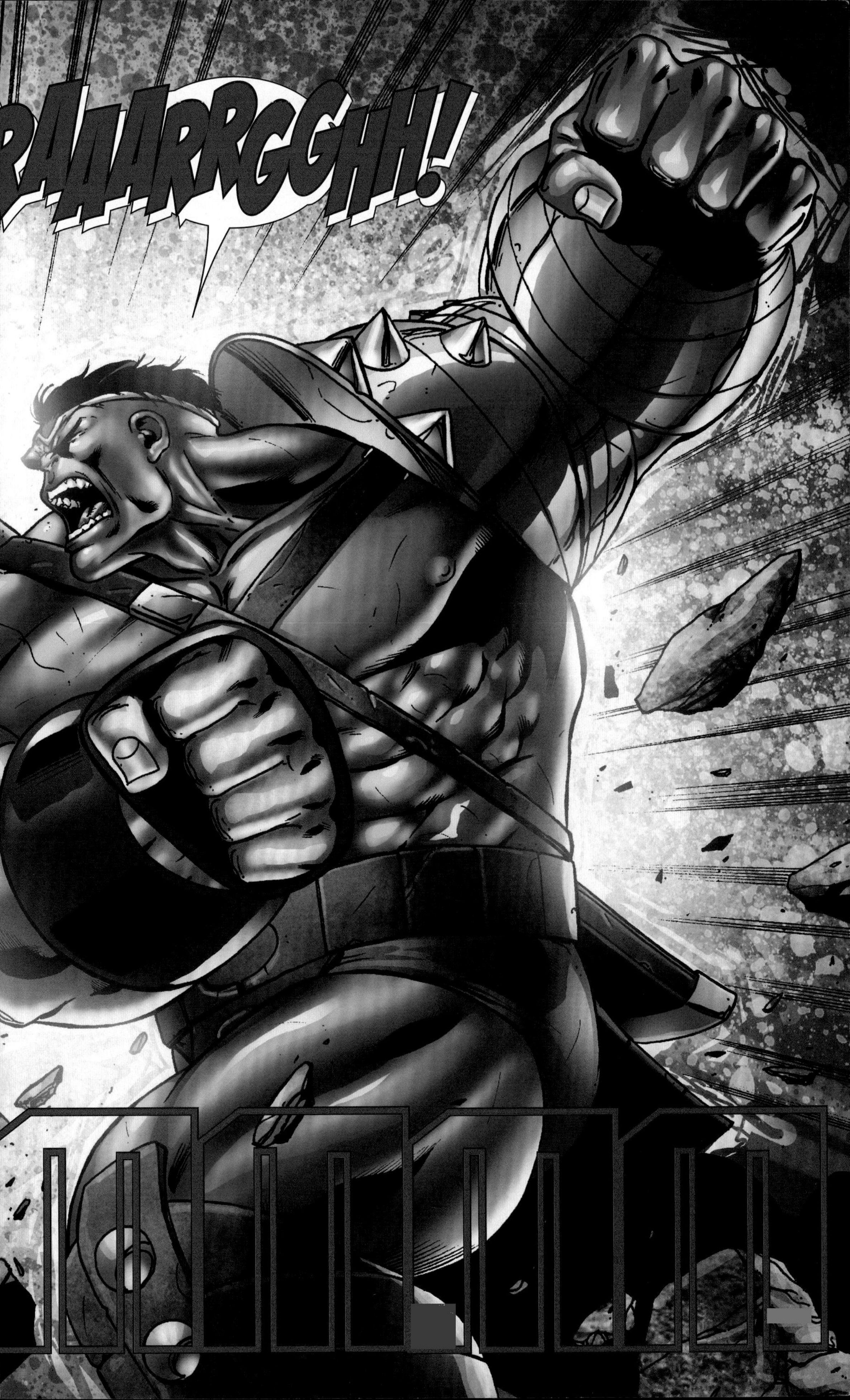
RAAARRGGHH!

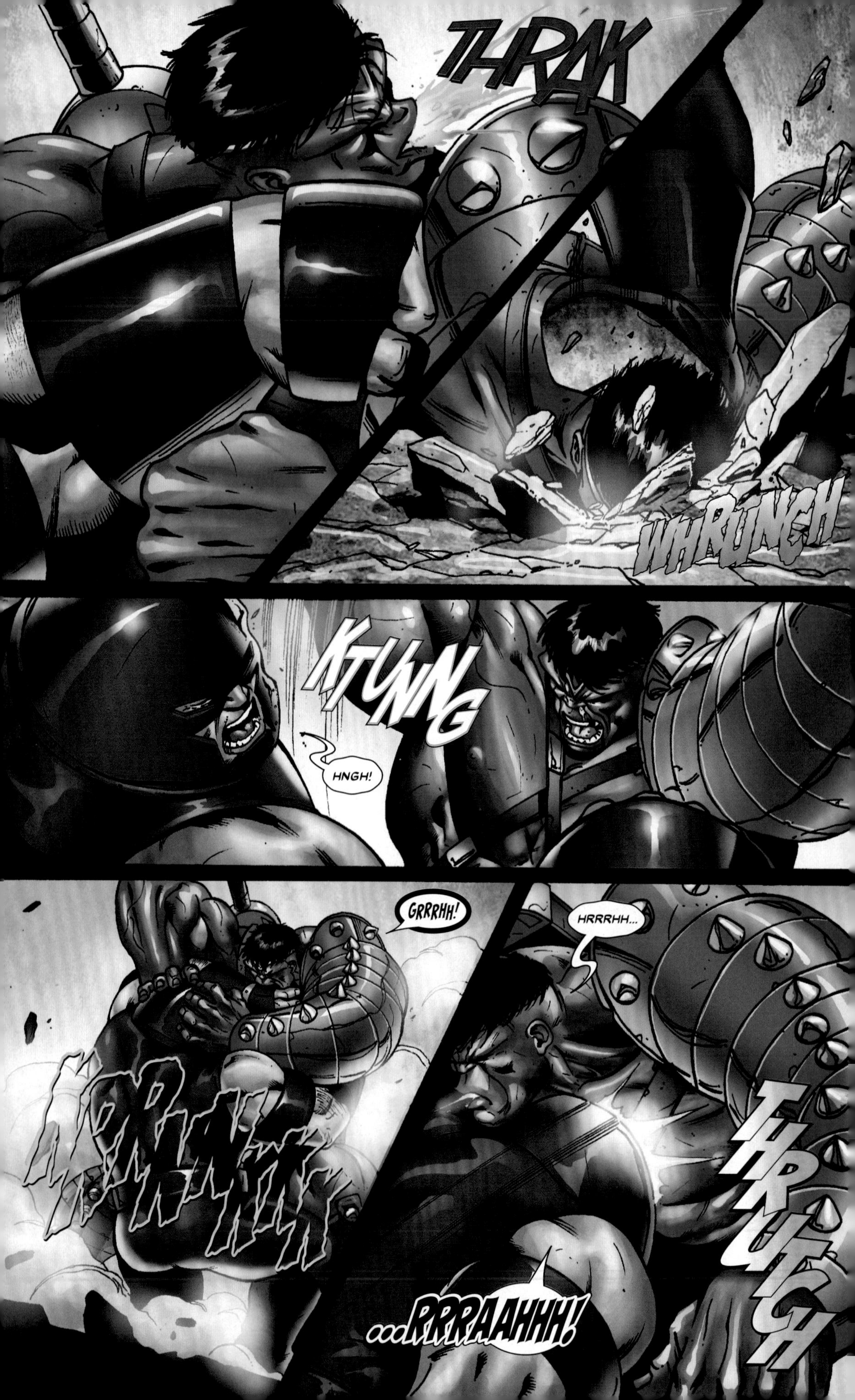
THRAK
WHRUNCH
KTUNNG
HNGH!
GRRRHH!
HRRRHH...
THRUTCH
...RRRAAHHH!

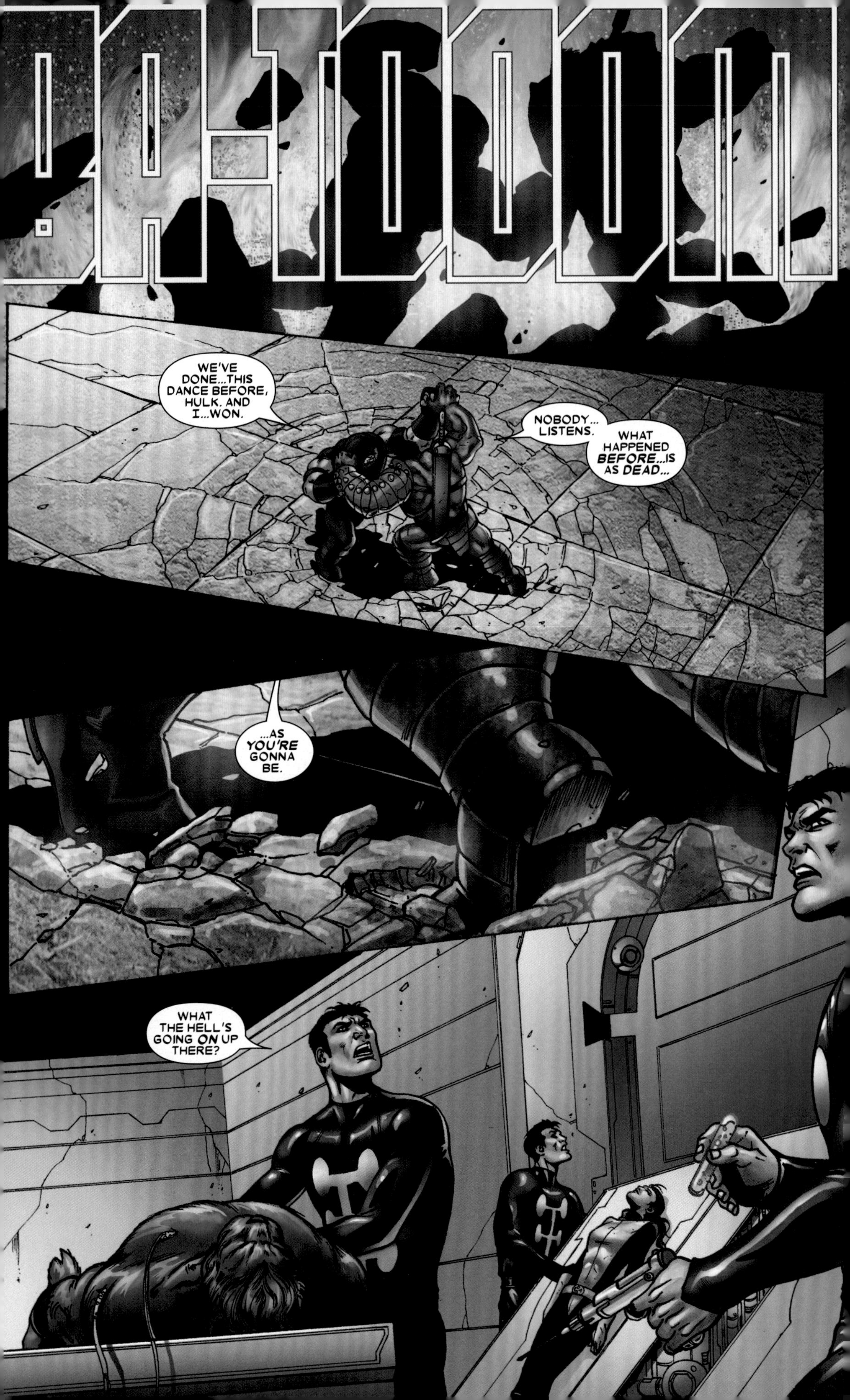
WE'VE DONE...THIS DANCE BEFORE, HULK. AND I...WON.
NOBODY... LISTENS.
WHAT HAPPENED BEFORE...IS AS DEAD...
...AS YOU'RE GONNA BE.
WHAT THE HELL'S GOING ON UP THERE?

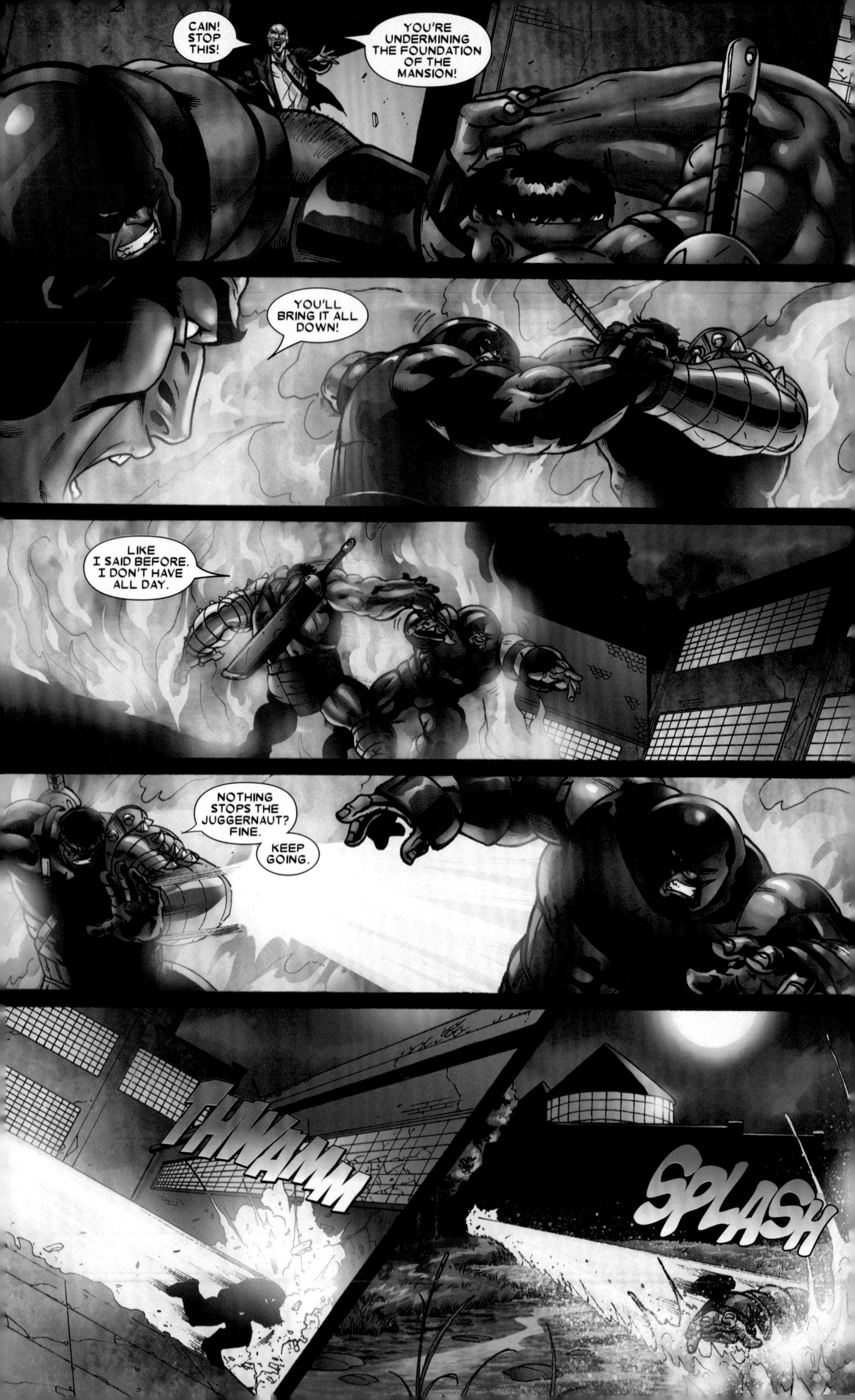
CAIN! STOP THIS!
YOU'RE UNDERMINING THE FOUNDATION OF THE MANSION!
YOU'LL BRING IT ALL DOWN!
LIKE I SAID BEFORE. I DON'T HAVE ALL DAY.
NOTHING STOPS THE JUGGERNAUT? FINE.
KEEP GOING.
THWAMM
SPLASH

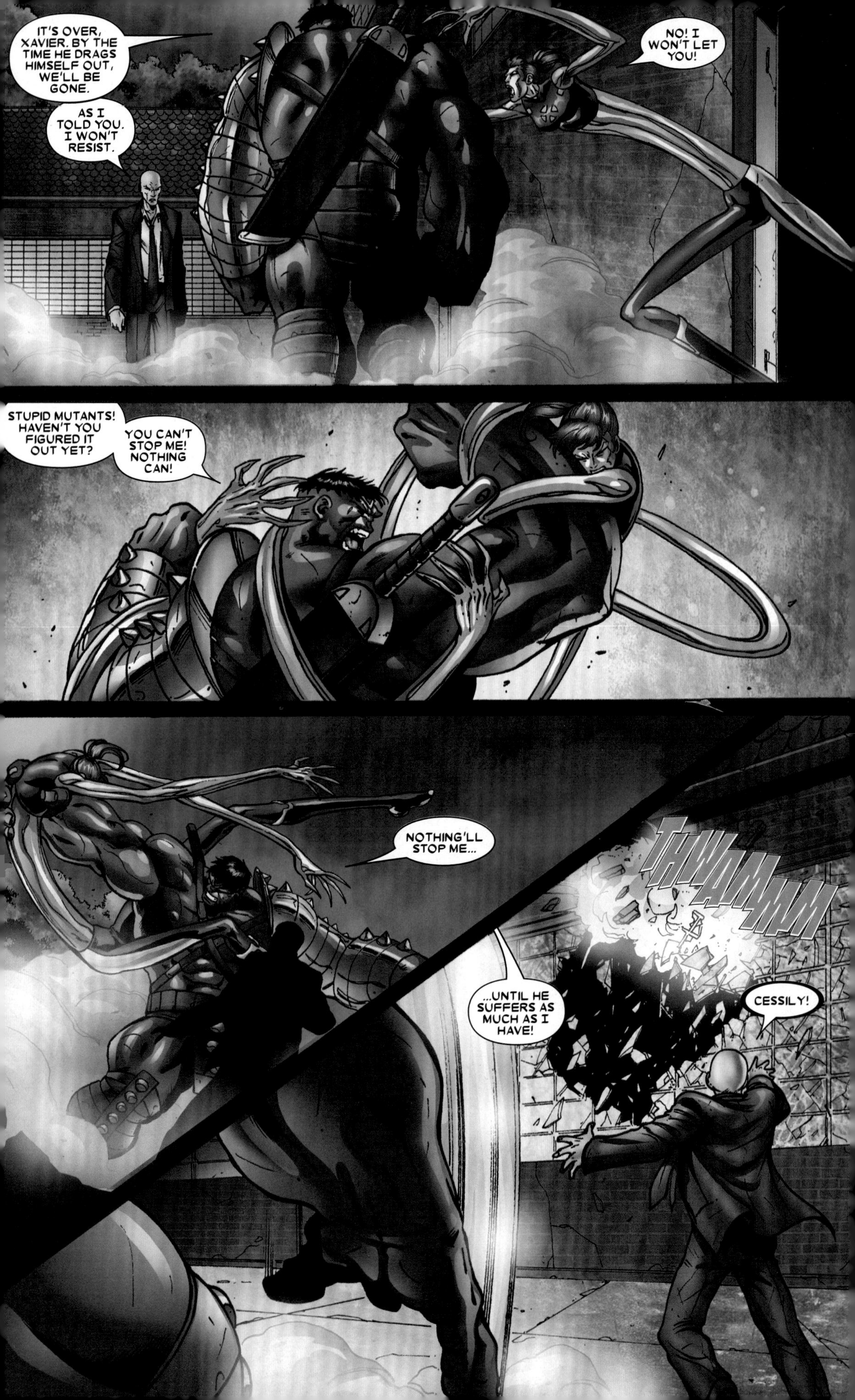
IT'S OVER, XAVIER. BY THE TIME HE DRAGS HIMSELF OUT, WE'LL BE GONE.
AS I TOLD YOU. I WON'T RESIST.
NO! I WON'T LET YOU!
STUPID MUTANTS! HAVEN'T YOU FIGURED IT OUT YET?
YOU CAN'T STOP ME! NOTHING CAN!
NOTHING'LL STOP ME...
THWAMMM
...UNTIL HE SUFFERS AS MUCH AS I HAVE!
CESSILY!

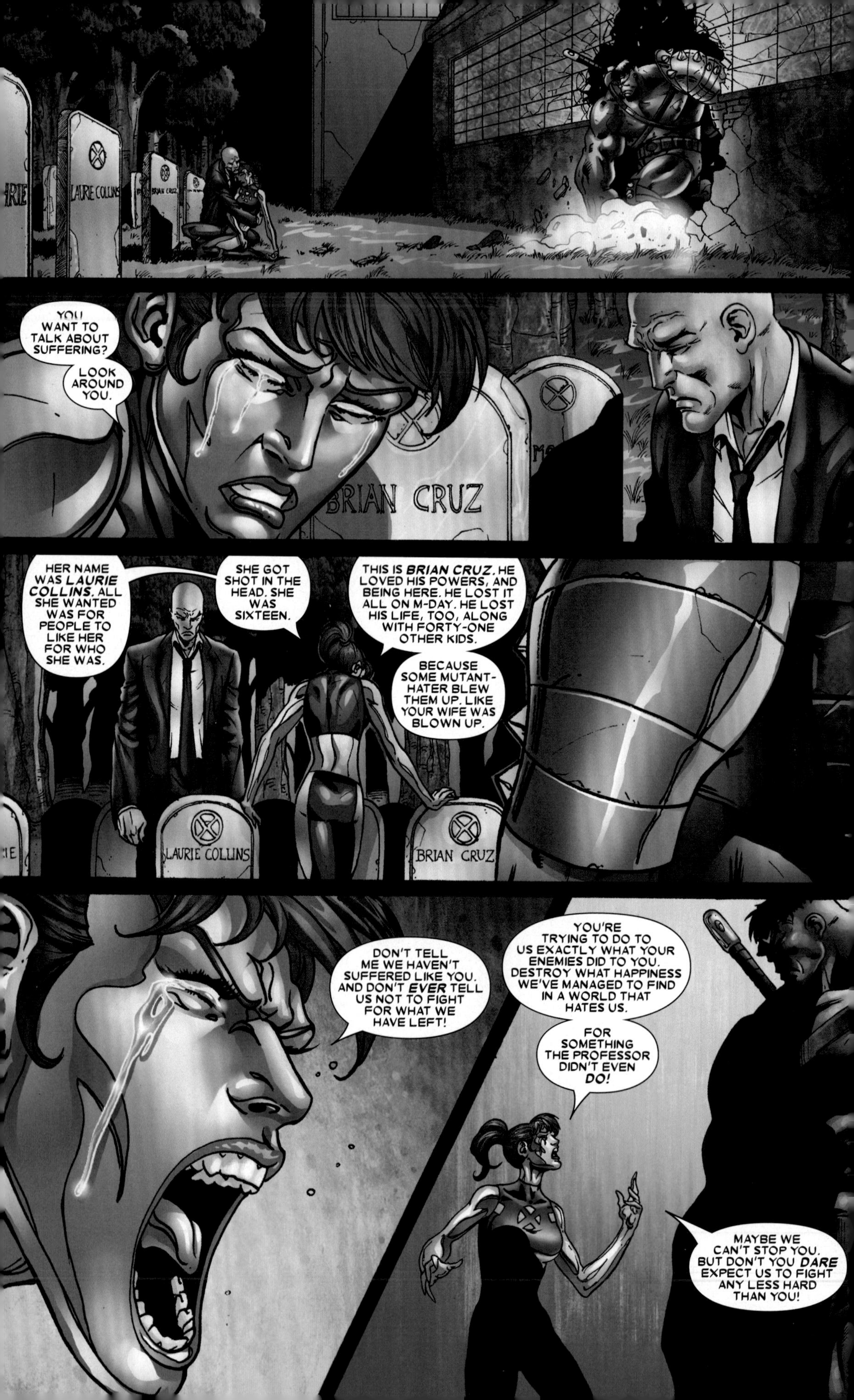

IRIE
LAURIE COLLINS
BRIAN CRUZ
YOU WANT TO TALK ABOUT SUFFERING?
LOOK AROUND YOU.
BRIAN CRUZ
HER NAME WAS LAURIE COLLINS. ALL SHE WANTED WAS FOR PEOPLE TO LIKE HER FOR WHO SHE WAS.
SHE GOT SHOT IN THE HEAD. SHE WAS SIXTEEN.
THIS IS BRIAN CRUZ. HE LOVED HIS POWERS, AND BEING HERE. HE LOST IT ALL ON M-DAY. HE LOST HIS LIFE, TOO, ALONG WITH FORTY-ONE OTHER KIDS.
BECAUSE SOME MUTANT-HATER BLEW THEM UP. LIKE YOUR WIFE WAS BLOWN UP.
LAURIE COLLINS
BRIAN CRUZ
DON'T TELL ME WE HAVEN'T SUFFERED LIKE YOU. AND DON'T EVER TELL US NOT TO FIGHT FOR WHAT WE HAVE LEFT!
YOU'RE TRYING TO DO TO US EXACTLY WHAT YOUR ENEMIES DID TO YOU. DESTROY WHAT HAPPINESS WE'VE MANAGED TO FIND IN A WORLD THAT HATES US.
FOR SOMETHING THE PROFESSOR DIDN'T EVEN DO!
MAYBE WE CAN'T STOP YOU. BUT DON'T YOU DARE EXPECT US TO FIGHT ANY LESS HARD THAN YOU!

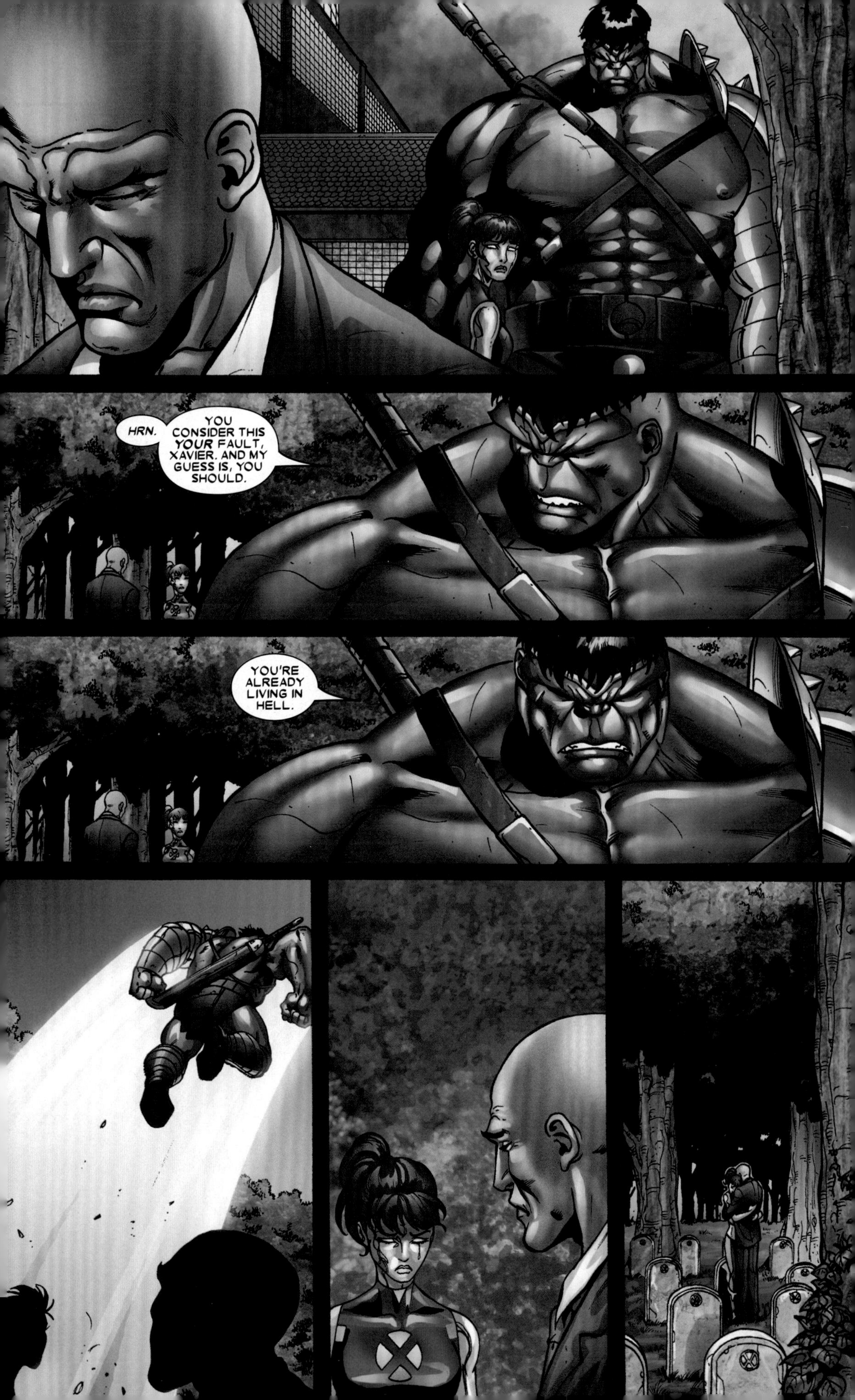

HRN.
YOU CONSIDER THIS YOUR FAULT, XAVIER. AND MY GUESS IS, YOU SHOULD.
YOU'RE ALREADY LIVING IN HELL.

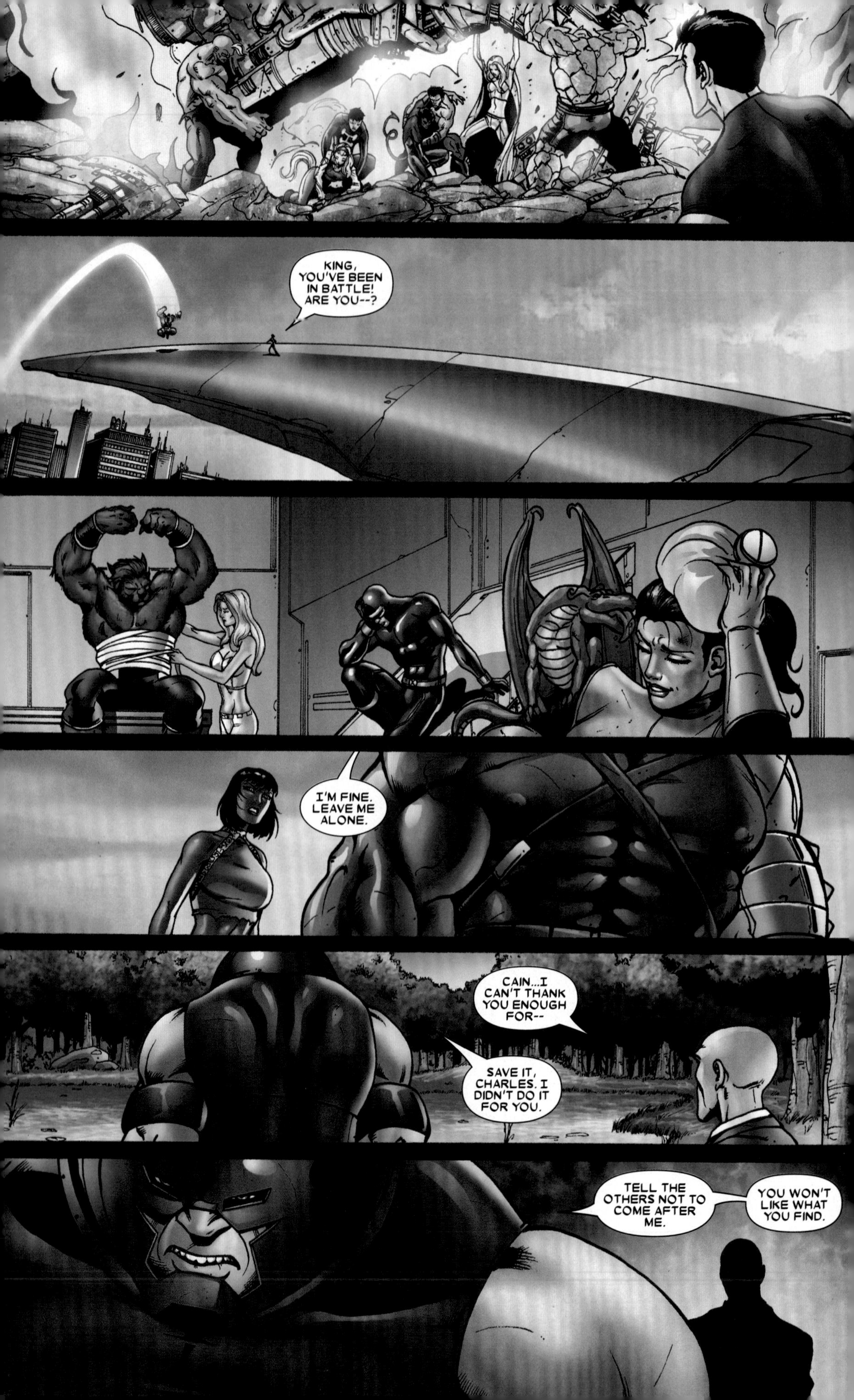
KING, YOU'VE BEEN IN BATTLE! ARE YOU--?
I'M FINE. LEAVE ME ALONE.
CAIN...I CAN'T THANK YOU ENOUGH FOR--
SAVE IT, CHARLES. I DIDN'T DO IT FOR YOU.
TELL THE OTHERS NOT TO COME AFTER ME.
YOU WON'T LIKE WHAT YOU FIND.

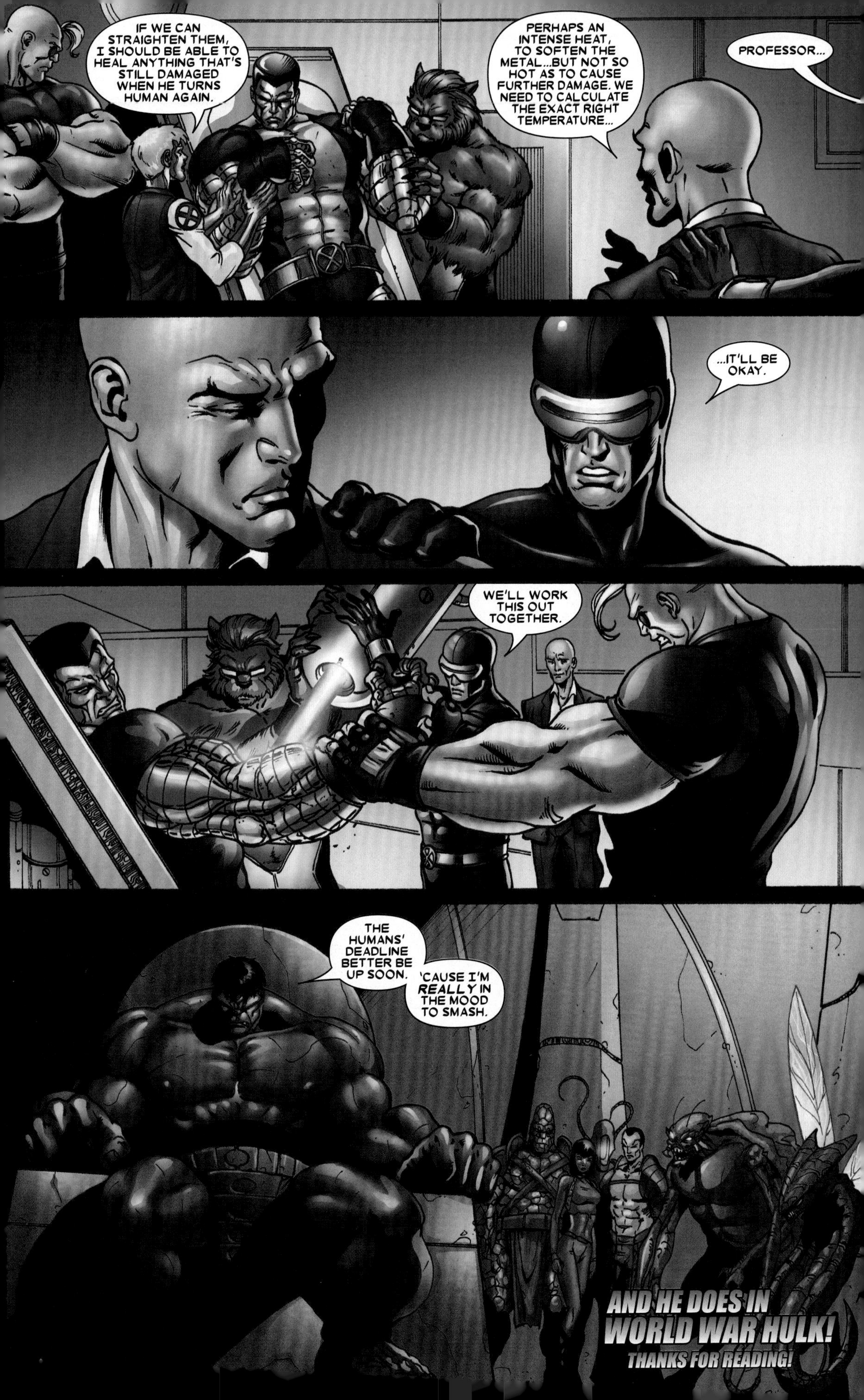
IF WE CAN STRAIGHTEN THEM, I SHOULD BE ABLE TO HEAL ANYTHING THAT'S STILL DAMAGED WHEN HE TURNS HUMAN AGAIN.
PERHAPS AN INTENSE HEAT, TO SOFTEN THE METAL...BUT NOT SO HOT AS TO CAUSE FURTHER DAMAGE. WE NEED TO CALCULATE THE EXACT RIGHT TEMPERATURE...
PROFESSOR...
...IT'LL BE OKAY.
WE'LL WORK THIS OUT TOGETHER.
THE HUMANS' DEADLINE BETTER BE UP SOON.
'CAUSE I'M REALLY IN THE MOOD TO SMASH.
AND HE DOES IN WORLD WAR HULK!
THANKS FOR READING!

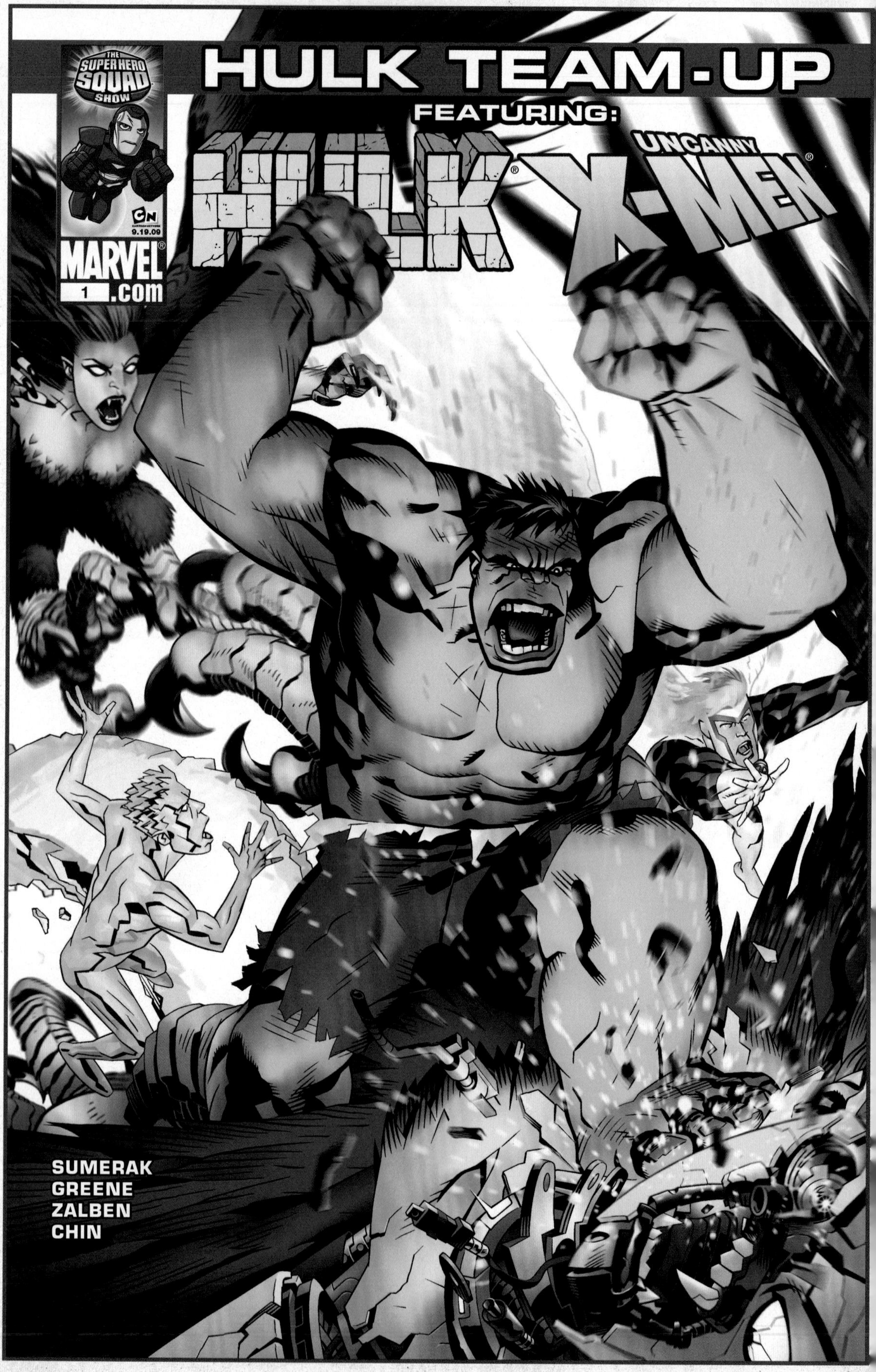
HULK TEAM-UP
FEATURING:
HULK
UNCANNY X-MEN
THE SUPER HERO SQUAD SHOW
9.19.09
MARVEL
1 .com
SUMERAK
GREENE
ZALBEN
CHIN

★ ★ ★ ROUND 4 ★ ★ ★

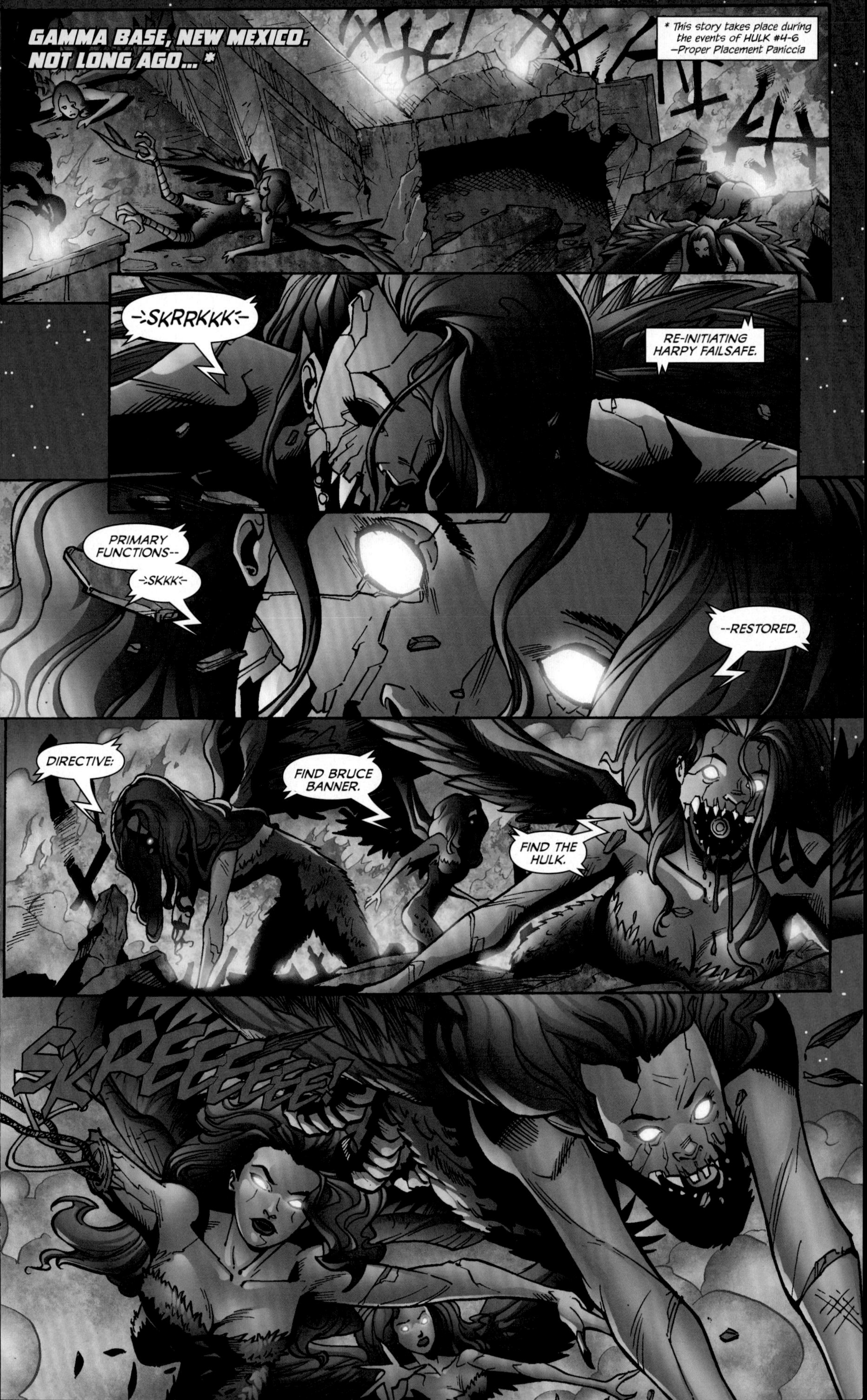
GAMMA BASE, NEW MEXICO. NOT LONG AGO... *
* This story takes place during the events of HULK #4-6 —Proper Placement Paniccia
-SKRRKKK-
RE-INITIATING HARPY FAILSAFE.
PRIMARY FUNCTIONS--
-SKKK-
--RESTORED.
DIRECTIVE:
FIND BRUCE BANNER.
FIND THE HULK.
SKREEEEEE!

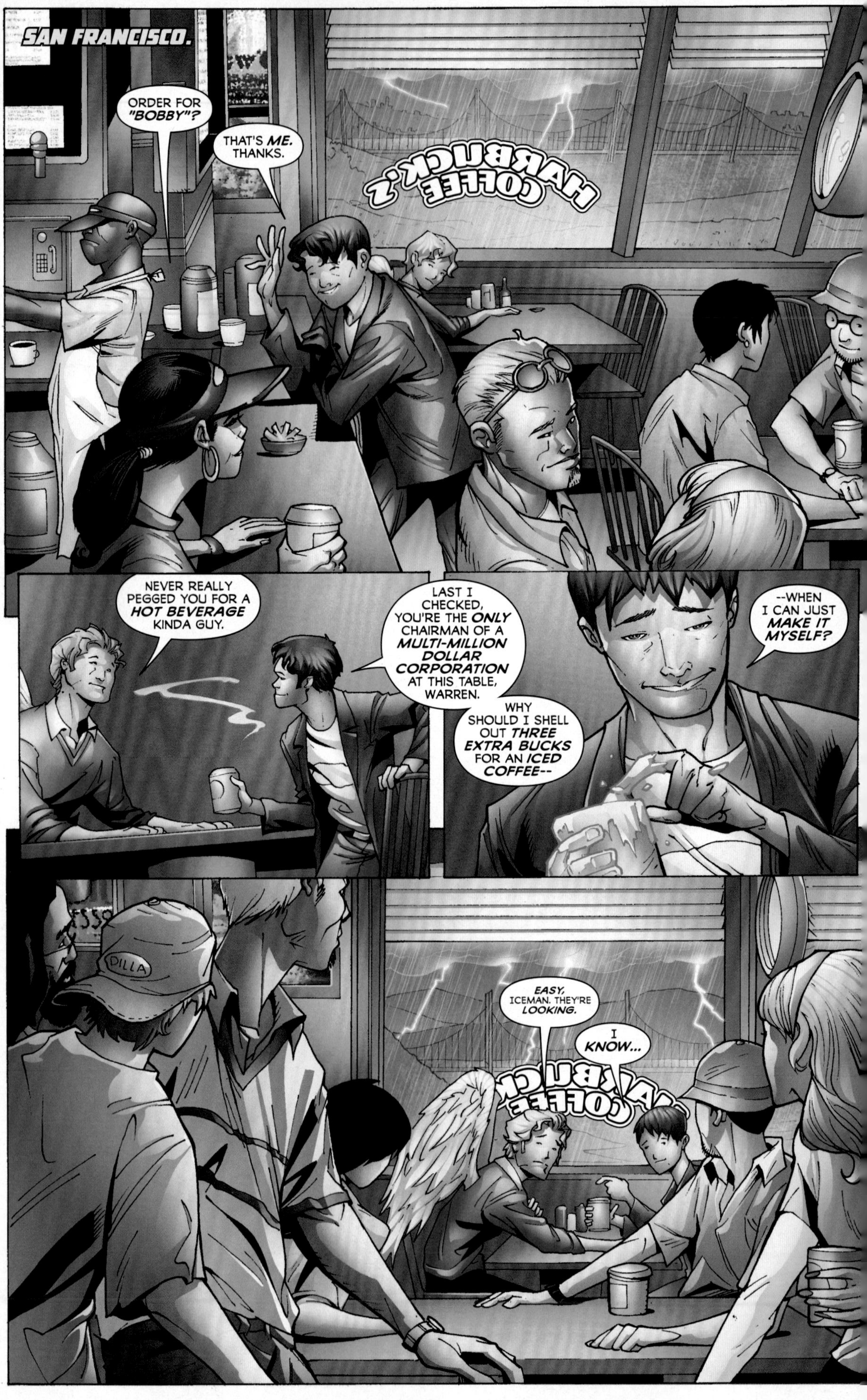
SAN FRANCISCO.
ORDER FOR "BOBBY"?
THAT'S ME. THANKS.
HARBUCK'S COFFEE
NEVER REALLY PEGGED YOU FOR A HOT BEVERAGE KINDA GUY.
LAST I CHECKED, YOU'RE THE ONLY CHAIRMAN OF A MULTI-MILLION DOLLAR CORPORATION AT THIS TABLE, WARREN.
WHY SHOULD I SHELL OUT THREE EXTRA BUCKS FOR AN ICED COFFEE--
--WHEN I CAN JUST MAKE IT MYSELF?
DILLA
EASY, ICEMAN. THEY'RE LOOKING.
I KNOW...
COFFEE

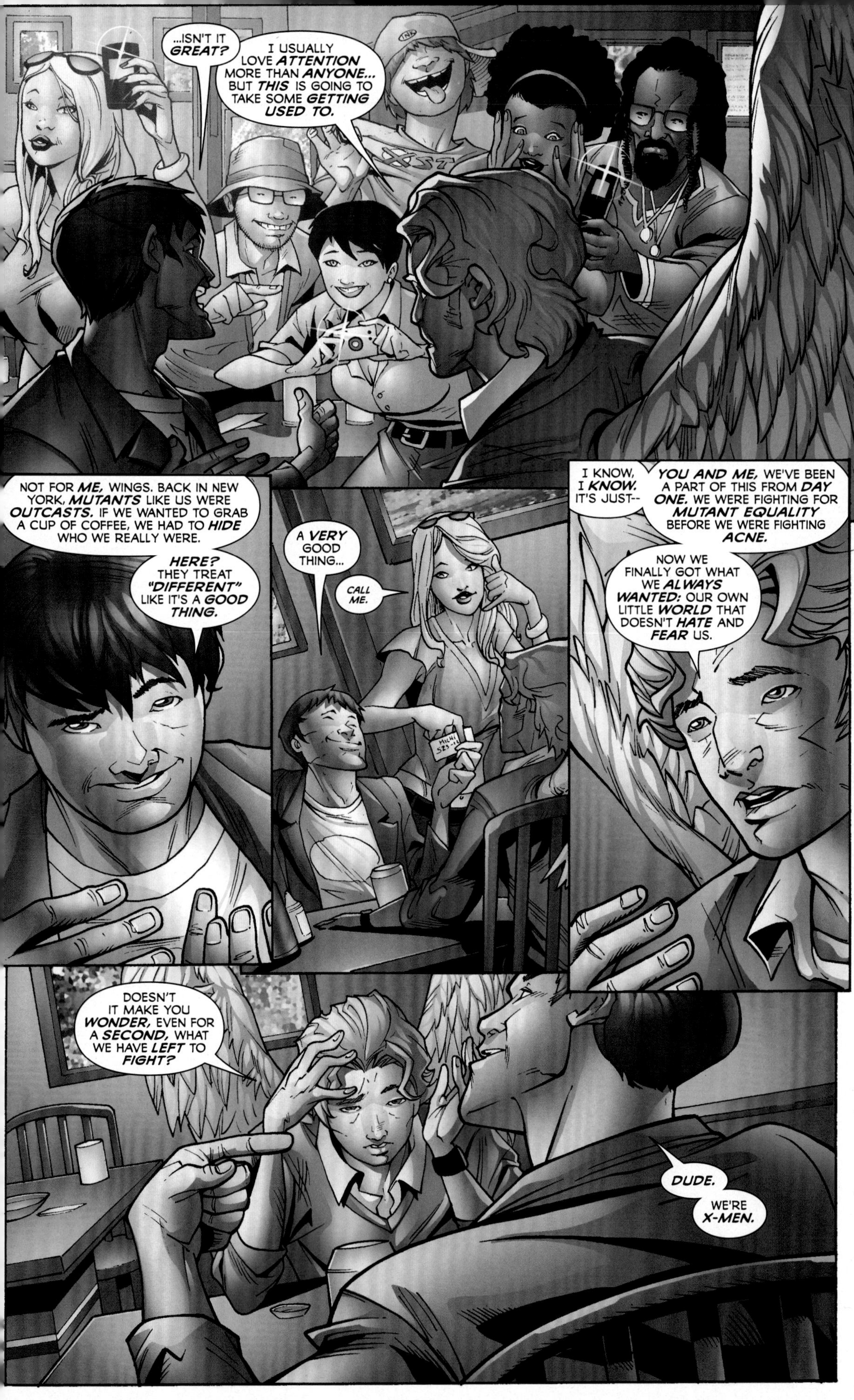
...ISN'T IT GREAT?
I USUALLY LOVE ATTENTION MORE THAN ANYONE... BUT THIS IS GOING TO TAKE SOME GETTING USED TO.
NOT FOR ME, WINGS. BACK IN NEW YORK, MUTANTS LIKE US WERE OUTCASTS. IF WE WANTED TO GRAB A CUP OF COFFEE, WE HAD TO HIDE WHO WE REALLY WERE.
HERE? THEY TREAT "DIFFERENT" LIKE IT'S A GOOD THING.
A VERY GOOD THING...
CALL ME.
I KNOW, I KNOW. IT'S JUST--
YOU AND ME, WE'VE BEEN A PART OF THIS FROM DAY ONE. WE WERE FIGHTING FOR MUTANT EQUALITY BEFORE WE WERE FIGHTING ACNE.
NOW WE FINALLY GOT WHAT WE ALWAYS WANTED: OUR OWN LITTLE WORLD THAT DOESN'T HATE AND FEAR US.
DOESN'T IT MAKE YOU WONDER, EVEN FOR A SECOND, WHAT WE HAVE LEFT TO FIGHT?
DUDE.
WE'RE X-MEN.

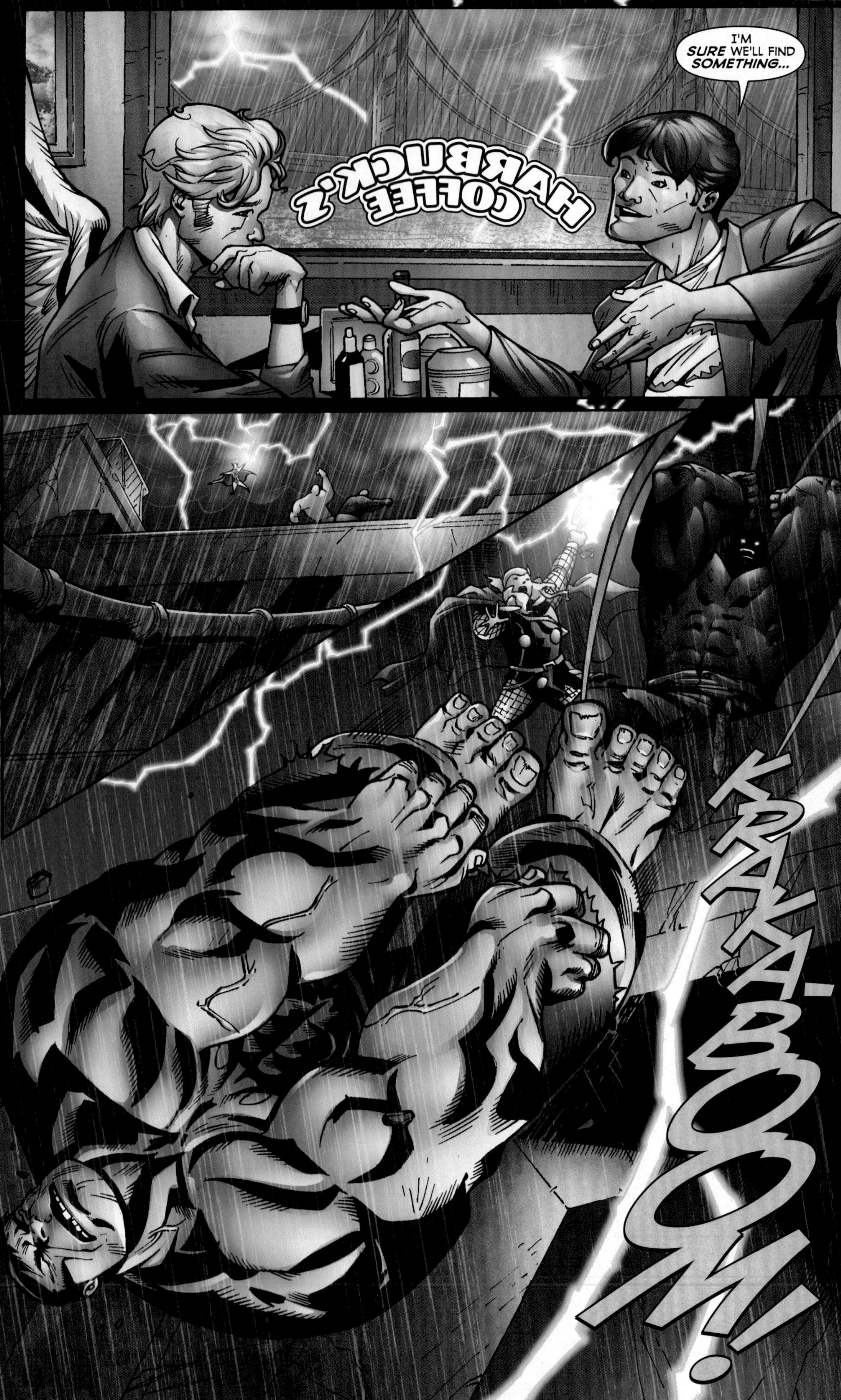
HARBUCK'S COFFEE
I'M SURE WE'LL FIND SOMETHING...
KRAKA-BOOOM!

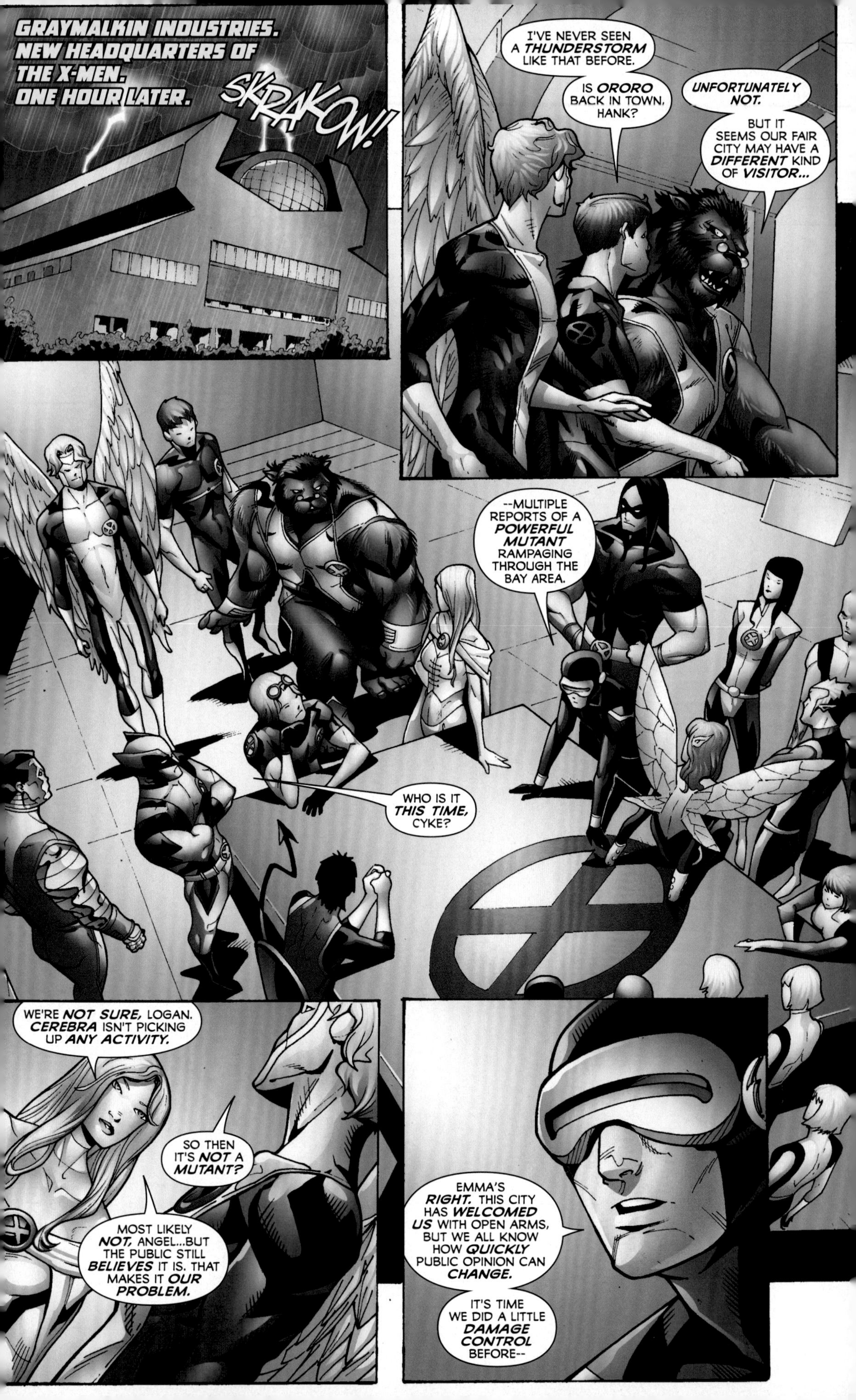
GRAYMALKIN INDUSTRIES. NEW HEADQUARTERS OF THE X-MEN. ONE HOUR LATER.
SKRAKOW!!
I'VE NEVER SEEN A THUNDERSTORM LIKE THAT BEFORE.
IS ORORO BACK IN TOWN, HANK?
UNFORTUNATELY NOT.
BUT IT SEEMS OUR FAIR CITY MAY HAVE A DIFFERENT KIND OF VISITOR...
--MULTIPLE REPORTS OF A POWERFUL MUTANT RAMPAGING THROUGH THE BAY AREA.
WHO IS IT THIS TIME, CYKE?
WE'RE NOT SURE, LOGAN. CEREBRA ISN'T PICKING UP ANY ACTIVITY.
SO THEN IT'S NOT A MUTANT?
MOST LIKELY NOT, ANGEL...BUT THE PUBLIC STILL BELIEVES IT IS. THAT MAKES IT OUR PROBLEM.
EMMA'S RIGHT. THIS CITY HAS WELCOMED US WITH OPEN ARMS, BUT WE ALL KNOW HOW QUICKLY PUBLIC OPINION CAN CHANGE.
IT'S TIME WE DID A LITTLE DAMAGE CONTROL BEFORE--

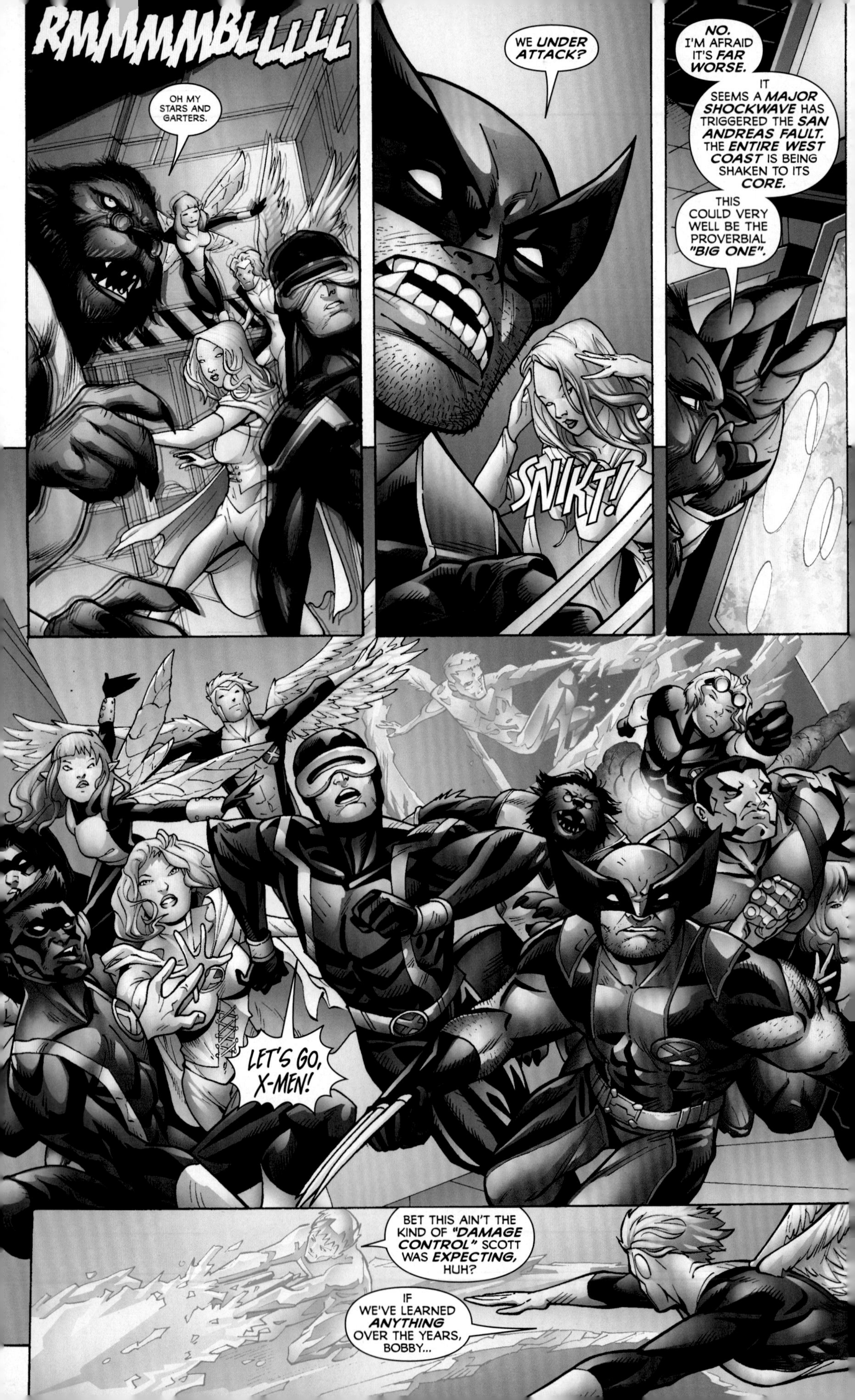
RMMMMBLLLLL
OH MY STARS AND GARTERS.
WE UNDER ATTACK?
NO. I'M AFRAID IT'S FAR WORSE.
IT SEEMS A MAJOR SHOCKWAVE HAS TRIGGERED THE SAN ANDREAS FAULT. THE ENTIRE WEST COAST IS BEING SHAKEN TO ITS CORE.
THIS COULD VERY WELL BE THE PROVERBIAL "BIG ONE".
SNIKT!
LET'S GO, X-MEN!
BET THIS AIN'T THE KIND OF "DAMAGE CONTROL" SCOTT WAS EXPECTING, HUH?
IF WE'VE LEARNED ANYTHING OVER THE YEARS, BOBBY...

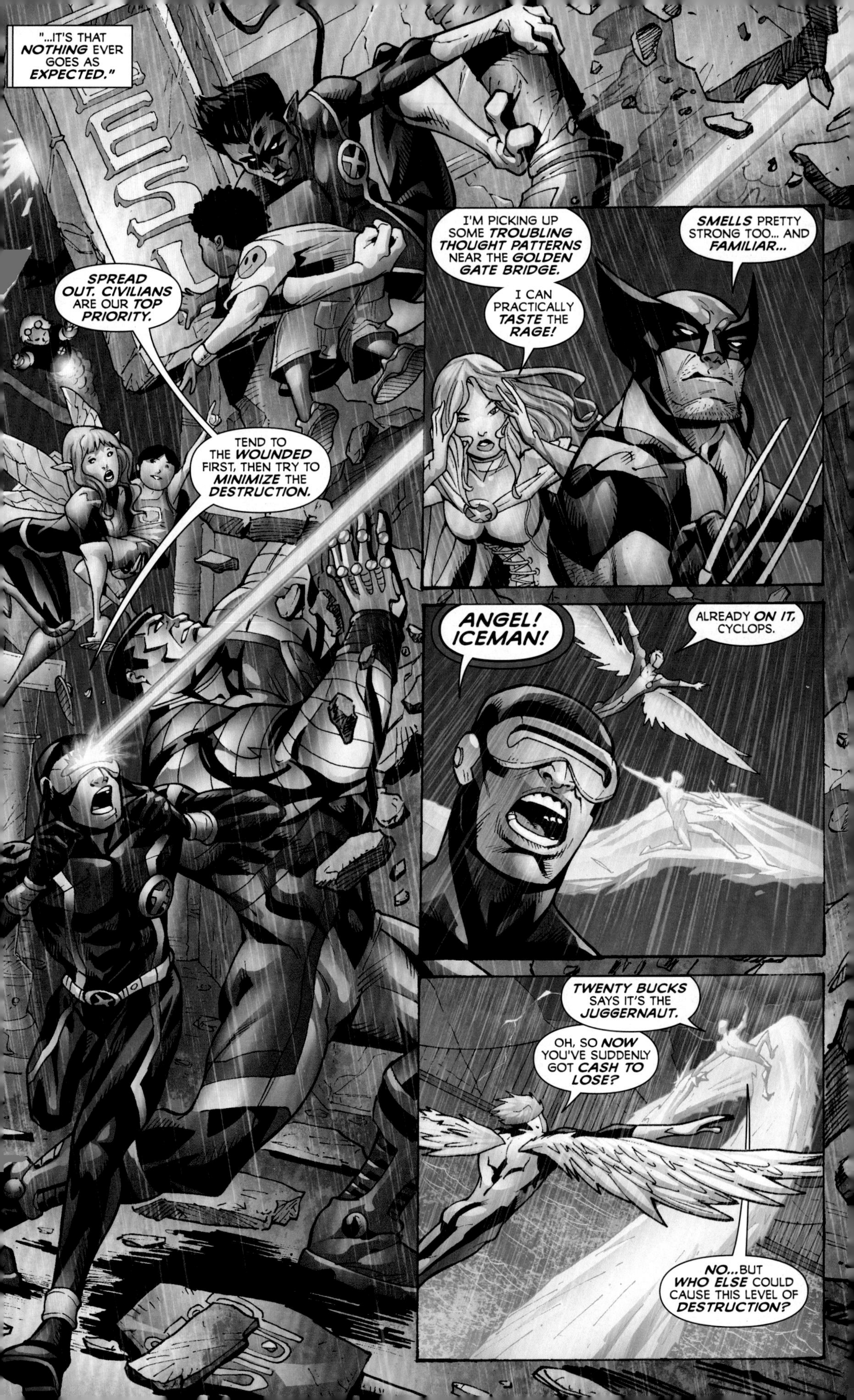
"...IT'S THAT NOTHING EVER GOES AS EXPECTED."
SPREAD OUT. CIVILIANS ARE OUR TOP PRIORITY.
TEND TO THE WOUNDED FIRST, THEN TRY TO MINIMIZE THE DESTRUCTION.
I'M PICKING UP SOME TROUBLING THOUGHT PATTERNS NEAR THE GOLDEN GATE BRIDGE.
I CAN PRACTICALLY TASTE THE RAGE!
SMELLS PRETTY STRONG TOO... AND FAMILIAR...
ANGEL! ICEMAN!
ALREADY ON IT, CYCLOPS.
TWENTY BUCKS SAYS IT'S THE JUGGERNAUT.
OH, SO NOW YOU'VE SUDDENLY GOT CASH TO LOSE?
NO...BUT WHO ELSE COULD CAUSE THIS LEVEL OF DESTRUCTION?

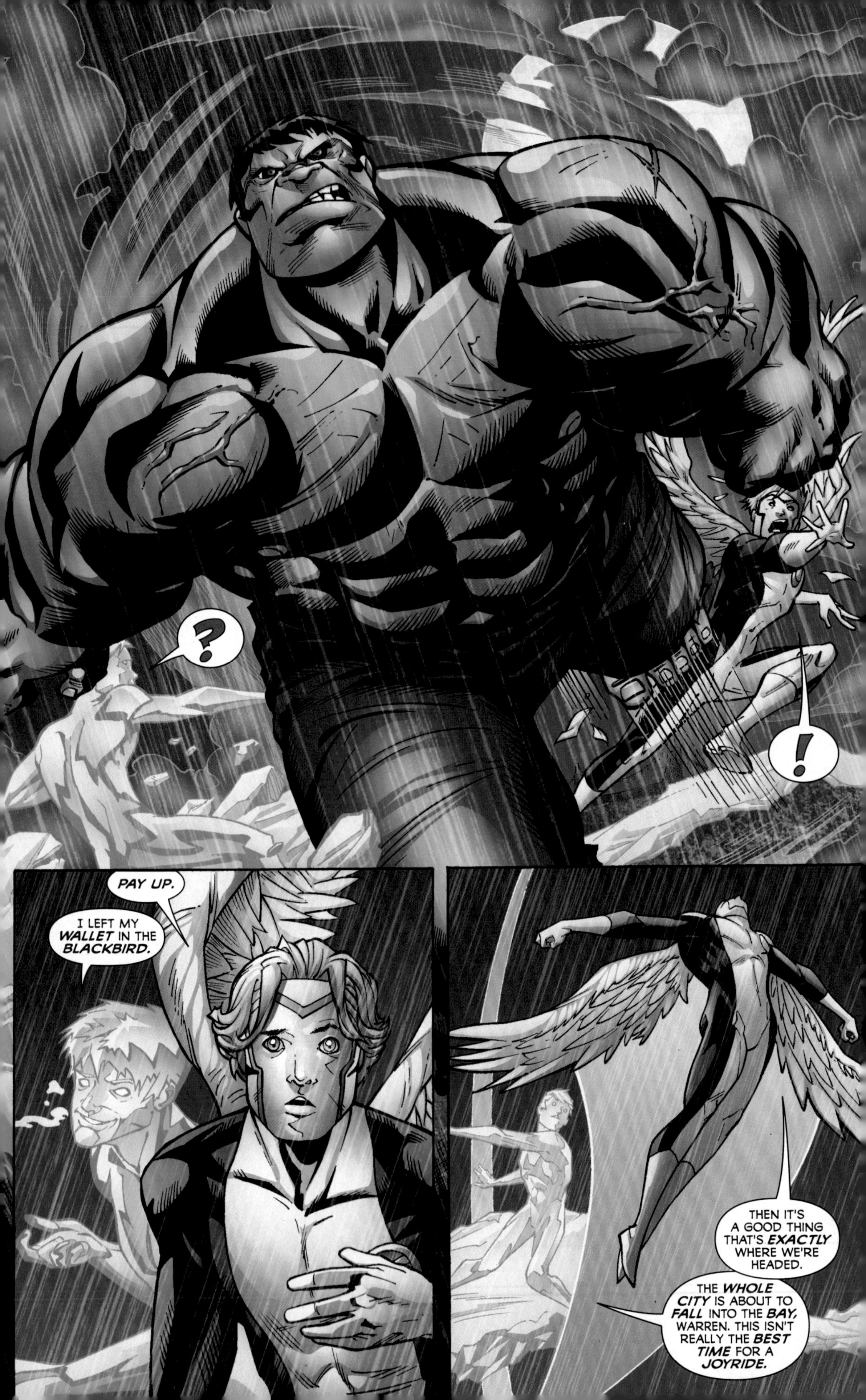
?
!
PAY UP.
I LEFT MY WALLET IN THE BLACKBIRD.
THEN IT'S A GOOD THING THAT'S EXACTLY WHERE WE'RE HEADED.
THE WHOLE CITY IS ABOUT TO FALL INTO THE BAY, WARREN. THIS ISN'T REALLY THE BEST TIME FOR A JOYRIDE.

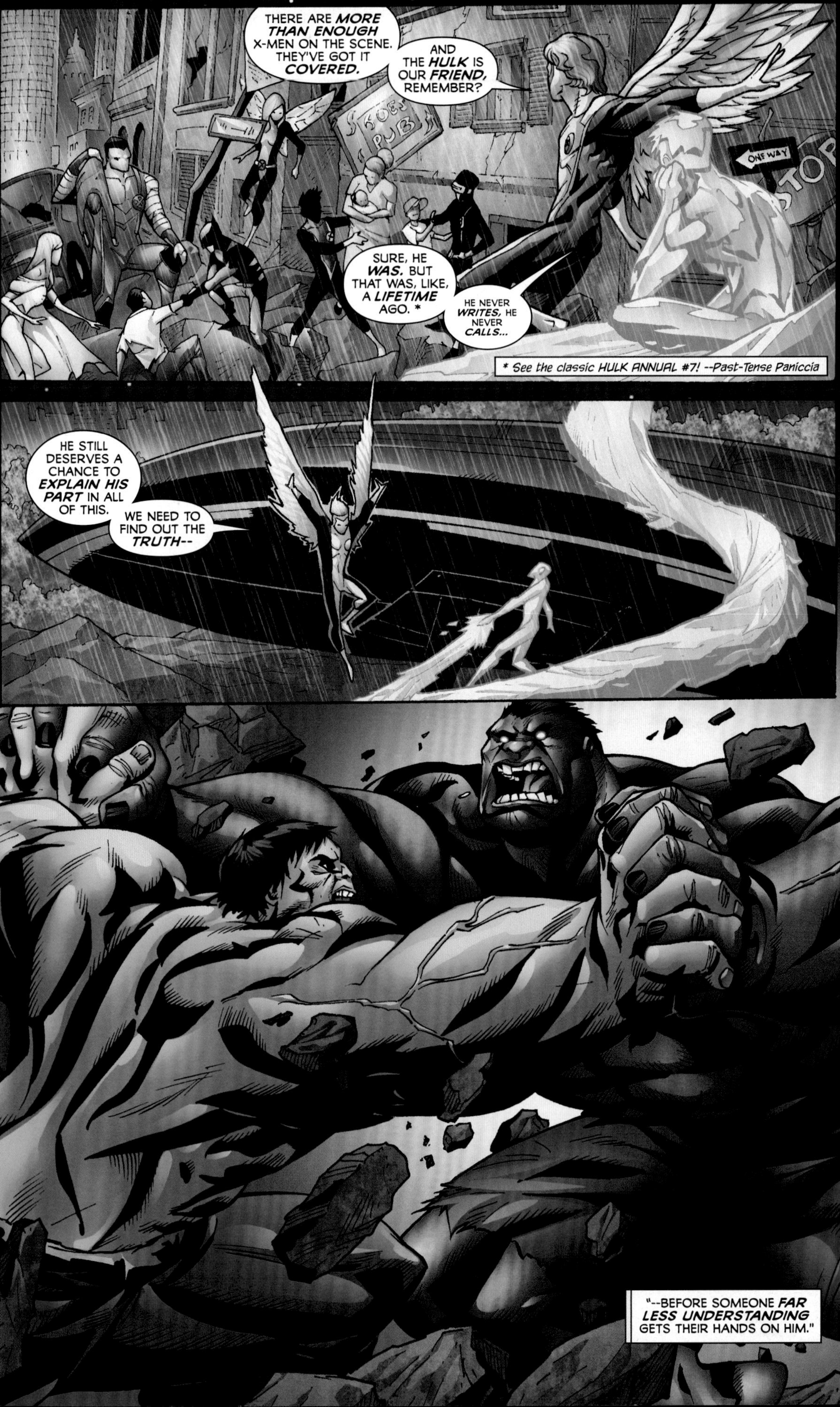
THERE ARE MORE THAN ENOUGH X-MEN ON THE SCENE. THEY'VE GOT IT COVERED.
AND THE HULK IS OUR FRIEND, REMEMBER?
SURE, HE WAS. BUT THAT WAS, LIKE, A LIFETIME AGO. *
HE NEVER WRITES, HE NEVER CALLS...
* See the classic HULK ANNUAL #7! --Past-Tense Paniccia
ONE WAY
STOP
HE STILL DESERVES A CHANCE TO EXPLAIN HIS PART IN ALL OF THIS.
WE NEED TO FIND OUT THE TRUTH--
"--BEFORE SOMEONE FAR LESS UNDERSTANDING GETS THEIR HANDS ON HIM."

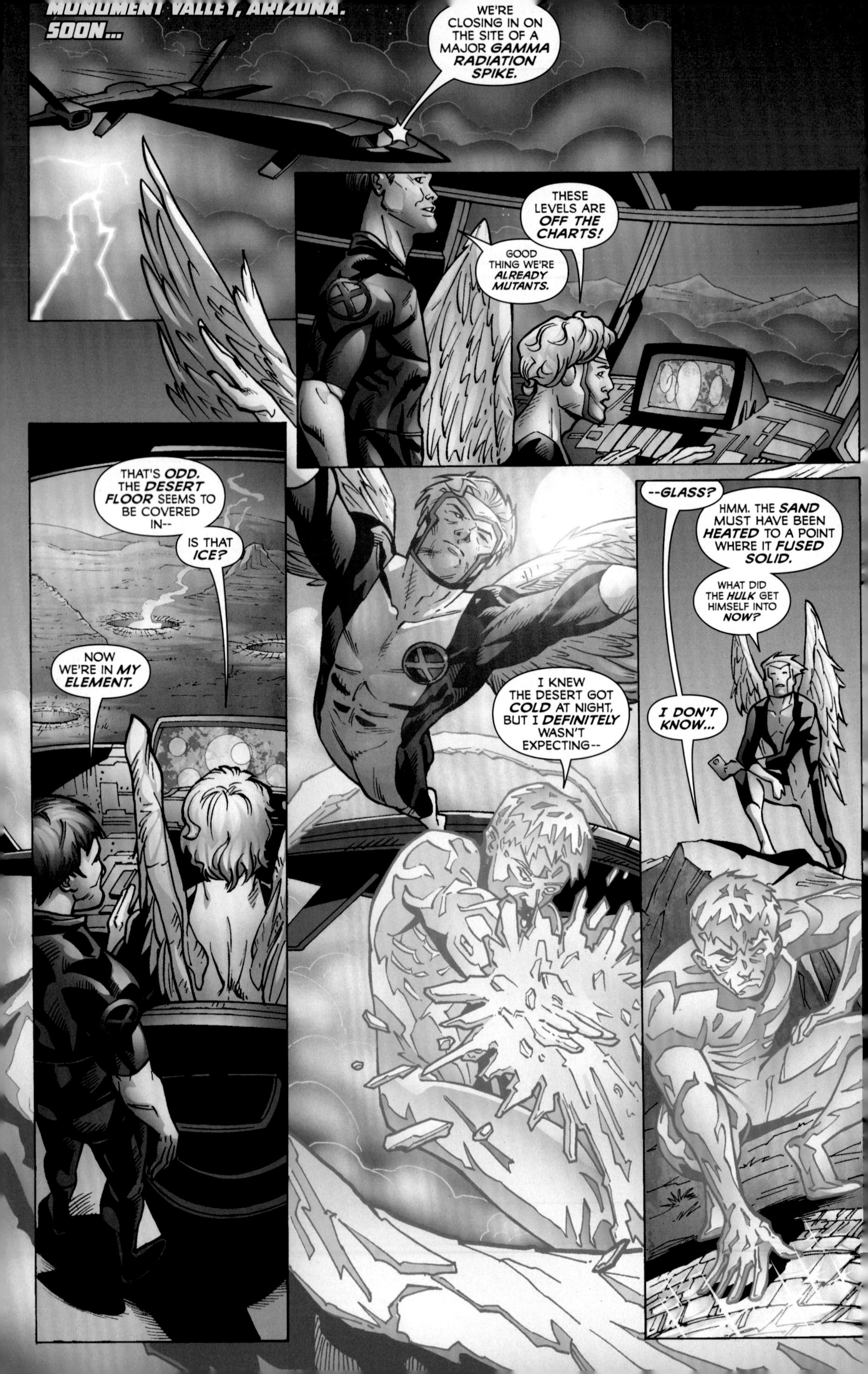
MONUMENT VALLEY, ARIZONA. SOON...
WE'RE CLOSING IN ON THE SITE OF A MAJOR GAMMA RADIATION SPIKE.
THESE LEVELS ARE OFF THE CHARTS!
GOOD THING WE'RE ALREADY MUTANTS.
THAT'S ODD. THE DESERT FLOOR SEEMS TO BE COVERED IN--
IS THAT ICE?
NOW WE'RE IN MY ELEMENT.
I KNEW THE DESERT GOT COLD AT NIGHT, BUT I DEFINITELY WASN'T EXPECTING--
--GLASS?
HMM. THE SAND MUST HAVE BEEN HEATED TO A POINT WHERE IT FUSED SOLID.
WHAT DID THE HULK GET HIMSELF INTO NOW?
I DON'T KNOW...

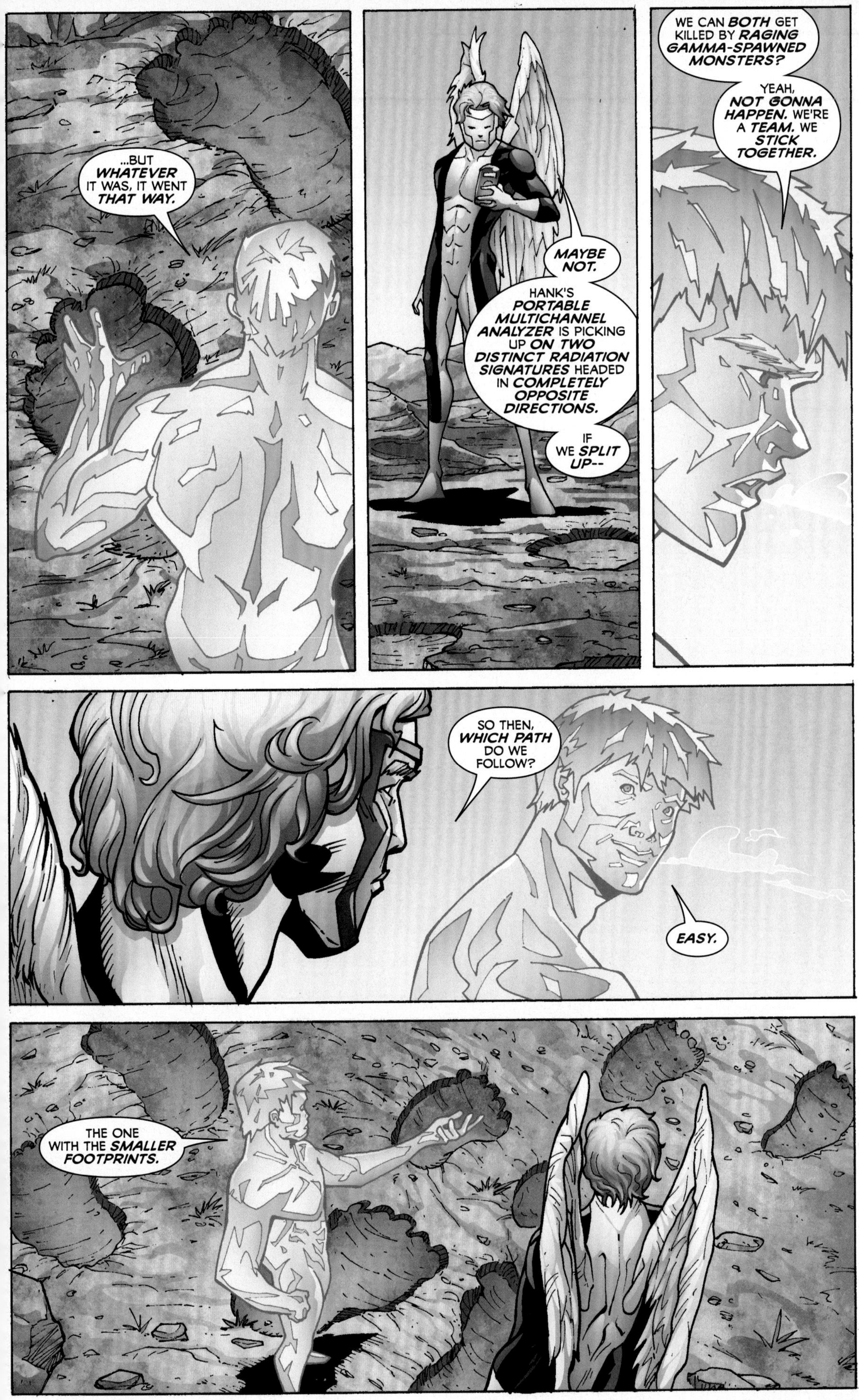
...BUT WHATEVER IT WAS, IT WENT THAT WAY.
MAYBE NOT.
HANK'S PORTABLE MULTICHANNEL ANALYZER IS PICKING UP ON TWO DISTINCT RADIATION SIGNATURES HEADED IN COMPLETELY OPPOSITE DIRECTIONS.
IF WE SPLIT UP--
WE CAN BOTH GET KILLED BY RAGING GAMMA-SPAWNED MONSTERS?
YEAH, NOT GONNA HAPPEN. WE'RE A TEAM. WE STICK TOGETHER.
SO THEN, WHICH PATH DO WE FOLLOW?
EASY.
THE ONE WITH THE SMALLER FOOTPRINTS.

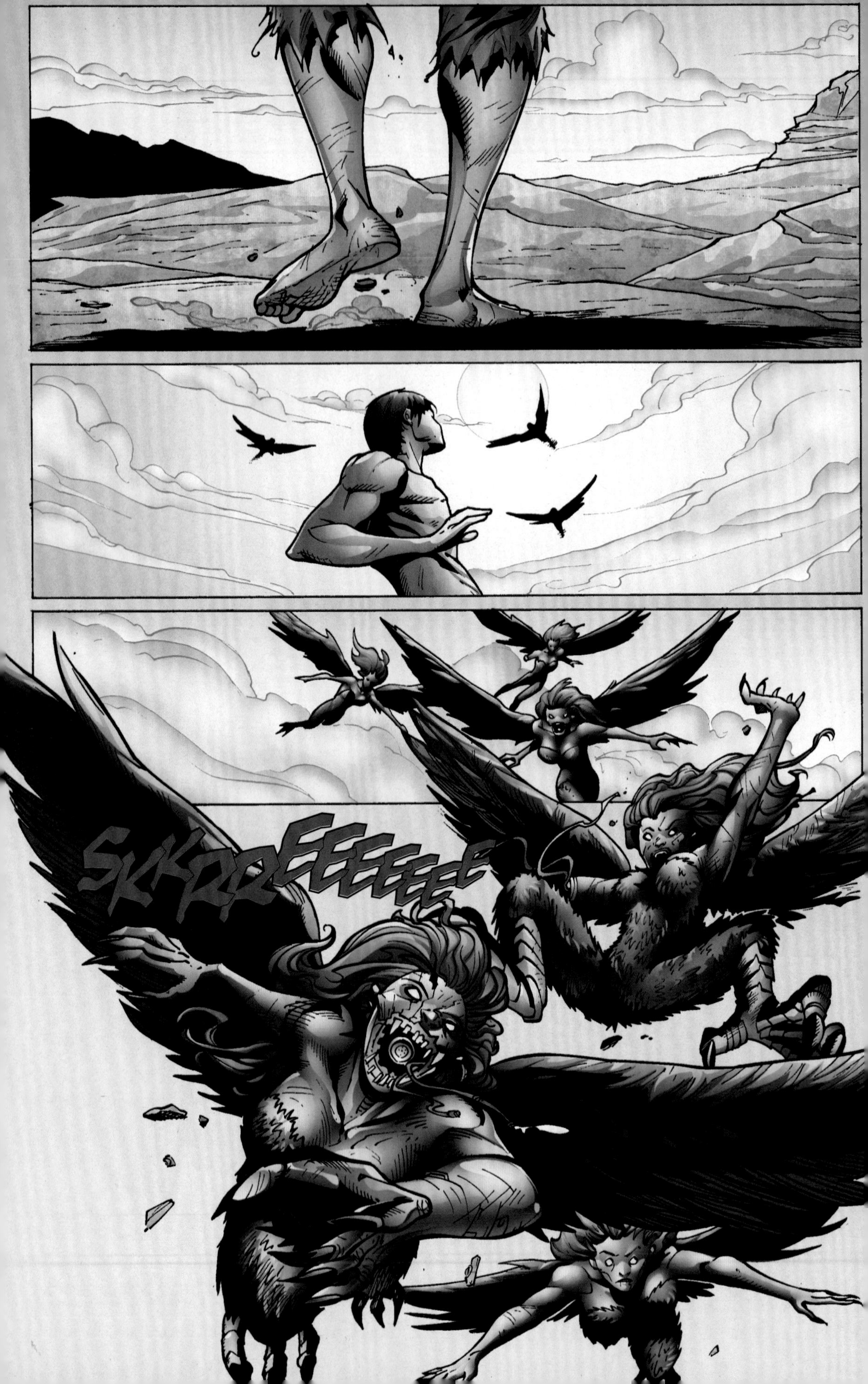
SKRREEEEEEE

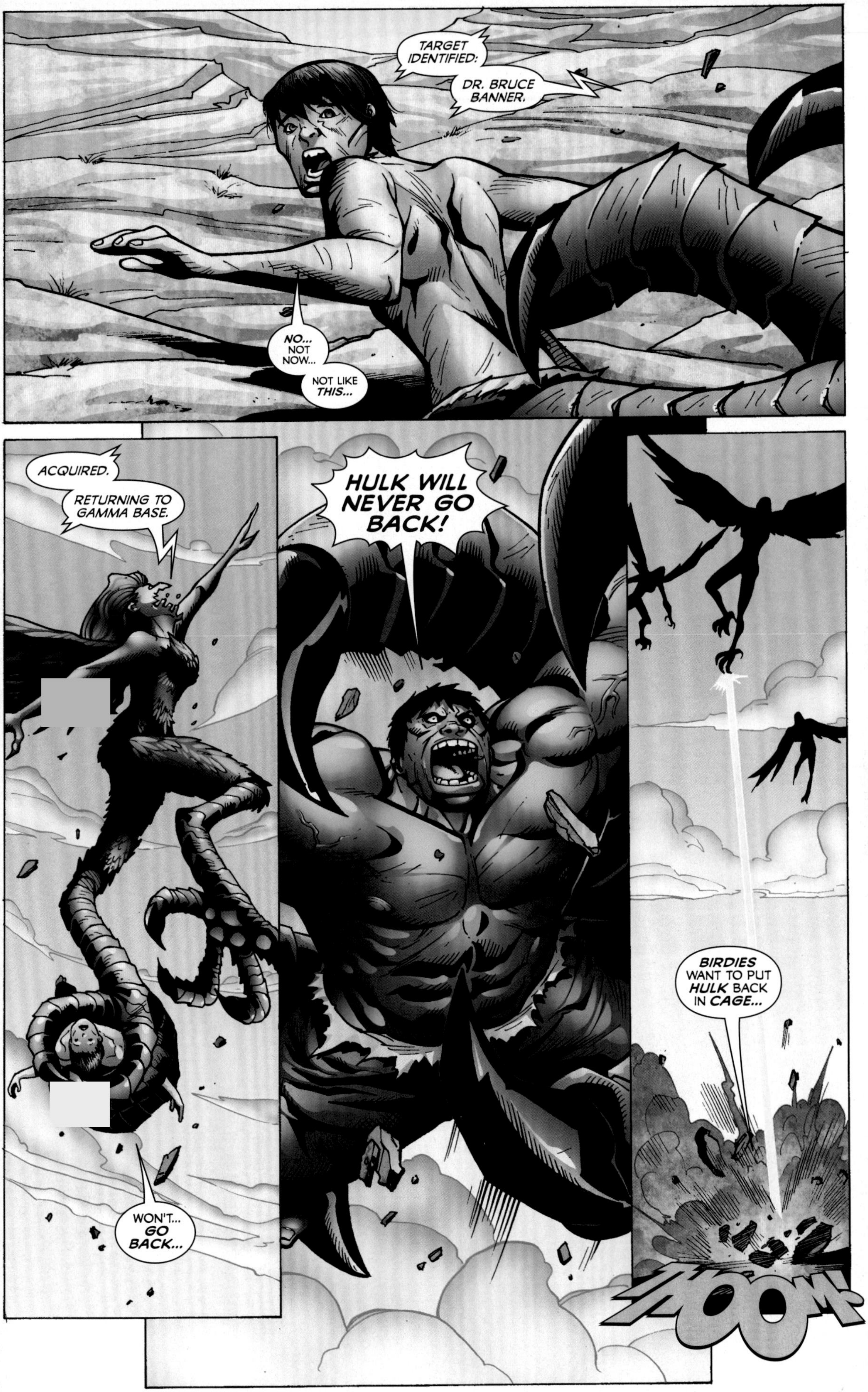
TARGET IDENTIFIED:
DR. BRUCE BANNER.
NO... NOT NOW...
NOT LIKE THIS...
ACQUIRED.
RETURNING TO GAMMA BASE.
WON'T... GO BACK...
HULK WILL NEVER GO BACK!
BIRDIES WANT TO PUT HULK BACK IN CAGE...
THOOM!

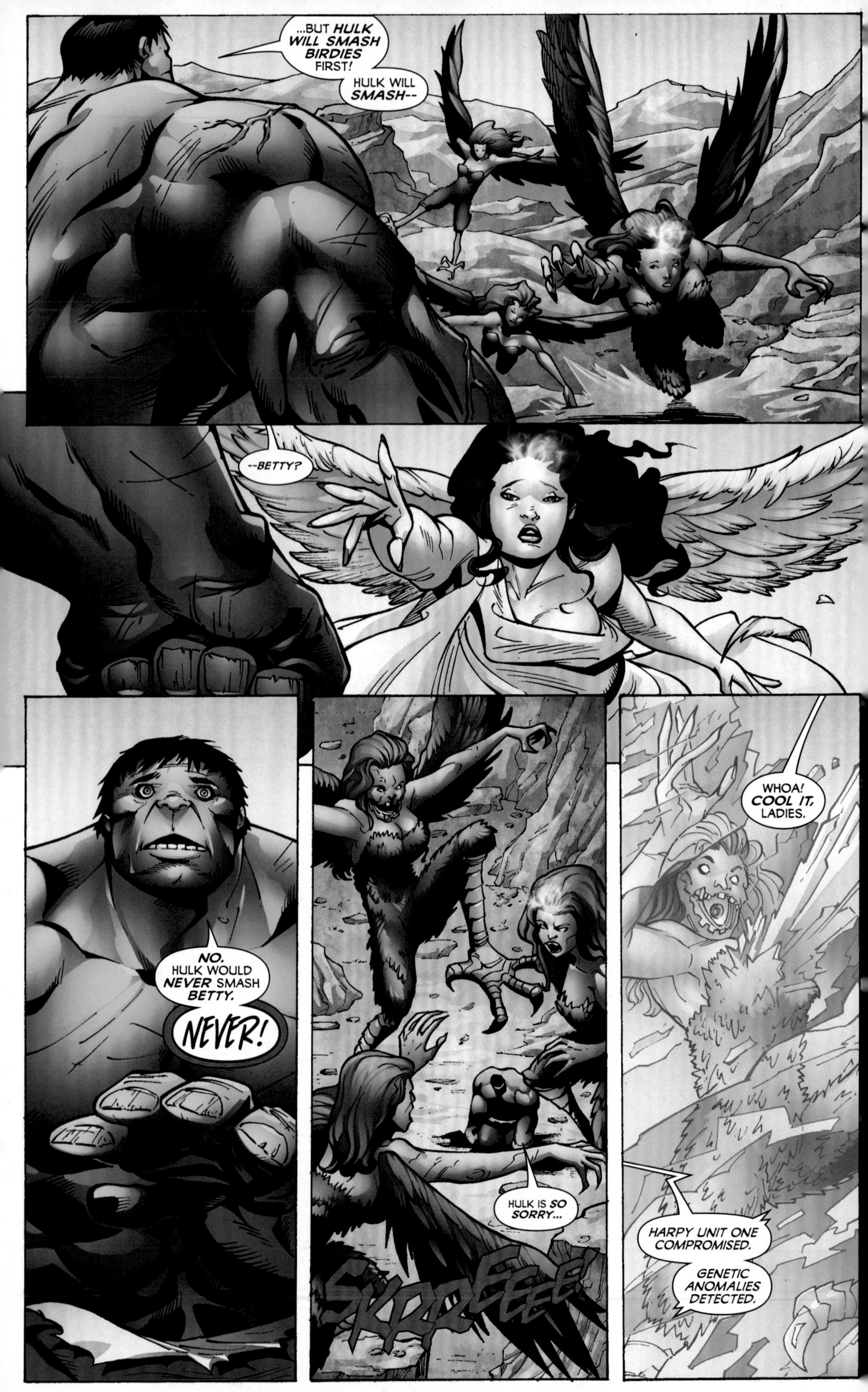
...BUT HULK WILL SMASH BIRDIES FIRST!
HULK WILL SMASH--
--BETTY?
NO. HULK WOULD NEVER SMASH BETTY.
NEVER!
HULK IS SO SORRY...
SKREEEEE
WHOA! COOL IT, LADIES.
HARPY UNIT ONE COMPROMISED.
GENETIC ANOMALIES DETECTED.

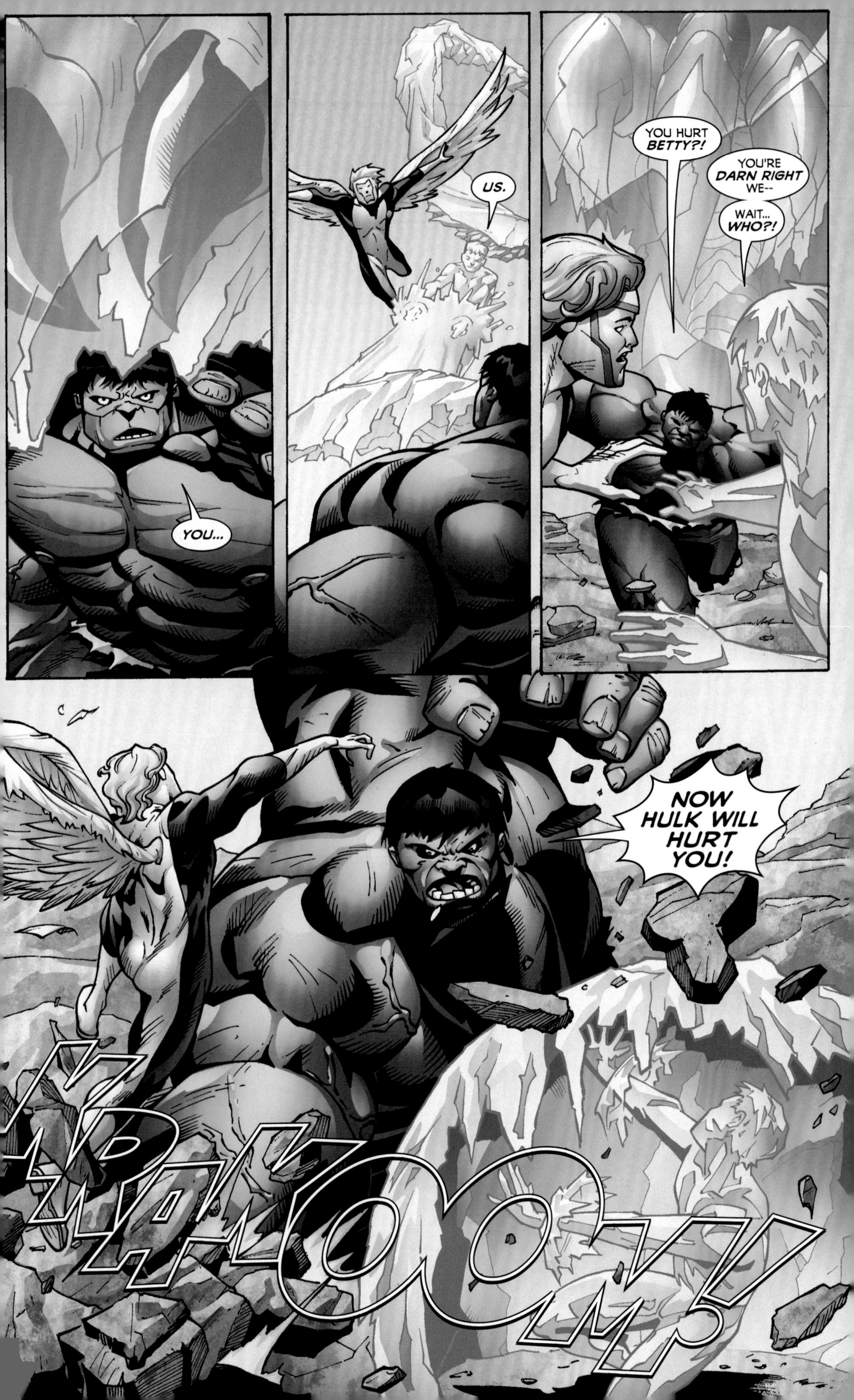
YOU...
US.
YOU HURT BETTY?!
YOU'RE DARN RIGHT WE--
WAIT... WHO?!
NOW HULK WILL HURT YOU!
KRAKOOM!

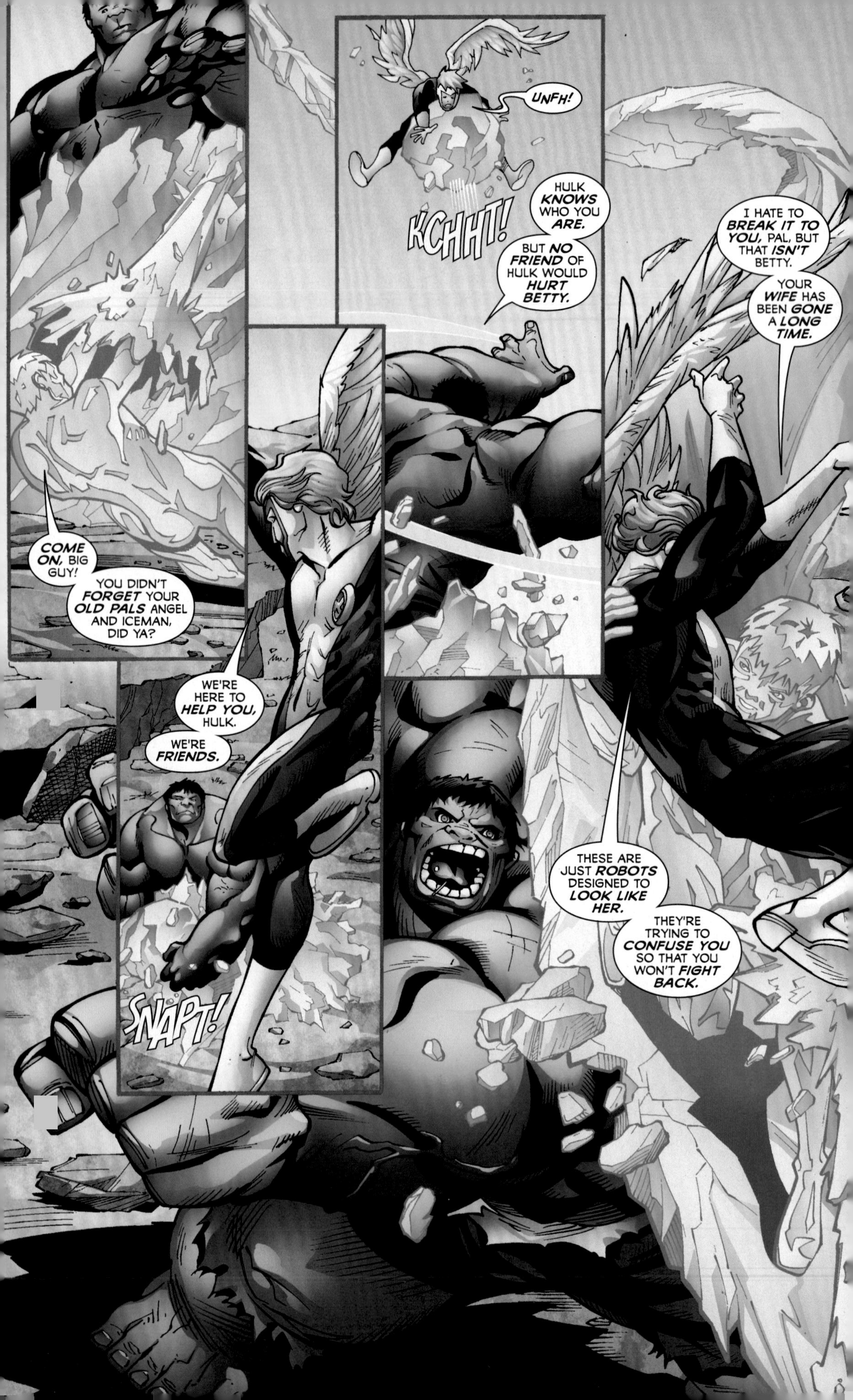
COME ON, BIG GUY!
YOU DIDN'T FORGET YOUR OLD PALS ANGEL AND ICEMAN, DID YA?
UNFH!
KCHHT!
HULK KNOWS WHO YOU ARE.
BUT NO FRIEND OF HULK WOULD HURT BETTY.
WE'RE HERE TO HELP YOU, HULK.
WE'RE FRIENDS.
SNAPT!
I HATE TO BREAK IT TO YOU, PAL, BUT THAT ISN'T BETTY.
YOUR WIFE HAS BEEN GONE A LONG TIME.
THESE ARE JUST ROBOTS DESIGNED TO LOOK LIKE HER.
THEY'RE TRYING TO CONFUSE YOU SO THAT YOU WON'T FIGHT BACK.

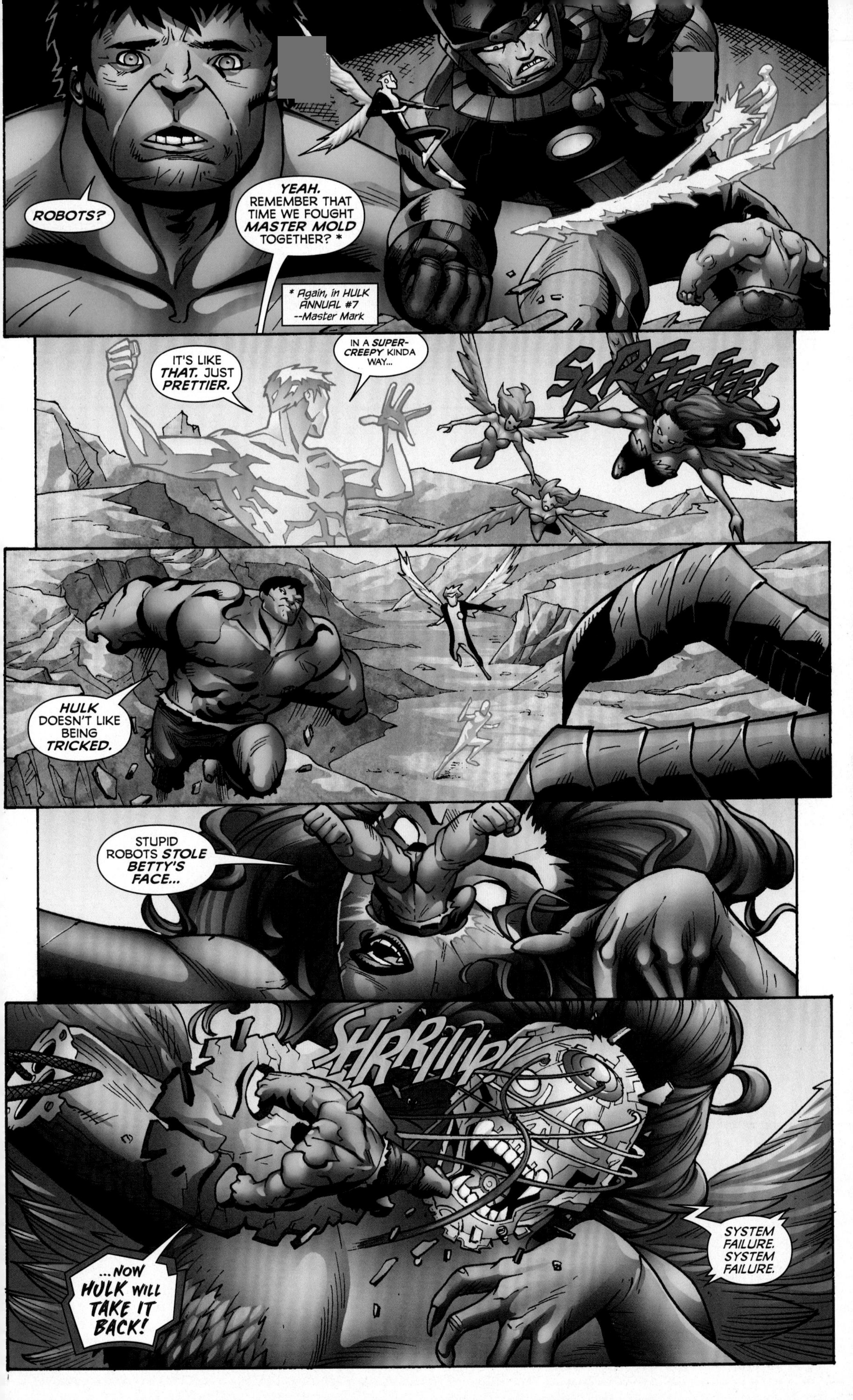
ROBOTS?
YEAH. REMEMBER THAT TIME WE FOUGHT MASTER MOLD TOGETHER? *
* Again, in HULK ANNUAL #7 --Master Mark
IT'S LIKE THAT. JUST PRETTIER.
IN A SUPER-CREEPY KINDA WAY...
SKREEEEEEE!
HULK DOESN'T LIKE BEING TRICKED.
STUPID ROBOTS STOLE BETTY'S FACE...
SHRUNNK!
SYSTEM FAILURE. SYSTEM FAILURE.
...NOW HULK WILL TAKE IT BACK!

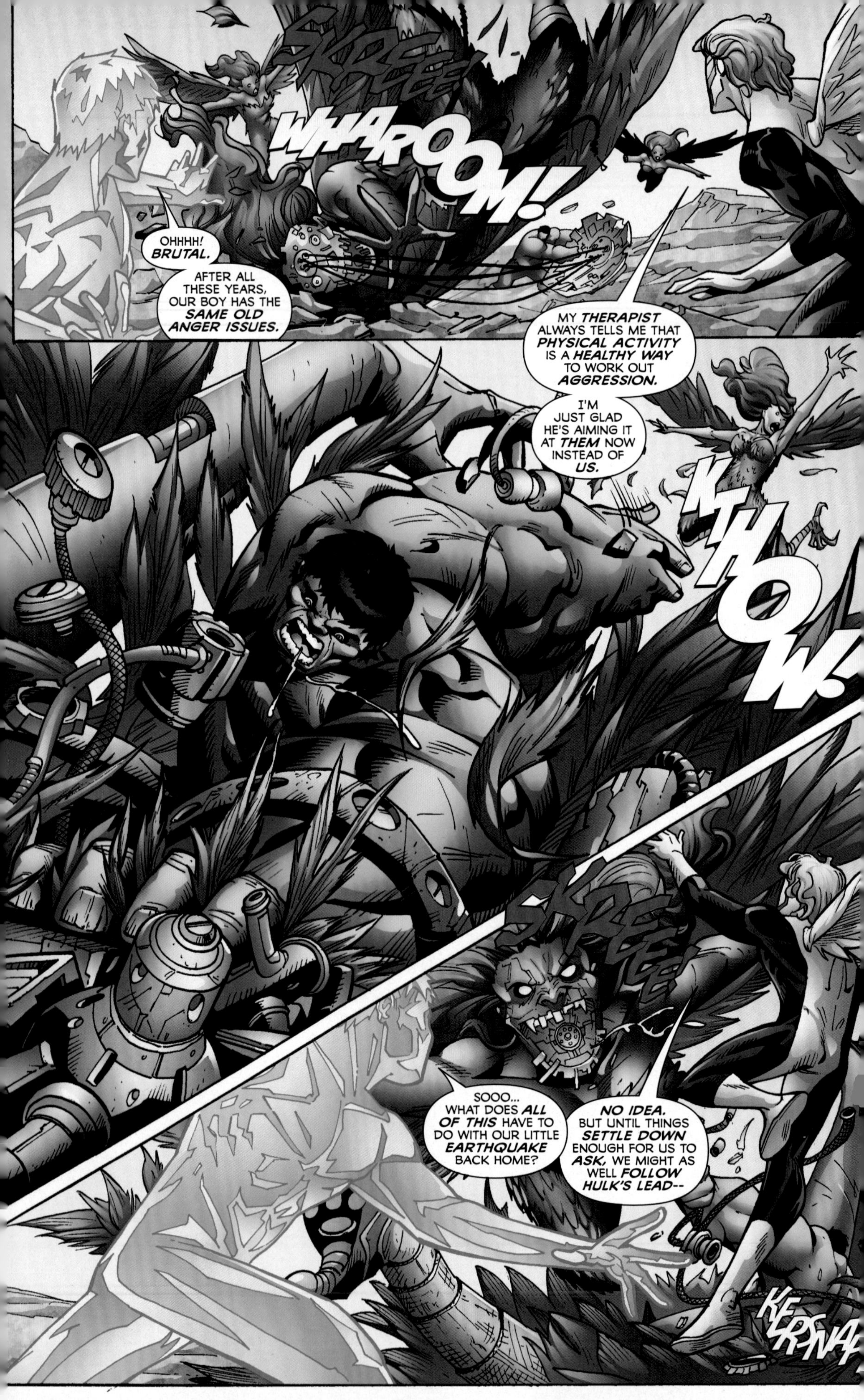
SKREEE
WHAROOOM!
OHHHH! BRUTAL.
AFTER ALL THESE YEARS, OUR BOY HAS THE SAME OLD ANGER ISSUES.
MY THERAPIST ALWAYS TELLS ME THAT PHYSICAL ACTIVITY IS A HEALTHY WAY TO WORK OUT AGGRESSION.
I'M JUST GLAD HE'S AIMING IT AT THEM NOW INSTEAD OF US.
KTHOW!
SKREEE
SOOO... WHAT DOES ALL OF THIS HAVE TO DO WITH OUR LITTLE EARTHQUAKE BACK HOME?
NO IDEA. BUT UNTIL THINGS SETTLE DOWN ENOUGH FOR US TO ASK, WE MIGHT AS WELL FOLLOW HULK'S LEAD--

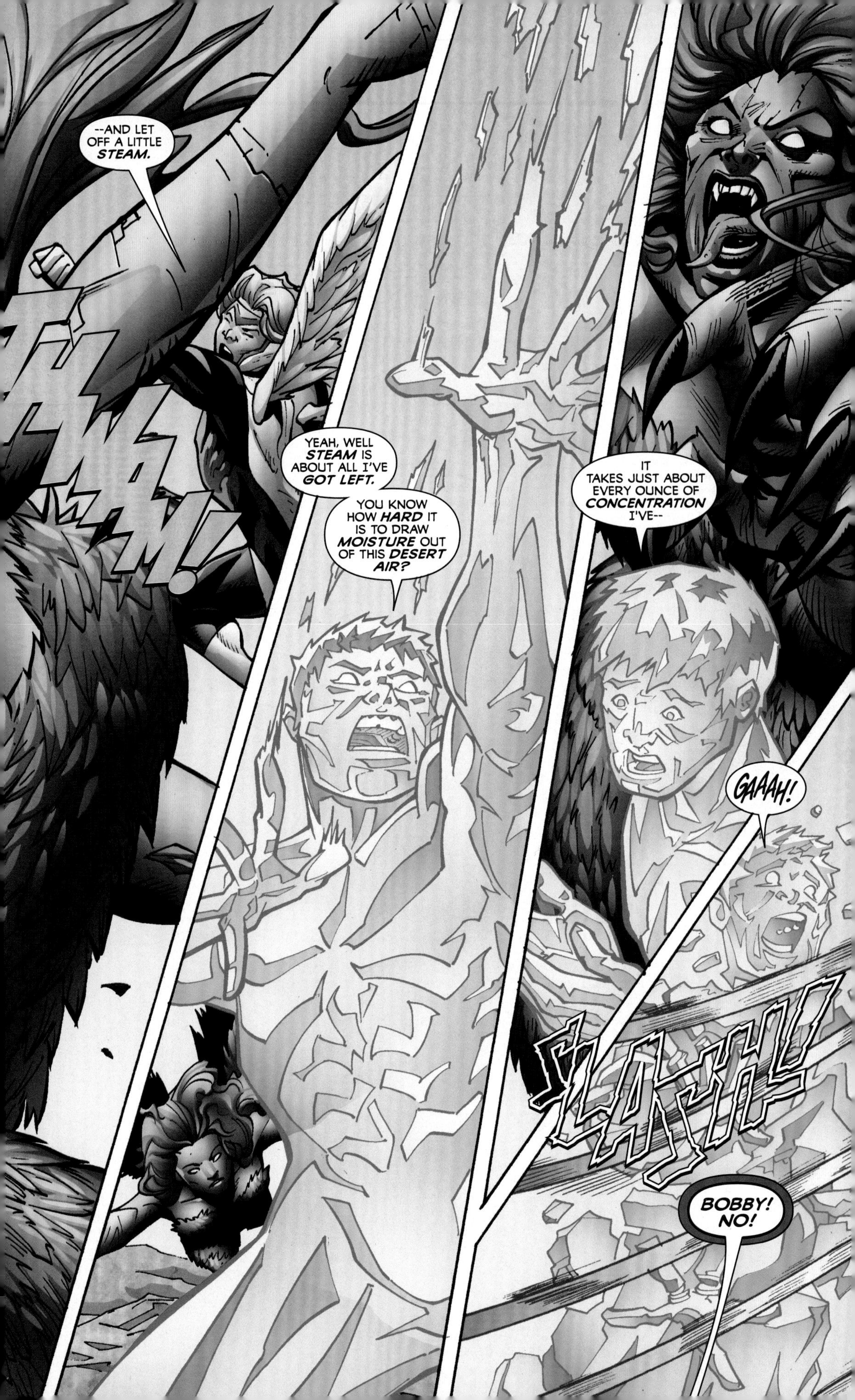
--AND LET OFF A LITTLE STEAM.
THWAM!
YEAH, WELL STEAM IS ABOUT ALL I'VE GOT LEFT.
YOU KNOW HOW HARD IT IS TO DRAW MOISTURE OUT OF THIS DESERT AIR?
IT TAKES JUST ABOUT EVERY OUNCE OF CONCENTRATION I'VE--
GAAAH!
SLASH!
BOBBY! NO!

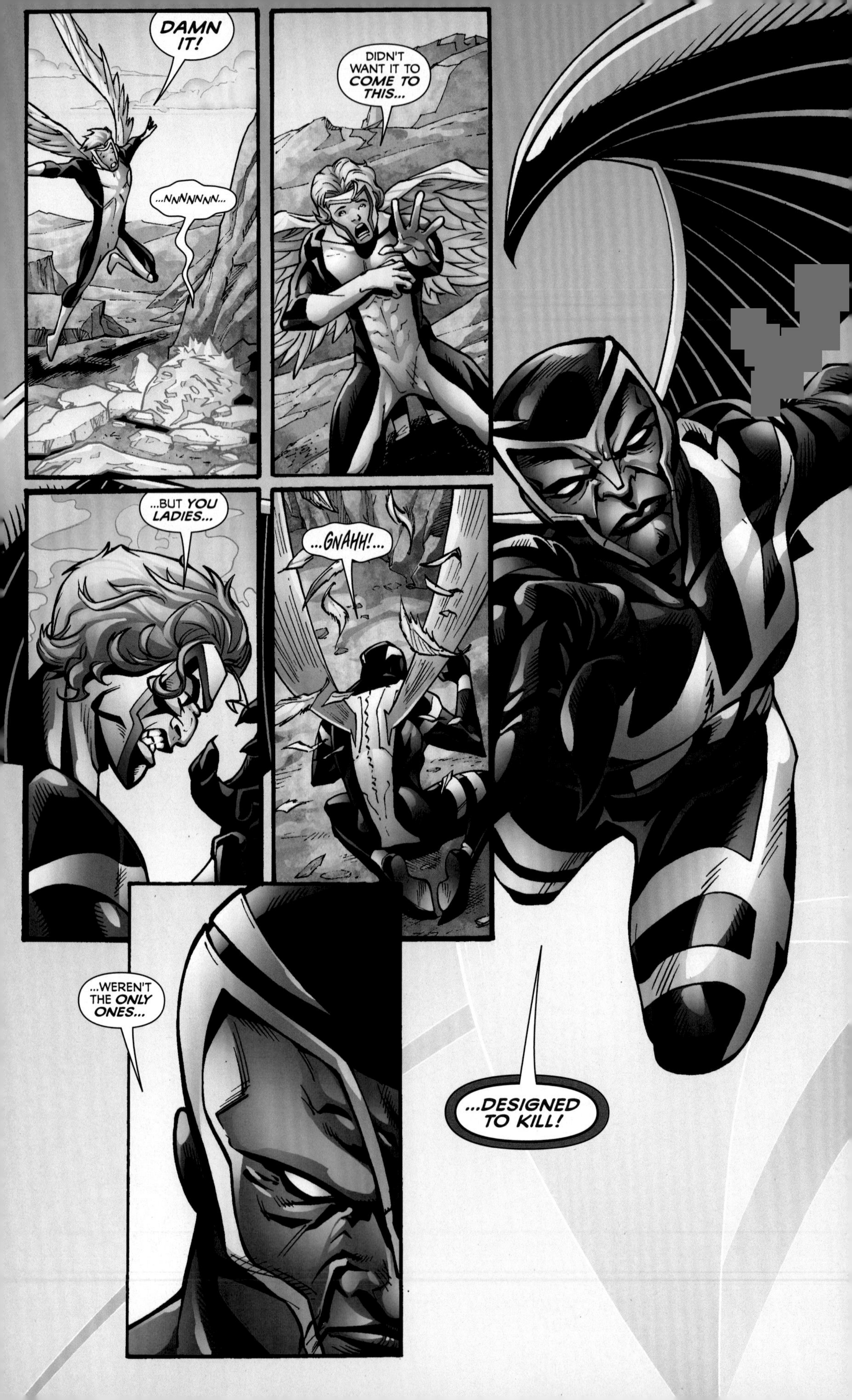

DAMN IT!
...NNNNNNN...
DIDN'T WANT IT TO COME TO THIS...
...BUT YOU LADIES...
...GNAHH!...
...WEREN'T THE ONLY ONES...
...DESIGNED TO KILL!

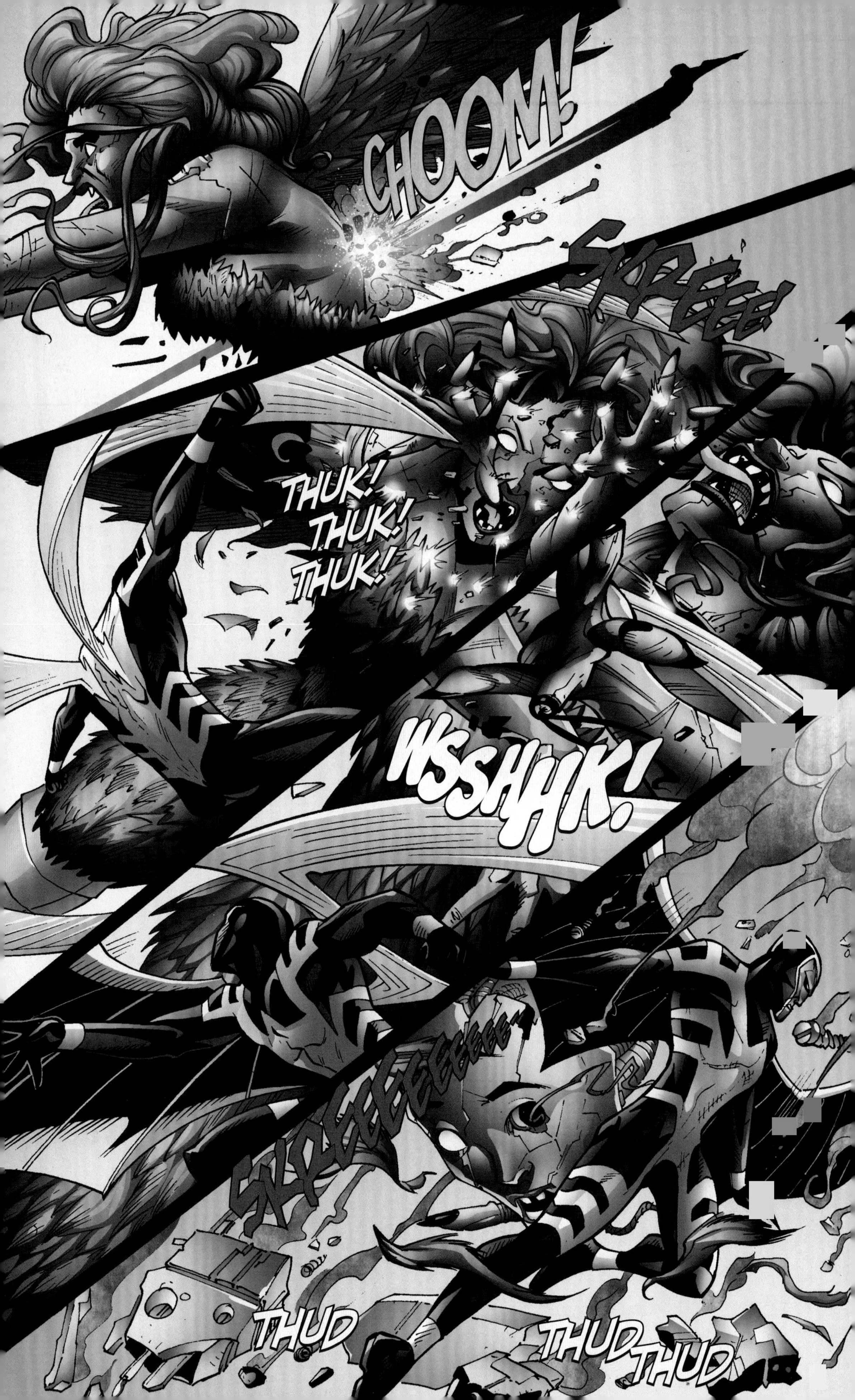
CHOOM!
SKREEE!
THUK! THUK! THUK!
WSSHHK!
THUD
THUD THUD

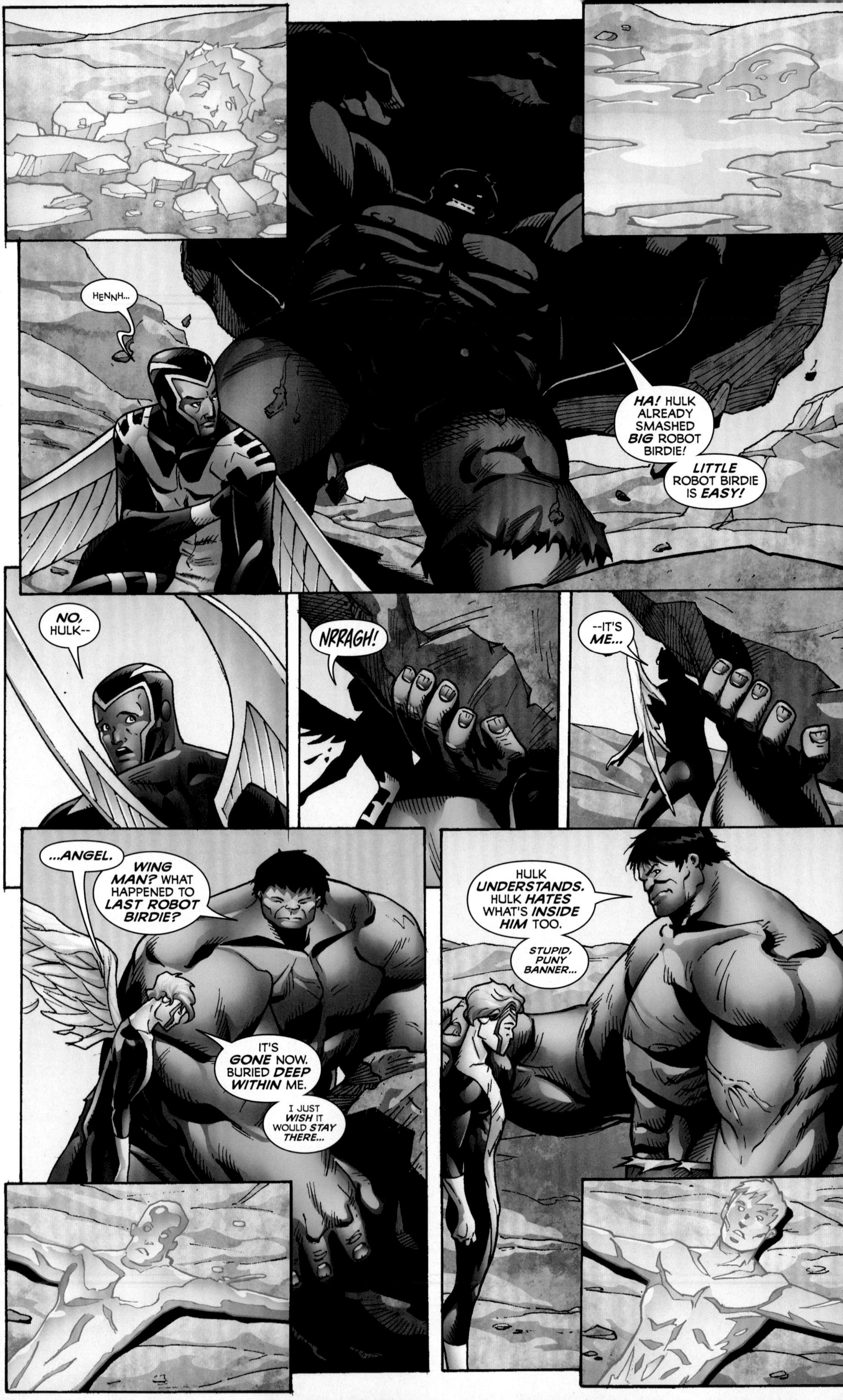
HENNH...
HA! HULK ALREADY SMASHED BIG ROBOT BIRDIE!
LITTLE ROBOT BIRDIE IS EASY!
NO, HULK--
NRRAGH!
--IT'S ME...
...ANGEL.
WING MAN? WHAT HAPPENED TO LAST ROBOT BIRDIE?
IT'S GONE NOW. BURIED DEEP WITHIN ME.
I JUST WISH IT WOULD STAY THERE...
HULK UNDERSTANDS. HULK HATES WHAT'S INSIDE HIM TOO.
STUPID, PUNY BANNER...

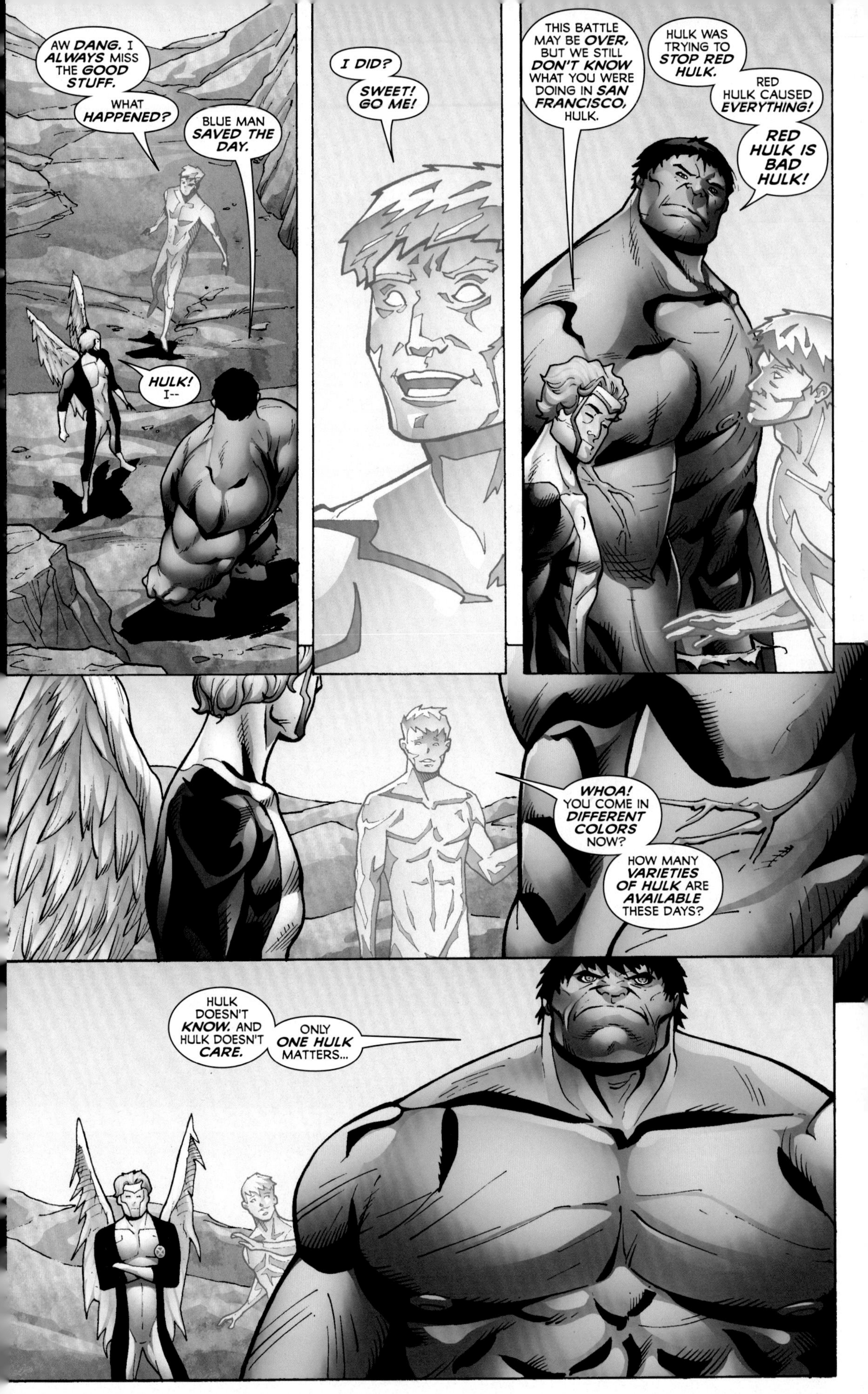

AW DANG. I ALWAYS MISS THE GOOD STUFF.
WHAT HAPPENED?
BLUE MAN SAVED THE DAY.
HULK! I--
I DID?
SWEET! GO ME!
THIS BATTLE MAY BE OVER, BUT WE STILL DON'T KNOW WHAT YOU WERE DOING IN SAN FRANCISCO, HULK.
HULK WAS TRYING TO STOP RED HULK.
RED HULK CAUSED EVERYTHING!
RED HULK IS BAD HULK!
WHOA! YOU COME IN DIFFERENT COLORS NOW?
HOW MANY VARIETIES OF HULK ARE AVAILABLE THESE DAYS?
HULK DOESN'T KNOW. AND HULK DOESN'T CARE.
ONLY ONE HULK MATTERS...

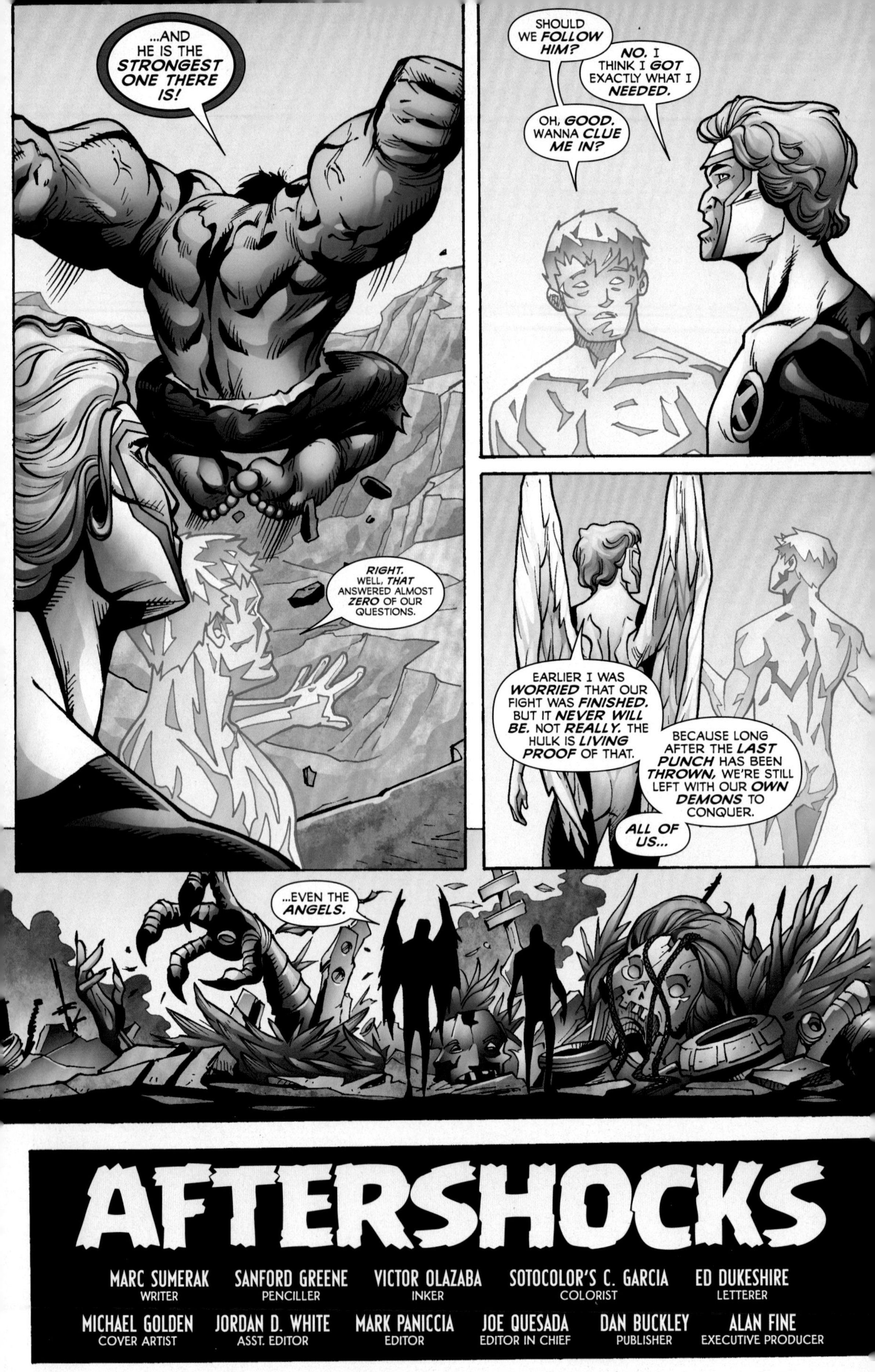

...AND HE IS THE STRONGEST ONE THERE IS!
RIGHT. WELL, THAT ANSWERED ALMOST ZERO OF OUR QUESTIONS.
SHOULD WE FOLLOW HIM?
NO. I THINK I GOT EXACTLY WHAT I NEEDED.
OH, GOOD. WANNA CLUE ME IN?
EARLIER I WAS WORRIED THAT OUR FIGHT WAS FINISHED. BUT IT NEVER WILL BE. NOT REALLY. THE HULK IS LIVING PROOF OF THAT.
BECAUSE LONG AFTER THE LAST PUNCH HAS BEEN THROWN, WE'RE STILL LEFT WITH OUR OWN DEMONS TO CONQUER.
ALL OF US...
...EVEN THE ANGELS.

AFTERSHOCKS

MARC SUMERAK
WRITER

SANFORD GREENE
PENCILLER

VICTOR OLAZABA
INKER

SOTOCOLOR'S C. GARCIA
COLORIST

ED DUKESHIRE
LETTERER

MICHAEL GOLDEN
COVER ARTIST

JORDAN D. WHITE
ASST. EDITOR

MARK PANICCIA
EDITOR

JOE QUESADA
EDITOR IN CHIEF

DAN BUCKLEY
PUBLISHER

ALAN FINE
EXECUTIVE PRODUCER

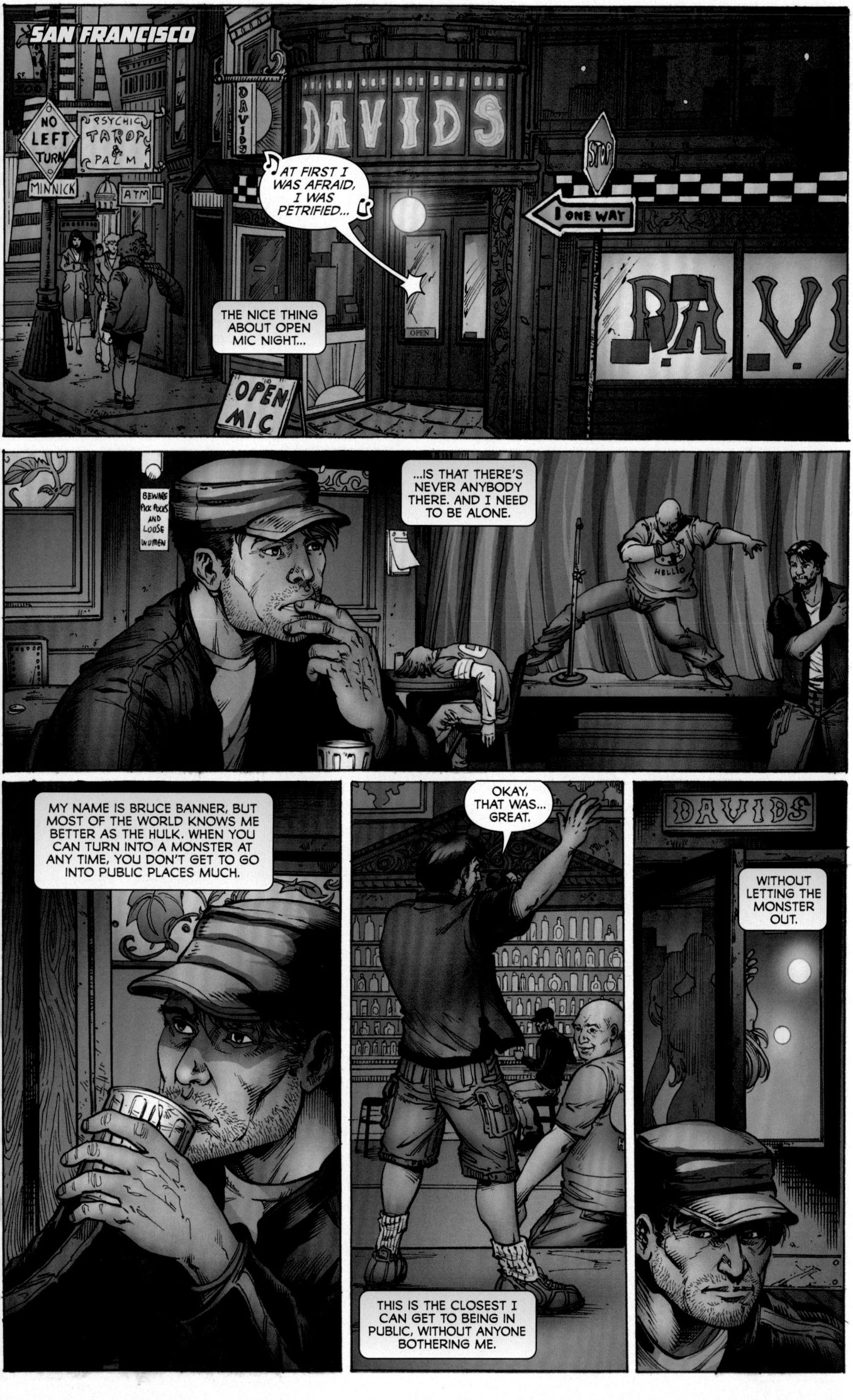
SAN FRANCISCO
NO LEFT TURN
PSYCHIC TAROT & PALM
MINNICK
ATM
DAVIDS
STOP
ONE WAY
OPEN
OPEN MIC
AT FIRST I WAS AFRAID, I WAS PETRIFIED...
THE NICE THING ABOUT OPEN MIC NIGHT...
BEWARE PICK POCKETS AND LOOSE WOMEN
...IS THAT THERE'S NEVER ANYBODY THERE. AND I NEED TO BE ALONE.
HELLO
MY NAME IS BRUCE BANNER, BUT MOST OF THE WORLD KNOWS ME BETTER AS THE HULK. WHEN YOU CAN TURN INTO A MONSTER AT ANY TIME, YOU DON'T GET TO GO INTO PUBLIC PLACES MUCH.
OKAY, THAT WAS... GREAT.
THIS IS THE CLOSEST I CAN GET TO BEING IN PUBLIC, WITHOUT ANYONE BOTHERING ME.
DAVIDS
WITHOUT LETTING THE MONSTER OUT.

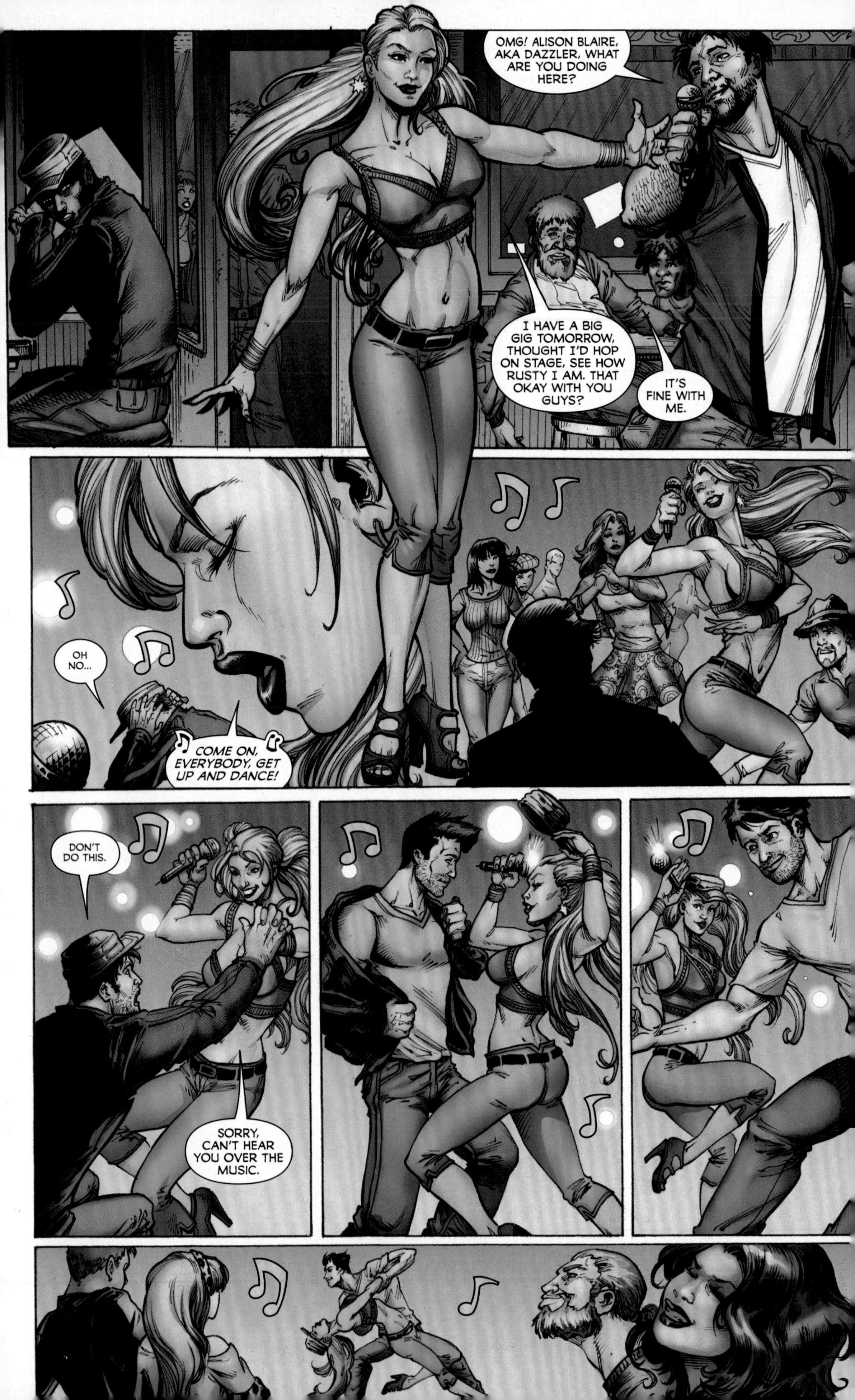
OMG! ALISON BLAIRE, AKA DAZZLER, WHAT ARE YOU DOING HERE?
I HAVE A BIG GIG TOMORROW, THOUGHT I'D HOP ON STAGE, SEE HOW RUSTY I AM. THAT OKAY WITH YOU GUYS?
IT'S FINE WITH ME.
OH NO...
COME ON, EVERYBODY, GET UP AND DANCE!
DON'T DO THIS.
SORRY, CAN'T HEAR YOU OVER THE MUSIC.

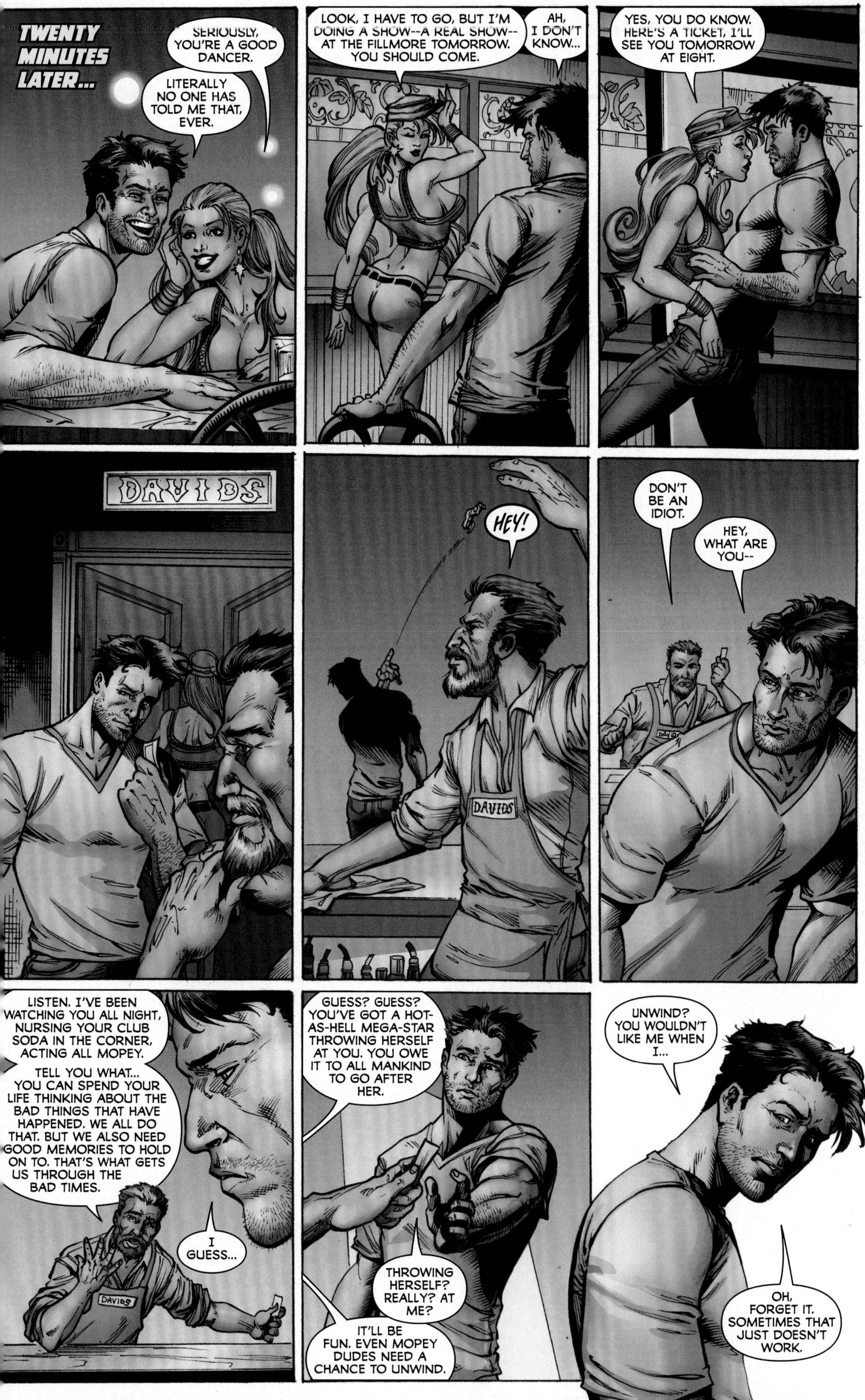
TWENTY MINUTES LATER...
SERIOUSLY, YOU'RE A GOOD DANCER.
LITERALLY NO ONE HAS TOLD ME THAT, EVER.
LOOK, I HAVE TO GO, BUT I'M DOING A SHOW--A REAL SHOW--AT THE FILLMORE TOMORROW. YOU SHOULD COME.
AH, I DON'T KNOW...
YES, YOU DO KNOW. HERE'S A TICKET, I'LL SEE YOU TOMORROW AT EIGHT.
DAVIDS
HEY!
DAVIDS
DON'T BE AN IDIOT.
HEY, WHAT ARE YOU--
LISTEN. I'VE BEEN WATCHING YOU ALL NIGHT, NURSING YOUR CLUB SODA IN THE CORNER, ACTING ALL MOPEY.
TELL YOU WHAT... YOU CAN SPEND YOUR LIFE THINKING ABOUT THE BAD THINGS THAT HAVE HAPPENED. WE ALL DO THAT. BUT WE ALSO NEED GOOD MEMORIES TO HOLD ON TO. THAT'S WHAT GETS US THROUGH THE BAD TIMES.
I GUESS...
DAVIDS
GUESS? GUESS? YOU'VE GOT A HOT-AS-HELL MEGA-STAR THROWING HERSELF AT YOU. YOU OWE IT TO ALL MANKIND TO GO AFTER HER.
THROWING HERSELF? REALLY? AT ME?
IT'LL BE FUN. EVEN MOPEY DUDES NEED A CHANCE TO UNWIND.
UNWIND? YOU WOULDN'T LIKE ME WHEN I...
OH, FORGET IT. SOMETIMES THAT JUST DOESN'T WORK.

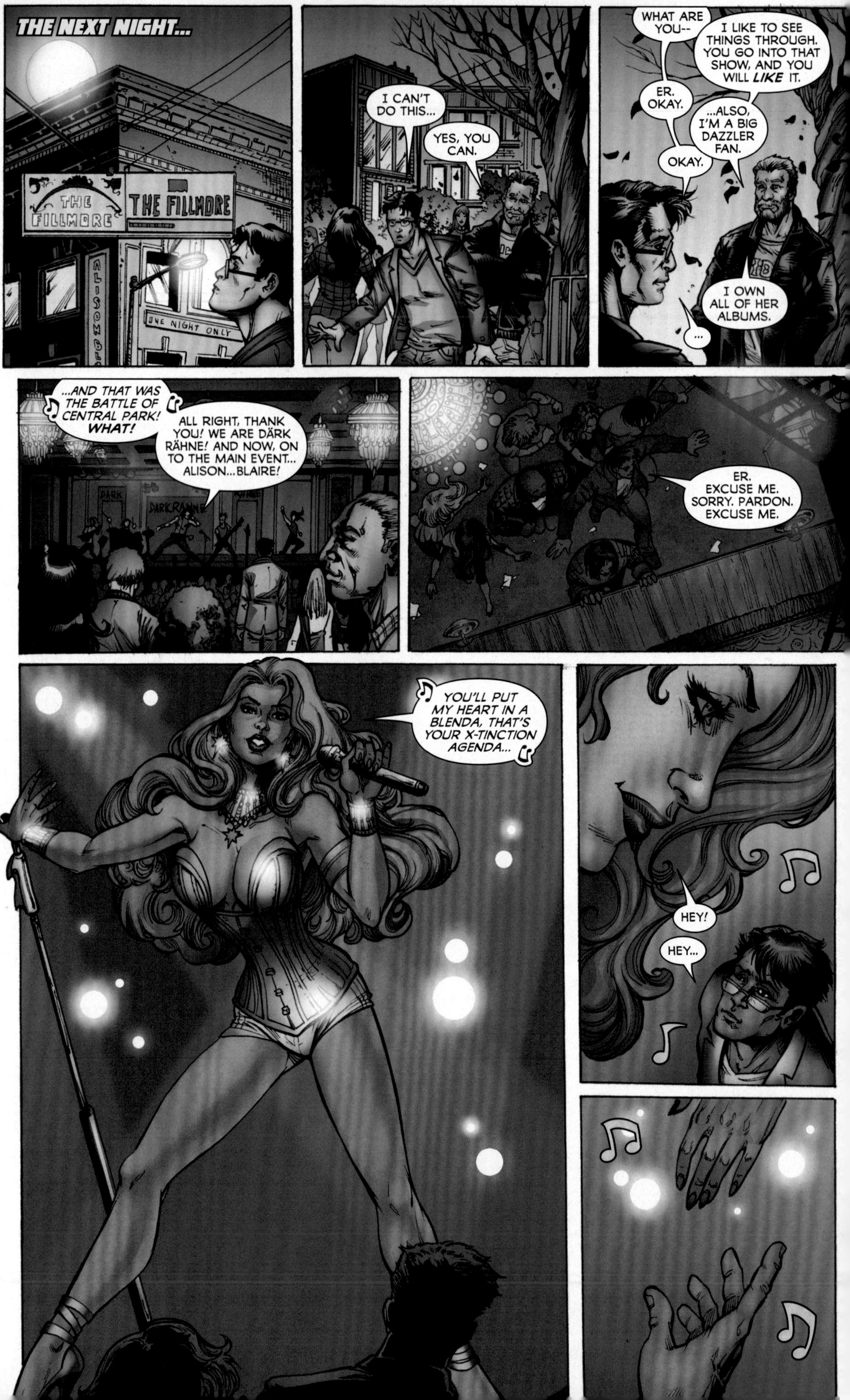
THE NEXT NIGHT...
THE FILLMORE
THE FILLMORE
ALISON BLAIRE
ONE NIGHT ONLY
I CAN'T DO THIS...
YES, YOU CAN.
WHAT ARE YOU--
I LIKE TO SEE THINGS THROUGH. YOU GO INTO THAT SHOW, AND YOU WILL LIKE IT.
ER. OKAY.
...ALSO, I'M A BIG DAZZLER FAN.
OKAY.
I OWN ALL OF HER ALBUMS.
...
...AND THAT WAS THE BATTLE OF CENTRAL PARK! WHAT!
ALL RIGHT, THANK YOU! WE ARE DÄRK RÄHNE! AND NOW, ON TO THE MAIN EVENT... ALISON...BLAIRE!
ER. EXCUSE ME. SORRY. PARDON. EXCUSE ME.
YOU'LL PUT MY HEART IN A BLENDA, THAT'S YOUR X-TINCTION AGENDA...
HEY!
HEY...

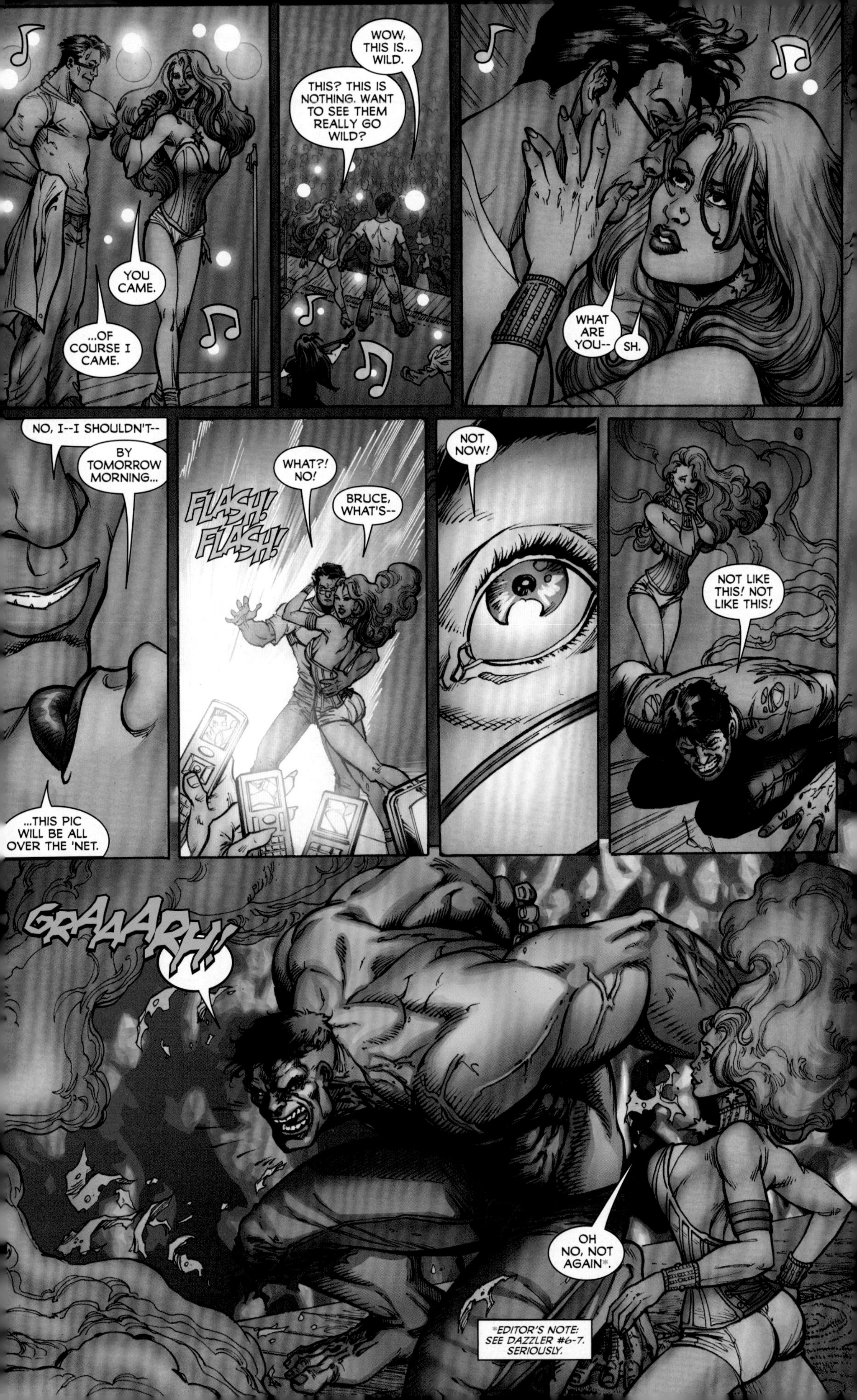
YOU CAME.
...OF COURSE I CAME.
WOW, THIS IS... WILD.
THIS? THIS IS NOTHING. WANT TO SEE THEM REALLY GO WILD?
WHAT ARE YOU--
SH.
NO, I--I SHOULDN'T--
BY TOMORROW MORNING...
...THIS PIC WILL BE ALL OVER THE 'NET.
FLASH! FLASH!
WHAT?! NO!
BRUCE, WHAT'S--
NOT NOW!
NOT LIKE THIS! NOT LIKE THIS!
GRAAARH!
OH NO, NOT AGAIN*.
*EDITOR'S NOTE: SEE DAZZLER #6-7. SERIOUSLY.

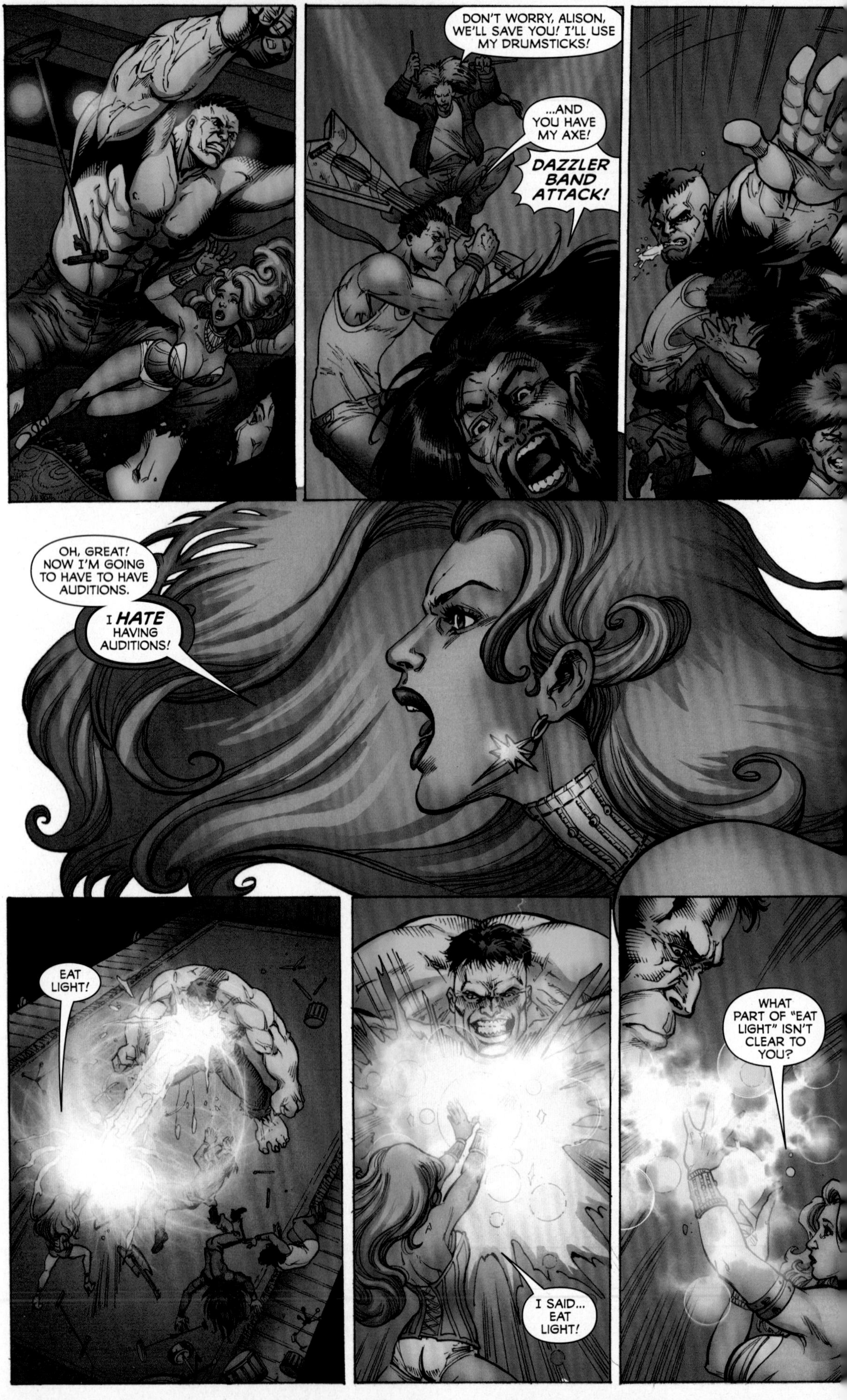
DON'T WORRY, ALISON, WE'LL SAVE YOU! I'LL USE MY DRUMSTICKS!
...AND YOU HAVE MY AXE!
DAZZLER BAND ATTACK!
OH, GREAT! NOW I'M GOING TO HAVE TO HAVE AUDITIONS.
I HATE HAVING AUDITIONS!
EAT LIGHT!
I SAID... EAT LIGHT!
WHAT PART OF "EAT LIGHT" ISN'T CLEAR TO YOU?

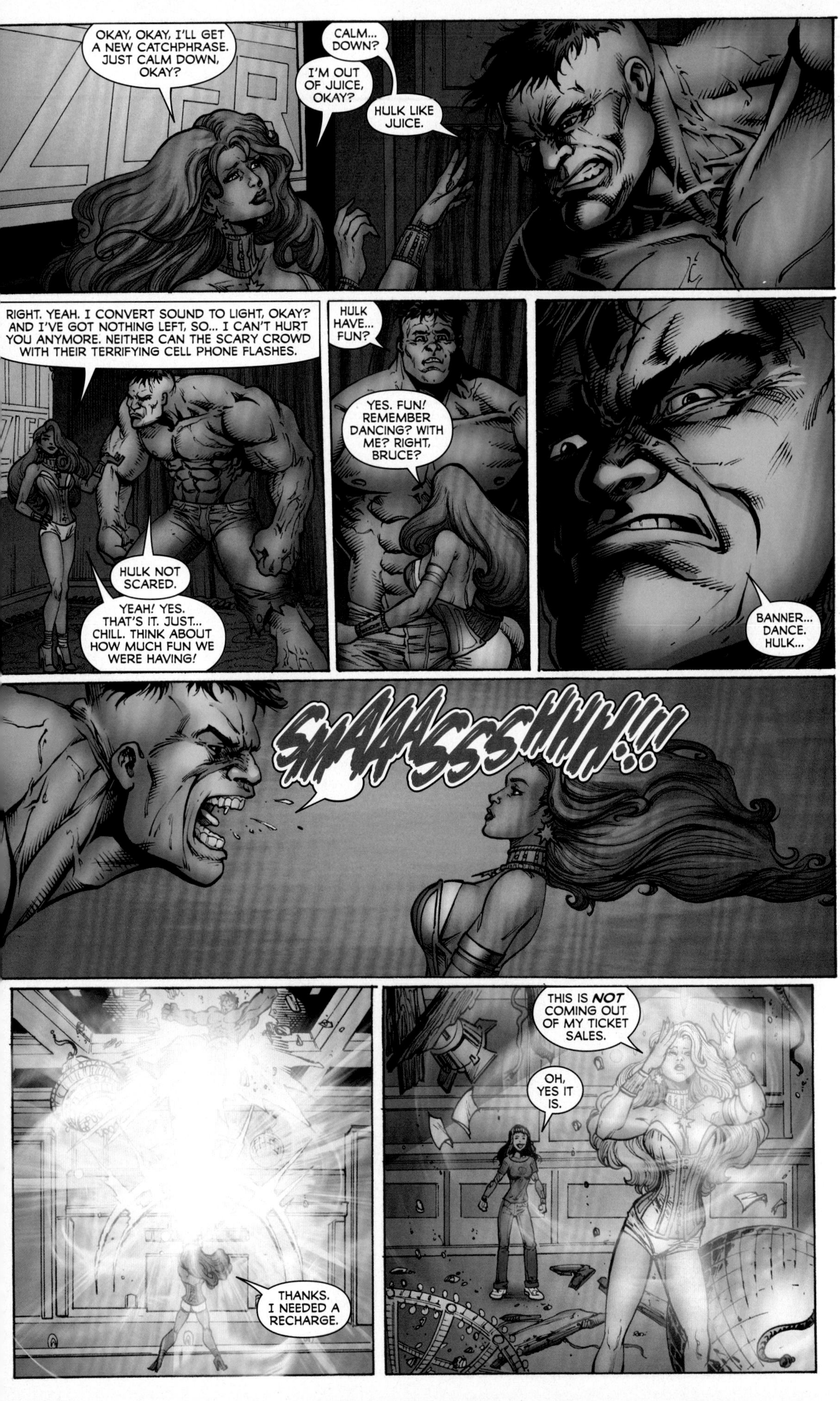
OKAY, OKAY, I'LL GET A NEW CATCHPHRASE. JUST CALM DOWN, OKAY?
CALM... DOWN?
I'M OUT OF JUICE, OKAY?
HULK LIKE JUICE.
RIGHT. YEAH. I CONVERT SOUND TO LIGHT, OKAY? AND I'VE GOT NOTHING LEFT, SO... I CAN'T HURT YOU ANYMORE. NEITHER CAN THE SCARY CROWD WITH THEIR TERRIFYING CELL PHONE FLASHES.
HULK NOT SCARED.
YEAH! YES. THAT'S IT. JUST... CHILL. THINK ABOUT HOW MUCH FUN WE WERE HAVING!
HULK HAVE... FUN?
YES. FUN! REMEMBER DANCING? WITH ME? RIGHT, BRUCE?
BANNER... DANCE. HULK...
SWAAASSSHHH!!!
THANKS. I NEEDED A RECHARGE.
THIS IS NOT COMING OUT OF MY TICKET SALES.
OH, YES IT IS.

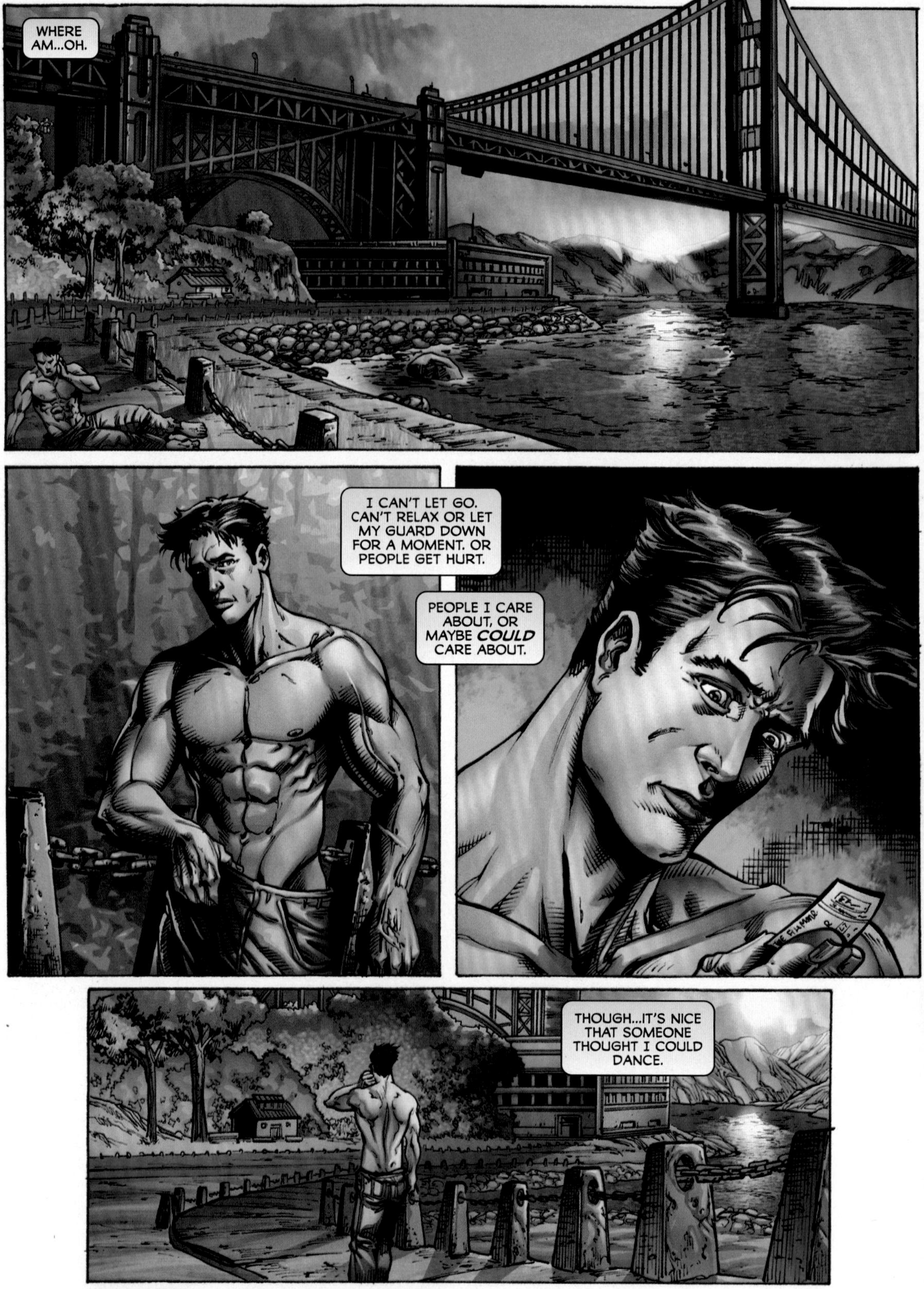
WHERE AM...OH.
I CAN'T LET GO. CAN'T RELAX OR LET MY GUARD DOWN FOR A MOMENT. OR PEOPLE GET HURT.
PEOPLE I CARE ABOUT, OR MAYBE *COULD* CARE ABOUT.
THOUGH...IT'S NICE THAT SOMEONE THOUGHT I COULD DANCE.

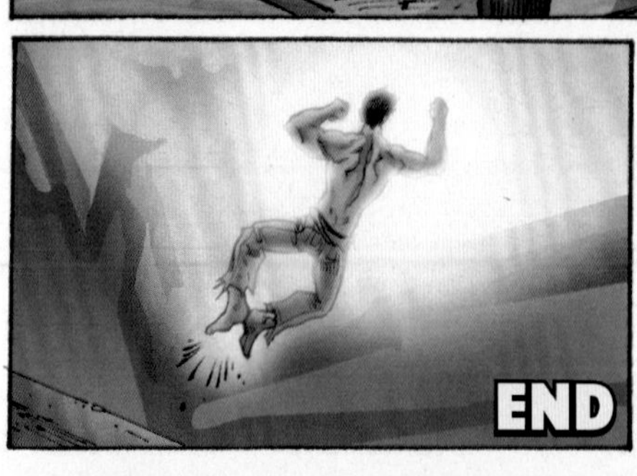
END

"SMASH HIT"
Writer: Alex Zalben
Pencils: Joyce Chin
Inks: Vicente Cifuentes
Colors: Sotocolor's A. Crossley
Letters: Ed Dukeshire
Production: Rev. Paul Acerios

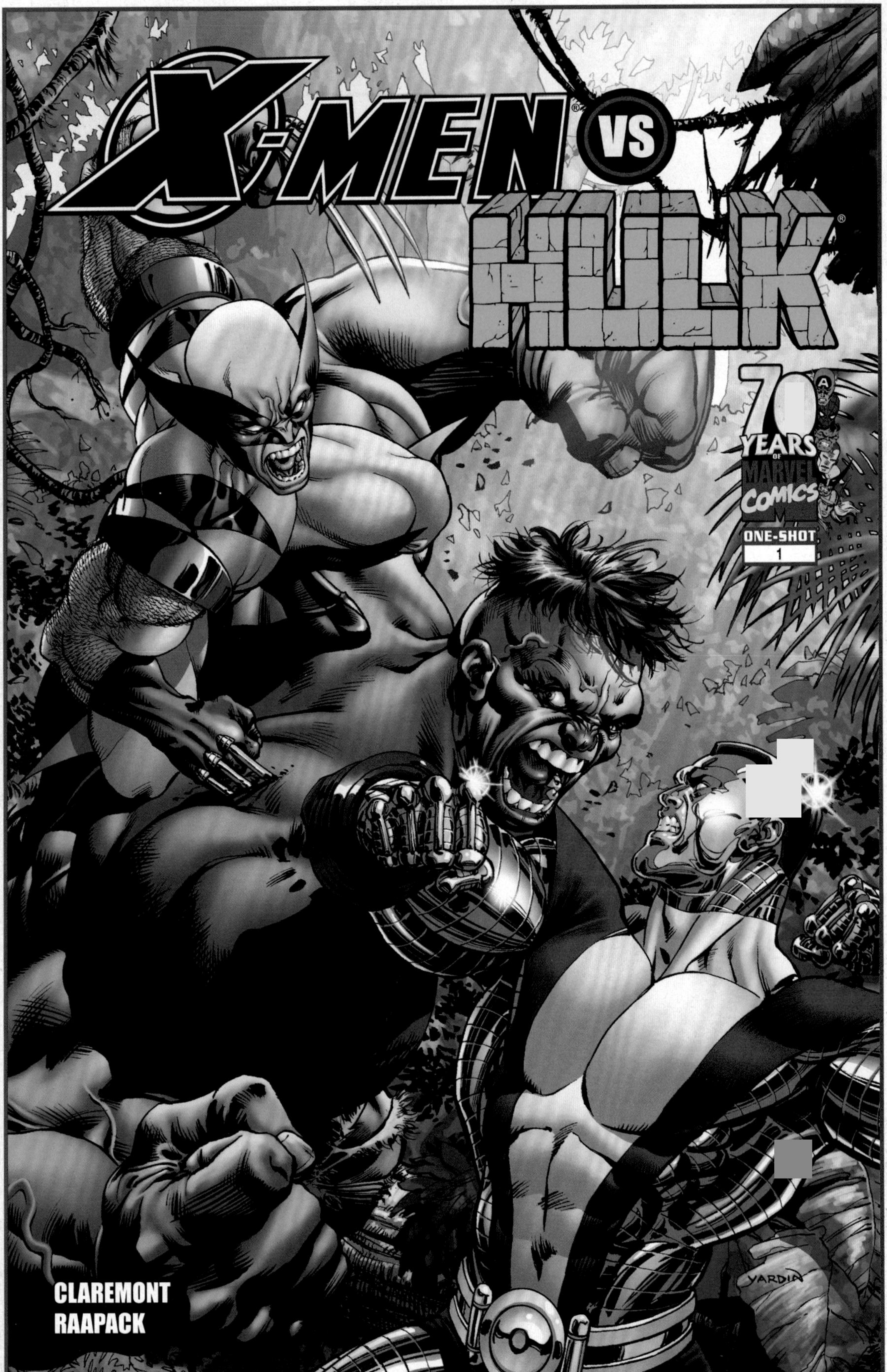
X-MEN VS HULK
70 YEARS OF MARVEL COMICS
ONE-SHOT
1
YARDIN
CLAREMONT
RAAPACK

★ ★ ★ ROUND 5 ★ ★ ★

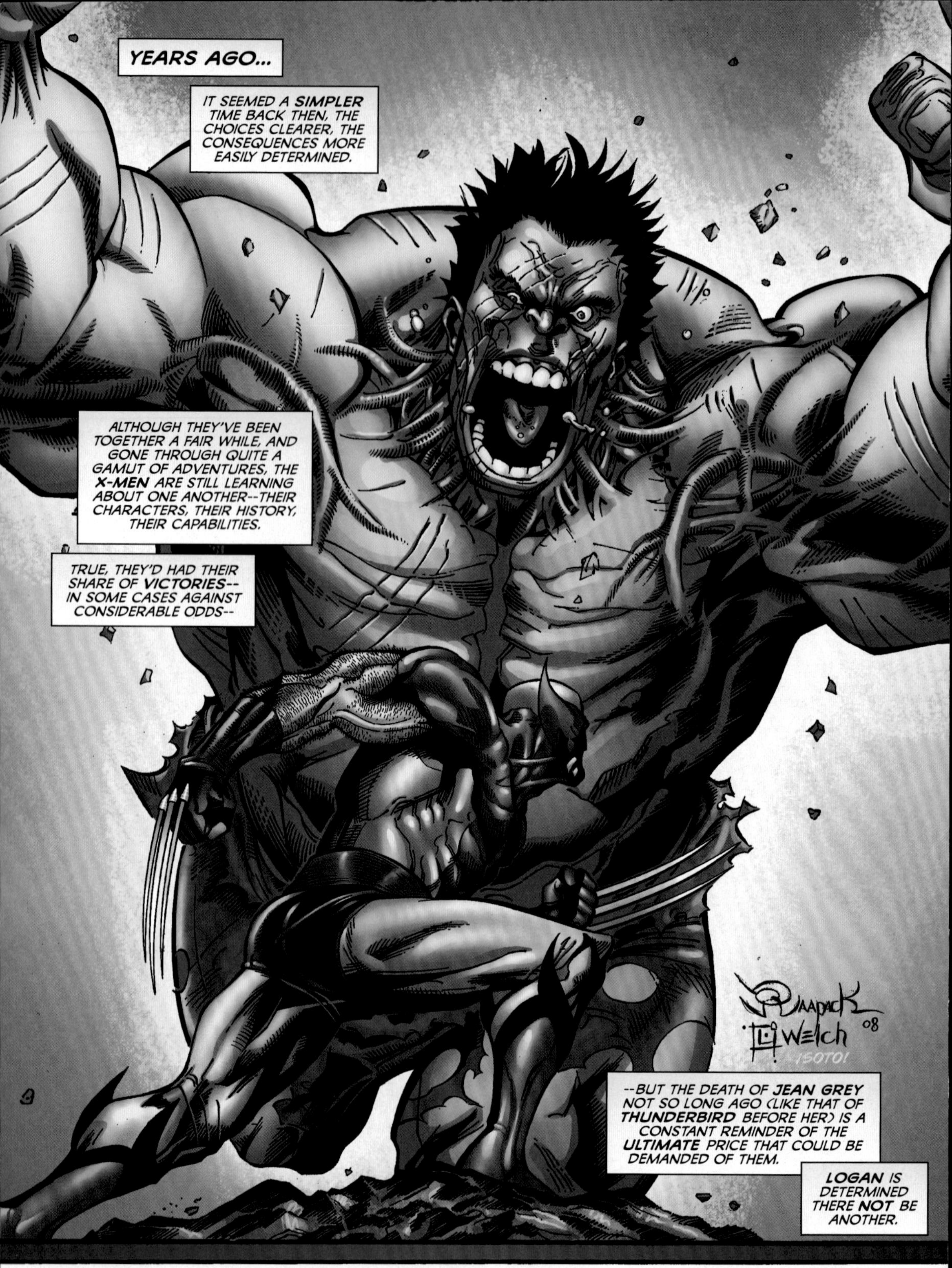
YEARS AGO...
IT SEEMED A SIMPLER TIME BACK THEN, THE CHOICES CLEARER, THE CONSEQUENCES MORE EASILY DETERMINED.
ALTHOUGH THEY'VE BEEN TOGETHER A FAIR WHILE, AND GONE THROUGH QUITE A GAMUT OF ADVENTURES, THE X-MEN ARE STILL LEARNING ABOUT ONE ANOTHER--THEIR CHARACTERS, THEIR HISTORY, THEIR CAPABILITIES.
TRUE, THEY'D HAD THEIR SHARE OF VICTORIES--IN SOME CASES AGAINST CONSIDERABLE ODDS--
--BUT THE DEATH OF JEAN GREY NOT SO LONG AGO (LIKE THAT OF THUNDERBIRD BEFORE HER) IS A CONSTANT REMINDER OF THE ULTIMATE PRICE THAT COULD BE DEMANDED OF THEM.
LOGAN IS DETERMINED THERE NOT BE ANOTHER.

THE MAKING OF A MAN...

By **CHRIS CLAREMONT & JHEREMY RAAPACK**

LARRY WELCH INKER

CHRIS SOTOMAYOR COLORIST

ED DUKESHIRE LETTERER

DAVID YARDIN & WIL QUINTANA COVER

CHARLIE BECKERMAN ASST. EDITOR

MARK PANICCIA EDITOR

JOE QUESADA EDITOR IN CHIEF

DAN BUCKLEY PUBLISHER

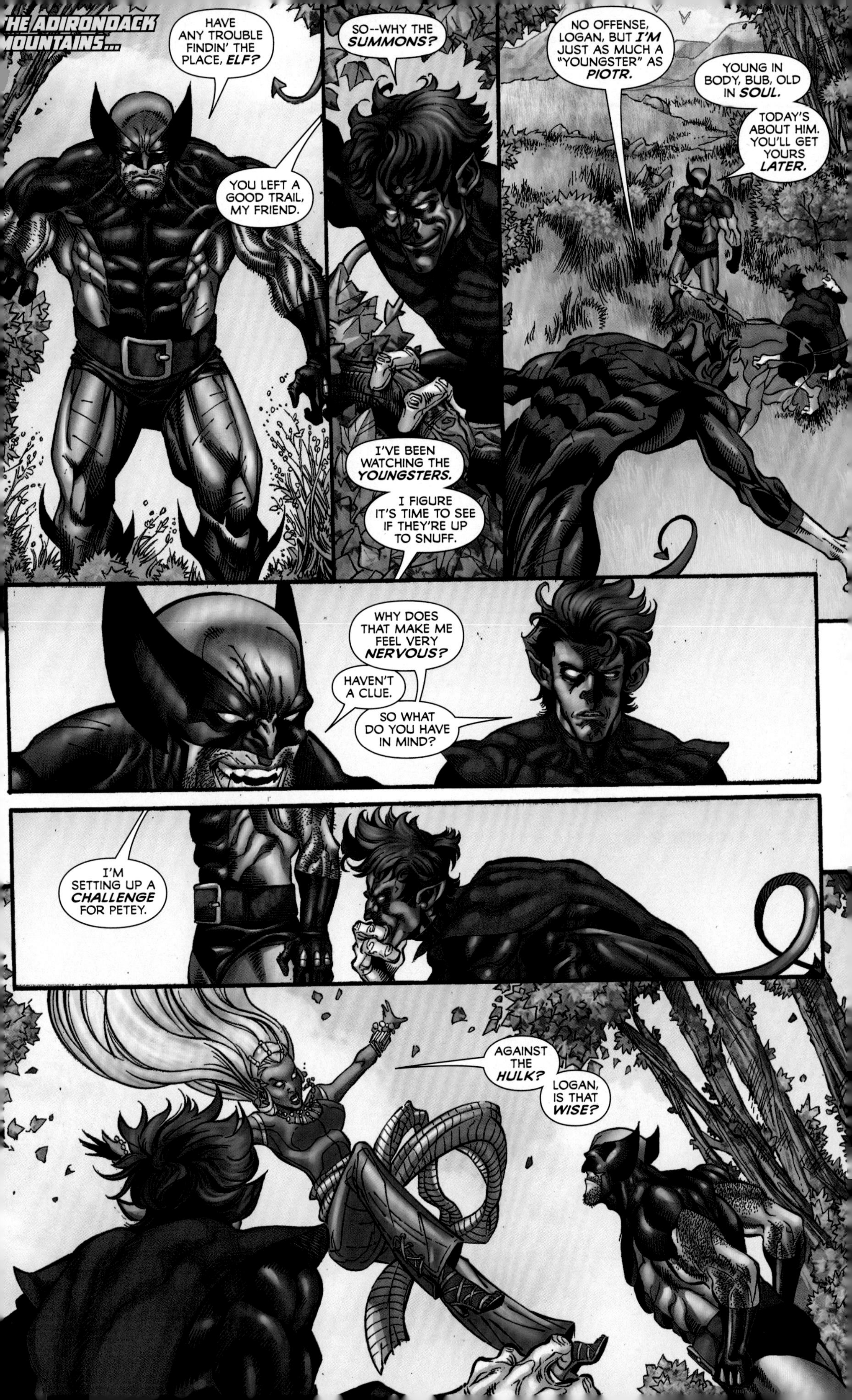
THE ADIRONDACK MOUNTAINS...
HAVE ANY TROUBLE FINDIN' THE PLACE, ELF?
YOU LEFT A GOOD TRAIL, MY FRIEND.
SO--WHY THE SUMMONS?
I'VE BEEN WATCHING THE YOUNGSTERS.
I FIGURE IT'S TIME TO SEE IF THEY'RE UP TO SNUFF.
NO OFFENSE, LOGAN, BUT I'M JUST AS MUCH A "YOUNGSTER" AS PIOTR.
YOUNG IN BODY, BUB, OLD IN SOUL.
TODAY'S ABOUT HIM. YOU'LL GET YOURS LATER.
WHY DOES THAT MAKE ME FEEL VERY NERVOUS?
HAVEN'T A CLUE.
SO WHAT DO YOU HAVE IN MIND?
I'M SETTING UP A CHALLENGE FOR PETEY.
AGAINST THE HULK?
LOGAN, IS THAT WISE?

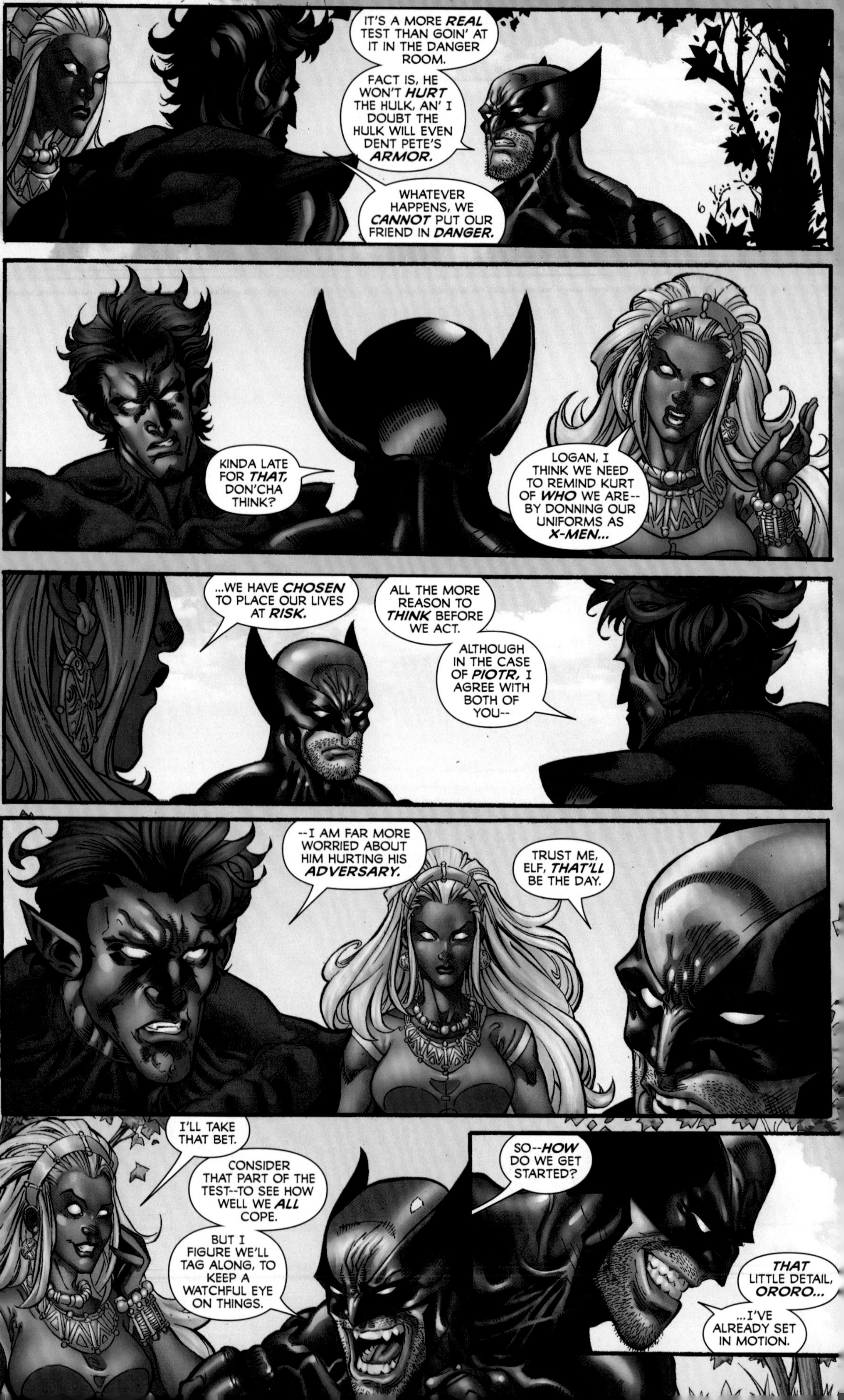

IT'S A MORE REAL TEST THAN GOIN' AT IT IN THE DANGER ROOM.
FACT IS, HE WON'T HURT THE HULK, AN' I DOUBT THE HULK WILL EVEN DENT PETE'S ARMOR.
WHATEVER HAPPENS, WE CANNOT PUT OUR FRIEND IN DANGER.
KINDA LATE FOR THAT, DON'CHA THINK?
LOGAN, I THINK WE NEED TO REMIND KURT OF WHO WE ARE-- BY DONNING OUR UNIFORMS AS X-MEN...
...WE HAVE CHOSEN TO PLACE OUR LIVES AT RISK.
ALL THE MORE REASON TO THINK BEFORE WE ACT.
ALTHOUGH IN THE CASE OF PIOTR, I AGREE WITH BOTH OF YOU--
--I AM FAR MORE WORRIED ABOUT HIM HURTING HIS ADVERSARY.
TRUST ME, ELF, THAT'LL BE THE DAY.
I'LL TAKE THAT BET.
CONSIDER THAT PART OF THE TEST--TO SEE HOW WELL WE ALL COPE.
BUT I FIGURE WE'LL TAG ALONG, TO KEEP A WATCHFUL EYE ON THINGS.
SO--HOW DO WE GET STARTED?
THAT LITTLE DETAIL, ORORO...
...I'VE ALREADY SET IN MOTION.

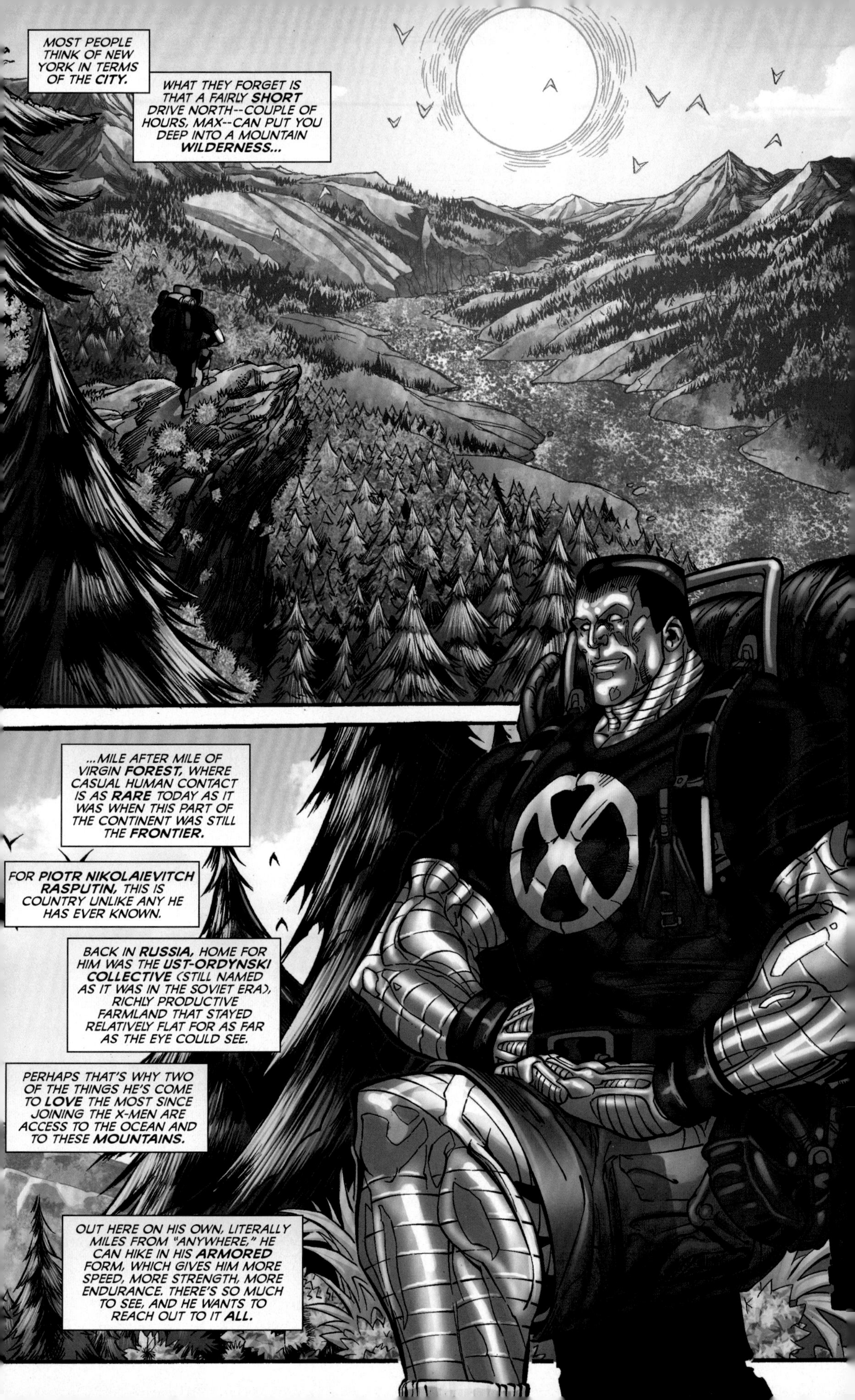

MOST PEOPLE THINK OF NEW YORK IN TERMS OF THE CITY.
WHAT THEY FORGET IS THAT A FAIRLY SHORT DRIVE NORTH--COUPLE OF HOURS, MAX--CAN PUT YOU DEEP INTO A MOUNTAIN WILDERNESS...
...MILE AFTER MILE OF VIRGIN FOREST, WHERE CASUAL HUMAN CONTACT IS AS RARE TODAY AS IT WAS WHEN THIS PART OF THE CONTINENT WAS STILL THE FRONTIER.
FOR PIOTR NIKOLAIEVITCH RASPUTIN, THIS IS COUNTRY UNLIKE ANY HE HAS EVER KNOWN.
BACK IN RUSSIA, HOME FOR HIM WAS THE UST-ORDYNSKI COLLECTIVE (STILL NAMED AS IT WAS IN THE SOVIET ERA), RICHLY PRODUCTIVE FARMLAND THAT STAYED RELATIVELY FLAT FOR AS FAR AS THE EYE COULD SEE.
PERHAPS THAT'S WHY TWO OF THE THINGS HE'S COME TO LOVE THE MOST SINCE JOINING THE X-MEN ARE ACCESS TO THE OCEAN AND TO THESE MOUNTAINS.
OUT HERE ON HIS OWN, LITERALLY MILES FROM "ANYWHERE," HE CAN HIKE IN HIS ARMORED FORM, WHICH GIVES HIM MORE SPEED, MORE STRENGTH, MORE ENDURANCE. THERE'S SO MUCH TO SEE, AND HE WANTS TO REACH OUT TO IT ALL.

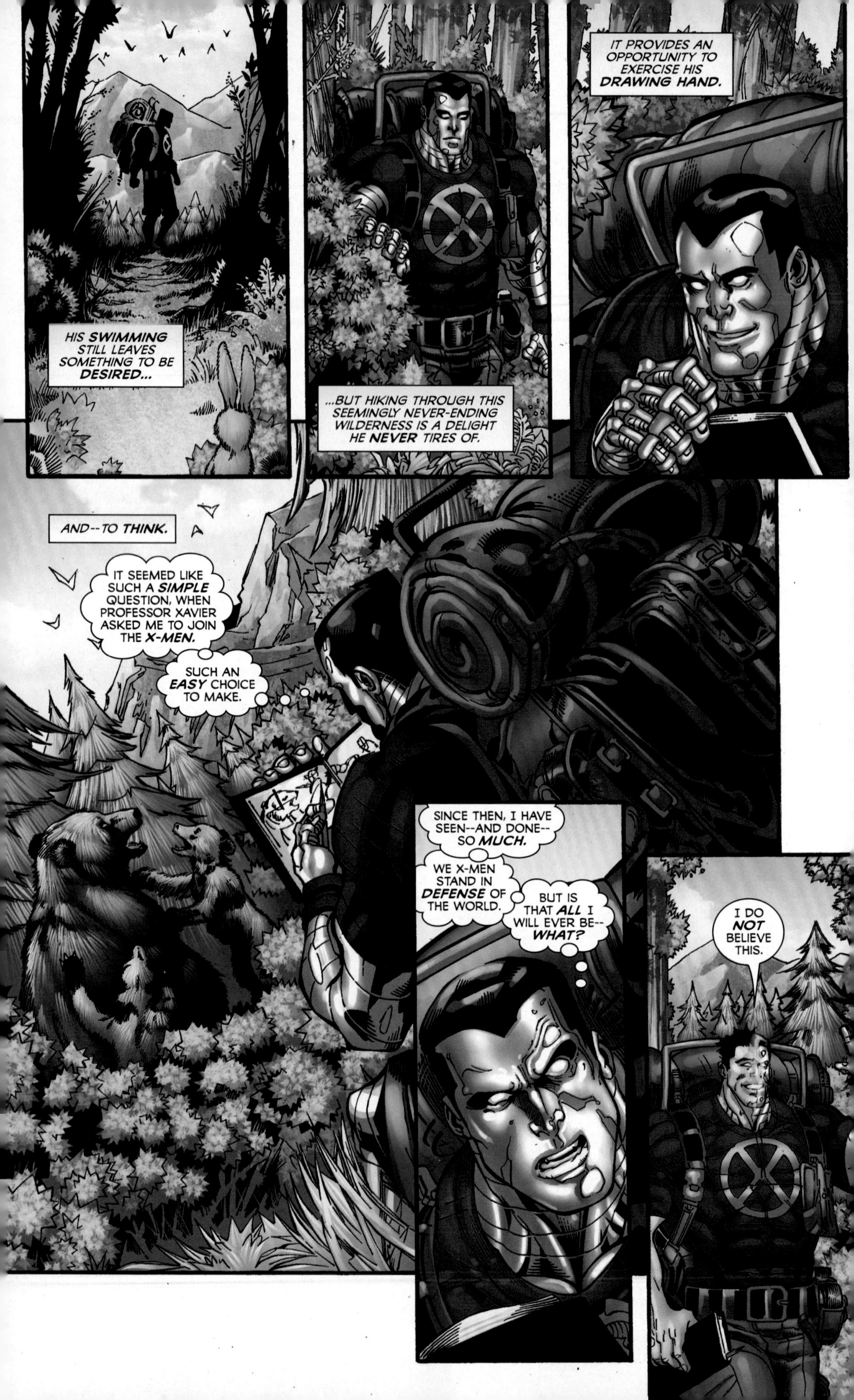
HIS SWIMMING STILL LEAVES SOMETHING TO BE DESIRED...
...BUT HIKING THROUGH THIS SEEMINGLY NEVER-ENDING WILDERNESS IS A DELIGHT HE NEVER TIRES OF.
IT PROVIDES AN OPPORTUNITY TO EXERCISE HIS DRAWING HAND.
AND--TO THINK.
IT SEEMED LIKE SUCH A SIMPLE QUESTION, WHEN PROFESSOR XAVIER ASKED ME TO JOIN THE X-MEN.
SUCH AN EASY CHOICE TO MAKE.
SINCE THEN, I HAVE SEEN--AND DONE--SO MUCH.
WE X-MEN STAND IN DEFENSE OF THE WORLD.
BUT IS THAT ALL I WILL EVER BE--WHAT?
I DO NOT BELIEVE THIS.

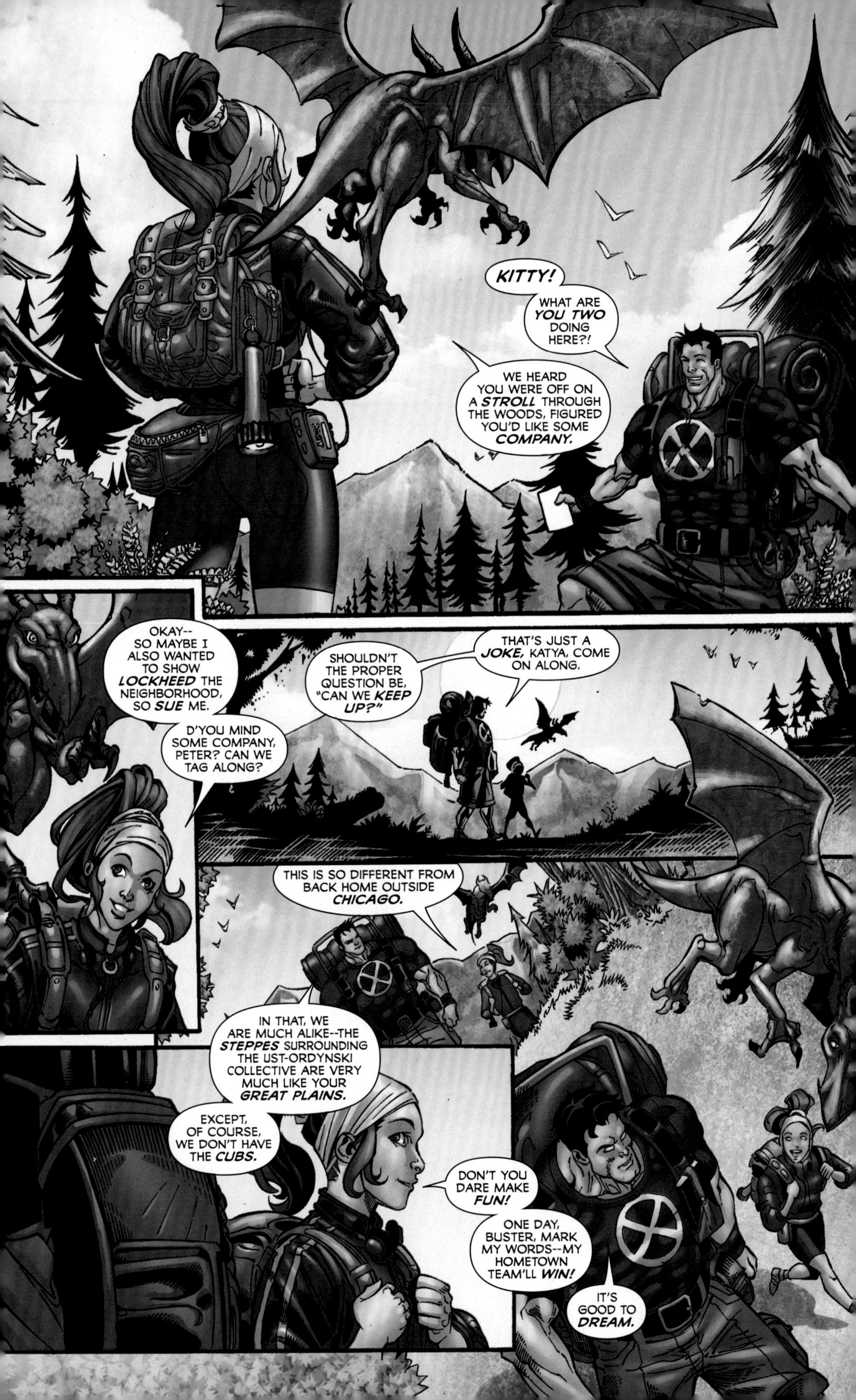
KITTY!
WHAT ARE YOU TWO DOING HERE?!
WE HEARD YOU WERE OFF ON A STROLL THROUGH THE WOODS, FIGURED YOU'D LIKE SOME COMPANY.
OKAY-- SO MAYBE I ALSO WANTED TO SHOW LOCKHEED THE NEIGHBORHOOD, SO SUE ME.
D'YOU MIND SOME COMPANY, PETER? CAN WE TAG ALONG?
SHOULDN'T THE PROPER QUESTION BE, "CAN WE KEEP UP?"
THAT'S JUST A JOKE, KATYA, COME ON ALONG.
THIS IS SO DIFFERENT FROM BACK HOME OUTSIDE CHICAGO.
IN THAT, WE ARE MUCH ALIKE--THE STEPPES SURROUNDING THE UST-ORDYNSKI COLLECTIVE ARE VERY MUCH LIKE YOUR GREAT PLAINS.
EXCEPT, OF COURSE, WE DON'T HAVE THE CUBS.
DON'T YOU DARE MAKE FUN!
ONE DAY, BUSTER, MARK MY WORDS--MY HOMETOWN TEAM'LL WIN!
IT'S GOOD TO DREAM.

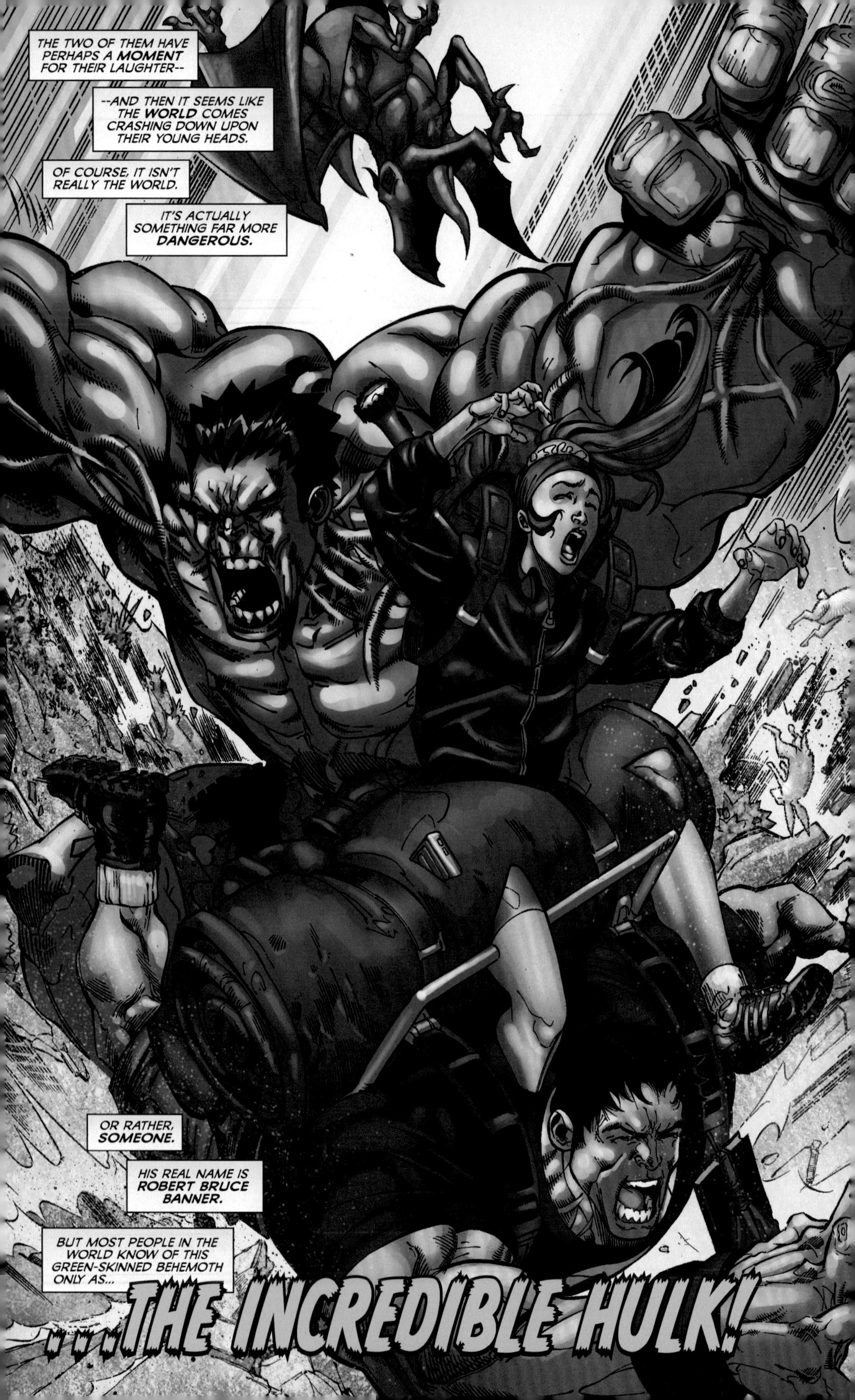
THE TWO OF THEM HAVE PERHAPS A MOMENT FOR THEIR LAUGHTER--
--AND THEN IT SEEMS LIKE THE WORLD COMES CRASHING DOWN UPON THEIR YOUNG HEADS.
OF COURSE, IT ISN'T REALLY THE WORLD.
IT'S ACTUALLY SOMETHING FAR MORE DANGEROUS.
OR RATHER, SOMEONE.
HIS REAL NAME IS ROBERT BRUCE BANNER.
BUT MOST PEOPLE IN THE WORLD KNOW OF THIS GREEN-SKINNED BEHEMOTH ONLY AS...
...THE INCREDIBLE HULK!

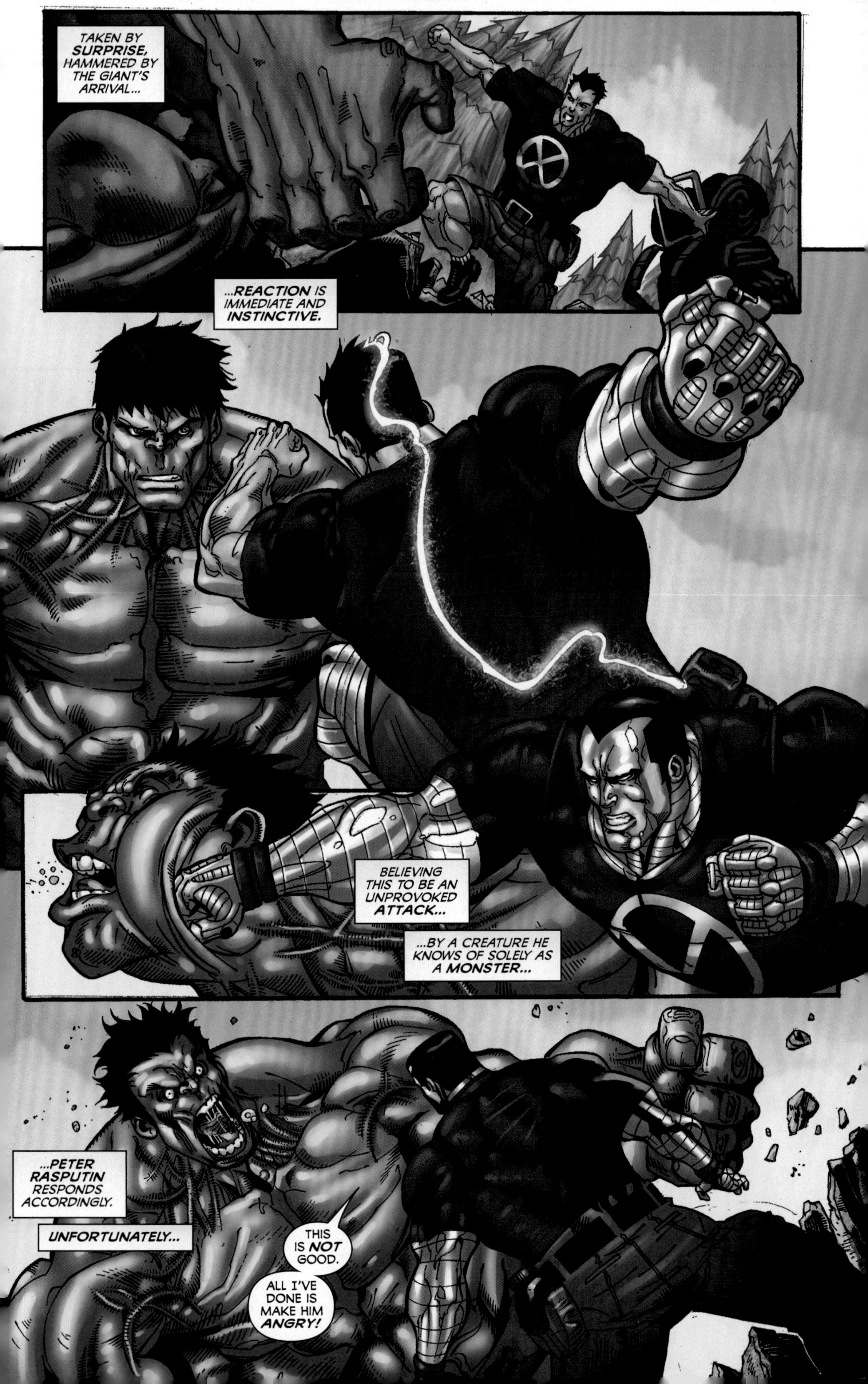
TAKEN BY SURPRISE, HAMMERED BY THE GIANT'S ARRIVAL...
...REACTION IS IMMEDIATE AND INSTINCTIVE.
BELIEVING THIS TO BE AN UNPROVOKED ATTACK...
...BY A CREATURE HE KNOWS OF SOLELY AS A MONSTER...
...PETER RASPUTIN RESPONDS ACCORDINGLY.
UNFORTUNATELY...
THIS IS NOT GOOD.
ALL I'VE DONE IS MAKE HIM ANGRY!

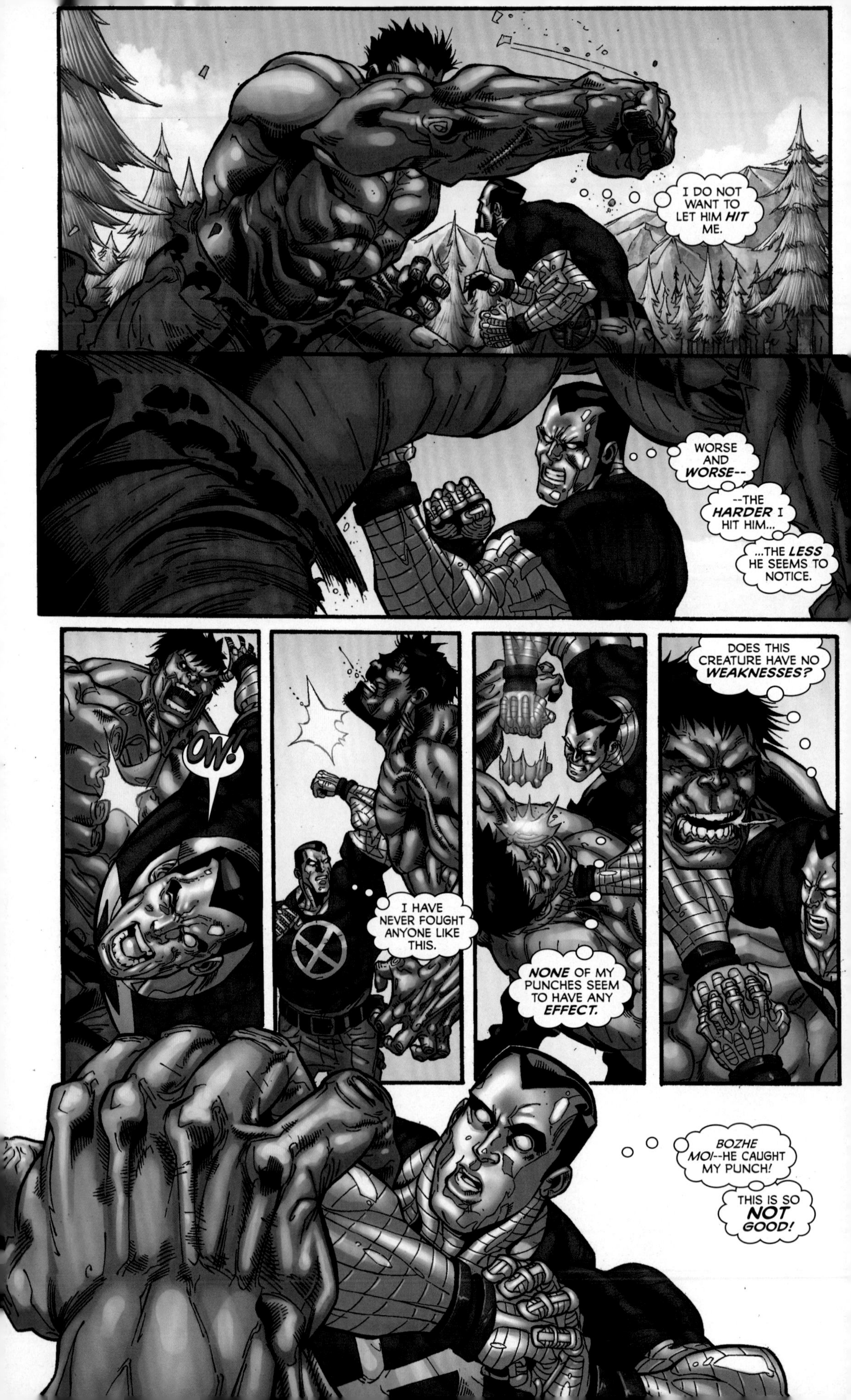
I DO NOT WANT TO LET HIM *HIT* ME.
WORSE AND *WORSE*--
--THE *HARDER* I HIT HIM...
...THE *LESS* HE SEEMS TO NOTICE.
OW!
I HAVE NEVER FOUGHT ANYONE LIKE THIS.
NONE OF MY PUNCHES SEEM TO HAVE ANY *EFFECT.*
DOES THIS CREATURE HAVE NO *WEAKNESSES?*
BOZHE MOI!--HE CAUGHT MY PUNCH!
THIS IS SO *NOT GOOD!*

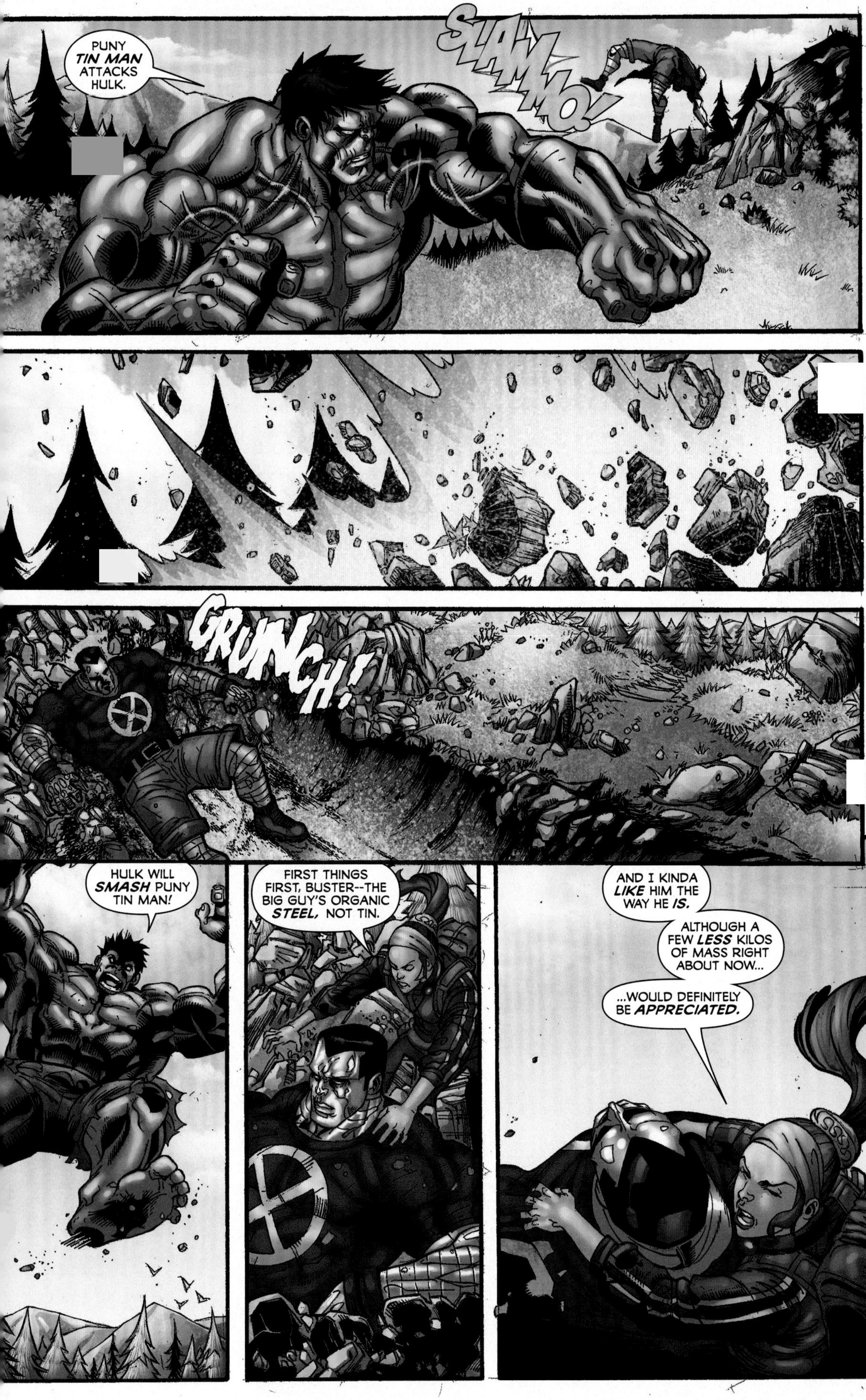

PUNY TIN MAN ATTACKS HULK.
SLAMMO!
GRUNCH!
HULK WILL SMASH PUNY TIN MAN!
FIRST THINGS FIRST, BUSTER--THE BIG GUY'S ORGANIC STEEL, NOT TIN.
AND I KINDA LIKE HIM THE WAY HE IS.
ALTHOUGH A FEW LESS KILOS OF MASS RIGHT ABOUT NOW...
...WOULD DEFINITELY BE APPRECIATED.

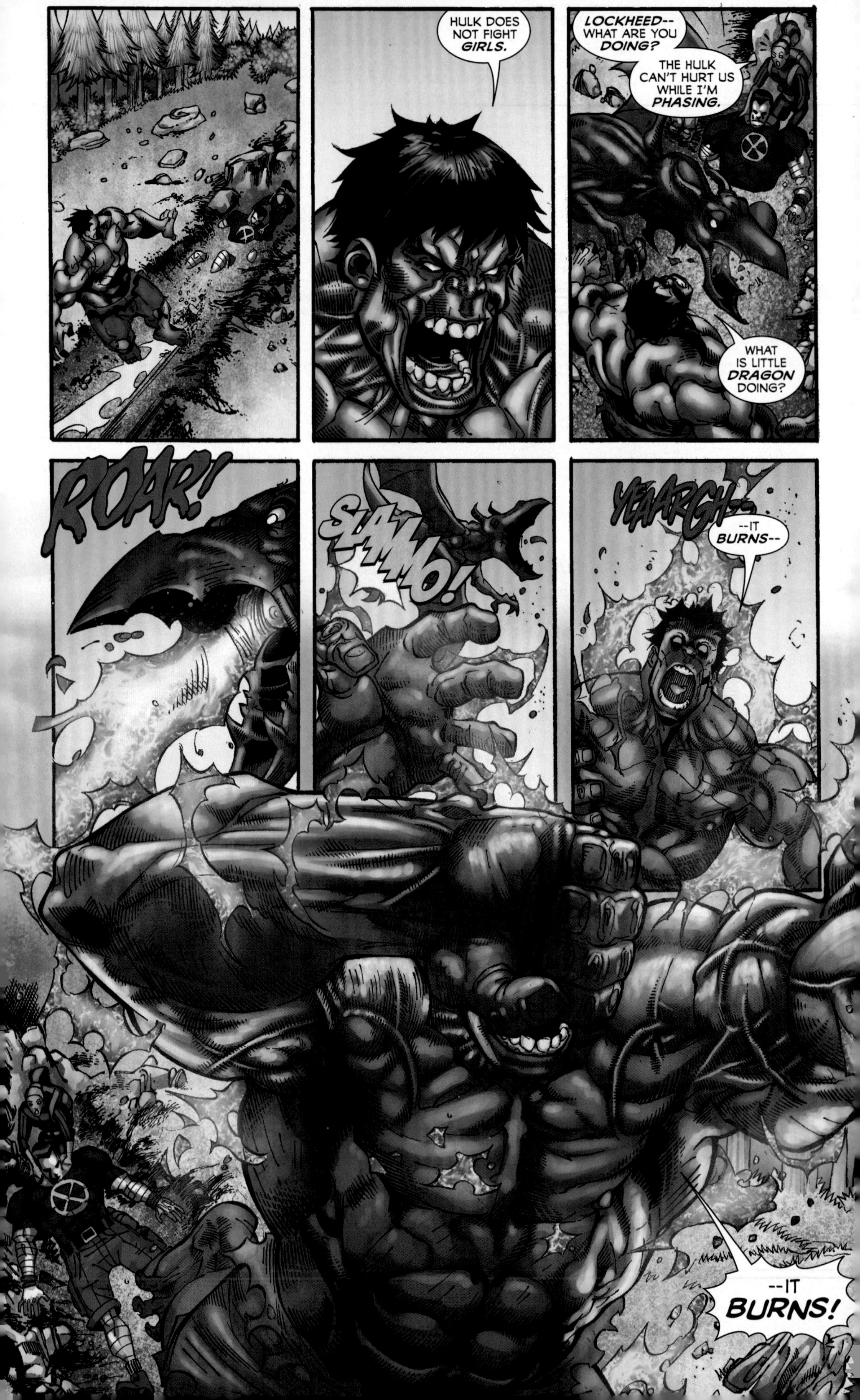
HULK DOES NOT FIGHT GIRLS.
LOCKHEED-- WHAT ARE YOU DOING?
THE HULK CAN'T HURT US WHILE I'M PHASING.
WHAT IS LITTLE DRAGON DOING?
ROAR!
SLAMM!
YEAARGH--
--IT BURNS--
--IT BURNS!

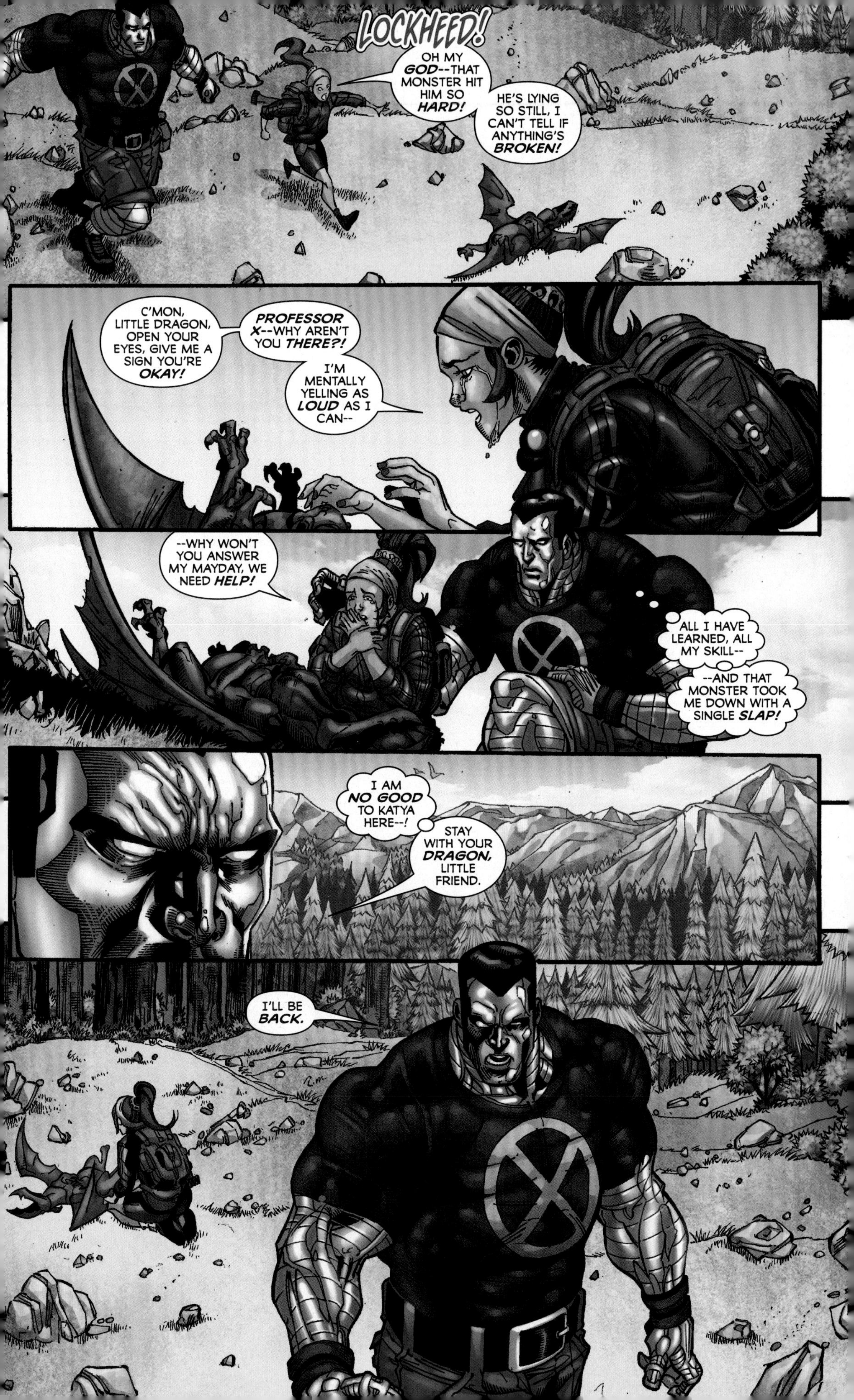
LOCKHEED!
OH MY GOD--THAT MONSTER HIT HIM SO HARD!
HE'S LYING SO STILL, I CAN'T TELL IF ANYTHING'S BROKEN!
C'MON, LITTLE DRAGON, OPEN YOUR EYES, GIVE ME A SIGN YOU'RE OKAY!
PROFESSOR X--WHY AREN'T YOU THERE?!
I'M MENTALLY YELLING AS LOUD AS I CAN--
--WHY WON'T YOU ANSWER MY MAYDAY, WE NEED HELP!
ALL I HAVE LEARNED, ALL MY SKILL--
--AND THAT MONSTER TOOK ME DOWN WITH A SINGLE SLAP!
I AM NO GOOD TO KATYA HERE--!
STAY WITH YOUR DRAGON, LITTLE FRIEND.
I'LL BE BACK.

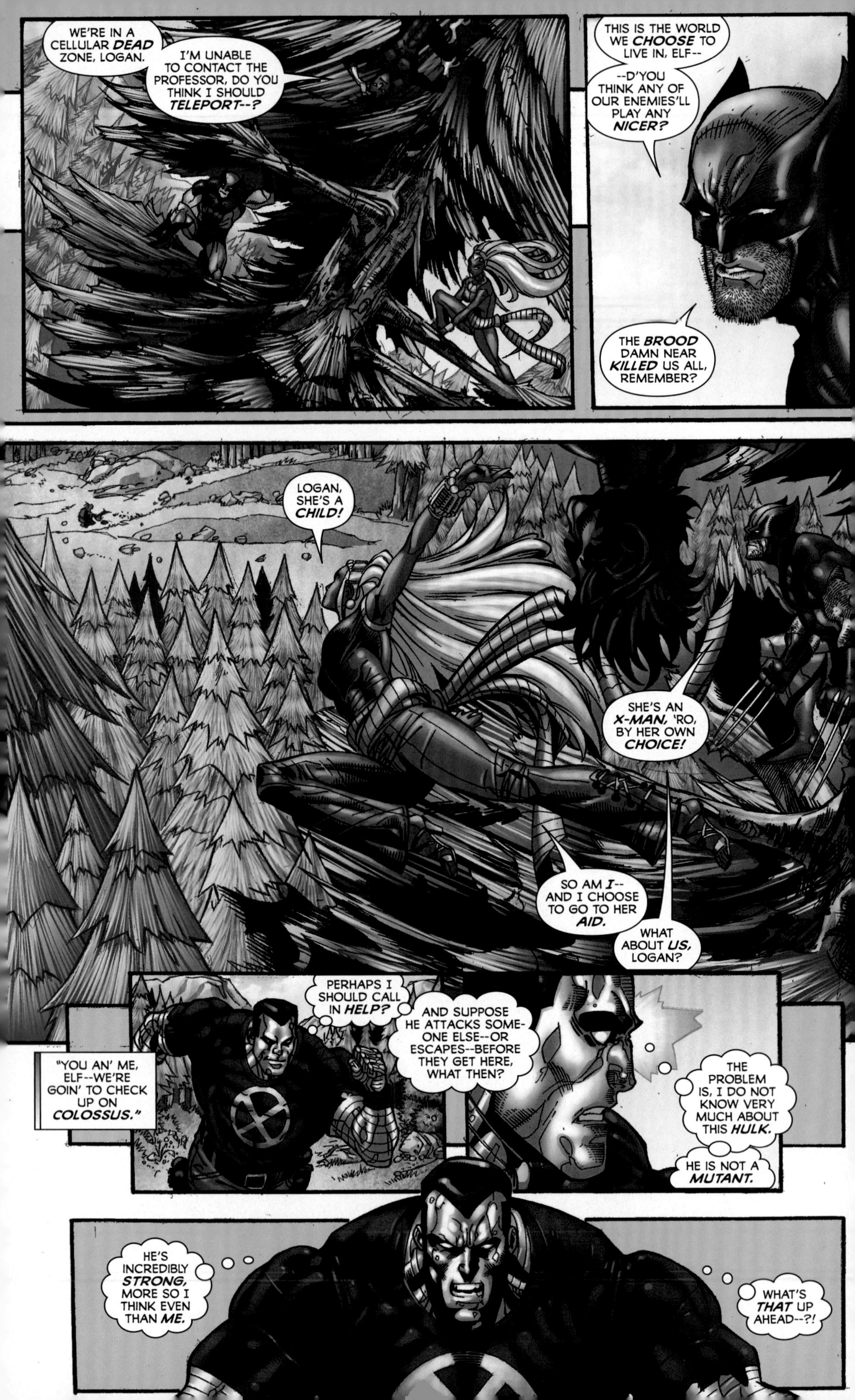
WE'RE IN A CELLULAR DEAD ZONE, LOGAN.
I'M UNABLE TO CONTACT THE PROFESSOR, DO YOU THINK I SHOULD TELEPORT--?
THIS IS THE WORLD WE CHOOSE TO LIVE IN, ELF--
--D'YOU THINK ANY OF OUR ENEMIES'LL PLAY ANY NICER?
THE BROOD DAMN NEAR KILLED US ALL, REMEMBER?
LOGAN, SHE'S A CHILD!
SHE'S AN X-MAN, 'RO, BY HER OWN CHOICE!
SO AM I-- AND I CHOOSE TO GO TO HER AID.
WHAT ABOUT US, LOGAN?
"YOU AN' ME, ELF--WE'RE GOIN' TO CHECK UP ON COLOSSUS."
PERHAPS I SHOULD CALL IN HELP?
AND SUPPOSE HE ATTACKS SOME-ONE ELSE--OR ESCAPES--BEFORE THEY GET HERE, WHAT THEN?
THE PROBLEM IS, I DO NOT KNOW VERY MUCH ABOUT THIS HULK.
HE IS NOT A MUTANT.
HE'S INCREDIBLY STRONG, MORE SO I THINK EVEN THAN ME.
WHAT'S THAT UP AHEAD--?!

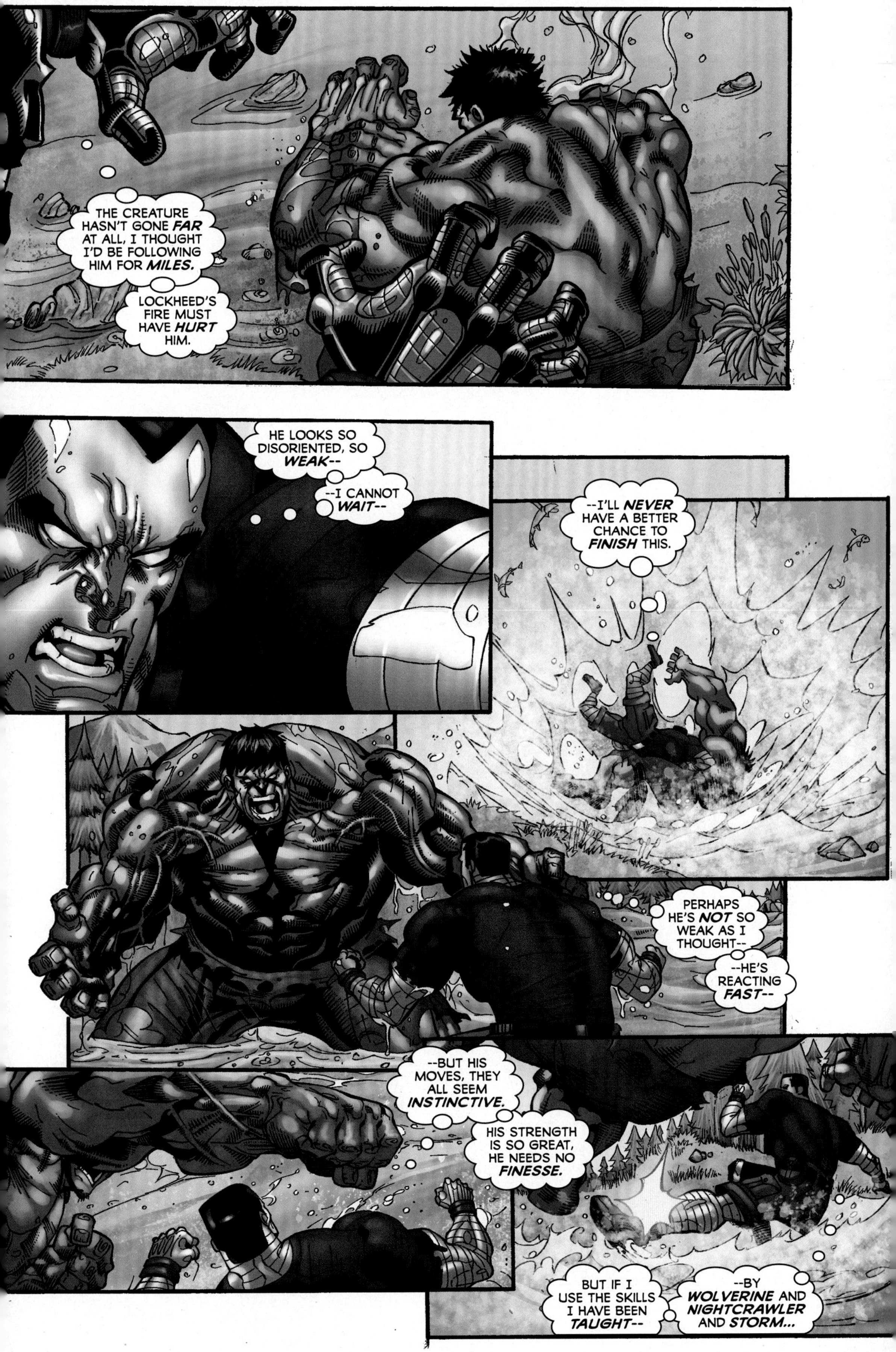
THE CREATURE HASN'T GONE FAR AT ALL, I THOUGHT I'D BE FOLLOWING HIM FOR MILES.
LOCKHEED'S FIRE MUST HAVE HURT HIM.
HE LOOKS SO DISORIENTED, SO WEAK--
--I CANNOT WAIT--
--I'LL NEVER HAVE A BETTER CHANCE TO FINISH THIS.
PERHAPS HE'S NOT SO WEAK AS I THOUGHT--
--HE'S REACTING FAST--
--BUT HIS MOVES, THEY ALL SEEM INSTINCTIVE.
HIS STRENGTH IS SO GREAT, HE NEEDS NO FINESSE.
BUT IF I USE THE SKILLS I HAVE BEEN TAUGHT--
--BY WOLVERINE AND NIGHTCRAWLER AND STORM...

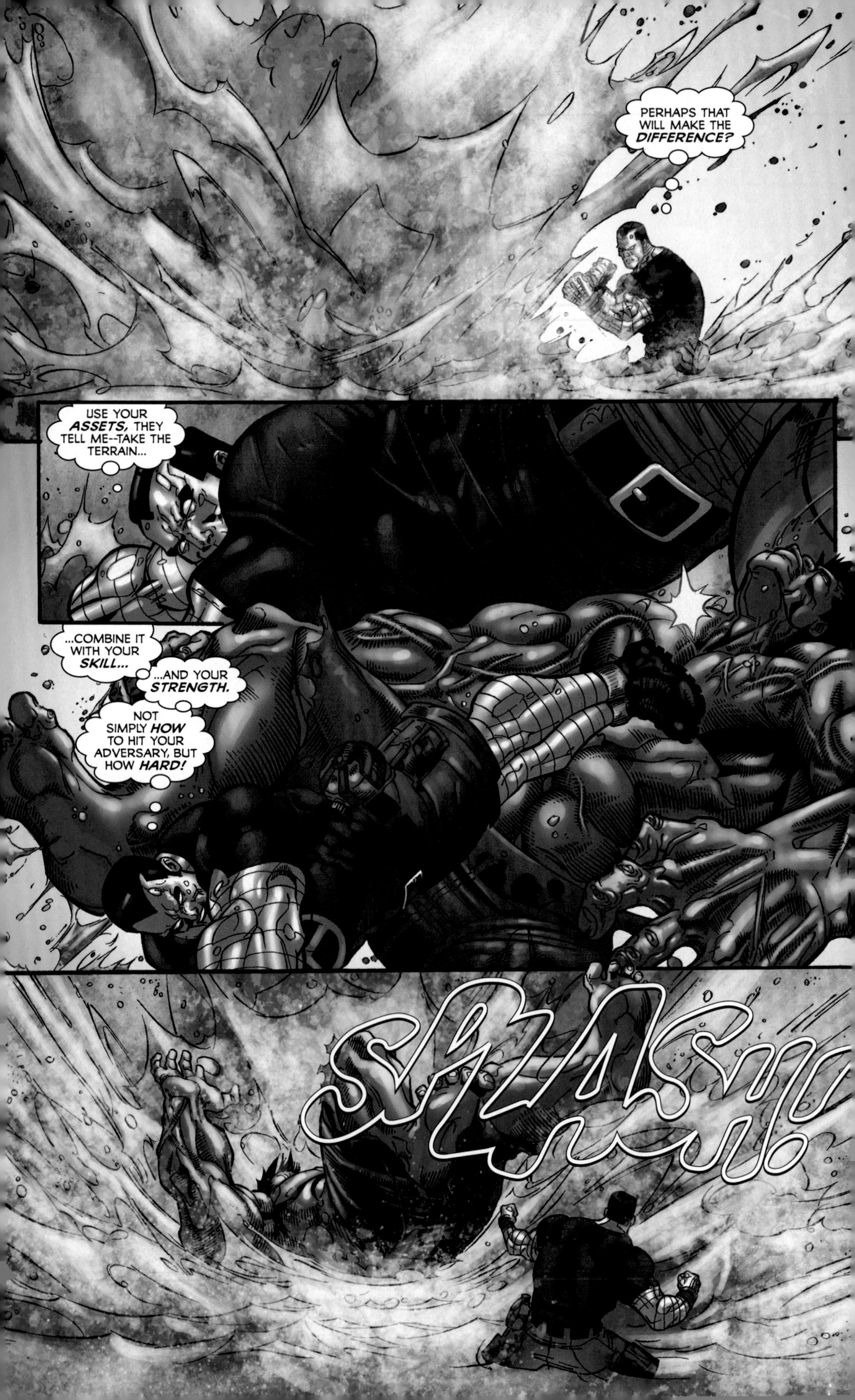
PERHAPS THAT WILL MAKE THE *DIFFERENCE?*
USE YOUR *ASSETS,* THEY TELL ME--TAKE THE TERRAIN...
...COMBINE IT WITH YOUR *SKILL...*
...AND YOUR *STRENGTH.*
NOT SIMPLY *HOW* TO HIT YOUR ADVERSARY, BUT HOW *HARD!*
SHASH

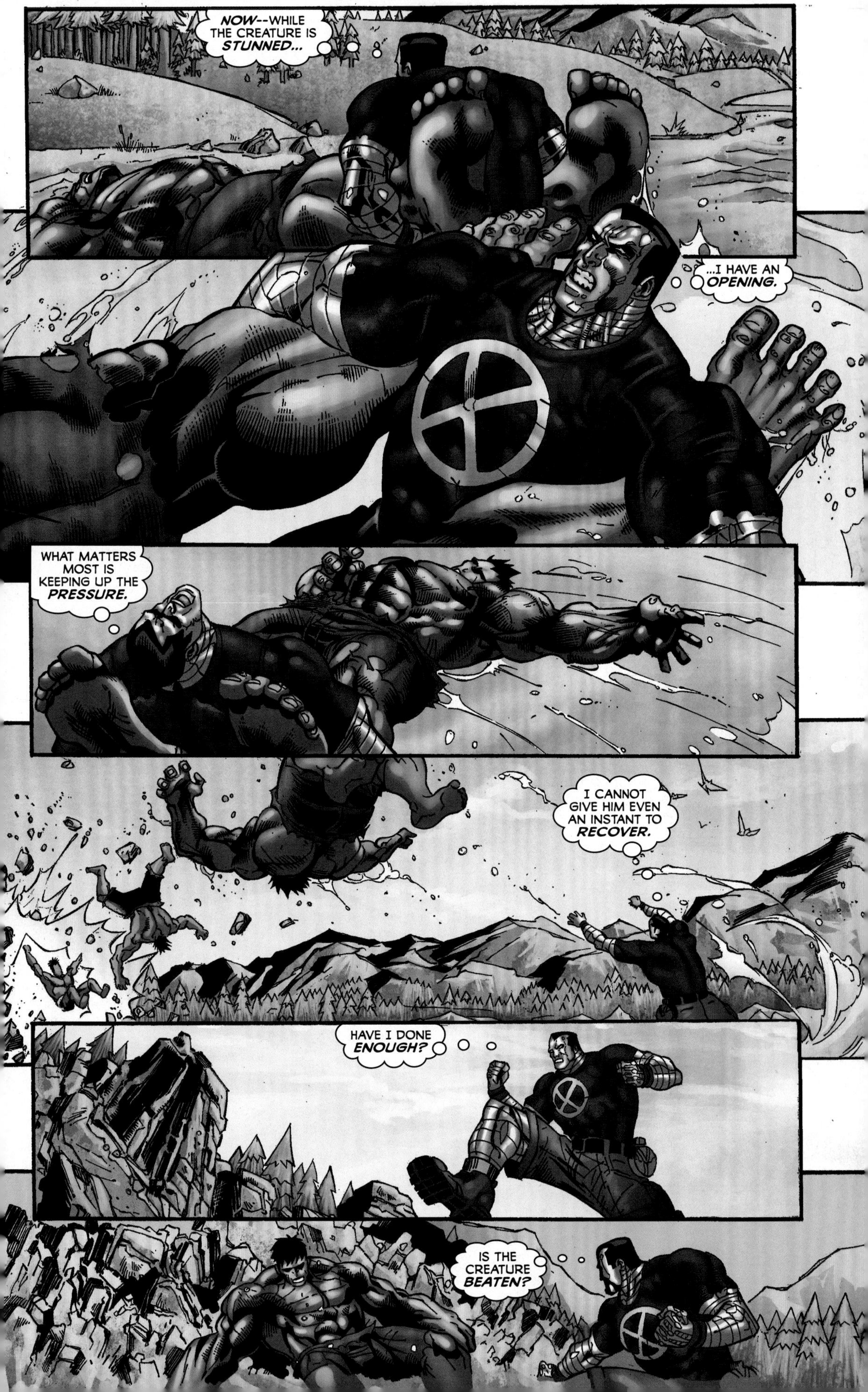

NOW--WHILE THE CREATURE IS STUNNED...
...I HAVE AN OPENING.
WHAT MATTERS MOST IS KEEPING UP THE PRESSURE.
I CANNOT GIVE HIM EVEN AN INSTANT TO RECOVER.
HAVE I DONE ENOUGH?
IS THE CREATURE BEATEN?

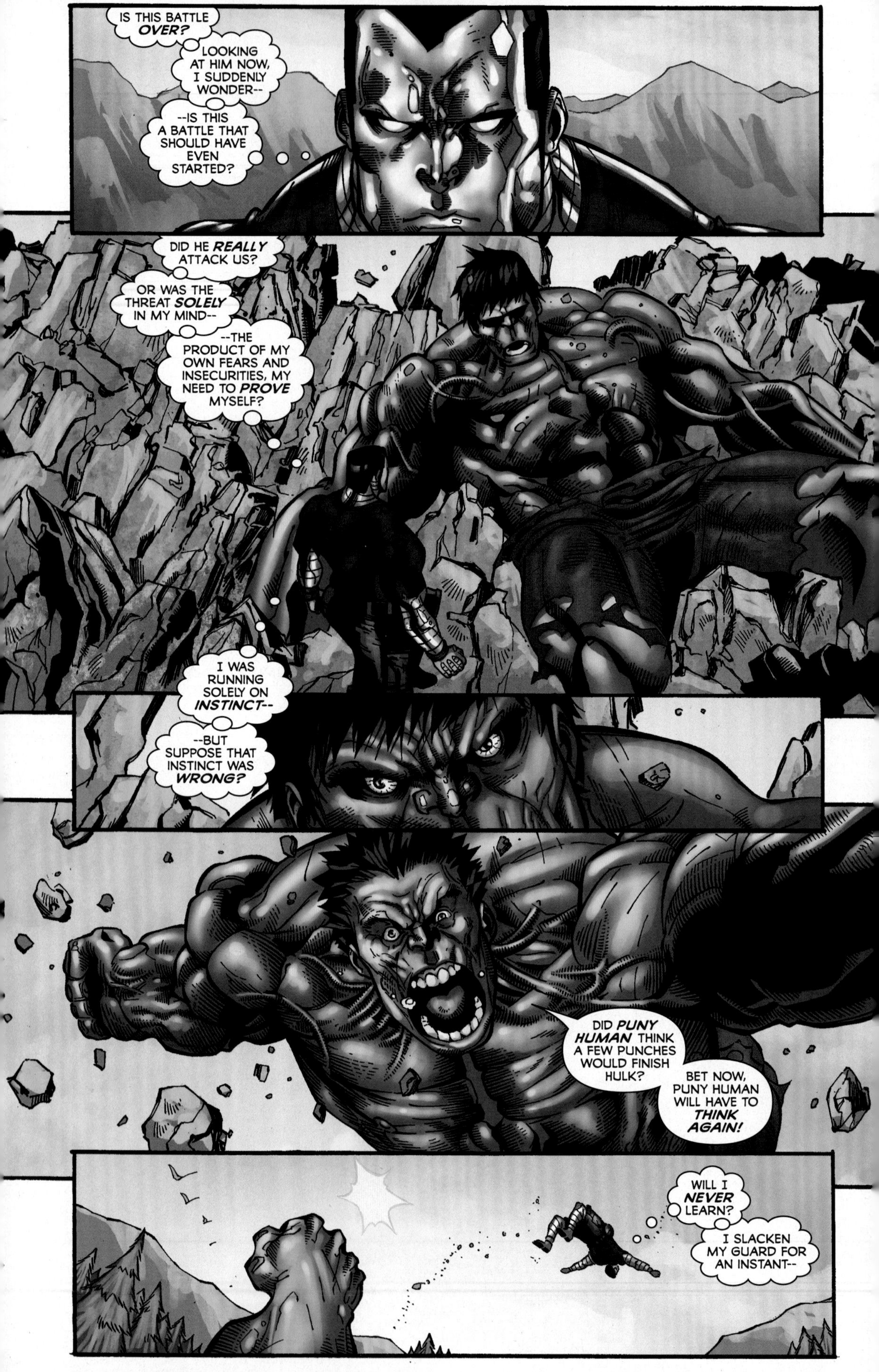
IS THIS BATTLE OVER?
LOOKING AT HIM NOW, I SUDDENLY WONDER--
--IS THIS A BATTLE THAT SHOULD HAVE EVEN STARTED?
DID HE REALLY ATTACK US?
OR WAS THE THREAT SOLELY IN MY MIND--
--THE PRODUCT OF MY OWN FEARS AND INSECURITIES, MY NEED TO PROVE MYSELF?
I WAS RUNNING SOLELY ON INSTINCT--
--BUT SUPPOSE THAT INSTINCT WAS WRONG?
DID PUNY HUMAN THINK A FEW PUNCHES WOULD FINISH HULK?
BET NOW, PUNY HUMAN WILL HAVE TO THINK AGAIN!
WILL I NEVER LEARN?
I SLACKEN MY GUARD FOR AN INSTANT--

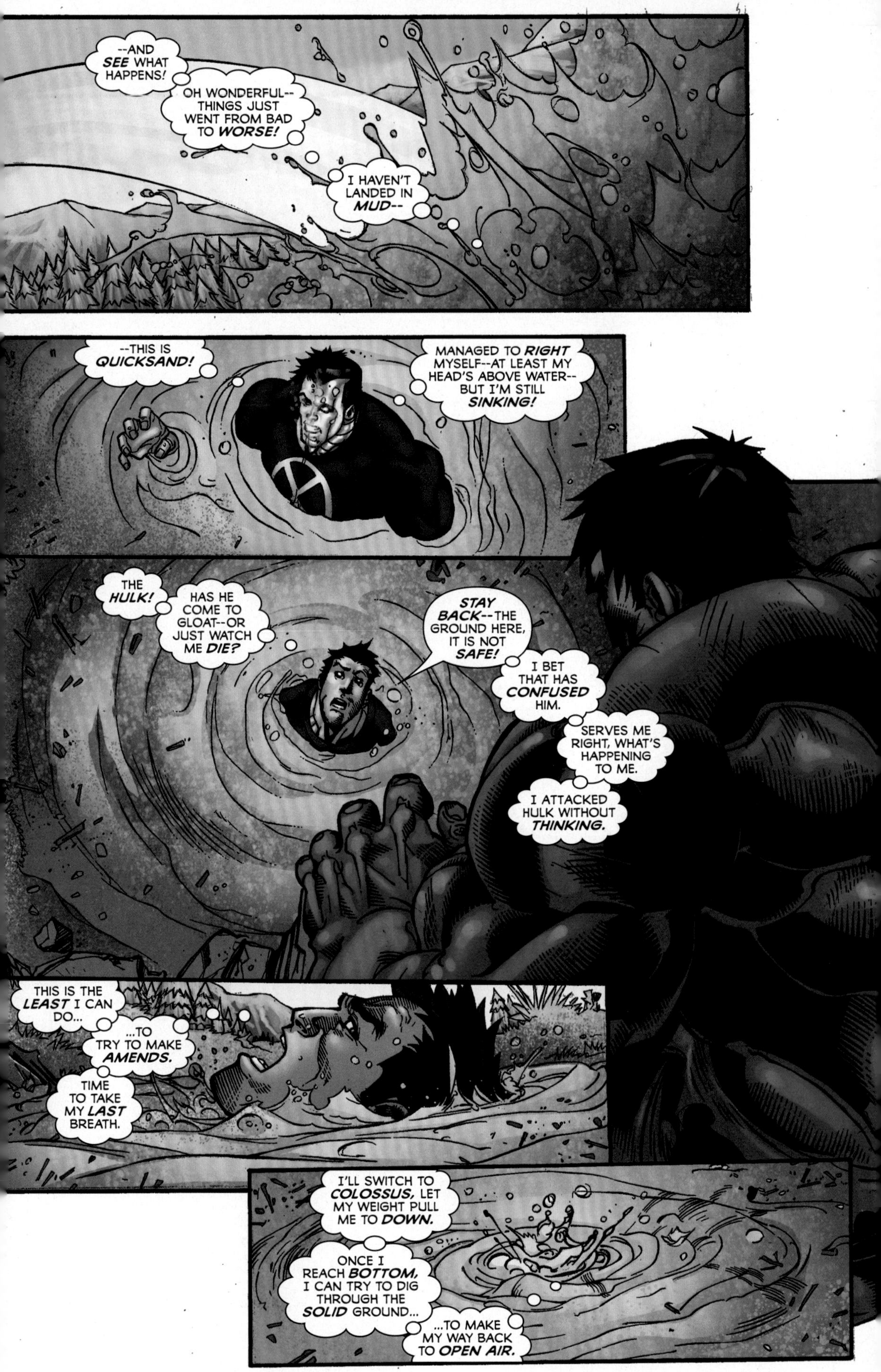
--AND SEE WHAT HAPPENS!
OH WONDERFUL-- THINGS JUST WENT FROM BAD TO WORSE!
I HAVEN'T LANDED IN MUD--
--THIS IS QUICKSAND!
MANAGED TO RIGHT MYSELF--AT LEAST MY HEAD'S ABOVE WATER-- BUT I'M STILL SINKING!
THE HULK!
HAS HE COME TO GLOAT--OR JUST WATCH ME DIE?
STAY BACK--THE GROUND HERE, IT IS NOT SAFE!
I BET THAT HAS CONFUSED HIM.
SERVES ME RIGHT, WHAT'S HAPPENING TO ME.
I ATTACKED HULK WITHOUT THINKING.
THIS IS THE LEAST I CAN DO...
...TO TRY TO MAKE AMENDS.
TIME TO TAKE MY LAST BREATH.
I'LL SWITCH TO COLOSSUS, LET MY WEIGHT PULL ME TO DOWN.
ONCE I REACH BOTTOM, I CAN TRY TO DIG THROUGH THE SOLID GROUND...
...TO MAKE MY WAY BACK TO OPEN AIR.

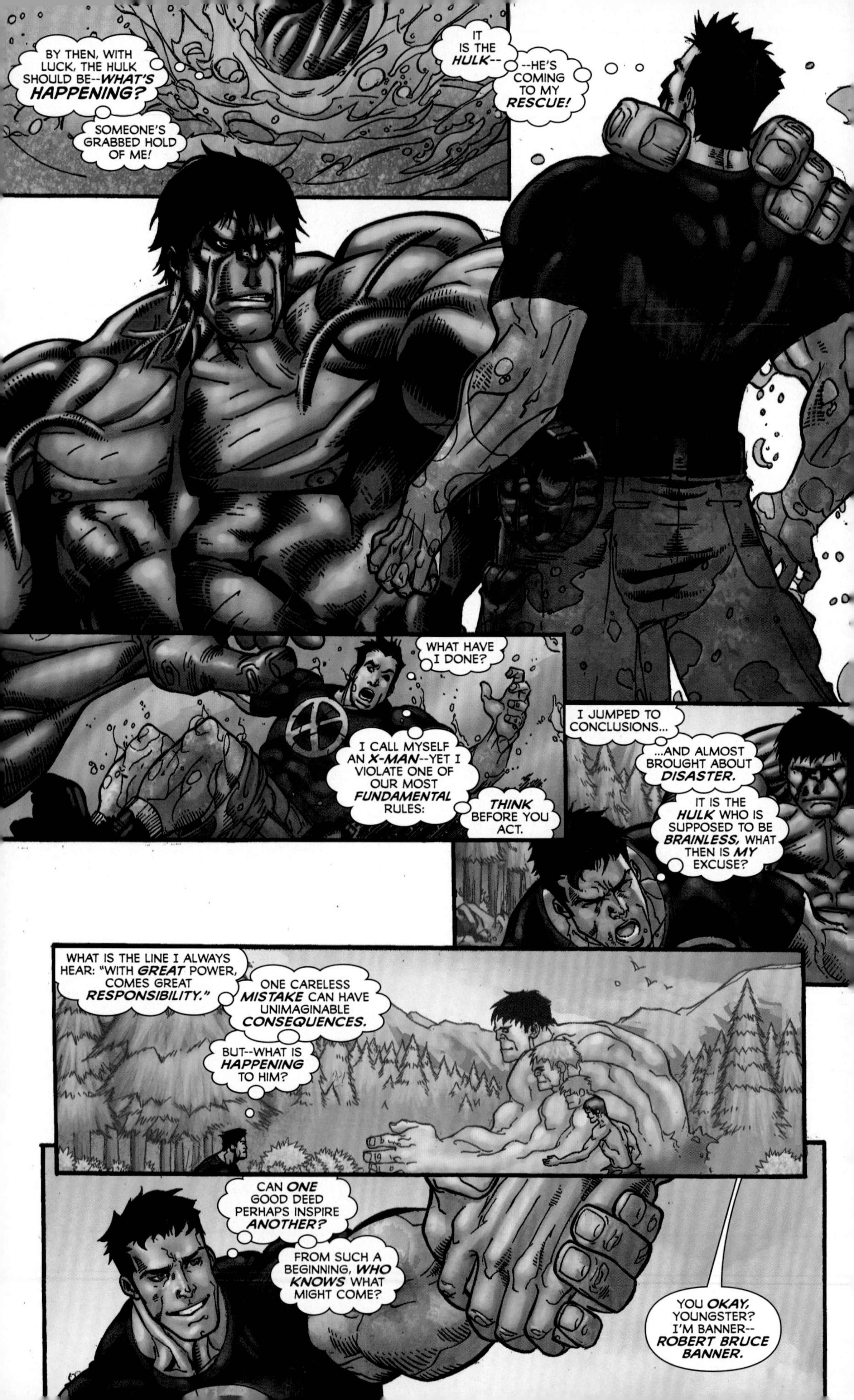
BY THEN, WITH LUCK, THE HULK SHOULD BE--WHAT'S HAPPENING?
SOMEONE'S GRABBED HOLD OF ME!
IT IS THE HULK--
--HE'S COMING TO MY RESCUE!
WHAT HAVE I DONE?
I CALL MYSELF AN X-MAN--YET I VIOLATE ONE OF OUR MOST FUNDAMENTAL RULES:
THINK BEFORE YOU ACT.
I JUMPED TO CONCLUSIONS...
...AND ALMOST BROUGHT ABOUT DISASTER.
IT IS THE HULK WHO IS SUPPOSED TO BE BRAINLESS, WHAT THEN IS MY EXCUSE?
WHAT IS THE LINE I ALWAYS HEAR: "WITH GREAT POWER, COMES GREAT RESPONSIBILITY."
ONE CARELESS MISTAKE CAN HAVE UNIMAGINABLE CONSEQUENCES.
BUT--WHAT IS HAPPENING TO HIM?
CAN ONE GOOD DEED PERHAPS INSPIRE ANOTHER?
FROM SUCH A BEGINNING, WHO KNOWS WHAT MIGHT COME?
YOU OKAY, YOUNGSTER? I'M BANNER-- ROBERT BRUCE BANNER.

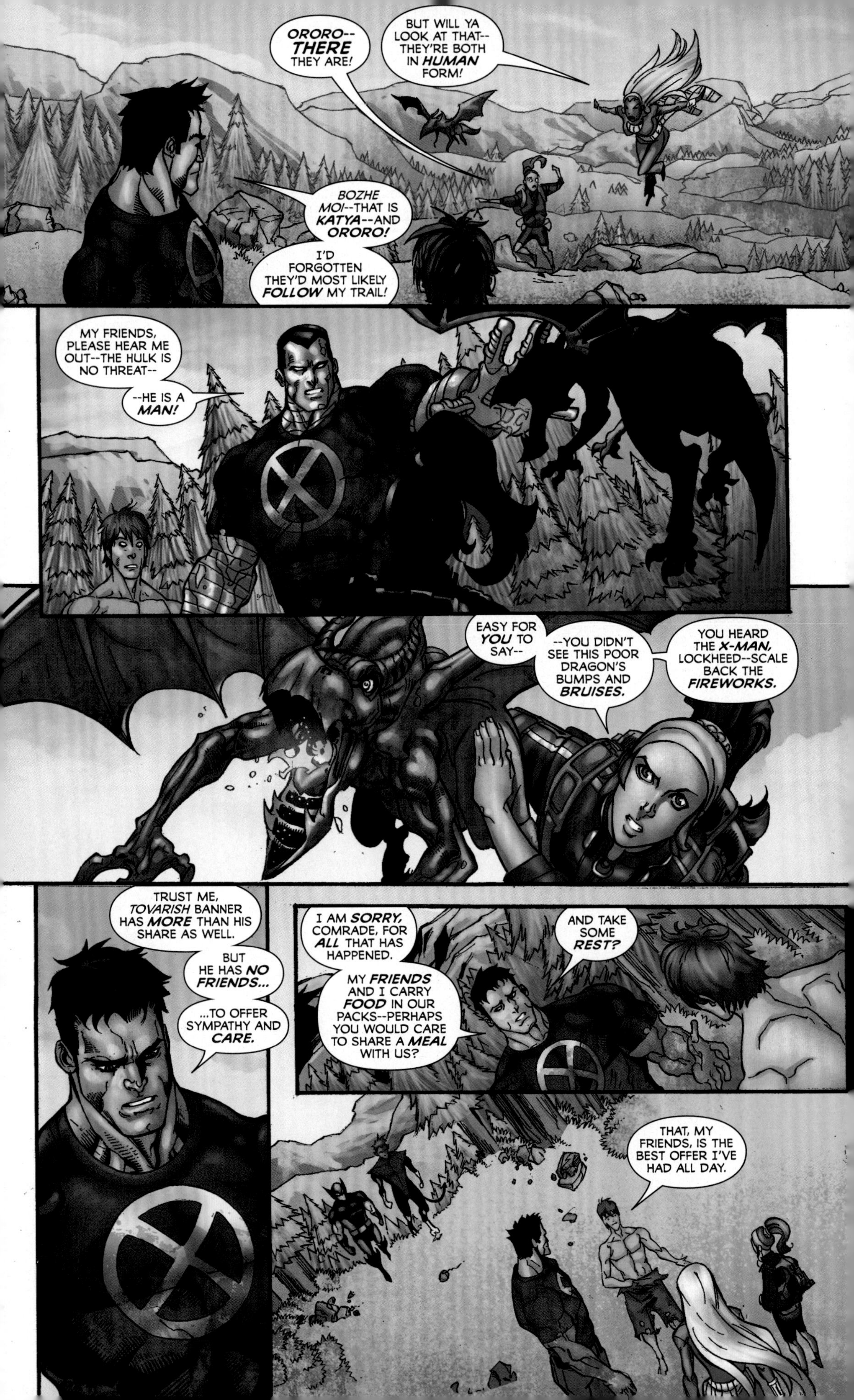
ORORO--THERE THEY ARE!
BUT WILL YA LOOK AT THAT--THEY'RE BOTH IN HUMAN FORM!
BOZHE MOI!--THAT IS KATYA--AND ORORO!
I'D FORGOTTEN THEY'D MOST LIKELY FOLLOW MY TRAIL!
MY FRIENDS, PLEASE HEAR ME OUT--THE HULK IS NO THREAT--
--HE IS A MAN!
EASY FOR YOU TO SAY--
--YOU DIDN'T SEE THIS POOR DRAGON'S BUMPS AND BRUISES.
YOU HEARD THE X-MAN, LOCKHEED--SCALE BACK THE FIREWORKS.
TRUST ME, TOVARISH BANNER HAS MORE THAN HIS SHARE AS WELL.
BUT HE HAS NO FRIENDS...
...TO OFFER SYMPATHY AND CARE.
I AM SORRY, COMRADE, FOR ALL THAT HAS HAPPENED.
MY FRIENDS AND I CARRY FOOD IN OUR PACKS--PERHAPS YOU WOULD CARE TO SHARE A MEAL WITH US?
AND TAKE SOME REST?
THAT, MY FRIENDS, IS THE BEST OFFER I'VE HAD ALL DAY.

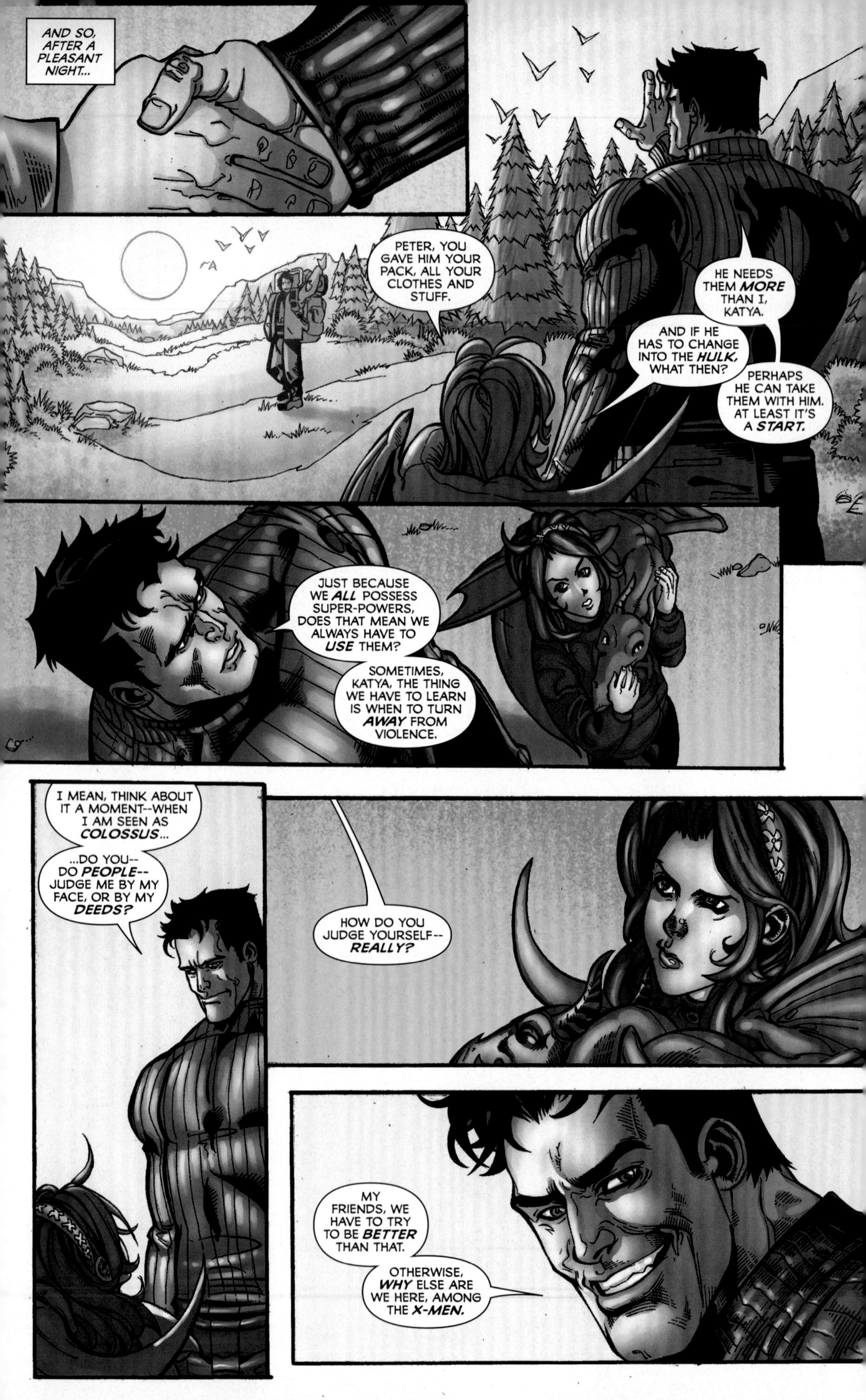
AND SO, AFTER A PLEASANT NIGHT...
PETER, YOU GAVE HIM YOUR PACK, ALL YOUR CLOTHES AND STUFF.
HE NEEDS THEM MORE THAN I, KATYA.
AND IF HE HAS TO CHANGE INTO THE HULK, WHAT THEN?
PERHAPS HE CAN TAKE THEM WITH HIM. AT LEAST IT'S A START.
JUST BECAUSE WE ALL POSSESS SUPER-POWERS, DOES THAT MEAN WE ALWAYS HAVE TO USE THEM?
SOMETIMES, KATYA, THE THING WE HAVE TO LEARN IS WHEN TO TURN AWAY FROM VIOLENCE.
I MEAN, THINK ABOUT IT A MOMENT--WHEN I AM SEEN AS COLOSSUS...
...DO YOU-- DO PEOPLE-- JUDGE ME BY MY FACE, OR BY MY DEEDS?
HOW DO YOU JUDGE YOURSELF-- REALLY?
MY FRIENDS, WE HAVE TO TRY TO BE BETTER THAN THAT.
OTHERWISE, WHY ELSE ARE WE HERE, AMONG THE X-MEN.

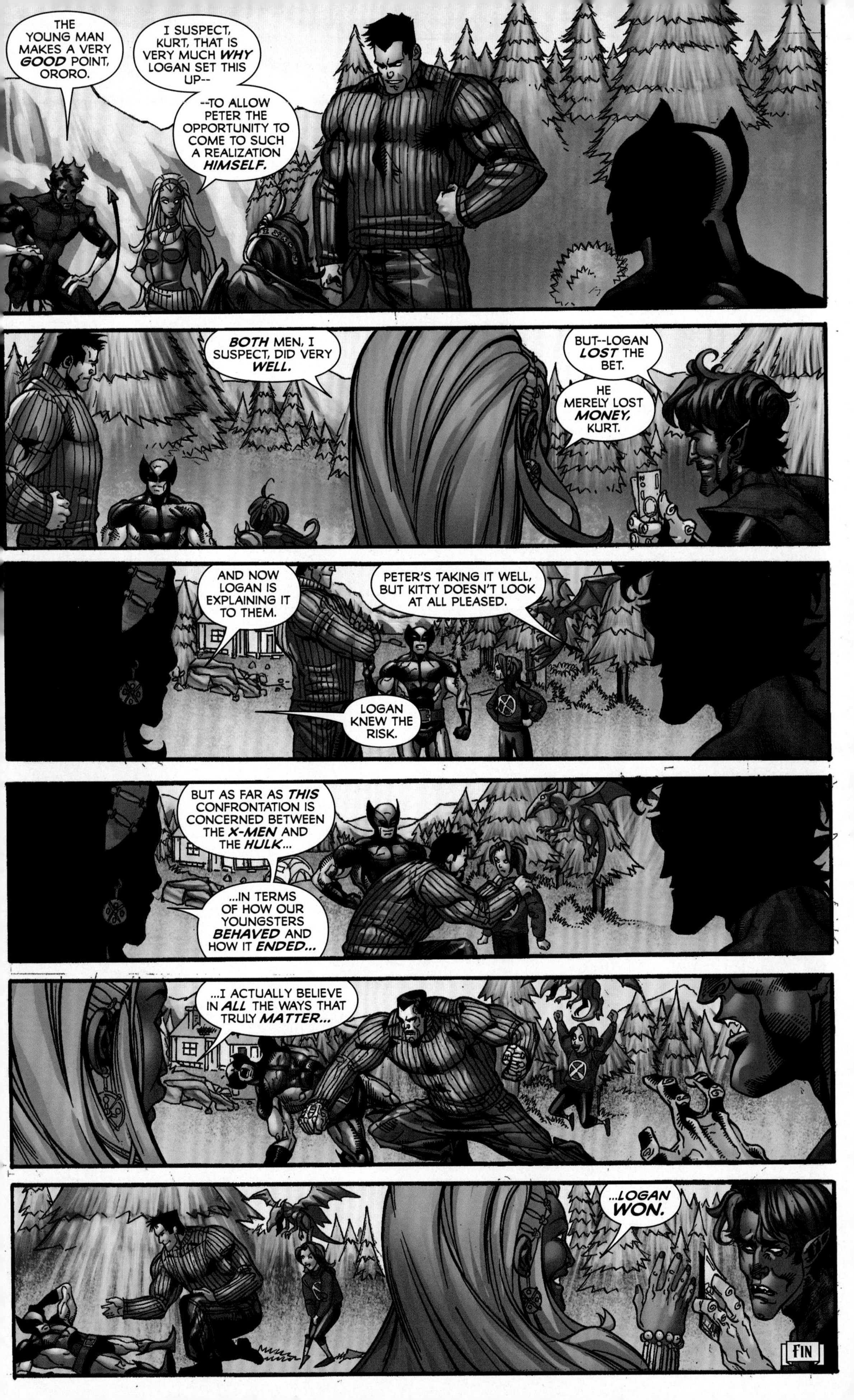
THE YOUNG MAN MAKES A VERY **GOOD** POINT, ORORO.
I SUSPECT, KURT, THAT IS VERY MUCH **WHY** LOGAN SET THIS UP--
--TO ALLOW PETER THE OPPORTUNITY TO COME TO SUCH A REALIZATION **HIMSELF.**
BOTH MEN, I SUSPECT, DID VERY **WELL.**
BUT--LOGAN **LOST** THE BET.
HE MERELY LOST **MONEY,** KURT.
AND NOW LOGAN IS EXPLAINING IT TO THEM.
PETER'S TAKING IT WELL, BUT KITTY DOESN'T LOOK AT ALL PLEASED.
LOGAN KNEW THE RISK.
BUT AS FAR AS **THIS** CONFRONTATION IS CONCERNED BETWEEN THE **X-MEN** AND THE **HULK**...
...IN TERMS OF HOW OUR YOUNGSTERS **BEHAVED** AND HOW IT **ENDED...**
...I ACTUALLY BELIEVE IN **ALL** THE WAYS THAT TRULY **MATTER...**
...**LOGAN WON.**
FIN

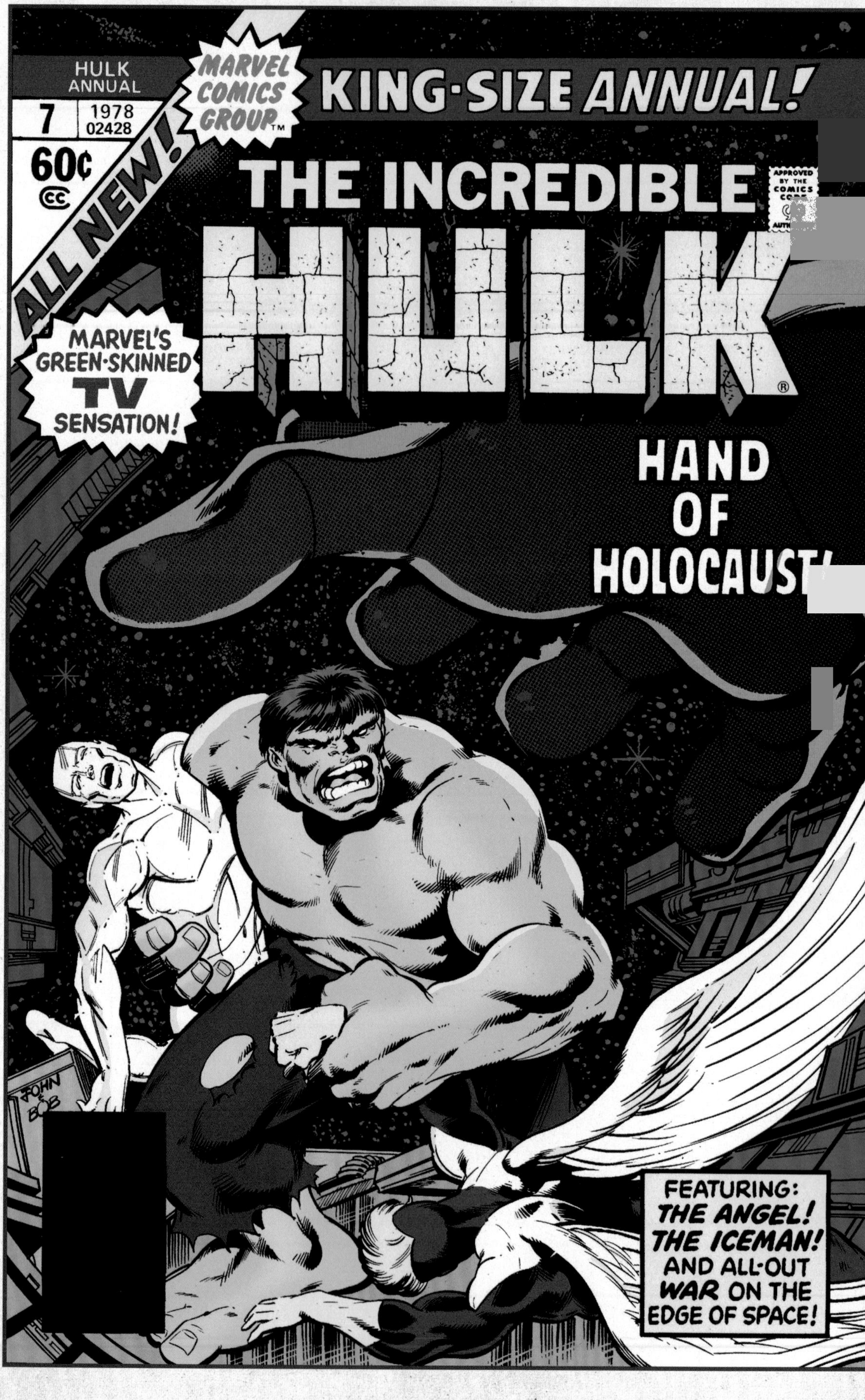

HULK ANNUAL
7
1978
02428
60¢
MARVEL COMICS GROUP
KING-SIZE ANNUAL!
ALL NEW!
THE INCREDIBLE
HULK
MARVEL'S GREEN-SKINNED TV SENSATION!
HAND OF HOLOCAUST!
JOHN & BOB
FEATURING: THE ANGEL! THE ICEMAN! AND ALL-OUT WAR ON THE EDGE OF SPACE!

★★★ ROUND 6 ★★★

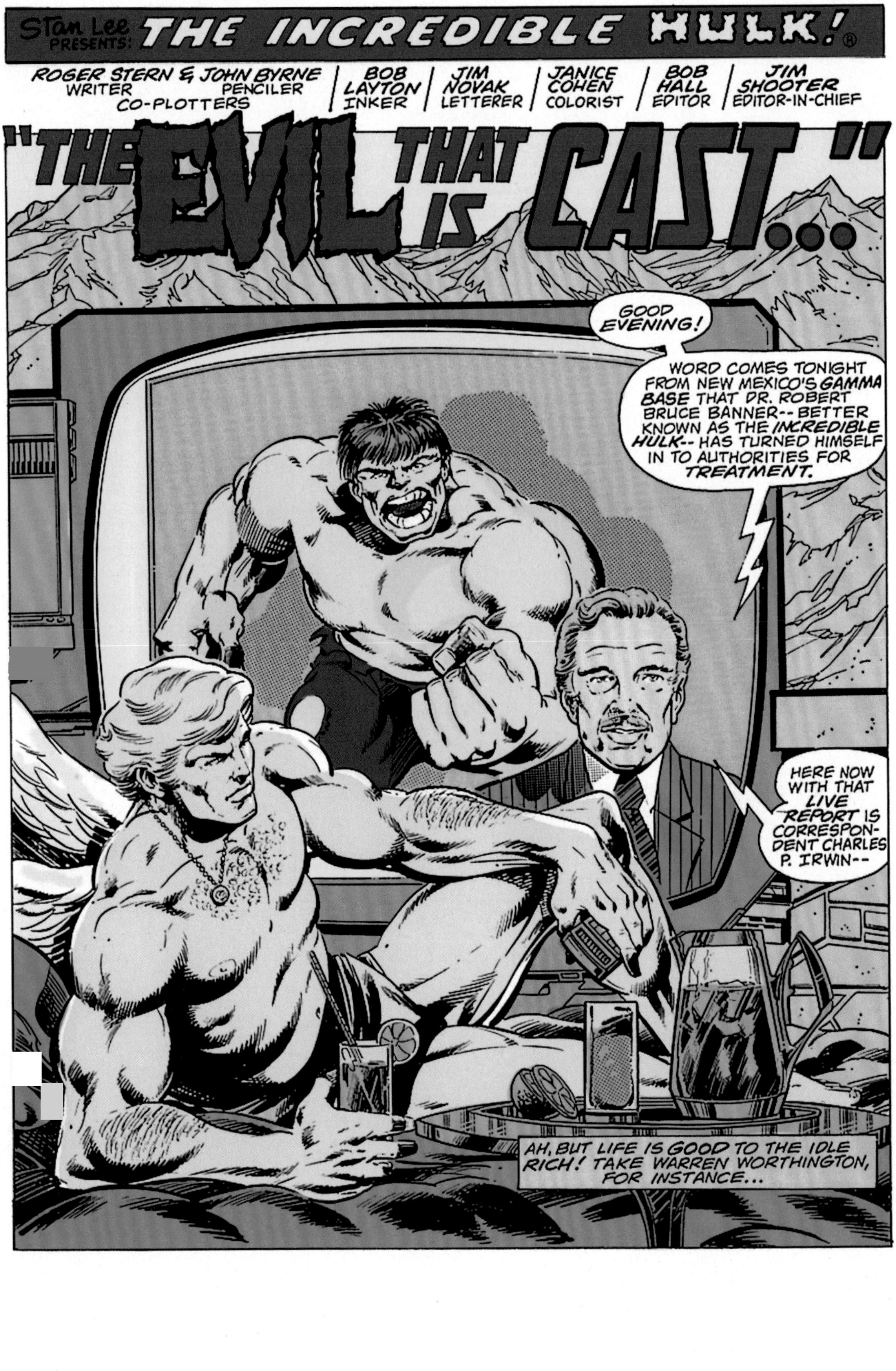
Stan Lee PRESENTS: THE INCREDIBLE HULK!®
ROGER STERN & JOHN BYRNE WRITER PENCILER CO-PLOTTERS
BOB LAYTON INKER
JIM NOVAK LETTERER
JANICE COHEN COLORIST
BOB HALL EDITOR
JIM SHOOTER EDITOR-IN-CHIEF
"THE EVIL THAT IS CAST..."
GOOD EVENING!
WORD COMES TONIGHT FROM NEW MEXICO'S GAMMA BASE THAT DR. ROBERT BRUCE BANNER-- BETTER KNOWN AS THE INCREDIBLE HULK-- HAS TURNED HIMSELF IN TO AUTHORITIES FOR TREATMENT.
HERE NOW WITH THAT LIVE REPORT IS CORRESPONDENT CHARLES P. IRWIN--
AH, BUT LIFE IS GOOD TO THE IDLE RICH! TAKE WARREN WORTHINGTON, FOR INSTANCE...

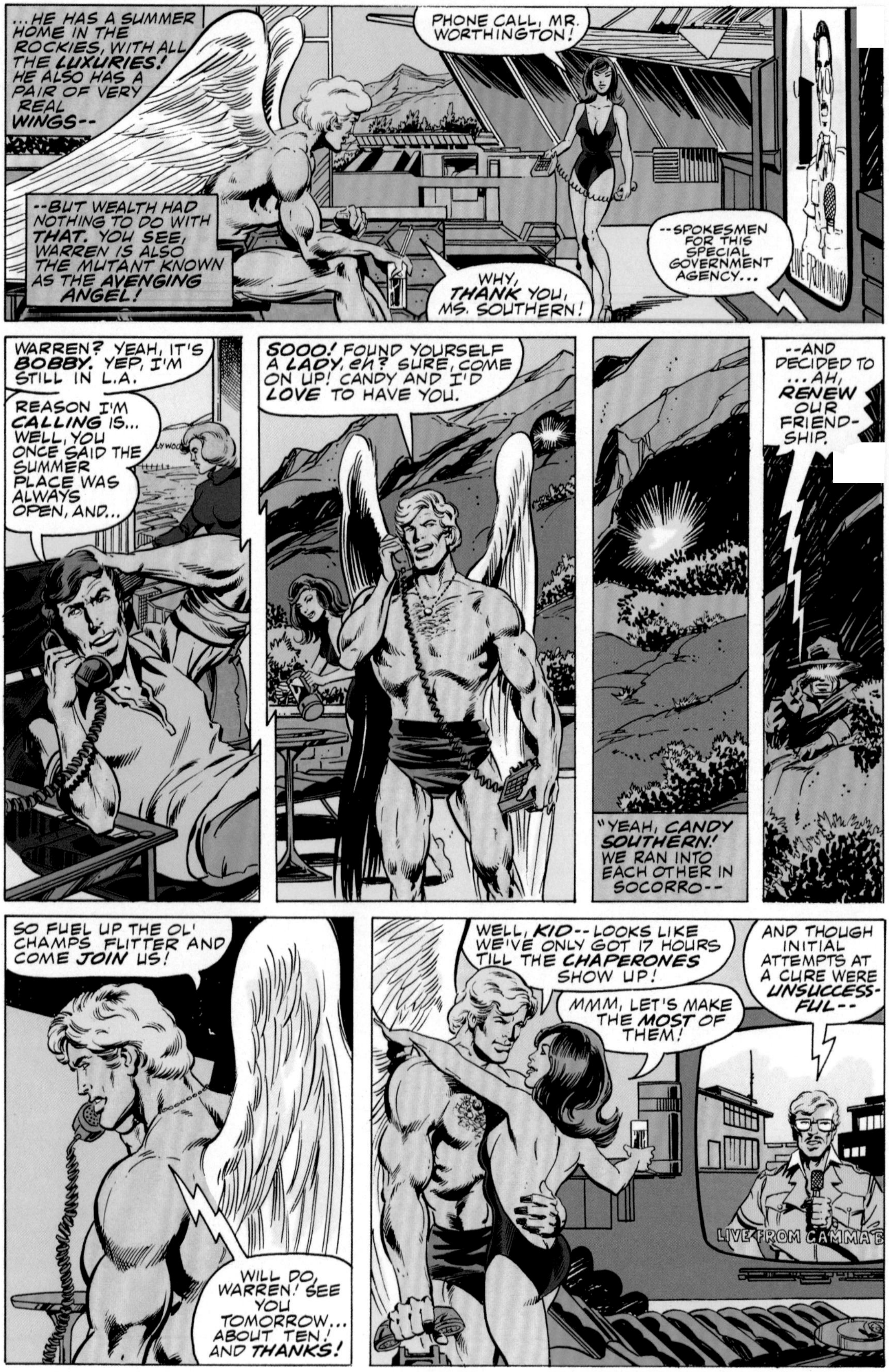
...HE HAS A SUMMER HOME IN THE ROCKIES, WITH ALL THE LUXURIES! HE ALSO HAS A PAIR OF VERY REAL WINGS--
PHONE CALL, MR. WORTHINGTON!
--BUT WEALTH HAD NOTHING TO DO WITH THAT. YOU SEE, WARREN IS ALSO THE MUTANT KNOWN AS THE AVENGING ANGEL!
--SPOKESMEN FOR THIS SPECIAL GOVERNMENT AGENCY...
WHY, THANK YOU, MS. SOUTHERN!
WARREN? YEAH, IT'S BOBBY. YEP, I'M STILL IN L.A.
REASON I'M CALLING IS... WELL, YOU ONCE SAID THE SUMMER PLACE WAS ALWAYS OPEN, AND...
SOOO! FOUND YOURSELF A LADY, eh? SURE, COME ON UP! CANDY AND I'D LOVE TO HAVE YOU.
"YEAH, CANDY SOUTHERN! WE RAN INTO EACH OTHER IN SOCORRO--
--AND DECIDED TO ...AH, RENEW OUR FRIENDSHIP.
SO FUEL UP THE OL' CHAMPS FLITTER AND COME JOIN US!
WILL DO, WARREN! SEE YOU TOMORROW... ABOUT TEN! AND THANKS!
WELL, KID--LOOKS LIKE WE'VE ONLY GOT 17 HOURS TILL THE CHAPERONES SHOW UP!
MMM, LET'S MAKE THE MOST OF THEM!
AND THOUGH INITIAL ATTEMPTS AT A CURE WERE UNSUCCESSFUL--
LIVE FROM GAMMA B

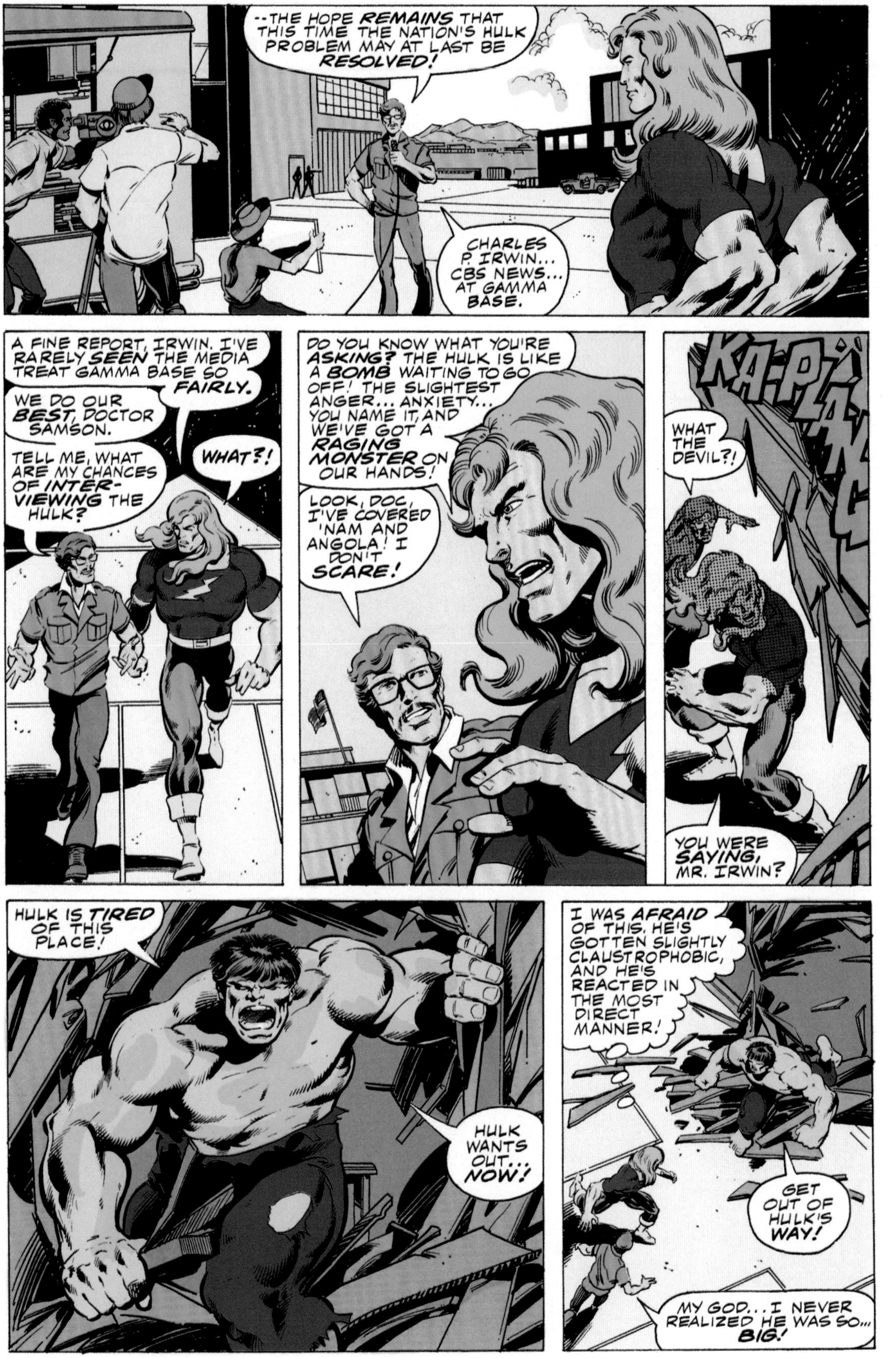

--THE HOPE REMAINS THAT THIS TIME THE NATION'S HULK PROBLEM MAY AT LAST BE RESOLVED!
CHARLES P. IRWIN... CBS NEWS... AT GAMMA BASE.
A FINE REPORT, IRWIN. I'VE RARELY SEEN THE MEDIA TREAT GAMMA BASE SO FAIRLY.
WE DO OUR BEST, DOCTOR SAMSON.
TELL ME, WHAT ARE MY CHANCES OF INTER-VIEWING THE HULK?
WHAT?!
DO YOU KNOW WHAT YOU'RE ASKING? THE HULK IS LIKE A BOMB WAITING TO GO OFF! THE SLIGHTEST ANGER... ANXIETY... YOU NAME IT, AND WE'VE GOT A RAGING MONSTER ON OUR HANDS!
LOOK, DOC, I'VE COVERED 'NAM AND ANGOLA! I DON'T SCARE!
KA-PLANG
WHAT THE DEVIL?!
YOU WERE SAYING, MR. IRWIN?
HULK IS TIRED OF THIS PLACE!
HULK WANTS OUT... NOW!
I WAS AFRAID OF THIS. HE'S GOTTEN SLIGHTLY CLAUSTROPHOBIC, AND HE'S REACTED IN THE MOST DIRECT MANNER!
GET OUT OF HULK'S WAY!
MY GOD... I NEVER REALIZED HE WAS SO... BIG!

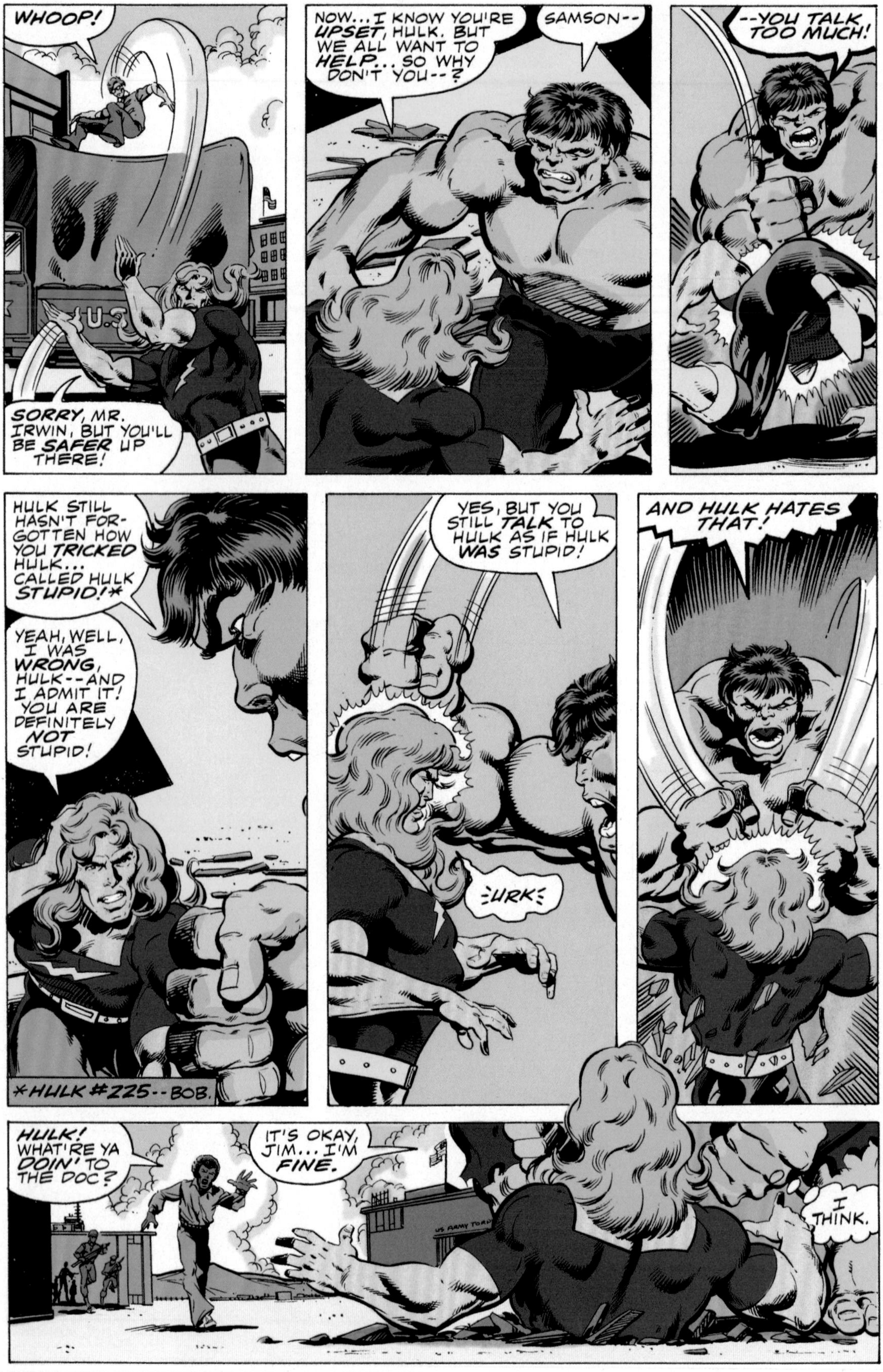
WHOOP!
SORRY, MR. IRWIN, BUT YOU'LL BE SAFER UP THERE!
NOW... I KNOW YOU'RE UPSET, HULK. BUT WE ALL WANT TO HELP... SO WHY DON'T YOU--?
SAMSON--
--YOU TALK TOO MUCH!
HULK STILL HASN'T FORGOTTEN HOW YOU TRICKED HULK... CALLED HULK STUPID!*
YEAH, WELL, I WAS WRONG, HULK--AND I ADMIT IT! YOU ARE DEFINITELY NOT STUPID!
*HULK #225--BOB.
YES, BUT YOU STILL TALK TO HULK AS IF HULK WAS STUPID!
URK
AND HULK HATES THAT!
HULK! WHAT'RE YA DOIN' TO THE DOC?
IT'S OKAY, JIM... I'M FINE.
I THINK.

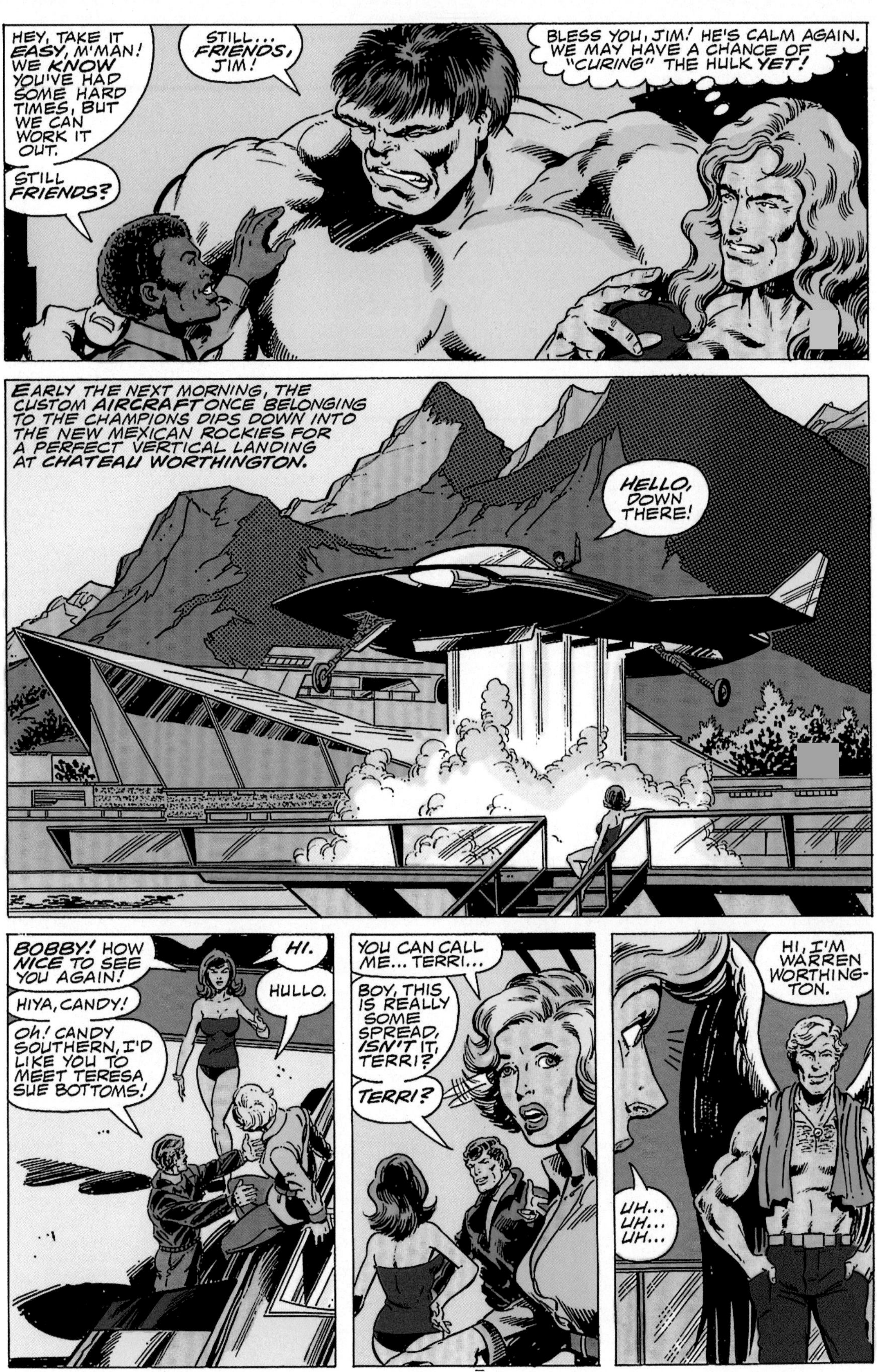
HEY, TAKE IT EASY, M'MAN! WE KNOW YOU'VE HAD SOME HARD TIMES, BUT WE CAN WORK IT OUT.
STILL FRIENDS?
STILL... FRIENDS, JIM!
BLESS YOU, JIM! HE'S CALM AGAIN. WE MAY HAVE A CHANCE OF "CURING" THE HULK YET!
EARLY THE NEXT MORNING, THE CUSTOM AIRCRAFT ONCE BELONGING TO THE CHAMPIONS DIPS DOWN INTO THE NEW MEXICAN ROCKIES FOR A PERFECT VERTICAL LANDING AT CHATEAU WORTHINGTON.
HELLO, DOWN THERE!
BOBBY! HOW NICE TO SEE YOU AGAIN!
HI.
HIYA, CANDY!
HULLO.
Oh! CANDY SOUTHERN, I'D LIKE YOU TO MEET TERESA SUE BOTTOMS!
...
YOU CAN CALL ME... TERRI...
BOY, THIS IS REALLY SOME SPREAD, ISN'T IT, TERRI?
TERRI?
HI, I'M WARREN WORTHINGTON.
UH... UH... UH...

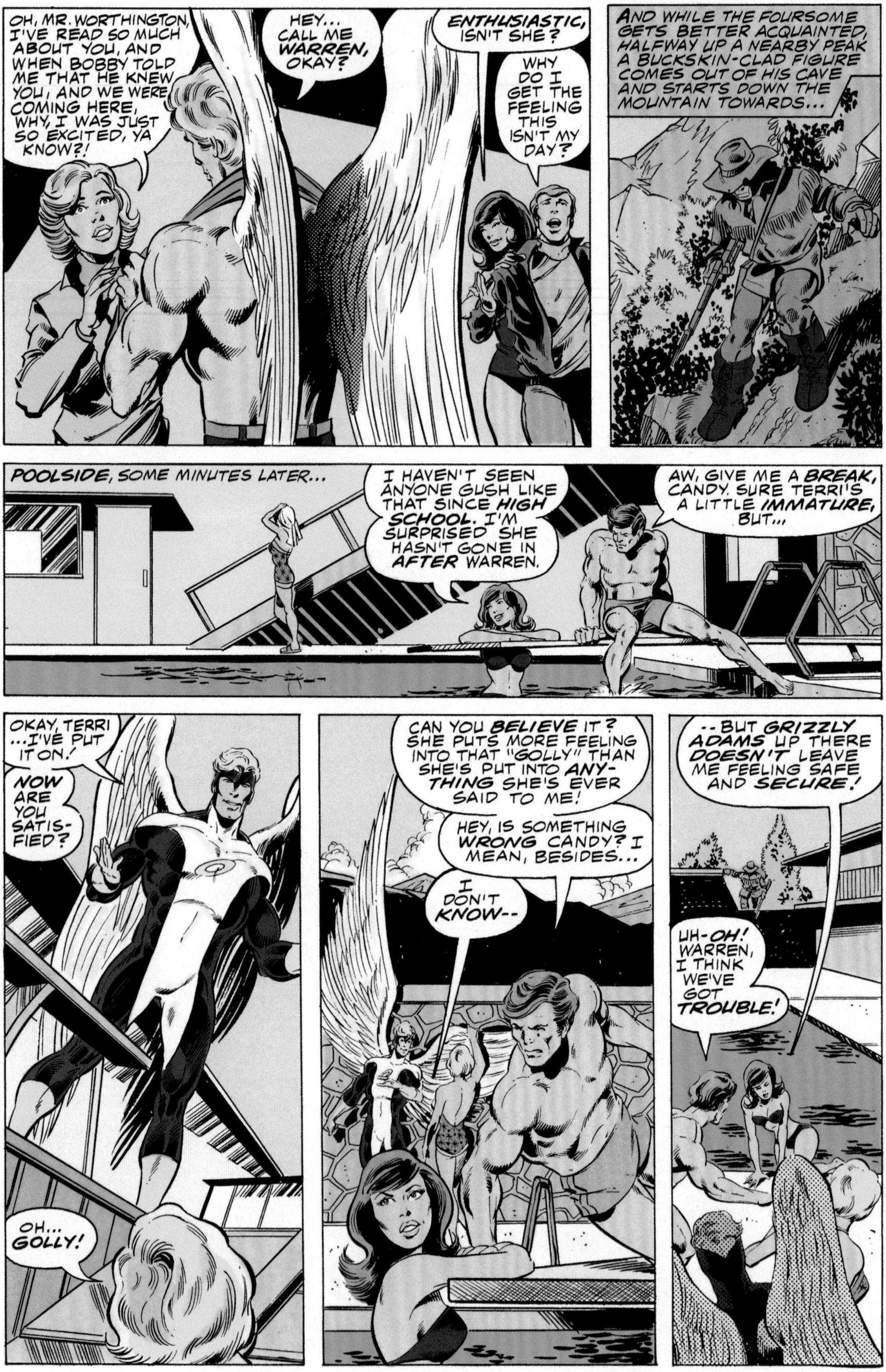
OH, MR. WORTHINGTON, I'VE READ SO MUCH ABOUT YOU, AND WHEN BOBBY TOLD ME THAT HE KNEW YOU, AND WE WERE COMING HERE, WHY, I WAS JUST SO EXCITED, YA KNOW?!
HEY... CALL ME WARREN, OKAY?
ENTHUSIASTIC, ISN'T SHE?
WHY DO I GET THE FEELING THIS ISN'T MY DAY?
AND WHILE THE FOURSOME GETS BETTER ACQUAINTED, HALFWAY UP A NEARBY PEAK A BUCKSKIN-CLAD FIGURE COMES OUT OF HIS CAVE AND STARTS DOWN THE MOUNTAIN TOWARDS...
POOLSIDE, SOME MINUTES LATER...
I HAVEN'T SEEN ANYONE GUSH LIKE THAT SINCE HIGH SCHOOL. I'M SURPRISED SHE HASN'T GONE IN AFTER WARREN.
AW, GIVE ME A BREAK, CANDY. SURE TERRI'S A LITTLE IMMATURE, BUT...
OKAY, TERRI ...I'VE PUT IT ON!
NOW ARE YOU SATIS-FIED?
OH... GOLLY!
CAN YOU BELIEVE IT? SHE PUTS MORE FEELING INTO THAT "GOLLY" THAN SHE'S PUT INTO ANY-THING SHE'S EVER SAID TO ME!
HEY, IS SOMETHING WRONG CANDY? I MEAN, BESIDES...
I DON'T KNOW--
--BUT GRIZZLY ADAMS UP THERE DOESN'T LEAVE ME FEELING SAFE AND SECURE!
UH-OH! WARREN, I THINK WE'VE GOT TROUBLE!

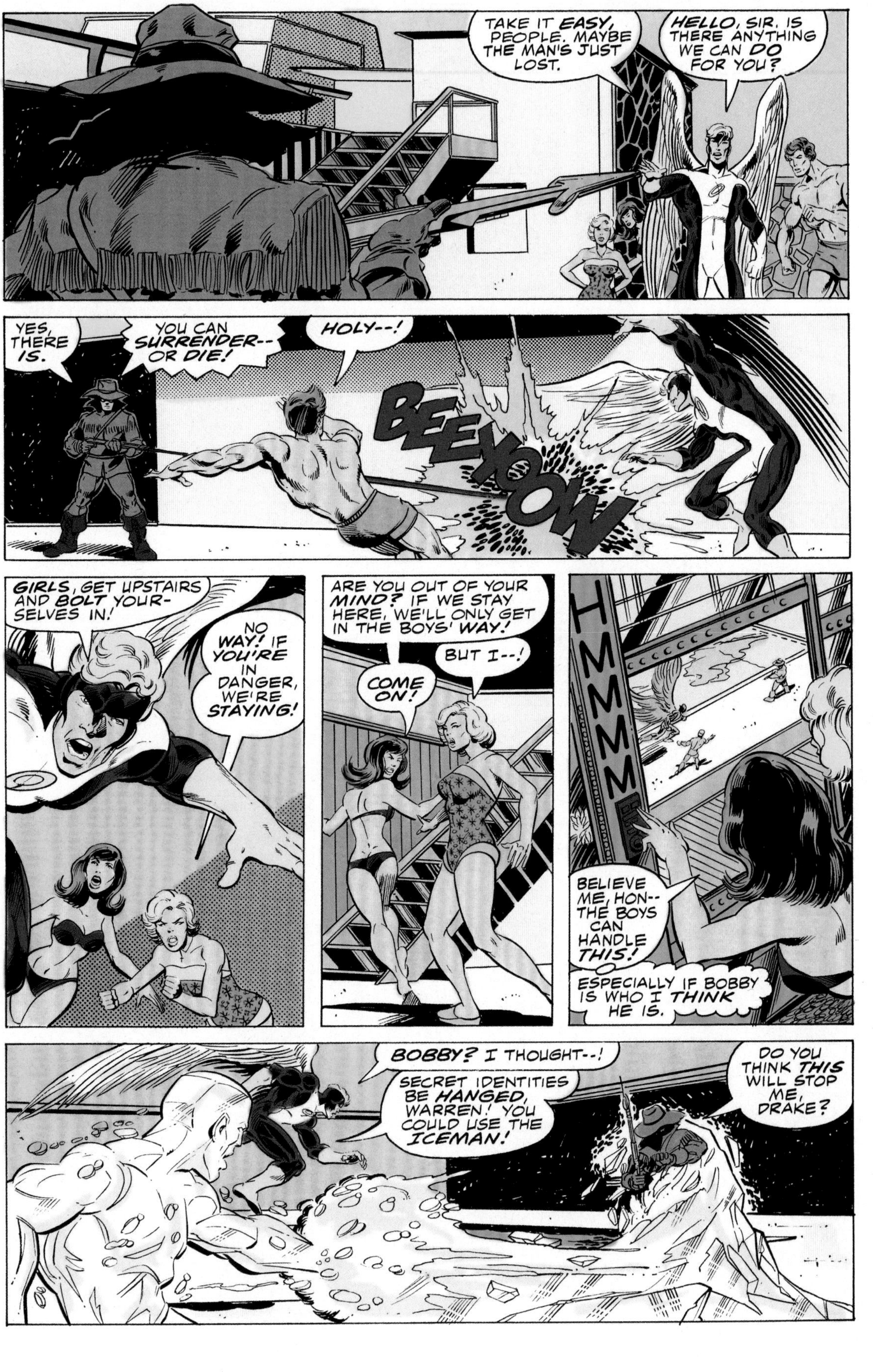
TAKE IT EASY, PEOPLE. MAYBE THE MAN'S JUST LOST.
HELLO, SIR. IS THERE ANYTHING WE CAN DO FOR YOU?
YES, THERE IS.
YOU CAN SURRENDER-- OR DIE!
HOLY--!
BEEYOOOW
GIRLS, GET UPSTAIRS AND BOLT YOURSELVES IN!
NO WAY! IF YOU'RE IN DANGER, WE'RE STAYING!
ARE YOU OUT OF YOUR MIND? IF WE STAY HERE, WE'LL ONLY GET IN THE BOYS' WAY!
COME ON!
BUT I--!
HMMMM
BELIEVE ME, HON-- THE BOYS CAN HANDLE THIS!
ESPECIALLY IF BOBBY IS WHO I THINK HE IS.
BOBBY? I THOUGHT--!
SECRET IDENTITIES BE HANGED, WARREN! YOU COULD USE THE ICEMAN!
DO YOU THINK THIS WILL STOP ME, DRAKE?

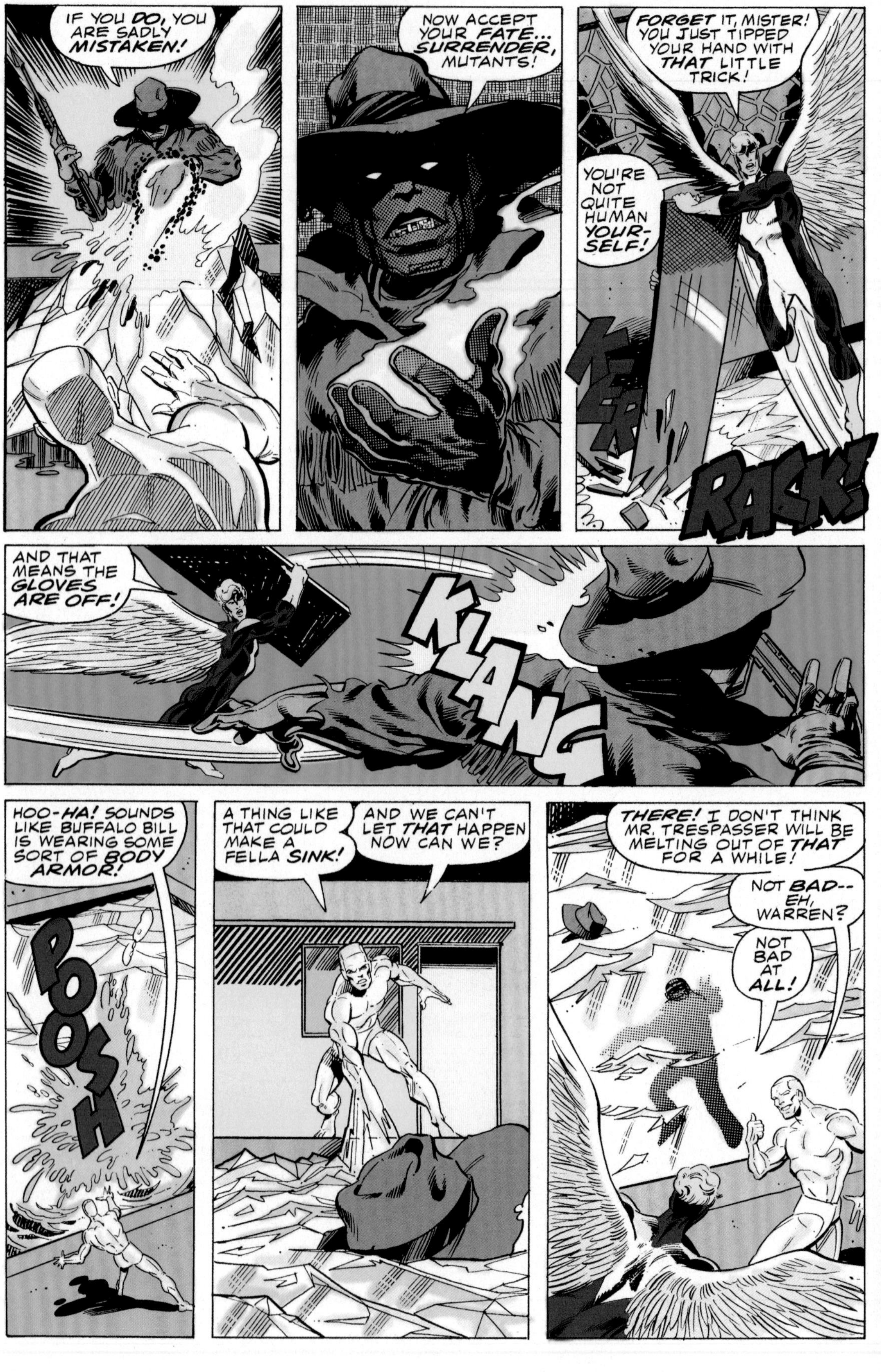
IF YOU DO, YOU ARE SADLY MISTAKEN!
NOW ACCEPT YOUR FATE... SURRENDER, MUTANTS!
FORGET IT, MISTER! YOU JUST TIPPED YOUR HAND WITH THAT LITTLE TRICK!
YOU'RE NOT QUITE HUMAN YOUR-SELF!
KEERRACK!
AND THAT MEANS THE GLOVES ARE OFF!
KLANG
HOO-HA! SOUNDS LIKE BUFFALO BILL IS WEARING SOME SORT OF BODY ARMOR!
POOSH
A THING LIKE THAT COULD MAKE A FELLA SINK!
AND WE CAN'T LET THAT HAPPEN NOW CAN WE?
THERE! I DON'T THINK MR. TRESPASSER WILL BE MELTING OUT OF THAT FOR A WHILE!
NOT BAD--EH, WARREN?
NOT BAD AT ALL!

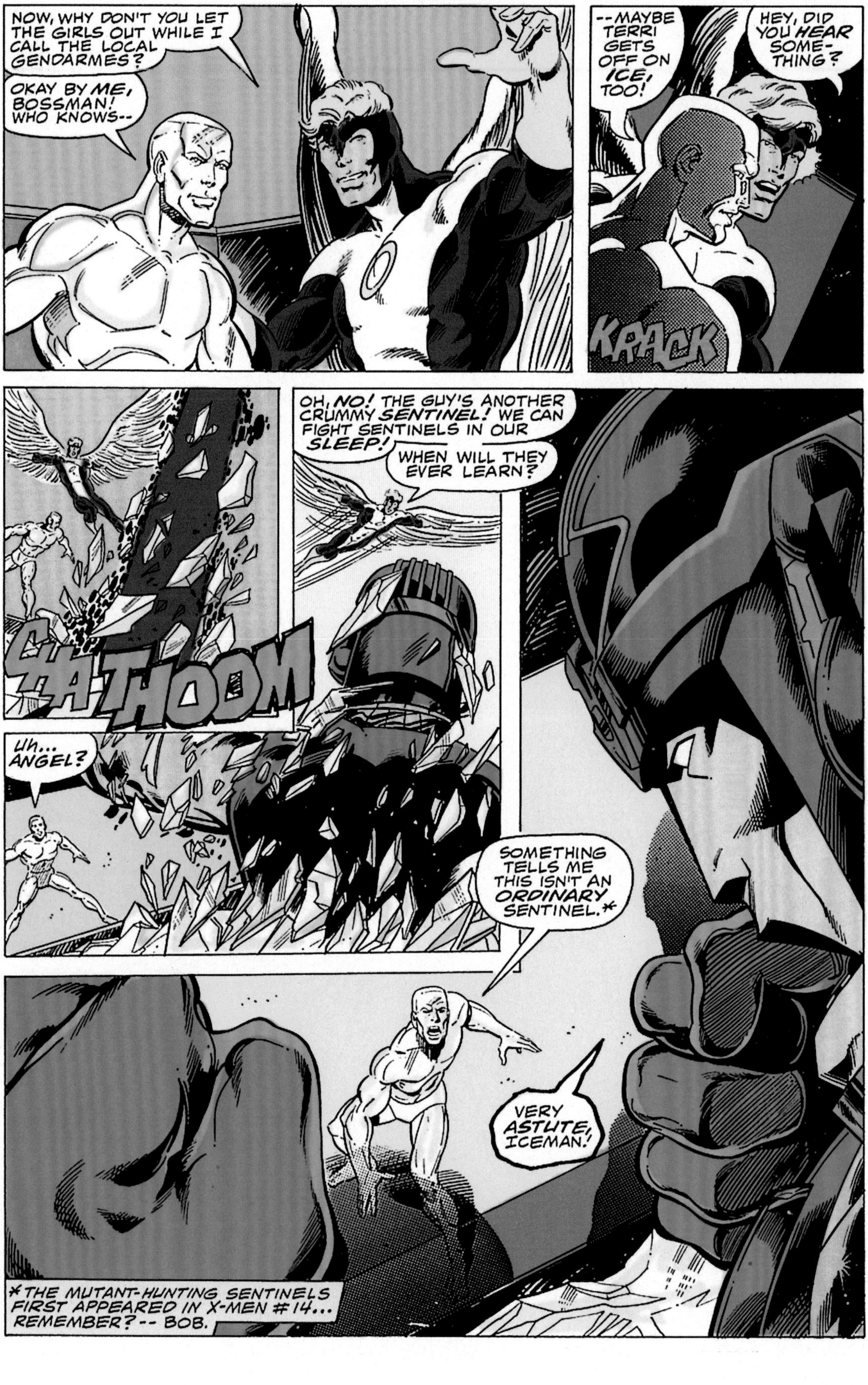

NOW, WHY DON'T YOU LET THE GIRLS OUT WHILE I CALL THE LOCAL GENDARMES?
OKAY BY ME, BOSSMAN! WHO KNOWS--
--MAYBE TERRI GETS OFF ON ICE, TOO!
HEY, DID YOU HEAR SOME-THING?
KRACK
CHATHOOM
OH, NO! THE GUY'S ANOTHER CRUMMY SENTINEL! WE CAN FIGHT SENTINELS IN OUR SLEEP!
WHEN WILL THEY EVER LEARN?
UH... ANGEL?
SOMETHING TELLS ME THIS ISN'T AN ORDINARY SENTINEL.*
VERY ASTUTE, ICEMAN!
*THE MUTANT-HUNTING SENTINELS FIRST APPEARED IN X-MEN #14... REMEMBER? -- BOB.

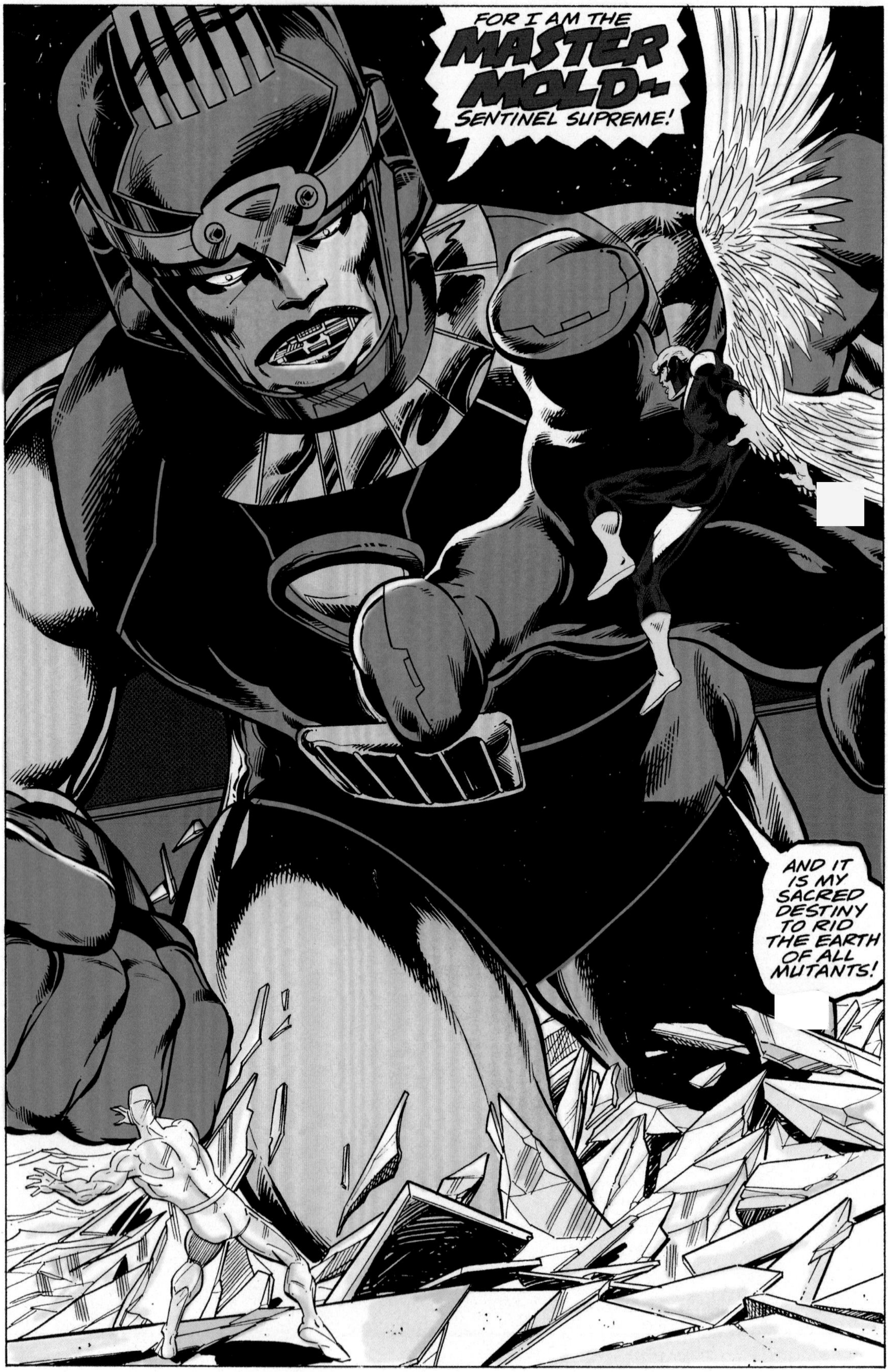
FOR I AM THE MASTER MOLD-- SENTINEL SUPREME!
AND IT IS MY SACRED DESTINY TO RID THE EARTH OF ALL MUTANTS!

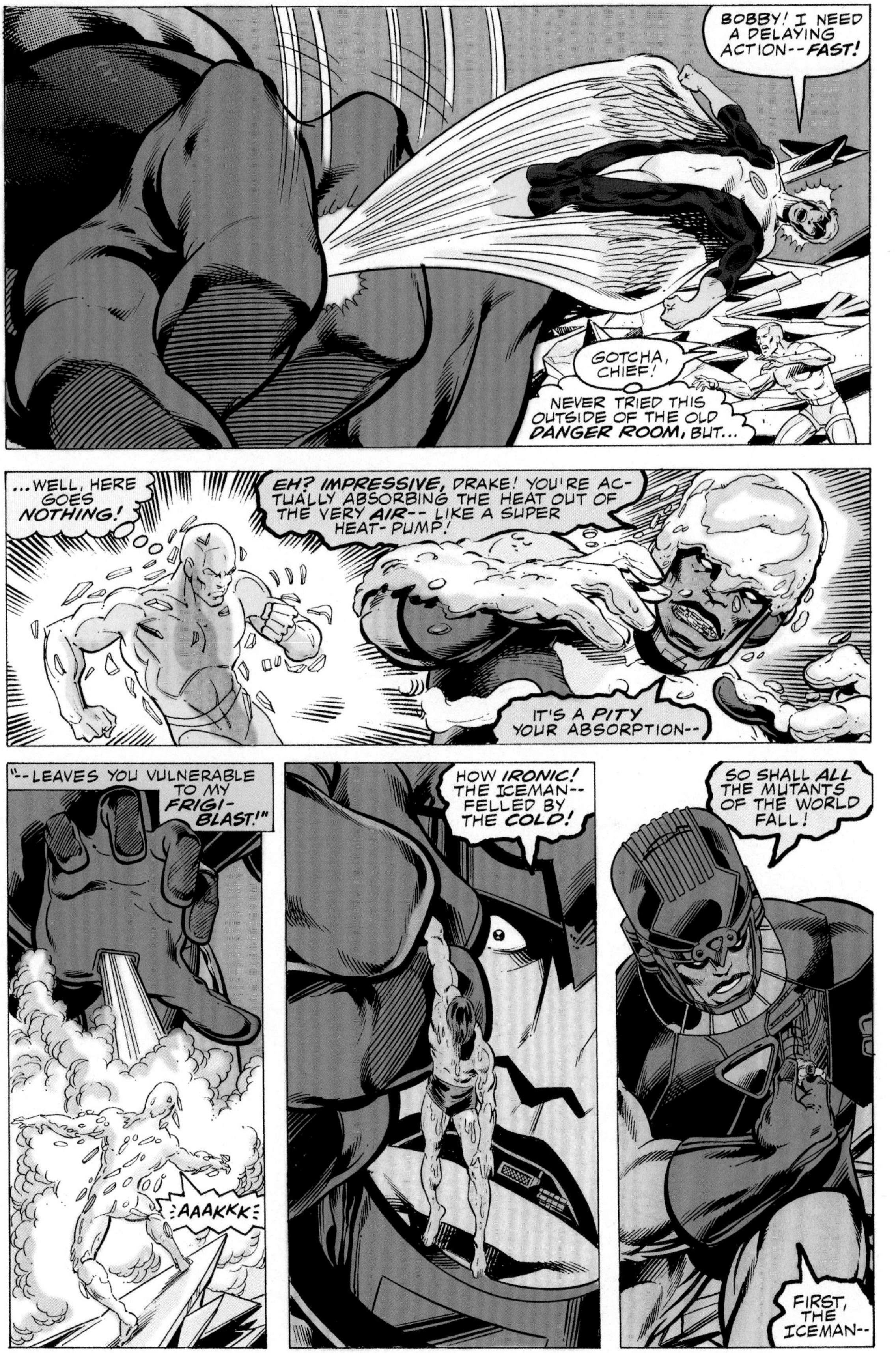
BOBBY! I NEED A DELAYING ACTION--FAST!
GOTCHA, CHIEF!
NEVER TRIED THIS OUTSIDE OF THE OLD DANGER ROOM, BUT...
...WELL, HERE GOES NOTHING!
EH? IMPRESSIVE, DRAKE! YOU'RE ACTUALLY ABSORBING THE HEAT OUT OF THE VERY AIR-- LIKE A SUPER HEAT-PUMP!
IT'S A PITY YOUR ABSORPTION--
"--LEAVES YOU VULNERABLE TO MY FRIGI-BLAST!"
AAAKKK
HOW IRONIC! THE ICEMAN-- FELLED BY THE COLD!
SO SHALL ALL THE MUTANTS OF THE WORLD FALL!
FIRST, THE ICEMAN--

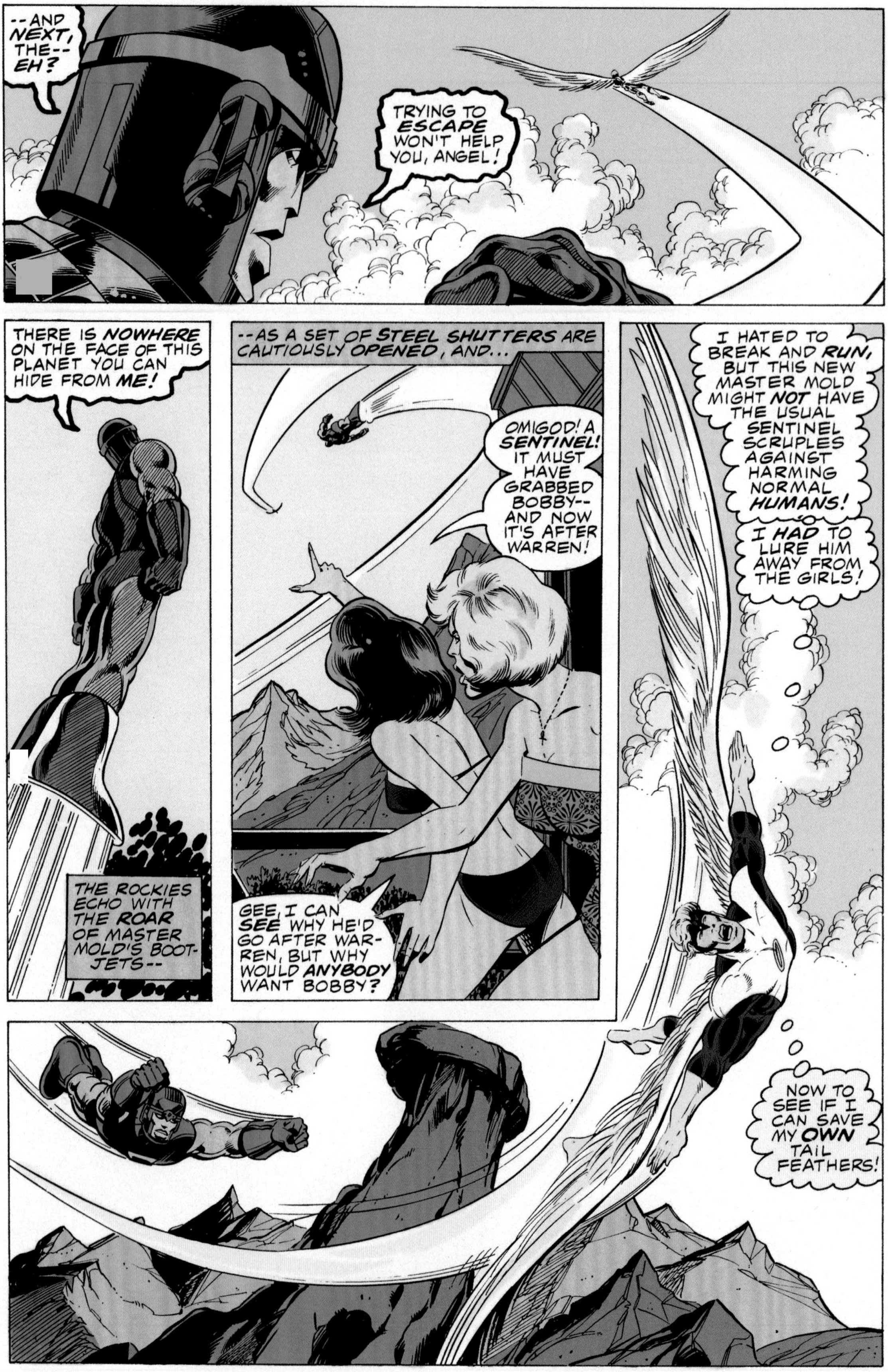
--AND NEXT, THE-- EH?
TRYING TO ESCAPE WON'T HELP YOU, ANGEL!
THERE IS NOWHERE ON THE FACE OF THIS PLANET YOU CAN HIDE FROM ME!
THE ROCKIES ECHO WITH THE ROAR OF MASTER MOLD'S BOOT-JETS--
--AS A SET OF STEEL SHUTTERS ARE CAUTIOUSLY OPENED, AND...
OMIGOD! A SENTINEL! IT MUST HAVE GRABBED BOBBY-- AND NOW IT'S AFTER WARREN!
GEE, I CAN SEE WHY HE'D GO AFTER WAR-REN, BUT WHY WOULD ANYBODY WANT BOBBY?
I HATED TO BREAK AND RUN, BUT THIS NEW MASTER MOLD MIGHT NOT HAVE THE USUAL SENTINEL SCRUPLES AGAINST HARMING NORMAL HUMANS!
I HAD TO LURE HIM AWAY FROM THE GIRLS!
NOW TO SEE IF I CAN SAVE MY OWN TAIL FEATHERS!

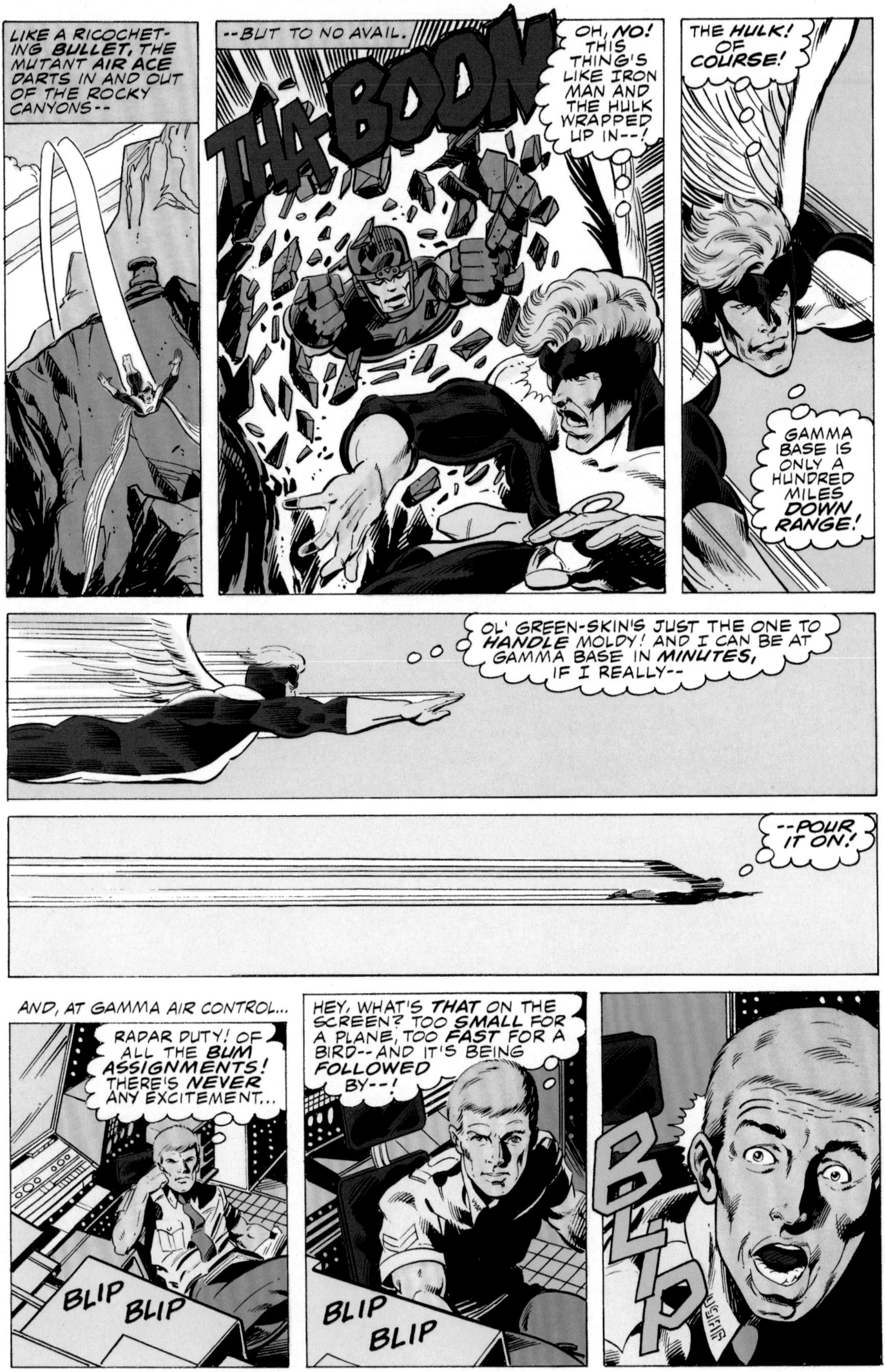
LIKE A RICOCHETING BULLET, THE MUTANT AIR ACE DARTS IN AND OUT OF THE ROCKY CANYONS--
--BUT TO NO AVAIL.
THA-BOOM
OH, NO! THIS THING'S LIKE IRON MAN AND THE HULK WRAPPED UP IN--!
THE HULK! OF COURSE!
GAMMA BASE IS ONLY A HUNDRED MILES DOWN RANGE!
OL' GREEN-SKIN'S JUST THE ONE TO HANDLE MOLDY! AND I CAN BE AT GAMMA BASE IN MINUTES, IF I REALLY--
--POUR IT ON!
AND, AT GAMMA AIR CONTROL...
RADAR DUTY! OF ALL THE BUM ASSIGNMENTS! THERE'S NEVER ANY EXCITEMENT...
BLIP
BLIP
HEY, WHAT'S THAT ON THE SCREEN? TOO SMALL FOR A PLANE, TOO FAST FOR A BIRD--AND IT'S BEING FOLLOWED BY--!
BLIP
BLIP
BLIP

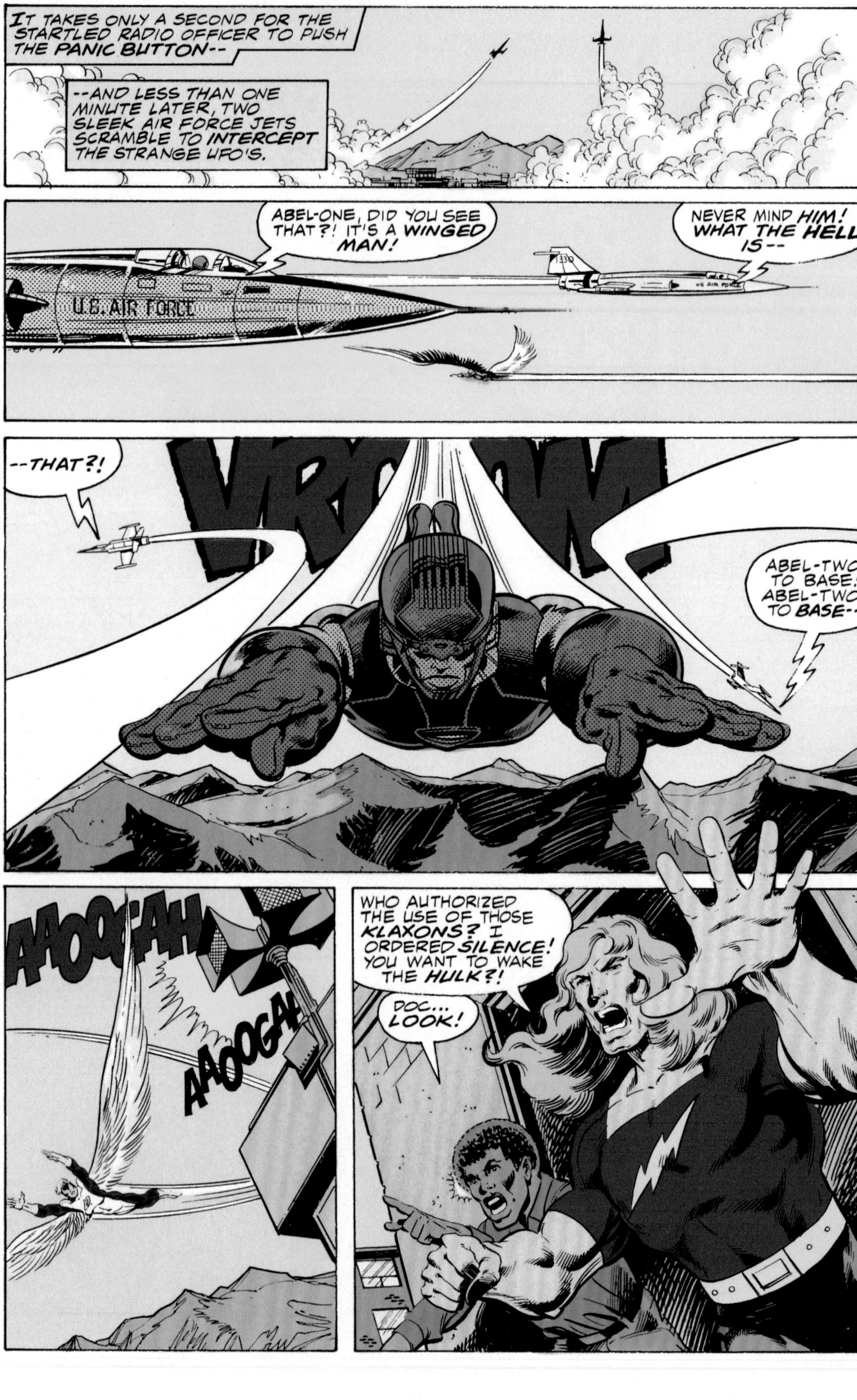
IT TAKES ONLY A SECOND FOR THE STARTLED RADIO OFFICER TO PUSH THE PANIC BUTTON--
--AND LESS THAN ONE MINUTE LATER, TWO SLEEK AIR FORCE JETS SCRAMBLE TO INTERCEPT THE STRANGE UFO'S.
ABEL-ONE, DID YOU SEE THAT?! IT'S A WINGED MAN!
NEVER MIND HIM! WHAT THE HELL IS--
U.S. AIR FORCE
--THAT?!
VROOOM
ABEL-TWO TO BASE! ABEL-TWO TO BASE--!
AAOOGAH
AAOOGAH
WHO AUTHORIZED THE USE OF THOSE KLAXONS? I ORDERED SILENCE! YOU WANT TO WAKE THE HULK?!
DOC... LOOK!

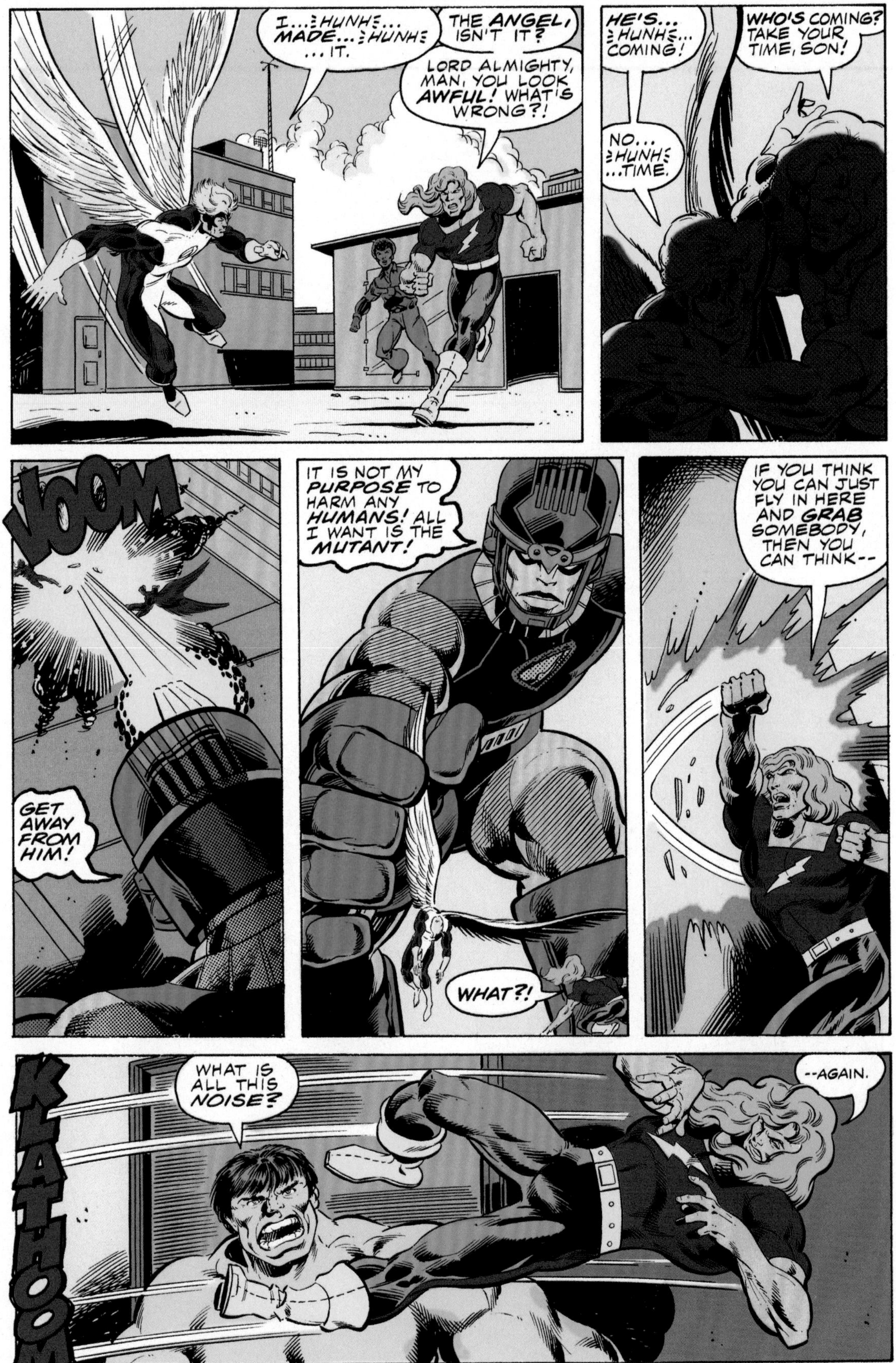
I...HUNH... MADE...HUNH ...IT.
THE ANGEL, ISN'T IT?
LORD ALMIGHTY, MAN, YOU LOOK AWFUL! WHAT'S WRONG?!
HE'S... HUNH... COMING!
WHO'S COMING? TAKE YOUR TIME, SON!
NO... HUNH ...TIME.
VOOM
GET AWAY FROM HIM!
IT IS NOT MY PURPOSE TO HARM ANY HUMANS! ALL I WANT IS THE MUTANT!
WHAT?!
IF YOU THINK YOU CAN JUST FLY IN HERE AND GRAB SOMEBODY, THEN YOU CAN THINK--
KLATHOOM
WHAT IS ALL THIS NOISE?
--AGAIN.

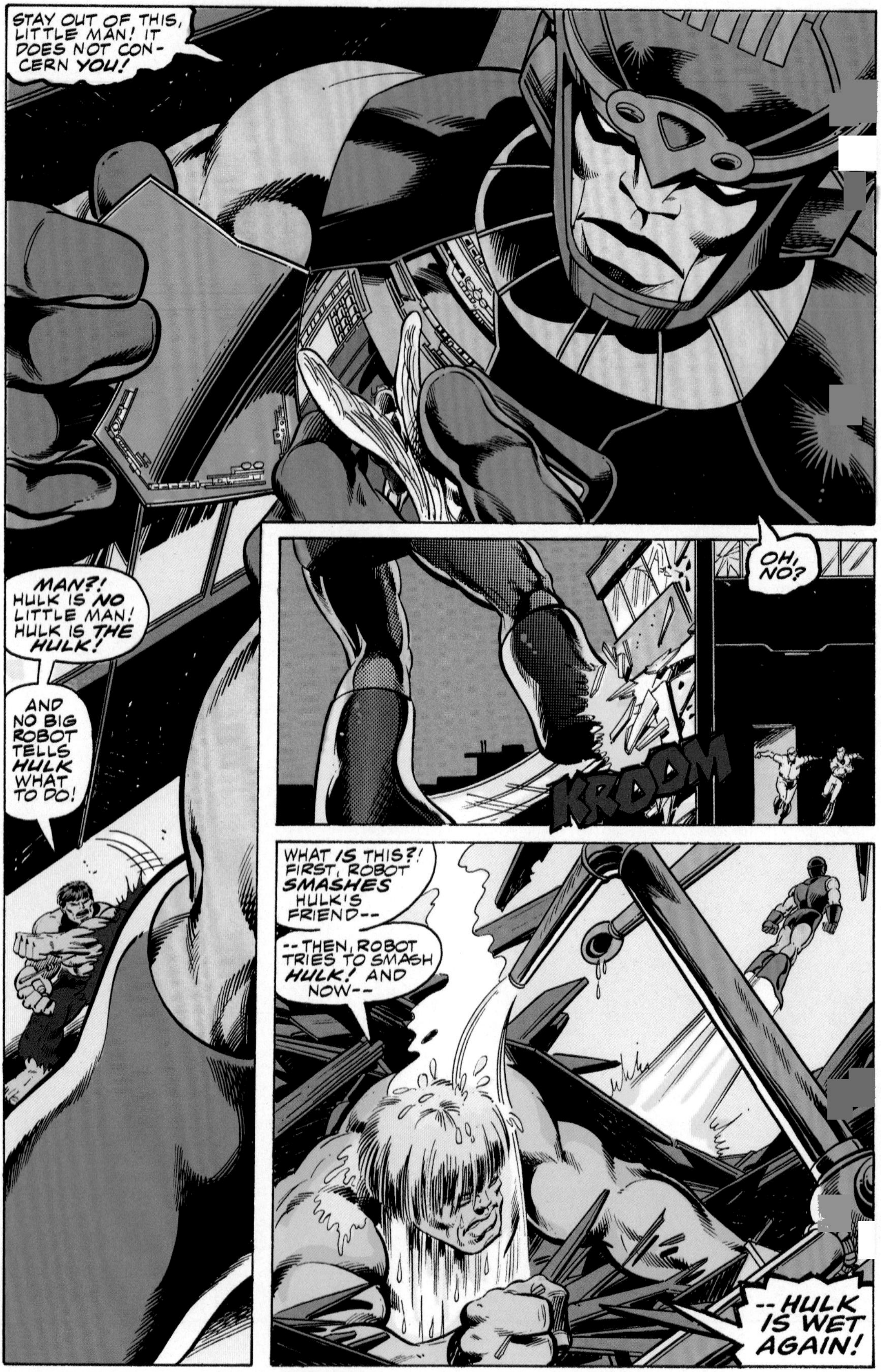
STAY OUT OF THIS, LITTLE MAN! IT DOES NOT CONCERN YOU!
MAN?! HULK IS NO LITTLE MAN! HULK IS THE HULK!
AND NO BIG ROBOT TELLS HULK WHAT TO DO!
OH, NO?
KROOM
WHAT IS THIS?! FIRST, ROBOT SMASHES HULK'S FRIEND--
--THEN, ROBOT TRIES TO SMASH HULK! AND NOW--
--HULK IS WET AGAIN!

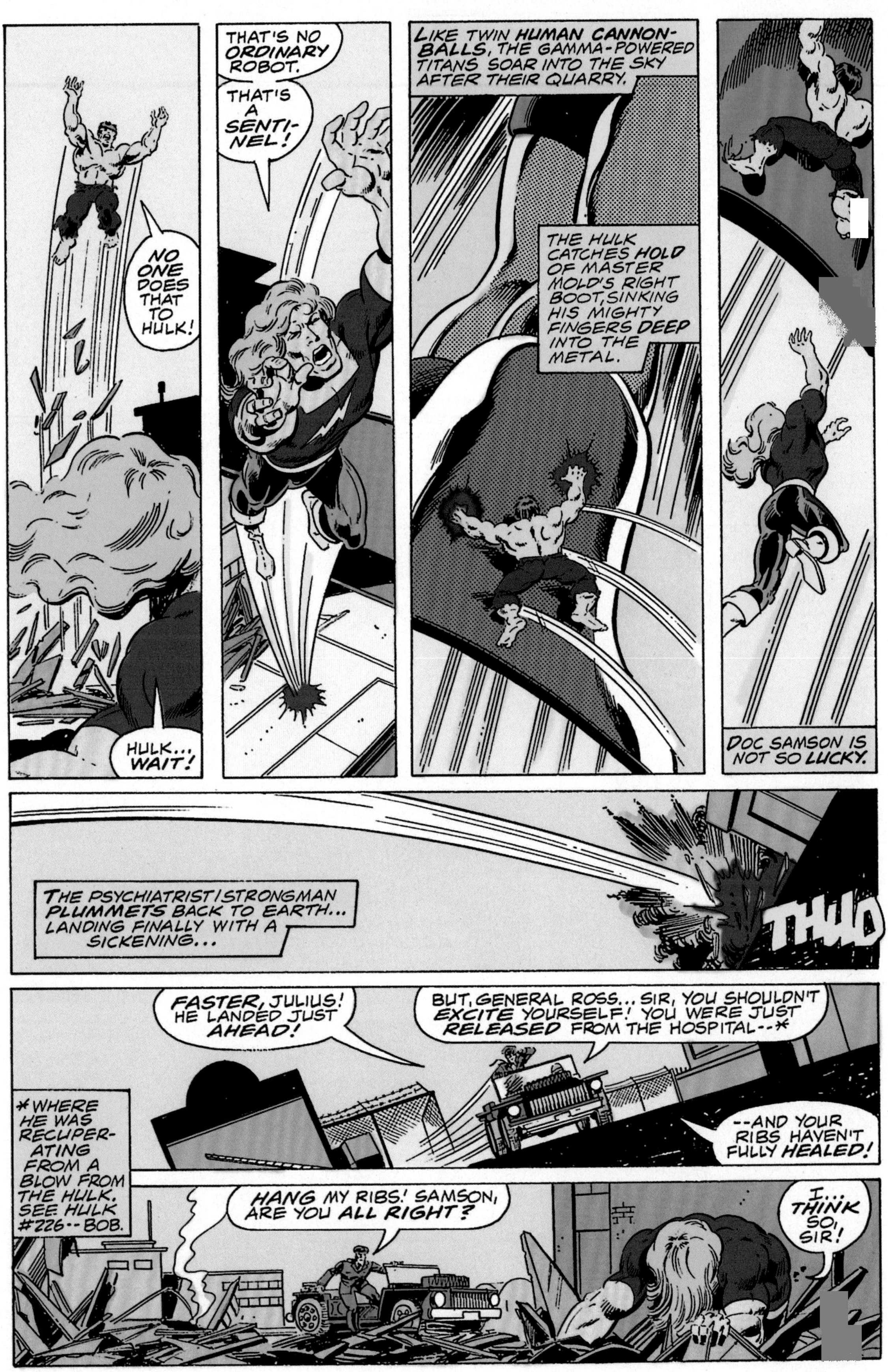
NO ONE DOES THAT TO HULK!
HULK... WAIT!
THAT'S NO ORDINARY ROBOT.
THAT'S A SENTI-NEL!
LIKE TWIN HUMAN CANNON-BALLS, THE GAMMA-POWERED TITANS SOAR INTO THE SKY AFTER THEIR QUARRY.
THE HULK CATCHES HOLD OF MASTER MOLD'S RIGHT BOOT, SINKING HIS MIGHTY FINGERS DEEP INTO THE METAL.
DOC SAMSON IS NOT SO LUCKY.
THE PSYCHIATRIST/STRONGMAN PLUMMETS BACK TO EARTH... LANDING FINALLY WITH A SICKENING...
THUD
FASTER, JULIUS! HE LANDED JUST AHEAD!
BUT, GENERAL ROSS... SIR, YOU SHOULDN'T EXCITE YOURSELF! YOU WERE JUST RELEASED FROM THE HOSPITAL--*
--AND YOUR RIBS HAVEN'T FULLY HEALED!
*WHERE HE WAS RECUPER-ATING FROM A BLOW FROM THE HULK. SEE HULK #226--BOB.
HANG MY RIBS! SAMSON, ARE YOU ALL RIGHT?
I... THINK SO, SIR!

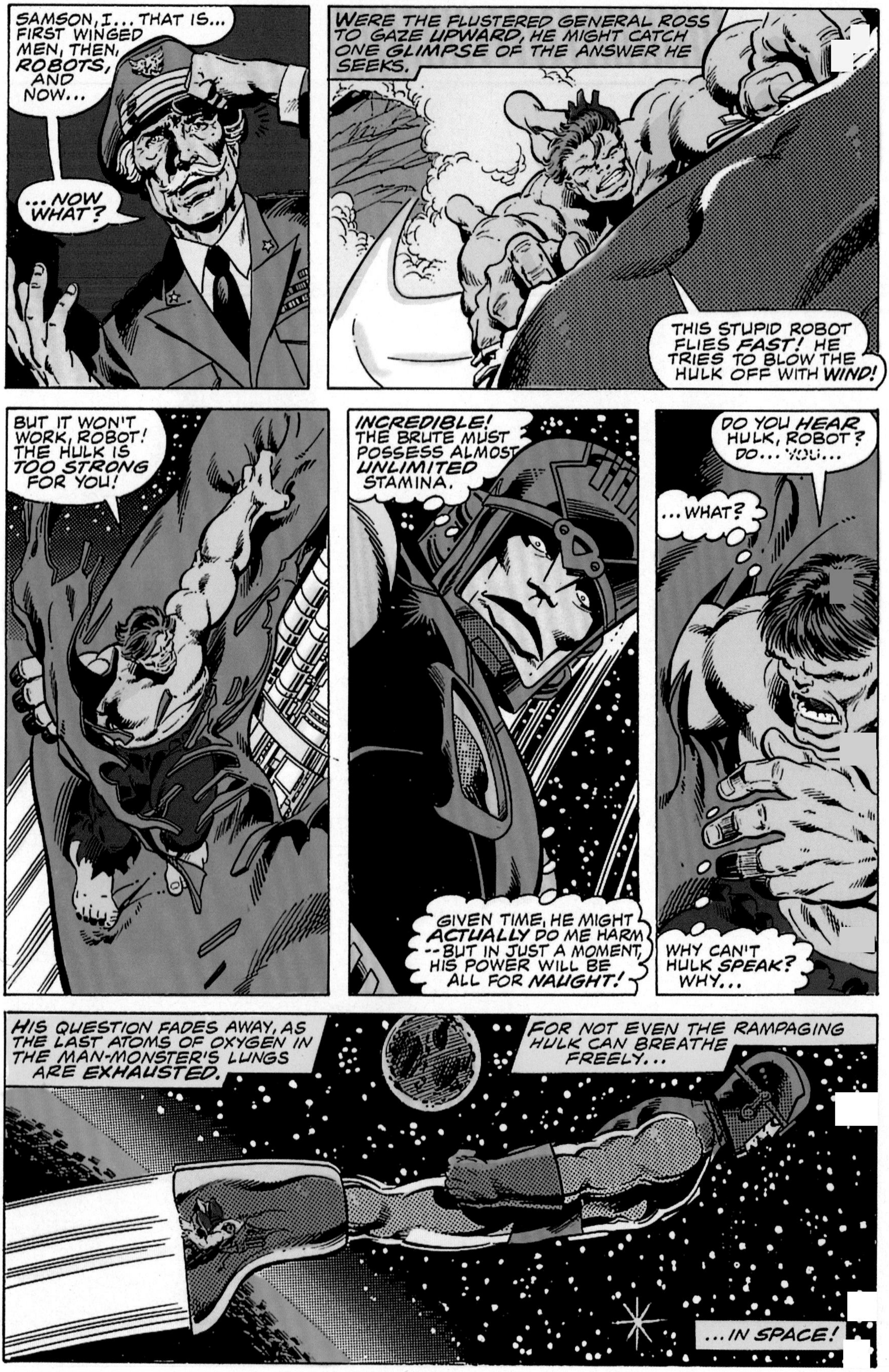

SAMSON, I... THAT IS... FIRST WINGED MEN, THEN, ROBOTS, AND NOW...
...NOW WHAT?
WERE THE FLUSTERED GENERAL ROSS TO GAZE UPWARD, HE MIGHT CATCH ONE GLIMPSE OF THE ANSWER HE SEEKS.
THIS STUPID ROBOT FLIES FAST! HE TRIES TO BLOW THE HULK OFF WITH WIND!
BUT IT WON'T WORK, ROBOT! THE HULK IS TOO STRONG FOR YOU!
INCREDIBLE! THE BRUTE MUST POSSESS ALMOST UNLIMITED STAMINA.
GIVEN TIME, HE MIGHT ACTUALLY DO ME HARM --BUT IN JUST A MOMENT, HIS POWER WILL BE ALL FOR NAUGHT!
DO YOU HEAR HULK, ROBOT? DO... YOU...
...WHAT?
WHY CAN'T HULK SPEAK? WHY...
HIS QUESTION FADES AWAY, AS THE LAST ATOMS OF OXYGEN IN THE MAN-MONSTER'S LUNGS ARE EXHAUSTED.
FOR NOT EVEN THE RAMPAGING HULK CAN BREATHE FREELY...
...IN SPACE!

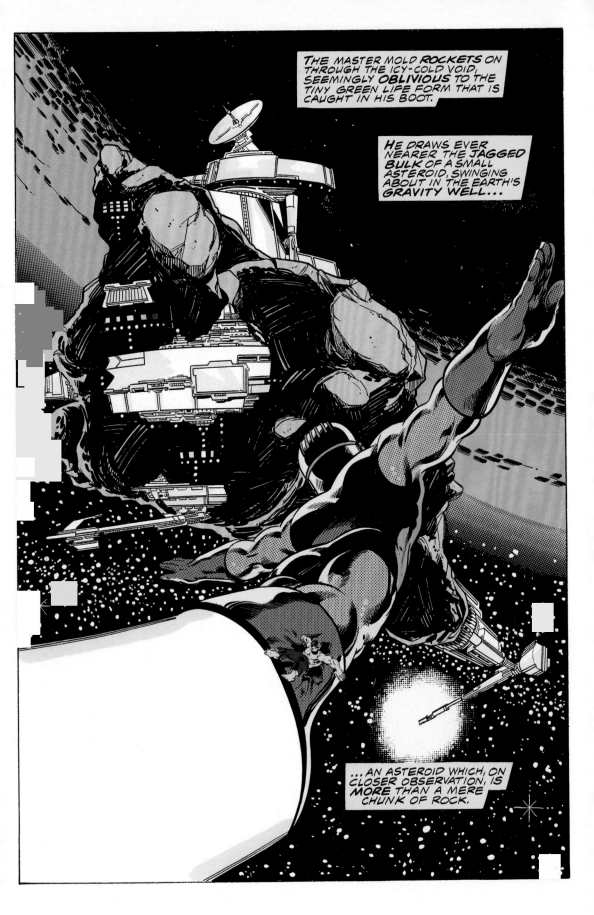

THE MASTER MOLD *ROCKETS* ON THROUGH THE ICY-COLD VOID, SEEMINGLY *OBLIVIOUS* TO THE TINY GREEN LIFE FORM THAT IS CAUGHT IN HIS BOOT.

HE DRAWS EVER NEARER THE JAGGED *BULK* OF A SMALL ASTEROID, SWINGING ABOUT IN THE EARTH'S *GRAVITY WELL...*

...AN ASTEROID WHICH, ON CLOSER OBSERVATION, IS MORE THAN A MERE CHUNK OF ROCK.

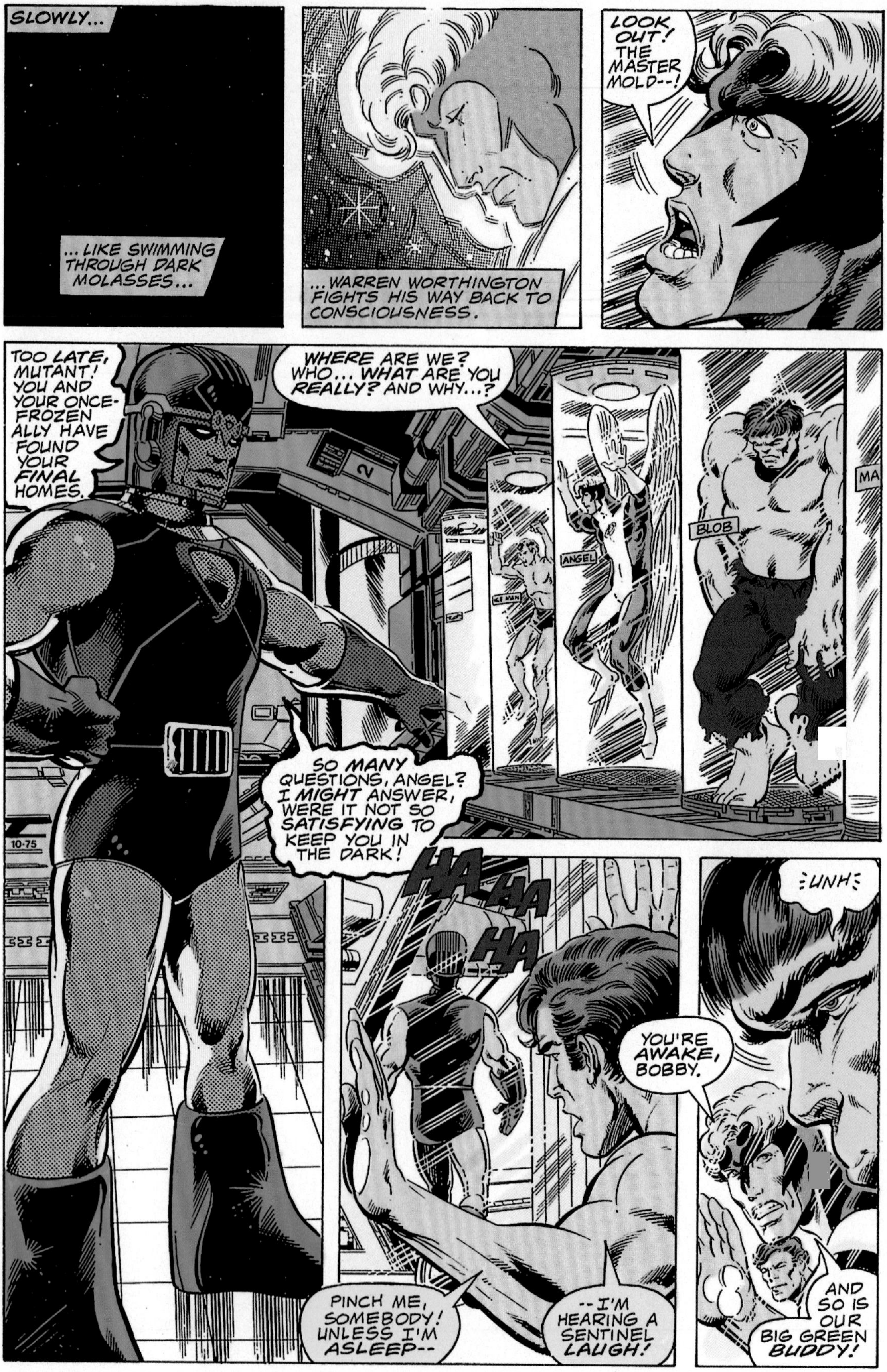
SLOWLY...
...LIKE SWIMMING THROUGH DARK MOLASSES...
...WARREN WORTHINGTON FIGHTS HIS WAY BACK TO CONSCIOUSNESS.
LOOK OUT! THE MASTER MOLD--!
TOO LATE, MUTANT! YOU AND YOUR ONCE-FROZEN ALLY HAVE FOUND YOUR FINAL HOMES.
WHERE ARE WE? WHO... WHAT ARE YOU REALLY? AND WHY...?
ICE MAN
ANGEL
BLOB
SO MANY QUESTIONS, ANGEL? I MIGHT ANSWER, WERE IT NOT SO SATISFYING TO KEEP YOU IN THE DARK!
HA HA HA
UNH
YOU'RE AWAKE, BOBBY.
AND SO IS OUR BIG GREEN BUDDY!
PINCH ME, SOMEBODY! UNLESS I'M ASLEEP--
--I'M HEARING A SENTINEL LAUGH!

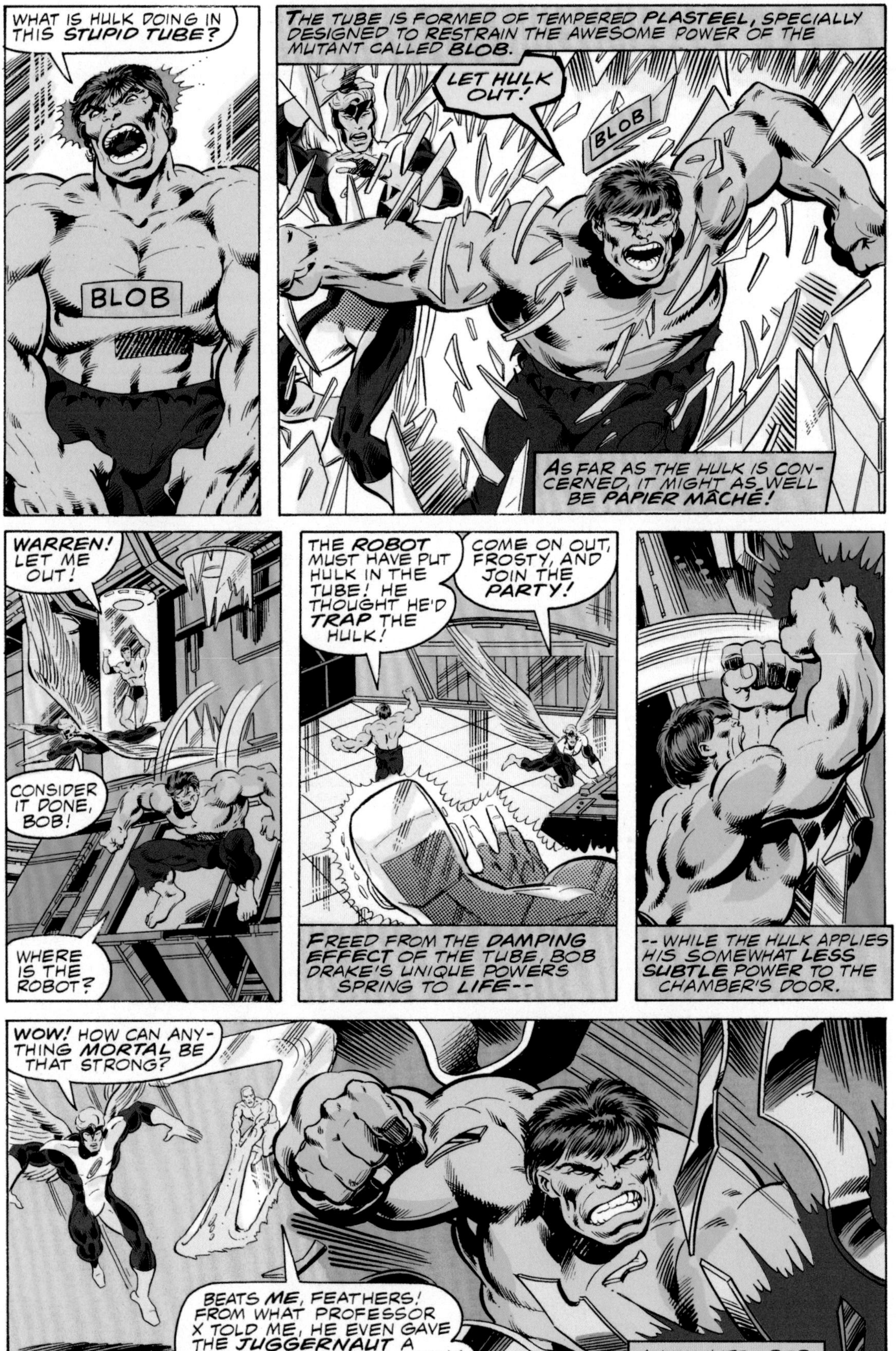
WHAT IS HULK DOING IN THIS STUPID TUBE?
BLOB
THE TUBE IS FORMED OF TEMPERED PLASTEEL, SPECIALLY DESIGNED TO RESTRAIN THE AWESOME POWER OF THE MUTANT CALLED BLOB.
LET HULK OUT!
BLOB
AS FAR AS THE HULK IS CONCERNED, IT MIGHT AS WELL BE PAPIER MÂCHÉ!
WARREN! LET ME OUT!
CONSIDER IT DONE, BOB!
WHERE IS THE ROBOT?
THE ROBOT MUST HAVE PUT HULK IN THE TUBE! HE THOUGHT HE'D TRAP THE HULK!
COME ON OUT, FROSTY, AND JOIN THE PARTY!
FREED FROM THE DAMPING EFFECT OF THE TUBE, BOB DRAKE'S UNIQUE POWERS SPRING TO LIFE--
-- WHILE THE HULK APPLIES HIS SOMEWHAT LESS SUBTLE POWER TO THE CHAMBER'S DOOR.
WOW! HOW CAN ANYTHING MORTAL BE THAT STRONG?
BEATS ME, FEATHERS! FROM WHAT PROFESSOR X TOLD ME, HE EVEN GAVE THE JUGGERNAUT A RUN FOR HIS MONEY ONCE!*
*HULK #172--BOB.

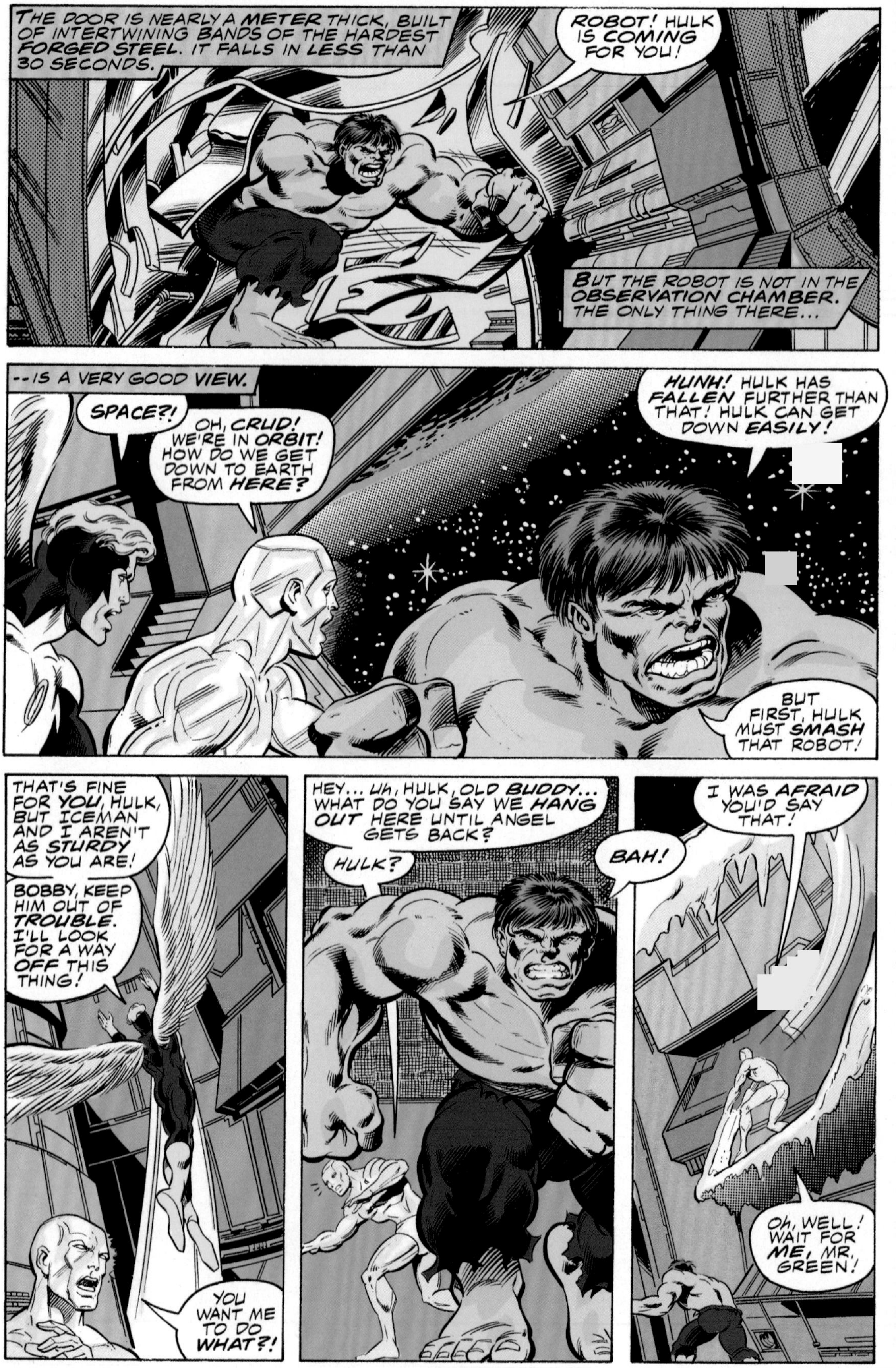
THE DOOR IS NEARLY A METER THICK, BUILT OF INTERTWINING BANDS OF THE HARDEST FORGED STEEL. IT FALLS IN LESS THAN 30 SECONDS.
ROBOT! HULK IS COMING FOR YOU!
BUT THE ROBOT IS NOT IN THE OBSERVATION CHAMBER. THE ONLY THING THERE...
--IS A VERY GOOD VIEW.
SPACE?!
OH, CRUD! WE'RE IN ORBIT! HOW DO WE GET DOWN TO EARTH FROM HERE?
HUNH! HULK HAS FALLEN FURTHER THAN THAT! HULK CAN GET DOWN EASILY!
BUT FIRST, HULK MUST SMASH THAT ROBOT!
THAT'S FINE FOR YOU, HULK, BUT ICEMAN AND I AREN'T AS STURDY AS YOU ARE!
BOBBY, KEEP HIM OUT OF TROUBLE. I'LL LOOK FOR A WAY OFF THIS THING!
YOU WANT ME TO DO WHAT?!
HEY... UH, HULK, OLD BUDDY... WHAT DO YOU SAY WE HANG OUT HERE UNTIL ANGEL GETS BACK?
HULK?
BAH!
I WAS AFRAID YOU'D SAY THAT!
OH, WELL! WAIT FOR ME, MR. GREEN!

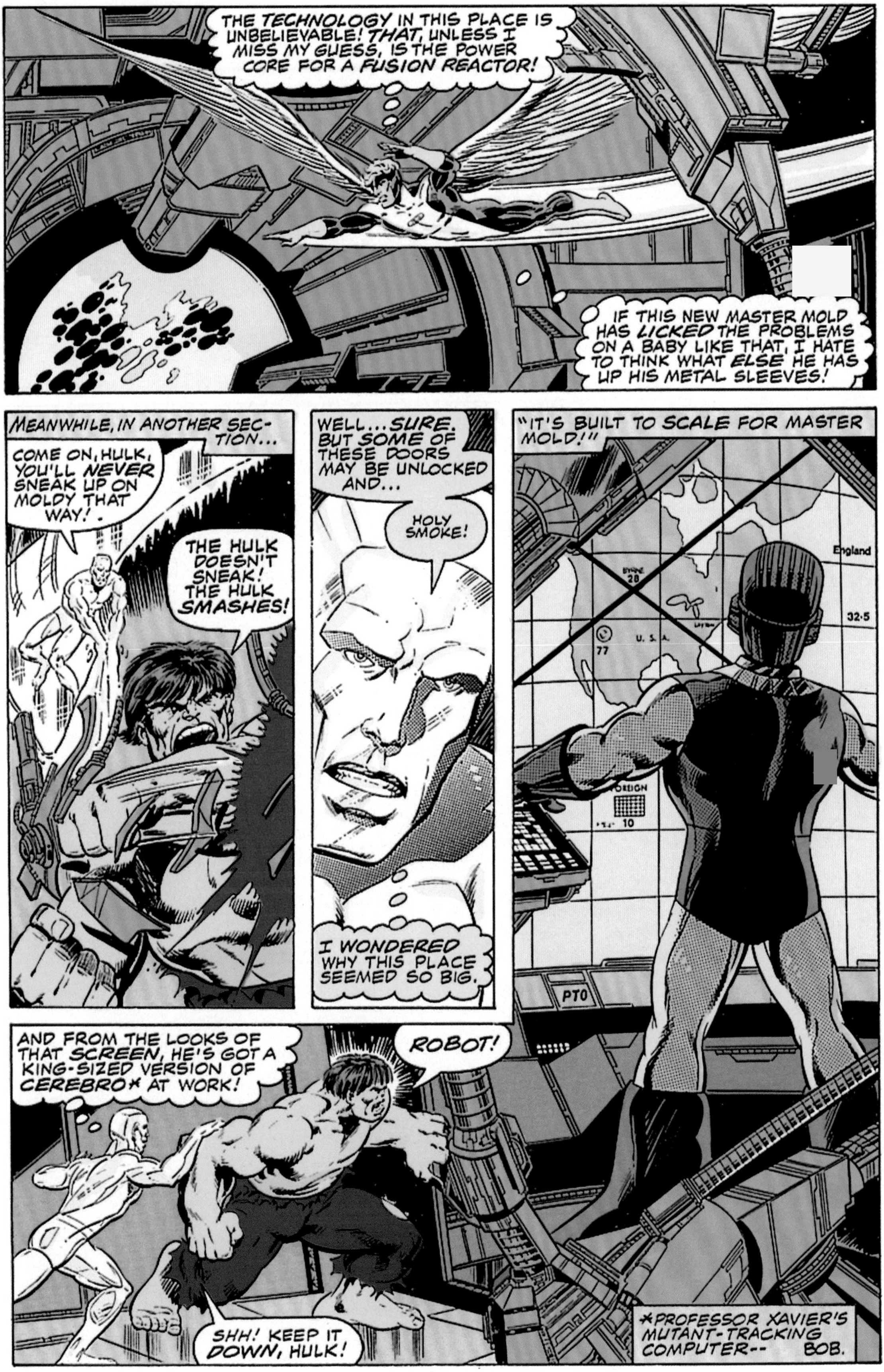
THE TECHNOLOGY IN THIS PLACE IS UNBELIEVABLE! THAT, UNLESS I MISS MY GUESS, IS THE POWER CORE FOR A FUSION REACTOR!
IF THIS NEW MASTER MOLD HAS LICKED THE PROBLEMS ON A BABY LIKE THAT, I HATE TO THINK WHAT ELSE HE HAS UP HIS METAL SLEEVES!
MEANWHILE, IN ANOTHER SECTION...
COME ON, HULK, YOU'LL NEVER SNEAK UP ON MOLDY THAT WAY!
THE HULK DOESN'T SNEAK! THE HULK SMASHES!
WELL... SURE. BUT SOME OF THESE DOORS MAY BE UNLOCKED AND...
HOLY SMOKE!
I WONDERED WHY THIS PLACE SEEMED SO BIG.
"IT'S BUILT TO SCALE FOR MASTER MOLD!"
AND FROM THE LOOKS OF THAT SCREEN, HE'S GOT A KING-SIZED VERSION OF CEREBRO* AT WORK!
ROBOT!
SHH! KEEP IT DOWN, HULK!
*PROFESSOR XAVIER'S MUTANT-TRACKING COMPUTER-- BOB.

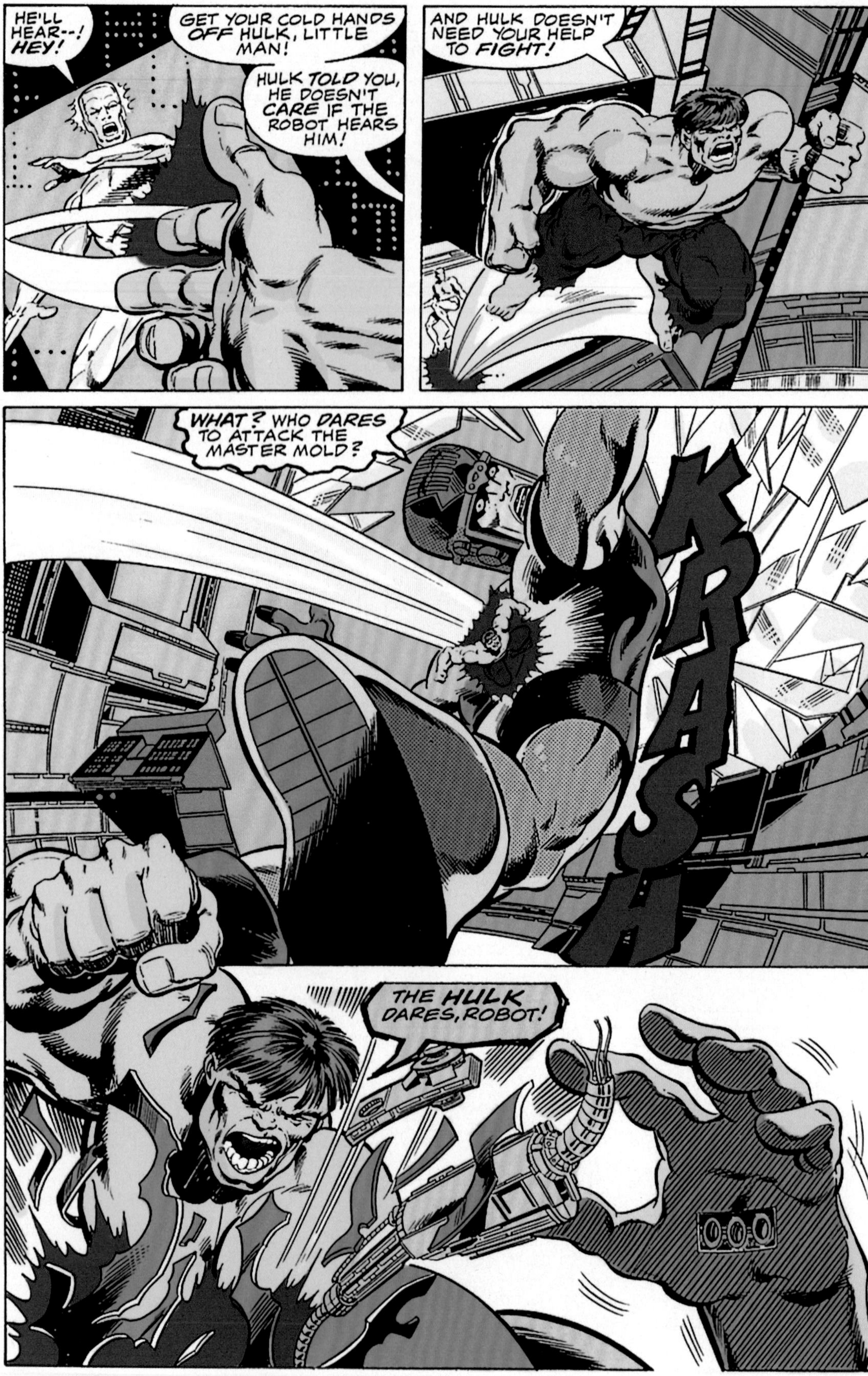
HE'LL HEAR--! HEY!
GET YOUR COLD HANDS OFF HULK, LITTLE MAN!
HULK TOLD YOU, HE DOESN'T CARE IF THE ROBOT HEARS HIM!
AND HULK DOESN'T NEED YOUR HELP TO FIGHT!
WHAT? WHO DARES TO ATTACK THE MASTER MOLD?
KRASH
THE HULK DARES, ROBOT!

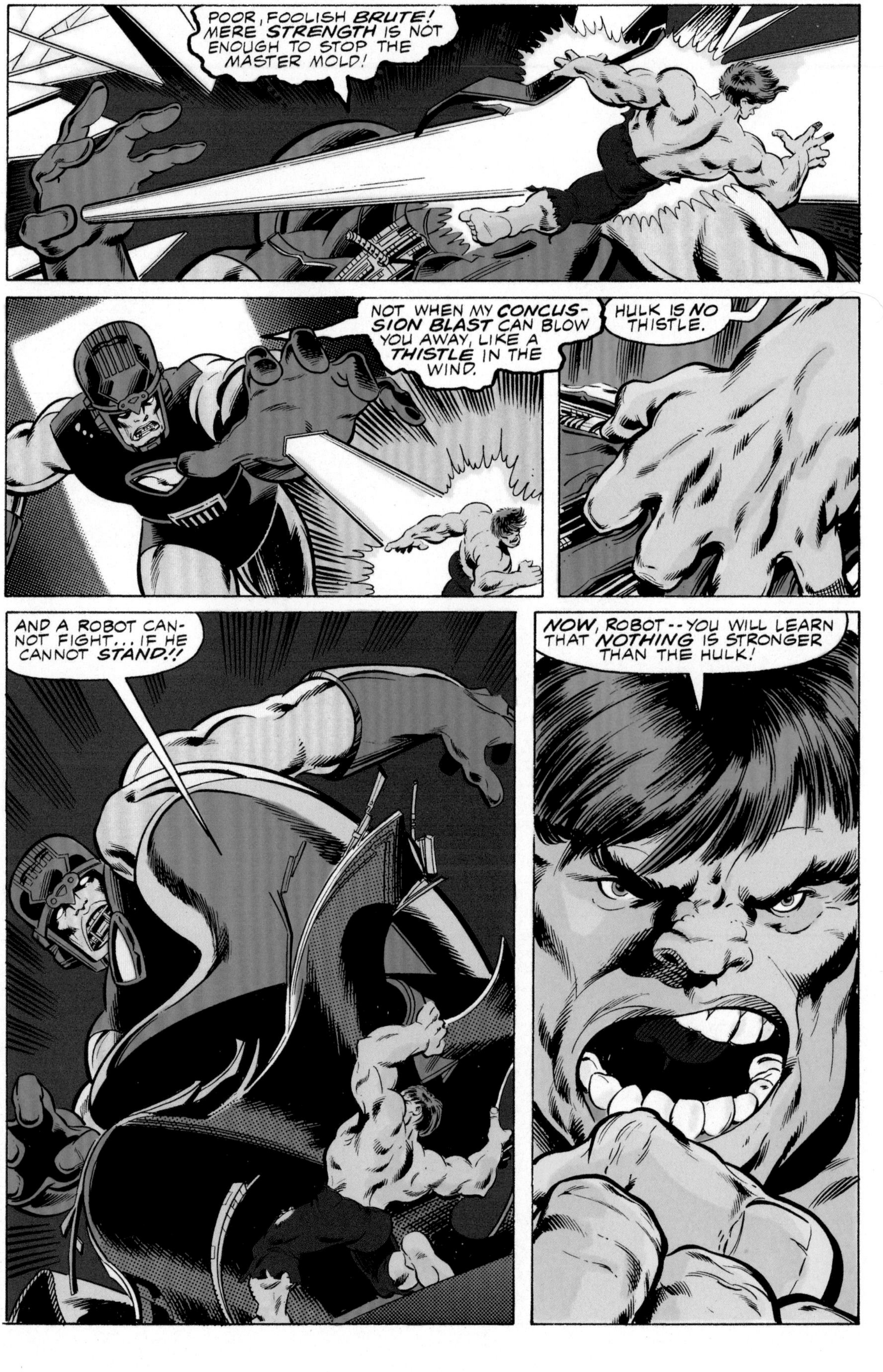
POOR, FOOLISH BRUTE! MERE STRENGTH IS NOT ENOUGH TO STOP THE MASTER MOLD!
NOT WHEN MY CONCUSSION BLAST CAN BLOW YOU AWAY, LIKE A THISTLE IN THE WIND.
HULK IS NO THISTLE.
AND A ROBOT CANNOT FIGHT... IF HE CANNOT STAND!!
NOW, ROBOT--YOU WILL LEARN THAT NOTHING IS STRONGER THAN THE HULK!

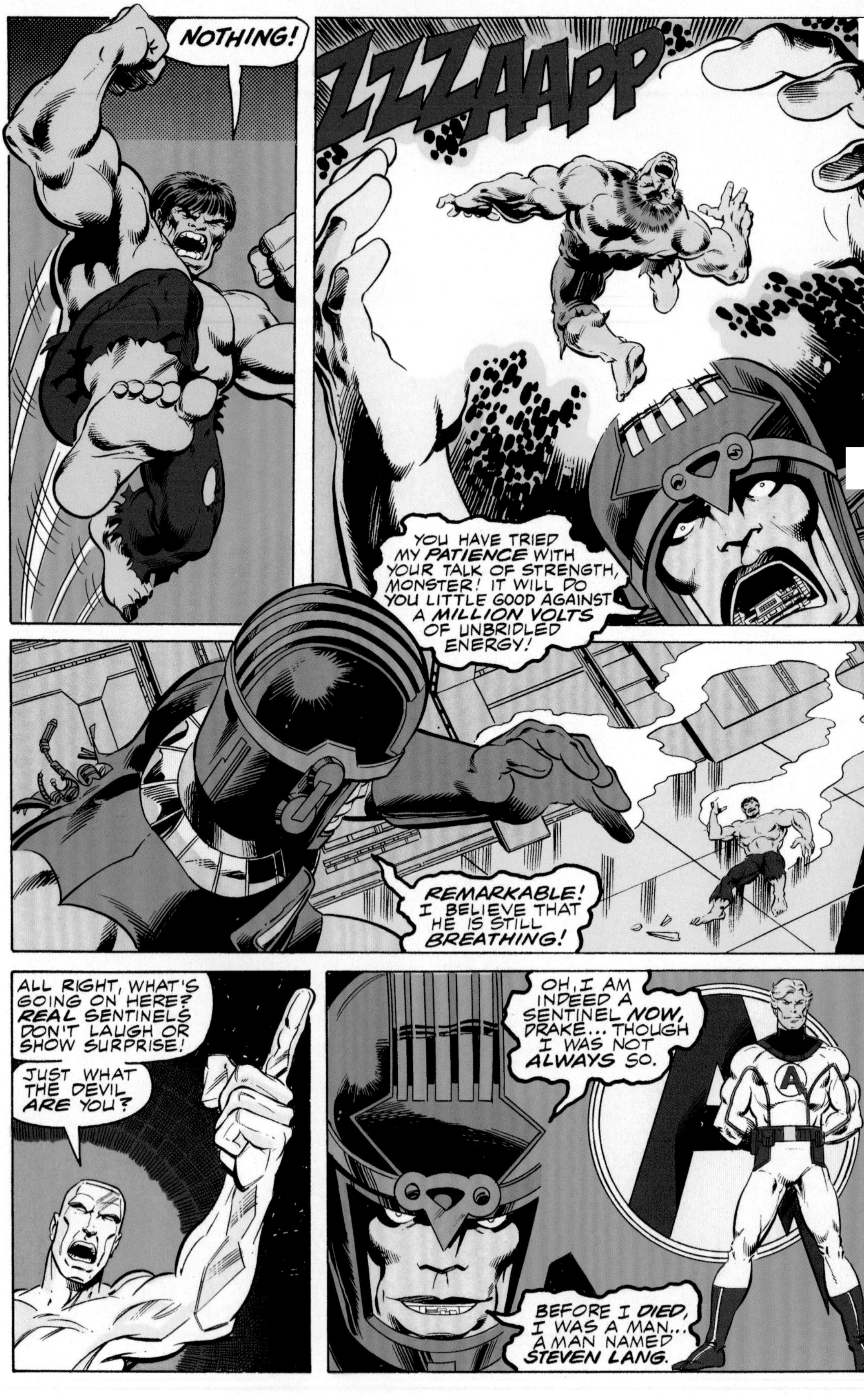
NOTHING!
ZZZAAPP
YOU HAVE TRIED MY PATIENCE WITH YOUR TALK OF STRENGTH, MONSTER! IT WILL DO YOU LITTLE GOOD AGAINST A MILLION VOLTS OF UNBRIDLED ENERGY!
REMARKABLE! I BELIEVE THAT HE IS STILL BREATHING!
ALL RIGHT, WHAT'S GOING ON HERE? REAL SENTINELS DON'T LAUGH OR SHOW SURPRISE!
JUST WHAT THE DEVIL ARE YOU?
OH, I AM INDEED A SENTINEL NOW, DRAKE... THOUGH I WAS NOT ALWAYS SO.
A
BEFORE I DIED, I WAS A MAN... A MAN NAMED STEVEN LANG.

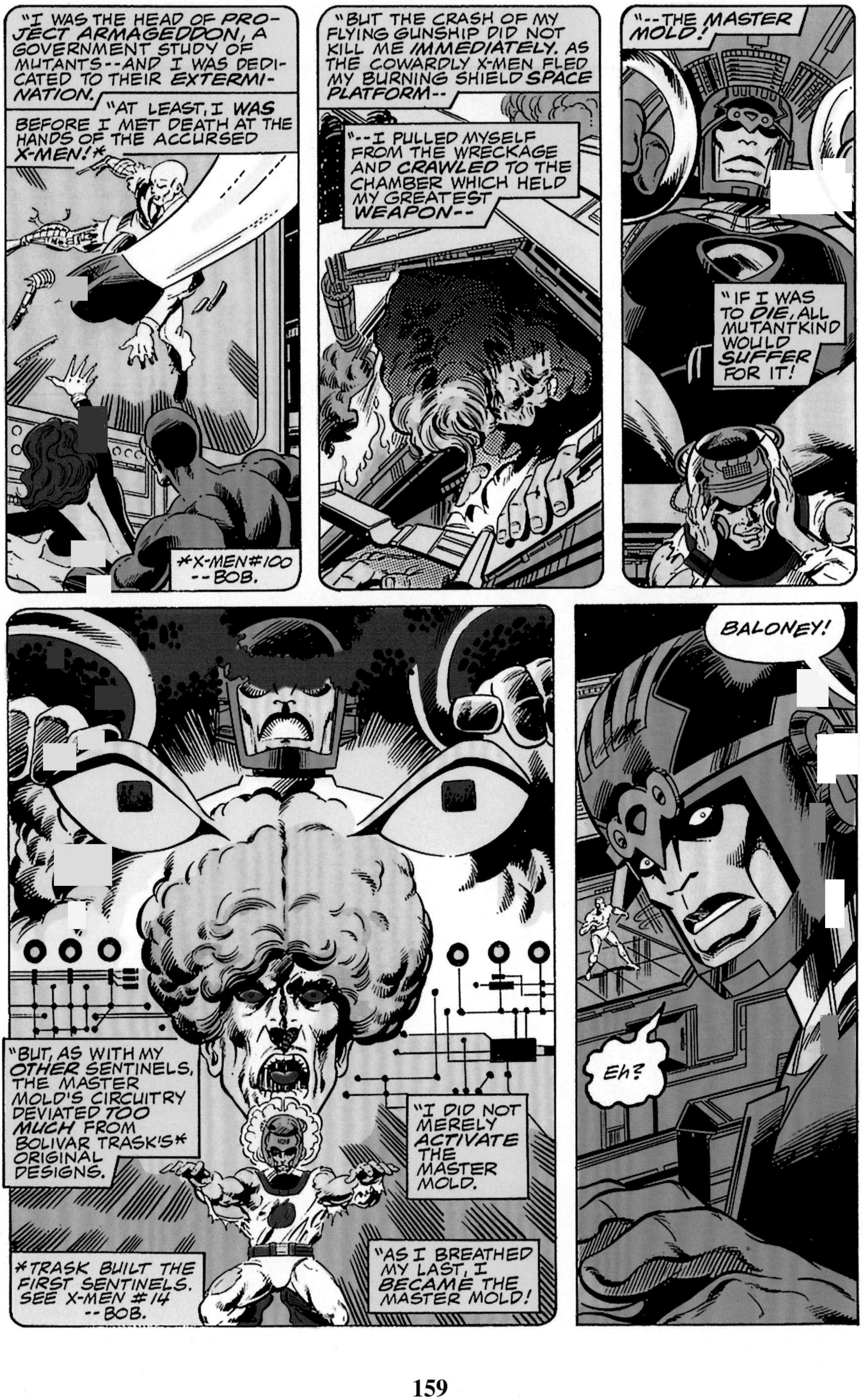
"I WAS THE HEAD OF PROJECT ARMAGEDDON, A GOVERNMENT STUDY OF MUTANTS--AND I WAS DEDICATED TO THEIR EXTERMINATION.
"AT LEAST, I WAS BEFORE I MET DEATH AT THE HANDS OF THE ACCURSED X-MEN!*
*X-MEN #100 --BOB.
"BUT THE CRASH OF MY FLYING GUNSHIP DID NOT KILL ME IMMEDIATELY. AS THE COWARDLY X-MEN FLED MY BURNING SHIELD SPACE PLATFORM--
"--I PULLED MYSELF FROM THE WRECKAGE AND CRAWLED TO THE CHAMBER WHICH HELD MY GREATEST WEAPON--
"--THE MASTER MOLD!
"IF I WAS TO DIE, ALL MUTANTKIND WOULD SUFFER FOR IT!
"BUT, AS WITH MY OTHER SENTINELS, THE MASTER MOLD'S CIRCUITRY DEVIATED TOO MUCH FROM BOLIVAR TRASK'S* ORIGINAL DESIGNS.
"I DID NOT MERELY ACTIVATE THE MASTER MOLD.
"AS I BREATHED MY LAST, I BECAME THE MASTER MOLD!
*TRASK BUILT THE FIRST SENTINELS. SEE X-MEN #14 --BOB.
BALONEY!
Eh?

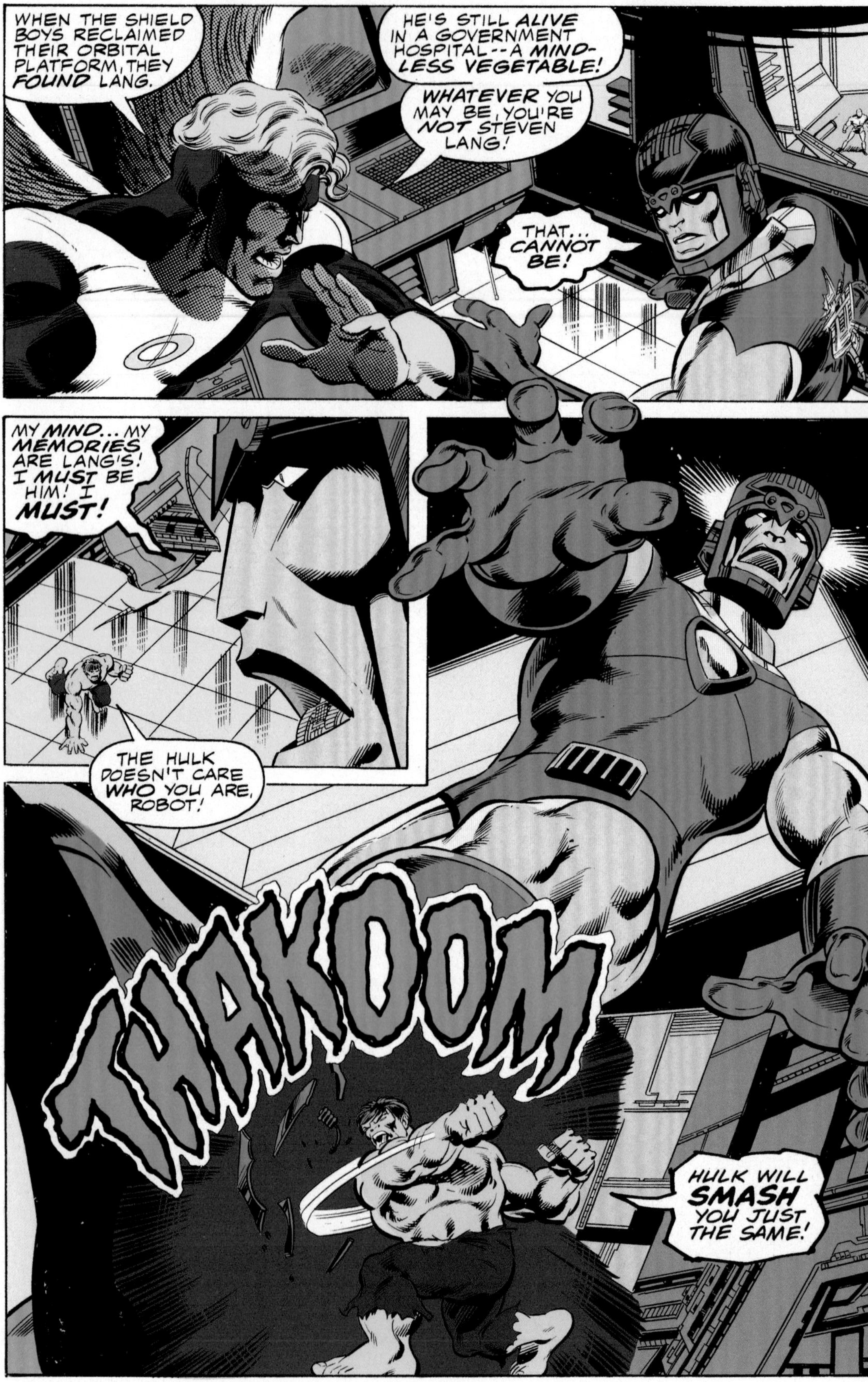
WHEN THE SHIELD BOYS RECLAIMED THEIR ORBITAL PLATFORM, THEY FOUND LANG.
HE'S STILL ALIVE IN A GOVERNMENT HOSPITAL--A MINDLESS VEGETABLE!
WHATEVER YOU MAY BE, YOU'RE NOT STEVEN LANG!
THAT... CANNOT BE!
MY MIND... MY MEMORIES ARE LANG'S! I MUST BE HIM! I MUST!
THE HULK DOESN'T CARE WHO YOU ARE, ROBOT!
THAKOOM
HULK WILL SMASH YOU JUST THE SAME!

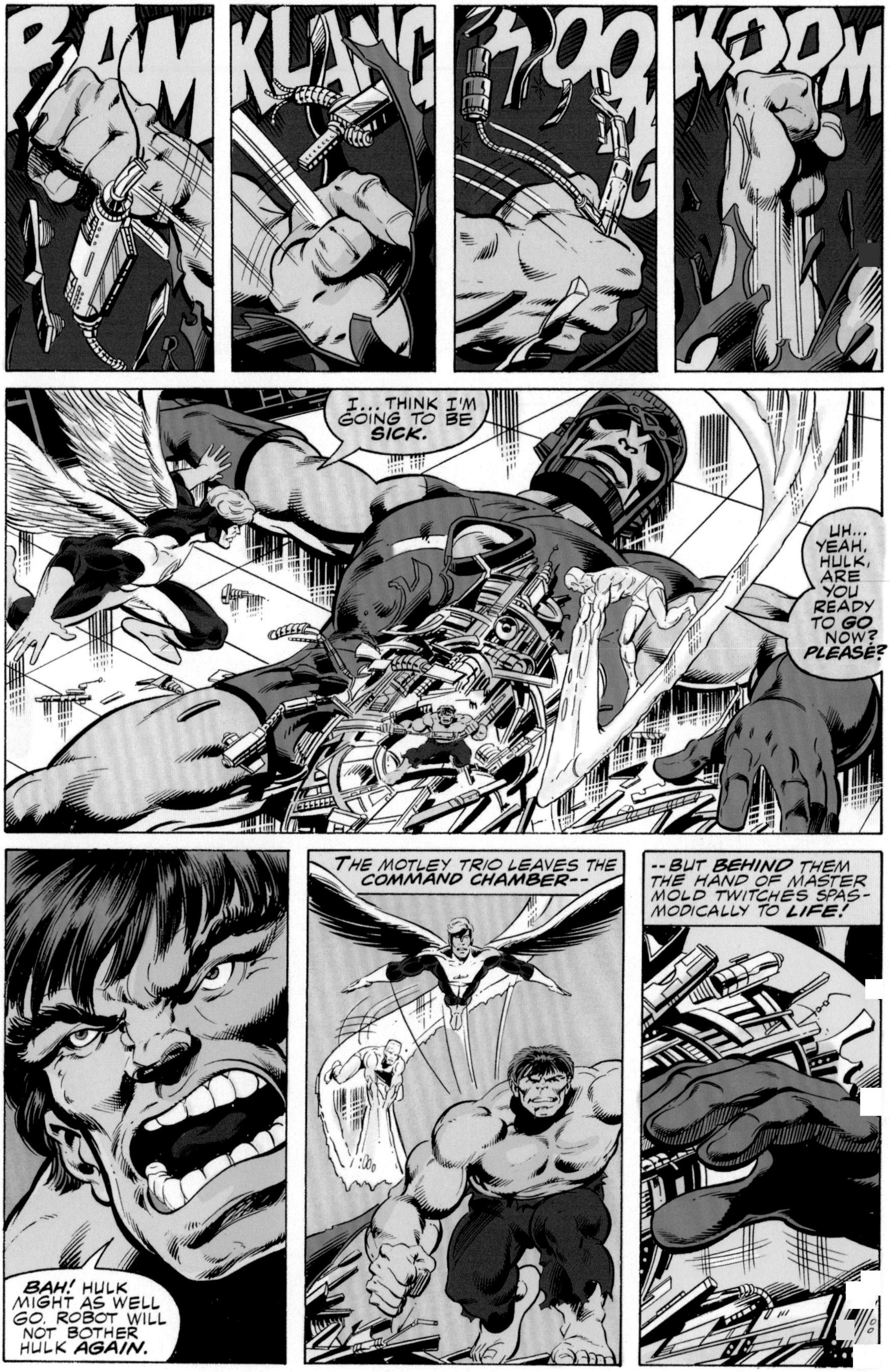
BAM
KLANG
KROOOOM
KOOM
I... THINK I'M GOING TO BE SICK.
UH... YEAH, HULK, ARE YOU READY TO GO NOW? PLEASE?
BAH! HULK MIGHT AS WELL GO. ROBOT WILL NOT BOTHER HULK AGAIN.
THE MOTLEY TRIO LEAVES THE COMMAND CHAMBER--
--BUT BEHIND THEM THE HAND OF MASTER MOLD TWITCHES SPASMODICALLY TO LIFE!

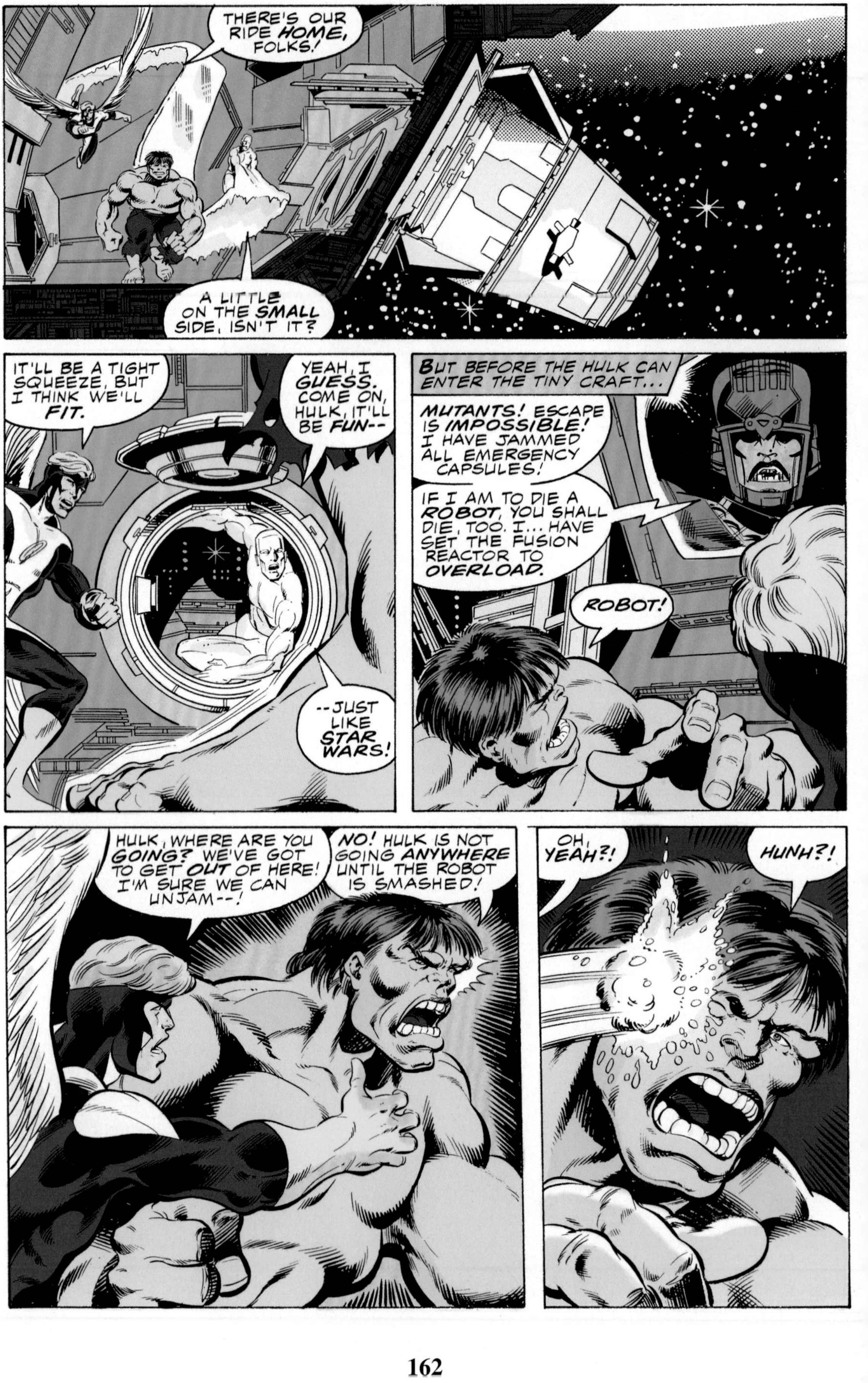
THERE'S OUR RIDE HOME, FOLKS!
A LITTLE ON THE SMALL SIDE, ISN'T IT?
IT'LL BE A TIGHT SQUEEZE, BUT I THINK WE'LL FIT.
YEAH, I GUESS. COME ON, HULK, IT'LL BE FUN--
--JUST LIKE STAR WARS!
BUT BEFORE THE HULK CAN ENTER THE TINY CRAFT...
MUTANTS! ESCAPE IS IMPOSSIBLE! I HAVE JAMMED ALL EMERGENCY CAPSULES!
IF I AM TO DIE A ROBOT, YOU SHALL DIE, TOO. I... HAVE SET THE FUSION REACTOR TO OVERLOAD.
ROBOT!
HULK, WHERE ARE YOU GOING? WE'VE GOT TO GET OUT OF HERE! I'M SURE WE CAN UNJAM--!
NO! HULK IS NOT GOING ANYWHERE UNTIL THE ROBOT IS SMASHED!
OH, YEAH?!
HUNH?!

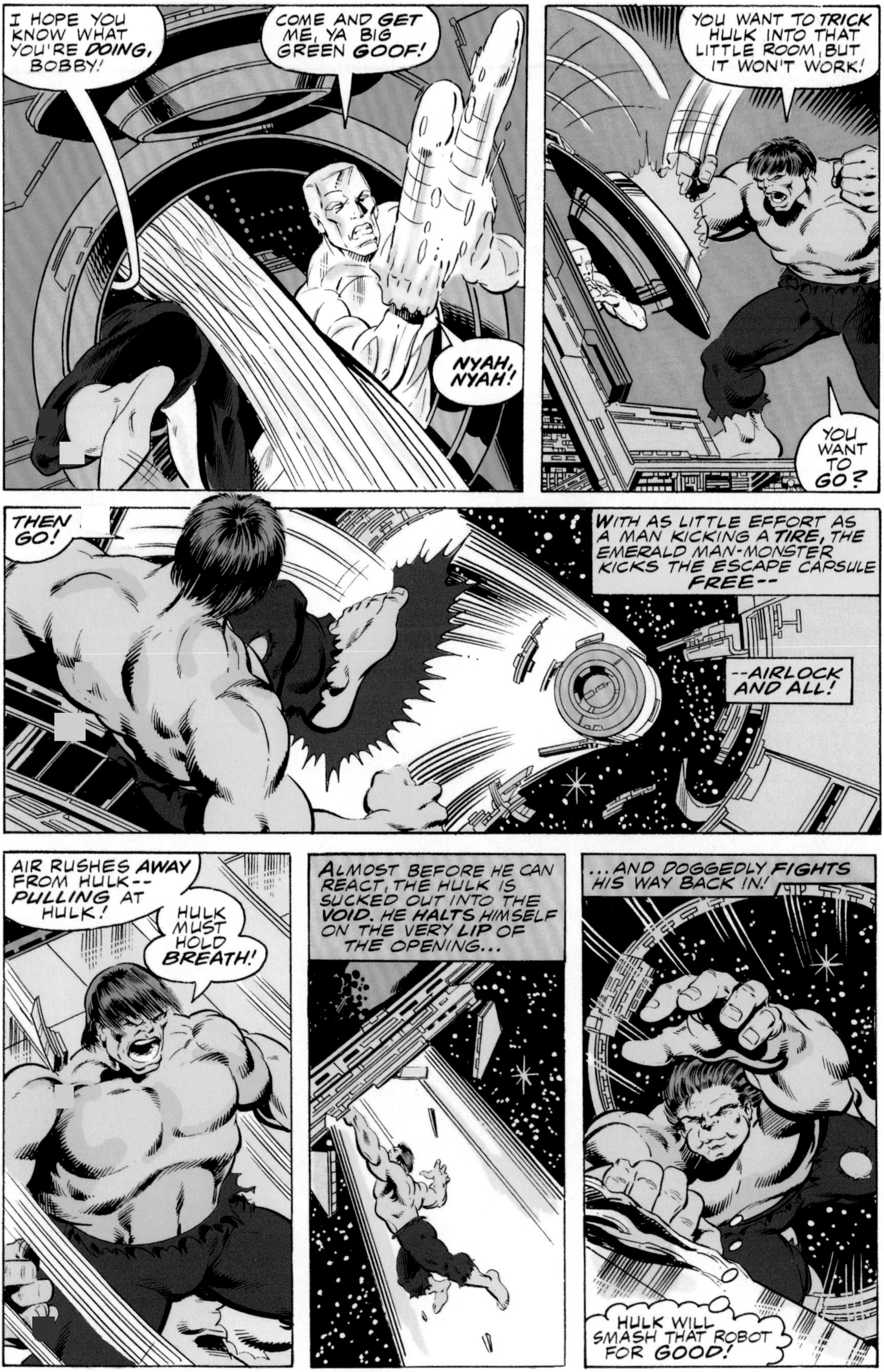
I HOPE YOU KNOW WHAT YOU'RE DOING, BOBBY!
COME AND GET ME, YA BIG GREEN GOOF!
NYAH, NYAH!
YOU WANT TO TRICK HULK INTO THAT LITTLE ROOM, BUT IT WON'T WORK!
YOU WANT TO GO?
THEN GO!
WITH AS LITTLE EFFORT AS A MAN KICKING A TIRE, THE EMERALD MAN-MONSTER KICKS THE ESCAPE CAPSULE FREE--
--AIRLOCK AND ALL!
AIR RUSHES AWAY FROM HULK-- PULLING AT HULK!
HULK MUST HOLD BREATH!
ALMOST BEFORE HE CAN REACT, THE HULK IS SUCKED OUT INTO THE VOID. HE HALTS HIMSELF ON THE VERY LIP OF THE OPENING...
...AND DOGGEDLY FIGHTS HIS WAY BACK IN!
HULK WILL SMASH THAT ROBOT FOR GOOD!

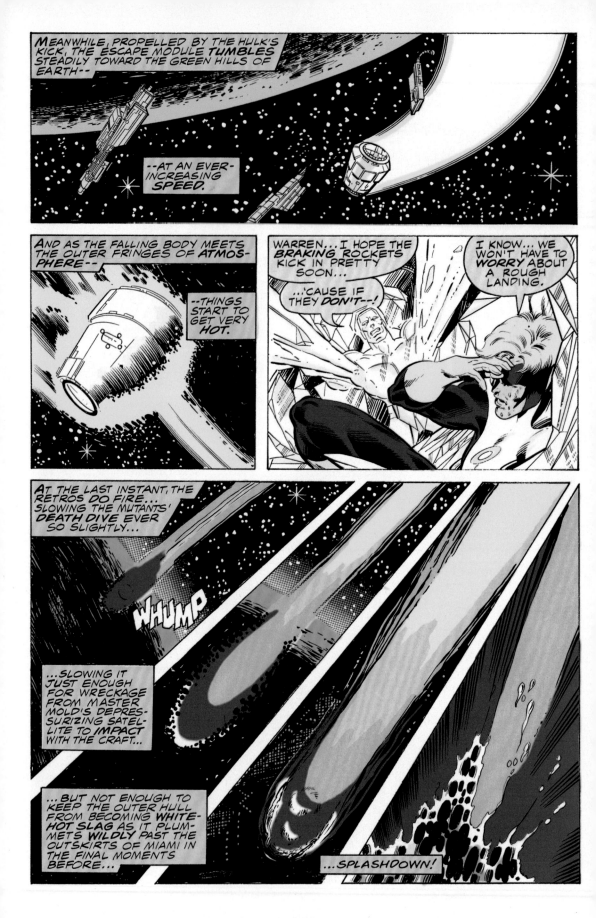

MEANWHILE, PROPELLED BY THE HULK'S KICK, THE ESCAPE MODULE *TUMBLES* STEADILY TOWARD THE GREEN HILLS OF EARTH--

--AT AN EVER-INCREASING *SPEED.*

AND AS THE FALLING BODY MEETS THE OUTER FRINGES OF *ATMOS-PHERE--*

--THINGS START TO GET VERY *HOT.*

WARREN... I HOPE THE *BRAKING* ROCKETS KICK IN PRETTY SOON...

...'CAUSE IF THEY *DON'T--!*

I KNOW... WE WON'T HAVE TO *WORRY* ABOUT A ROUGH LANDING.

AT THE LAST INSTANT, THE RETROS *DO* FIRE... SLOWING THE MUTANTS' *DEATH DIVE* EVER SO SLIGHTLY...

WHUMP

...SLOWING IT JUST ENOUGH FOR WRECKAGE FROM MASTER MOLD'S DEPRES-SURIZING SATEL-LITE TO *IMPACT* WITH THE CRAFT...

...BUT NOT ENOUGH TO KEEP THE OUTER HULL FROM BECOMING *WHITE-HOT SLAG* AS IT PLUM-METS *WILDLY* PAST THE OUTSKIRTS OF MIAMI IN THE FINAL MOMENTS BEFORE...

...SPLASHDOWN!

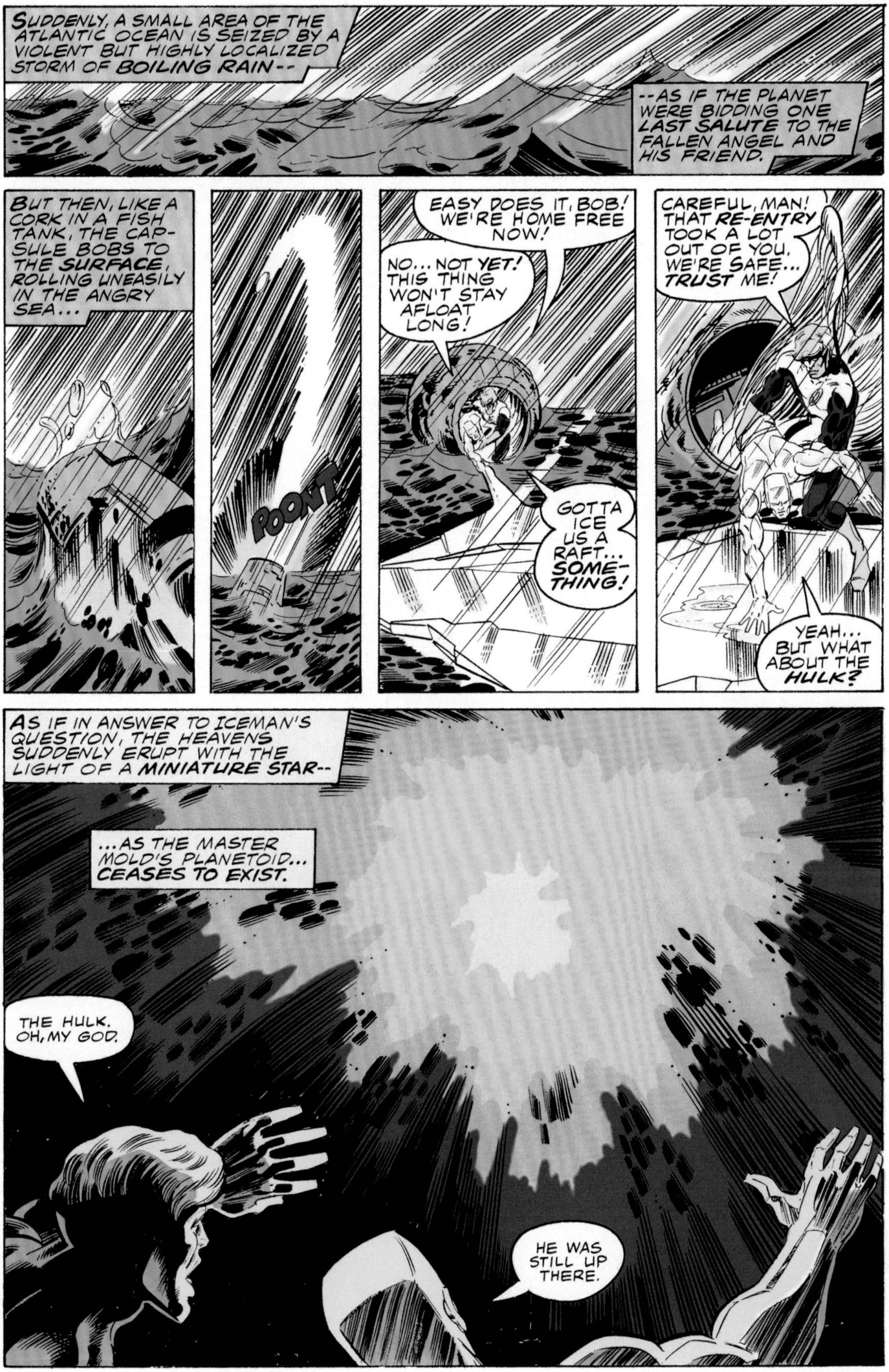
SUDDENLY, A SMALL AREA OF THE ATLANTIC OCEAN IS SEIZED BY A VIOLENT BUT HIGHLY LOCALIZED STORM OF BOILING RAIN--
--AS IF THE PLANET WERE BIDDING ONE LAST SALUTE TO THE FALLEN ANGEL AND HIS FRIEND.
BUT THEN, LIKE A CORK IN A FISH TANK, THE CAPSULE BOBS TO THE SURFACE, ROLLING UNEASILY IN THE ANGRY SEA...
POONT
EASY DOES IT, BOB! WE'RE HOME FREE NOW!
NO... NOT YET! THIS THING WON'T STAY AFLOAT LONG!
GOTTA ICE US A RAFT... SOMETHING!
CAREFUL, MAN! THAT RE-ENTRY TOOK A LOT OUT OF YOU. WE'RE SAFE... TRUST ME!
YEAH... BUT WHAT ABOUT THE HULK?
AS IF IN ANSWER TO ICEMAN'S QUESTION, THE HEAVENS SUDDENLY ERUPT WITH THE LIGHT OF A MINIATURE STAR--
...AS THE MASTER MOLD'S PLANETOID... CEASES TO EXIST.
THE HULK. OH, MY GOD.
HE WAS STILL UP THERE.

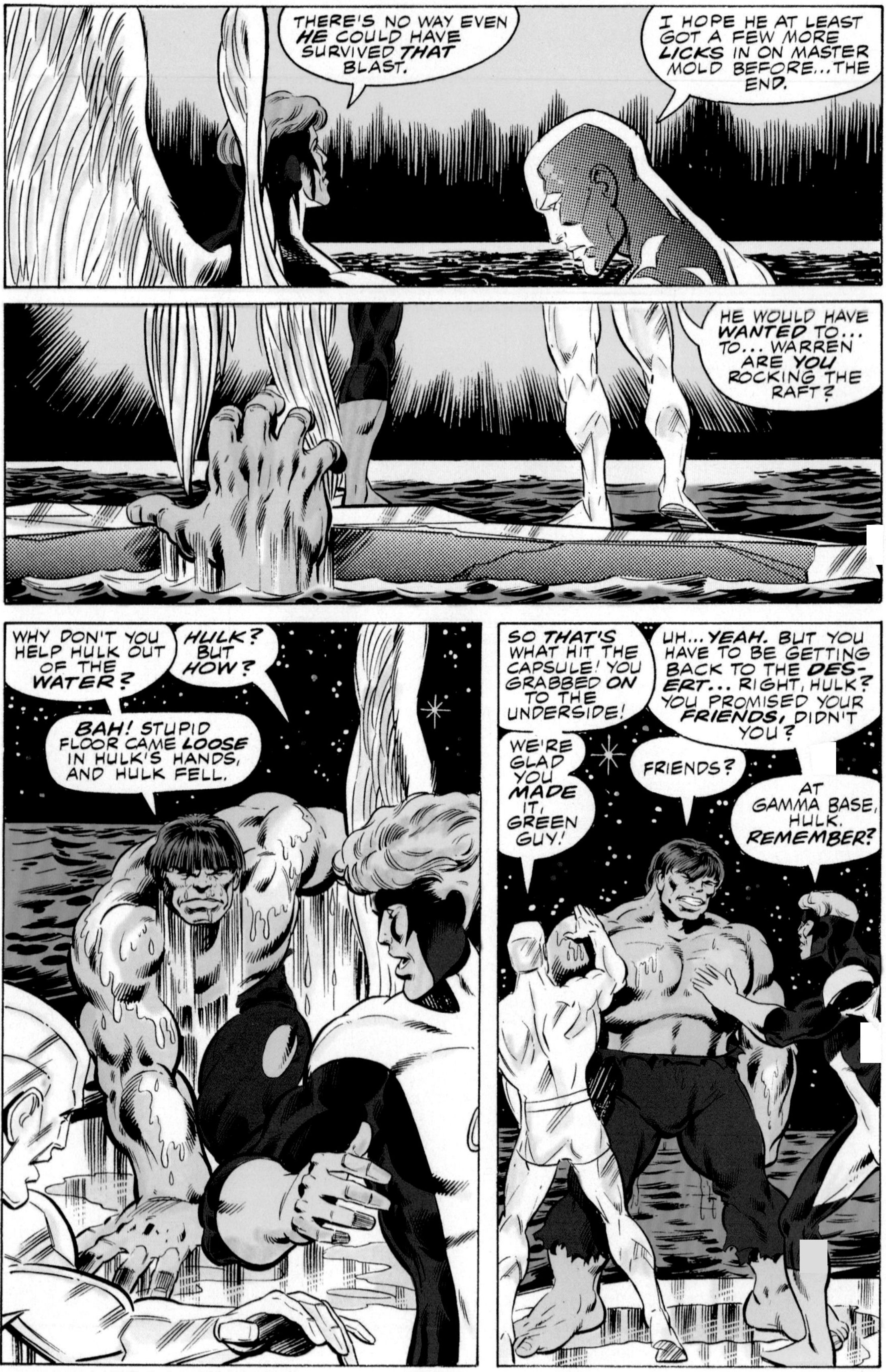
THERE'S NO WAY EVEN HE COULD HAVE SURVIVED THAT BLAST.
I HOPE HE AT LEAST GOT A FEW MORE LICKS IN ON MASTER MOLD BEFORE... THE END.
HE WOULD HAVE WANTED TO... TO... WARREN ARE YOU ROCKING THE RAFT?
WHY DON'T YOU HELP HULK OUT OF THE WATER?
HULK? BUT HOW?
BAH! STUPID FLOOR CAME LOOSE IN HULK'S HANDS, AND HULK FELL.
SO THAT'S WHAT HIT THE CAPSULE! YOU GRABBED ON TO THE UNDERSIDE!
UH... YEAH. BUT YOU HAVE TO BE GETTING BACK TO THE DES-ERT... RIGHT, HULK? YOU PROMISED YOUR FRIENDS, DIDN'T YOU?
WE'RE GLAD YOU MADE IT, GREEN GUY!
FRIENDS?
AT GAMMA BASE, HULK. REMEMBER?

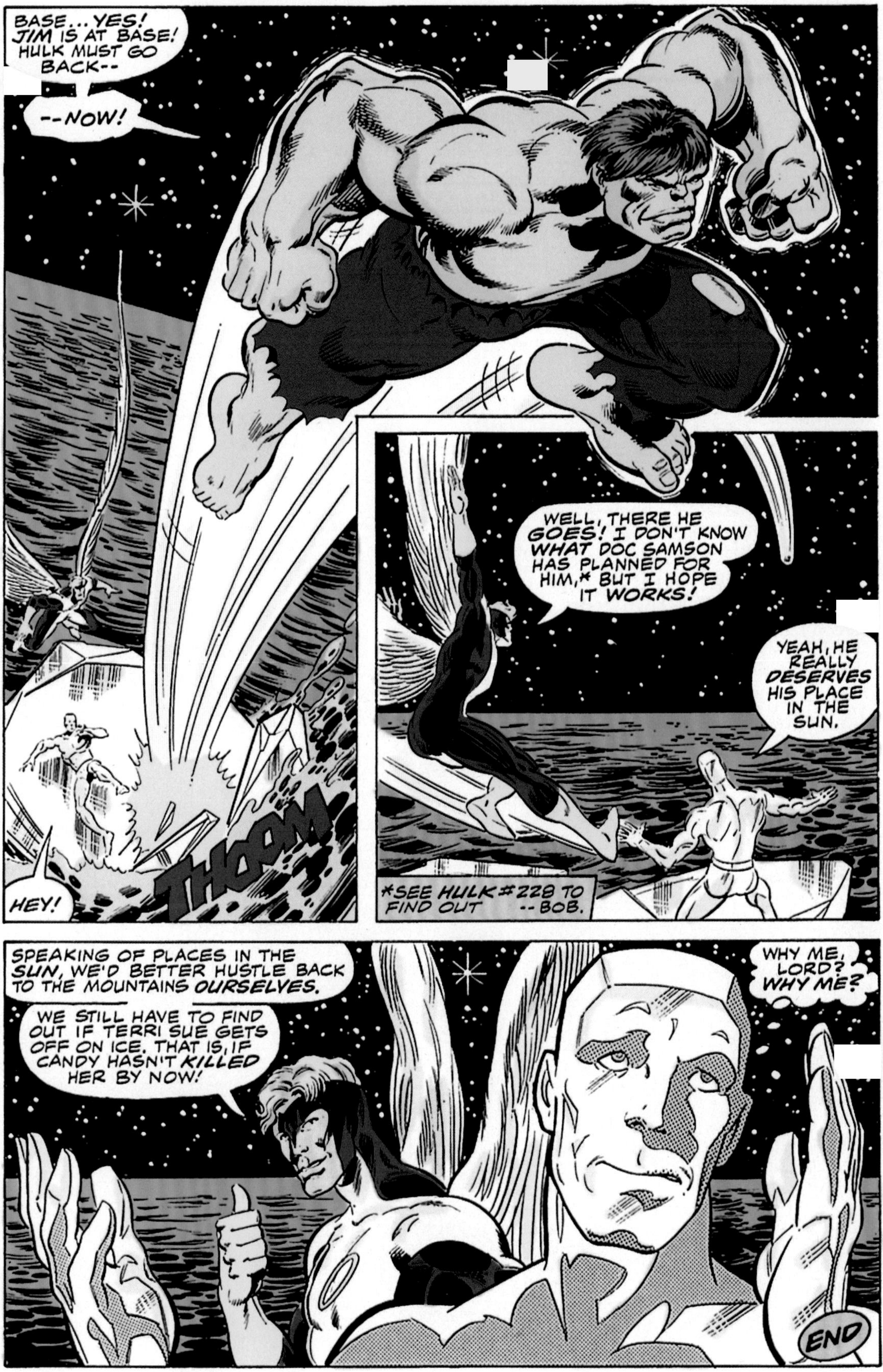
BASE... YES! JIM IS AT BASE! HULK MUST GO BACK--
--NOW!
HEY!
THOOM
WELL, THERE HE GOES! I DON'T KNOW WHAT DOC SAMSON HAS PLANNED FOR HIM,* BUT I HOPE IT WORKS!
YEAH, HE REALLY DESERVES HIS PLACE IN THE SUN.
*SEE HULK #228 TO FIND OUT --BOB.
SPEAKING OF PLACES IN THE SUN, WE'D BETTER HUSTLE BACK TO THE MOUNTAINS OURSELVES.
WE STILL HAVE TO FIND OUT IF TERRI SUE GETS OFF ON ICE. THAT IS, IF CANDY HASN'T KILLED HER BY NOW!
WHY ME, LORD? WHY ME?
END

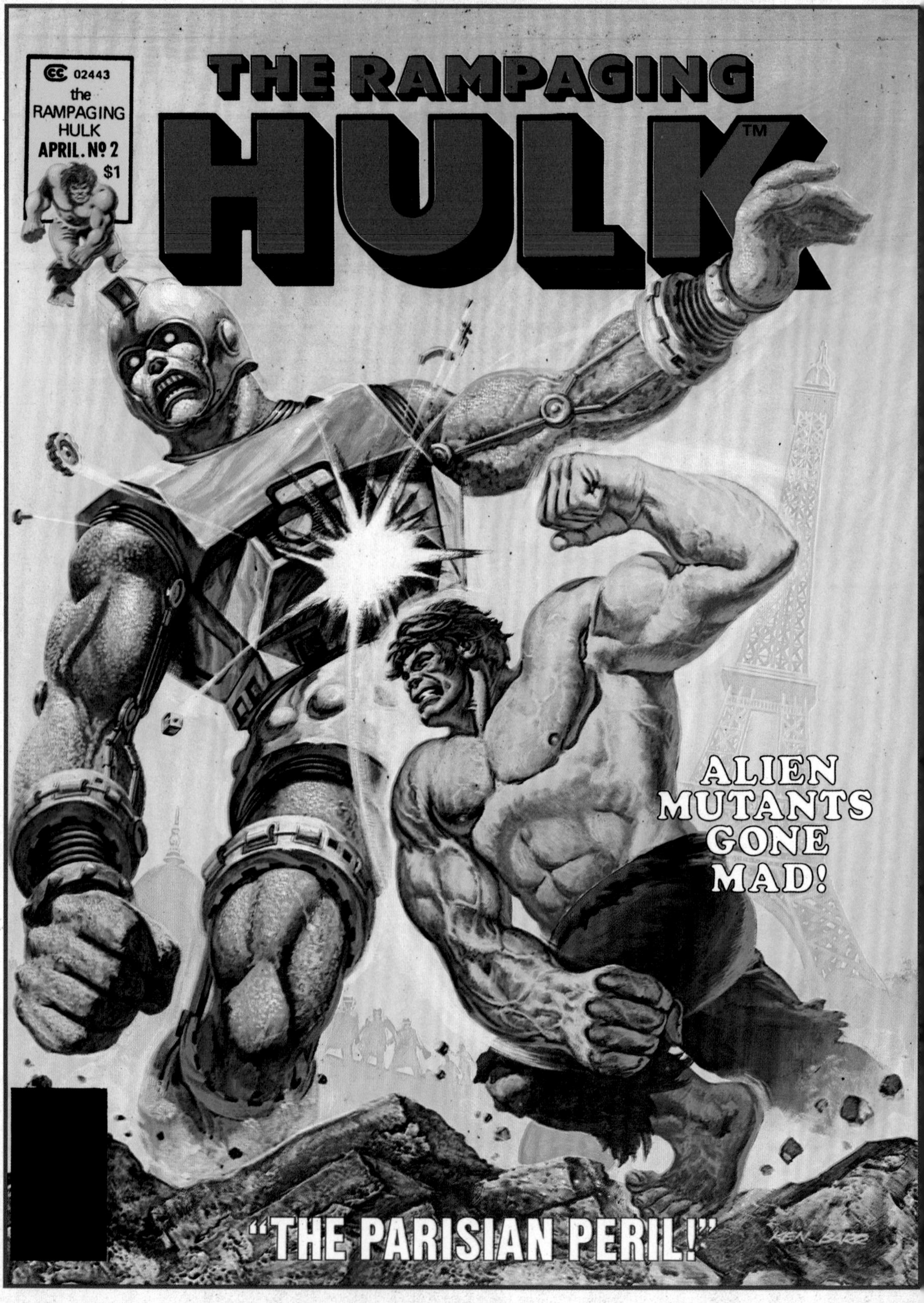
CC 02443
the
RAMPAGING
HULK
APRIL. Nº 2
$1
THE RAMPAGING
HULK™
ALIEN
MUTANTS
GONE
MAD!
"THE PARISIAN PERIL!"

★★★ ROUND 7 ★★★

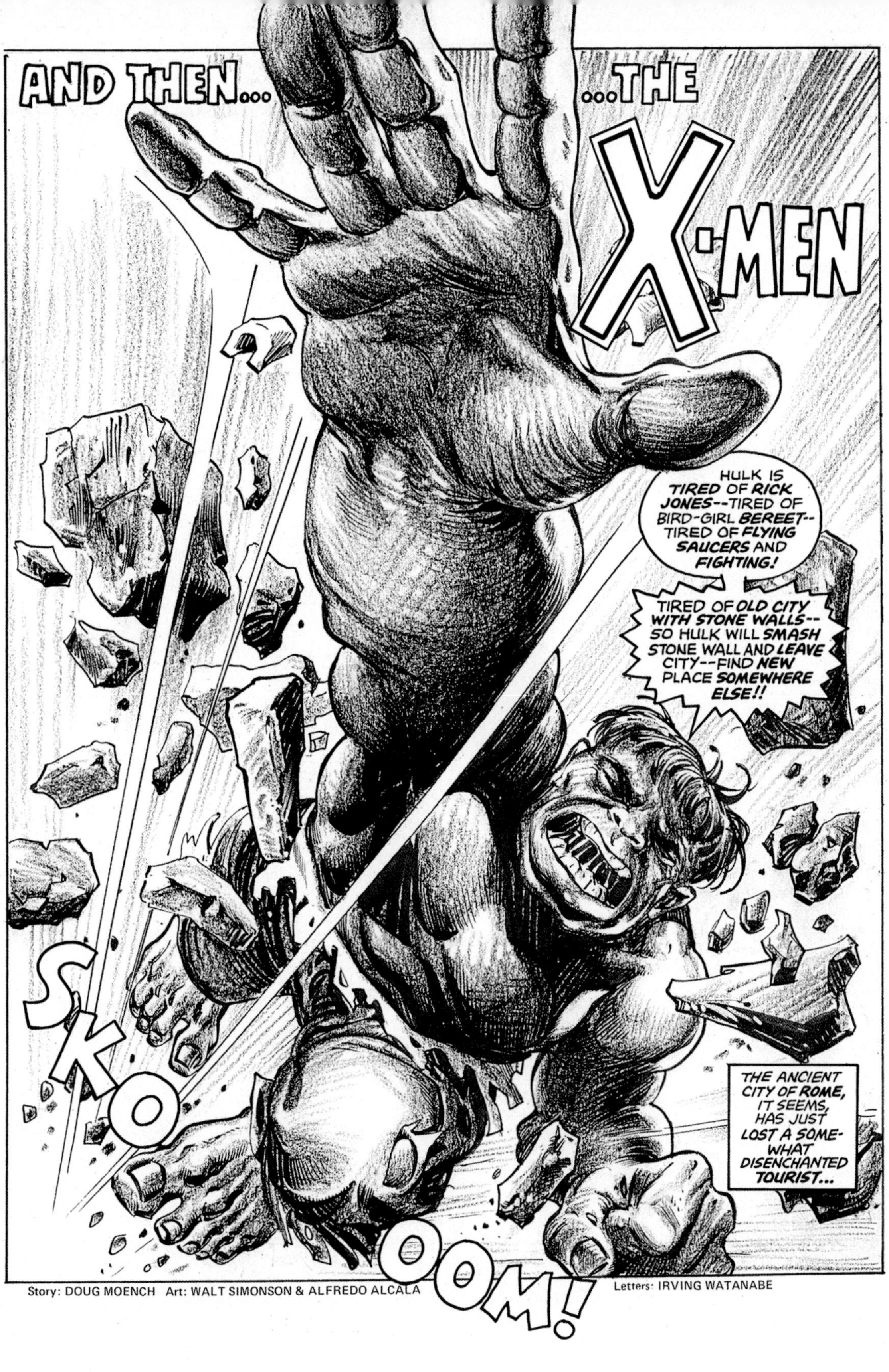
AND THEN... ...THE
X-MEN
HULK IS TIRED OF RICK JONES--TIRED OF BIRD-GIRL BEREET--TIRED OF FLYING SAUCERS AND FIGHTING!
TIRED OF OLD CITY WITH STONE WALLS--SO HULK WILL SMASH STONE WALL AND LEAVE CITY--FIND NEW PLACE SOMEWHERE ELSE!!
THE ANCIENT CITY OF ROME, IT SEEMS, HAS JUST LOST A SOME-WHAT DISENCHANTED TOURIST...
SKOOOM!
Story: DOUG MOENCH Art: WALT SIMONSON & ALFREDO ALCALA Letters: IRVING WATANABE

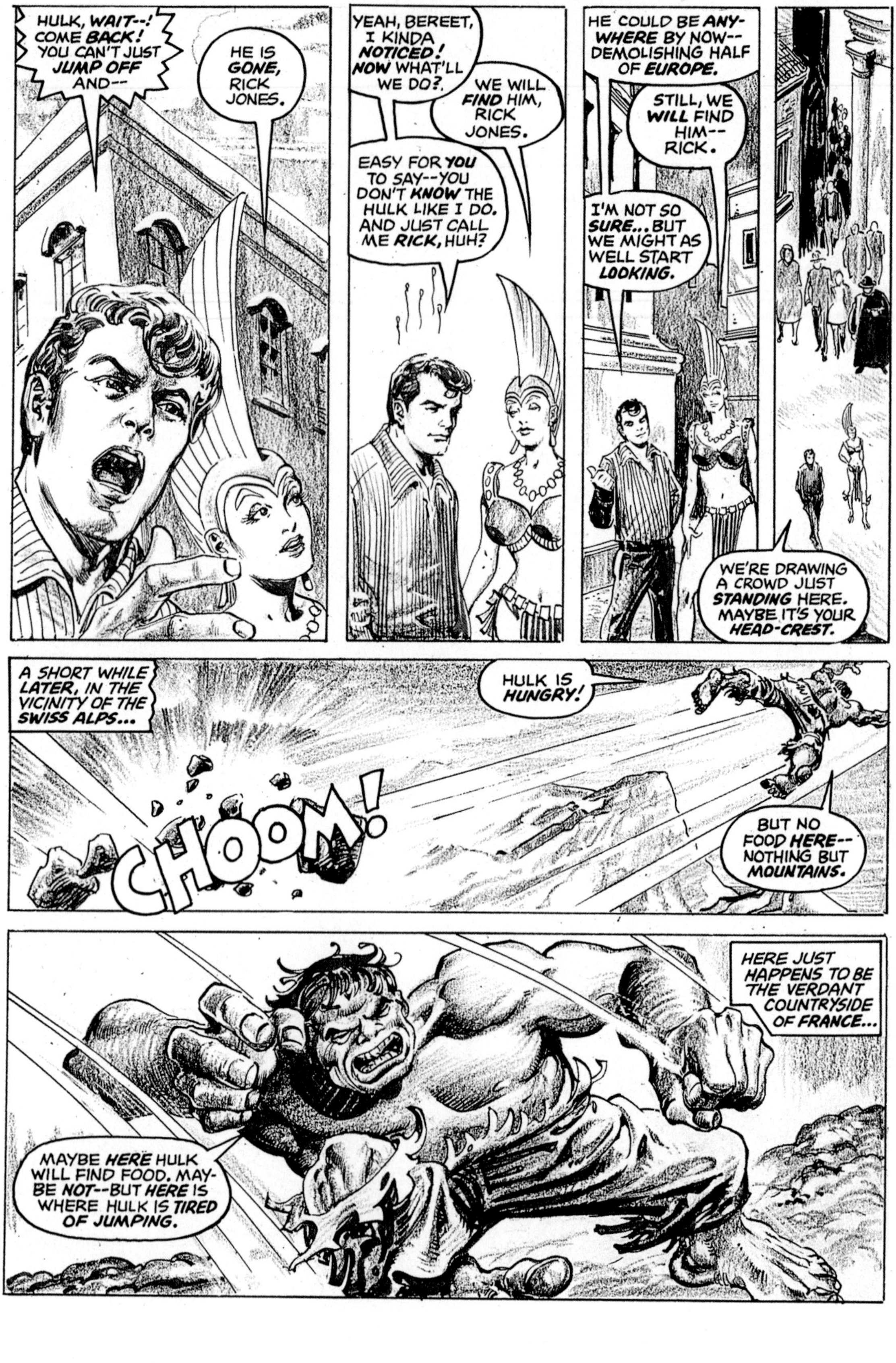
HULK, WAIT--! COME BACK! YOU CAN'T JUST JUMP OFF AND--
HE IS GONE, RICK JONES.
YEAH, BEREET, I KINDA NOTICED! NOW WHAT'LL WE DO?
WE WILL FIND HIM, RICK JONES.
EASY FOR YOU TO SAY--YOU DON'T KNOW THE HULK LIKE I DO. AND JUST CALL ME RICK, HUH?
HE COULD BE ANY-WHERE BY NOW--DEMOLISHING HALF OF EUROPE.
STILL, WE WILL FIND HIM--RICK.
I'M NOT SO SURE... BUT WE MIGHT AS WELL START LOOKING.
WE'RE DRAWING A CROWD JUST STANDING HERE. MAYBE IT'S YOUR HEAD-CREST.
A SHORT WHILE LATER, IN THE VICINITY OF THE SWISS ALPS...
HULK IS HUNGRY!
CHOOM!
BUT NO FOOD HERE--NOTHING BUT MOUNTAINS.
HERE JUST HAPPENS TO BE THE VERDANT COUNTRYSIDE OF FRANCE...
MAYBE HERE HULK WILL FIND FOOD. MAY-BE NOT--BUT HERE IS WHERE HULK IS TIRED OF JUMPING.

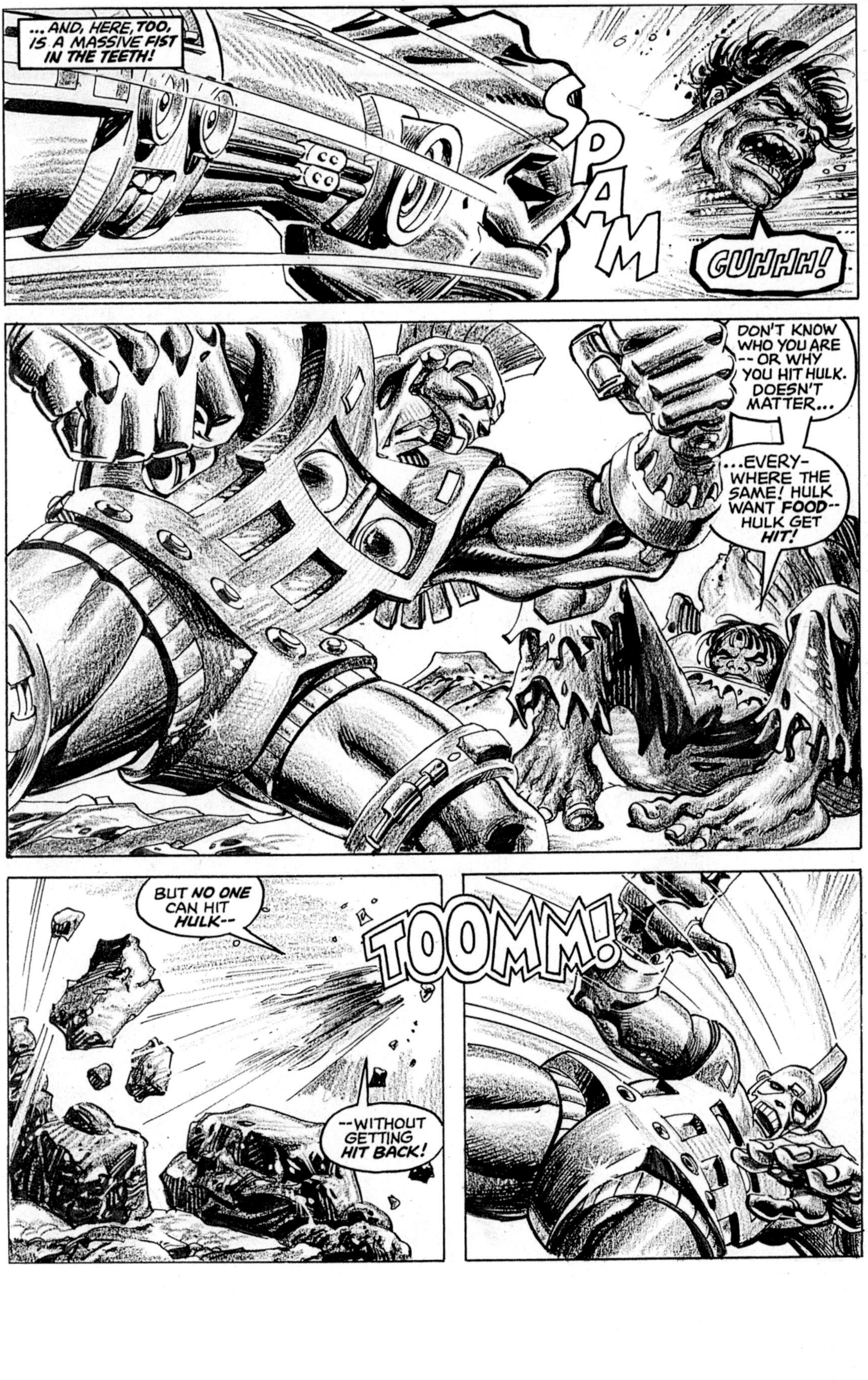
...AND, HERE, TOO, IS A MASSIVE FIST IN THE TEETH!
SPAM
GUHHH!
DON'T KNOW WHO YOU ARE -- OR WHY YOU HIT HULK. DOESN'T MATTER...
...EVERY-WHERE THE SAME! HULK WANT FOOD-- HULK GET HIT!
BUT NO ONE CAN HIT HULK--
TOOMM!
--WITHOUT GETTING HIT BACK!

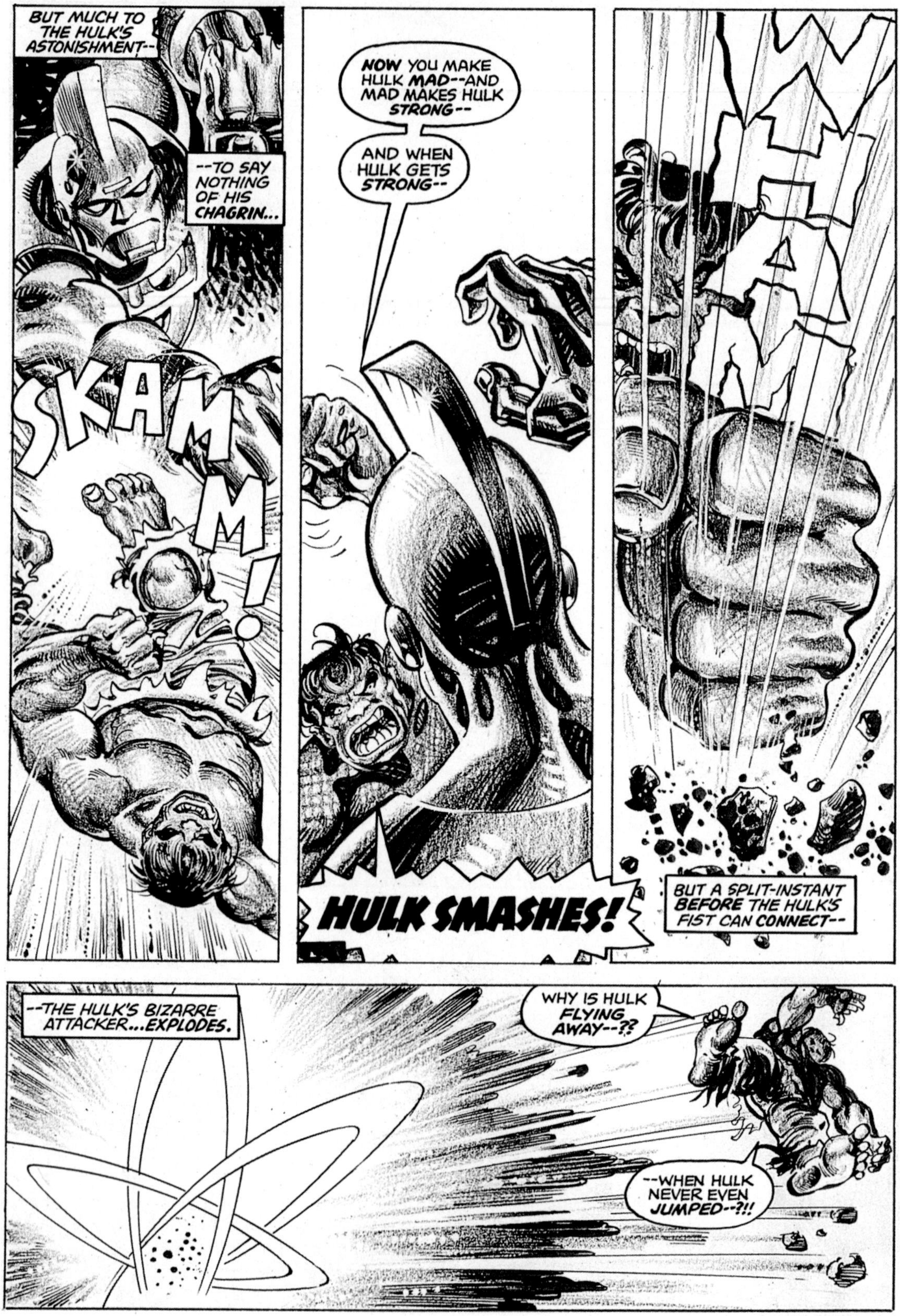
BUT MUCH TO THE HULK'S ASTONISHMENT--
--TO SAY NOTHING OF HIS CHAGRIN...
SKAMMM!
NOW YOU MAKE HULK MAD--AND MAD MAKES HULK STRONG--
AND WHEN HULK GETS STRONG--
HULK SMASHES!
BUT A SPLIT-INSTANT BEFORE THE HULK'S FIST CAN CONNECT--
--THE HULK'S BIZARRE ATTACKER...EXPLODES.
WHY IS HULK FLYING AWAY--??
--WHEN HULK NEVER EVEN JUMPED--?!!

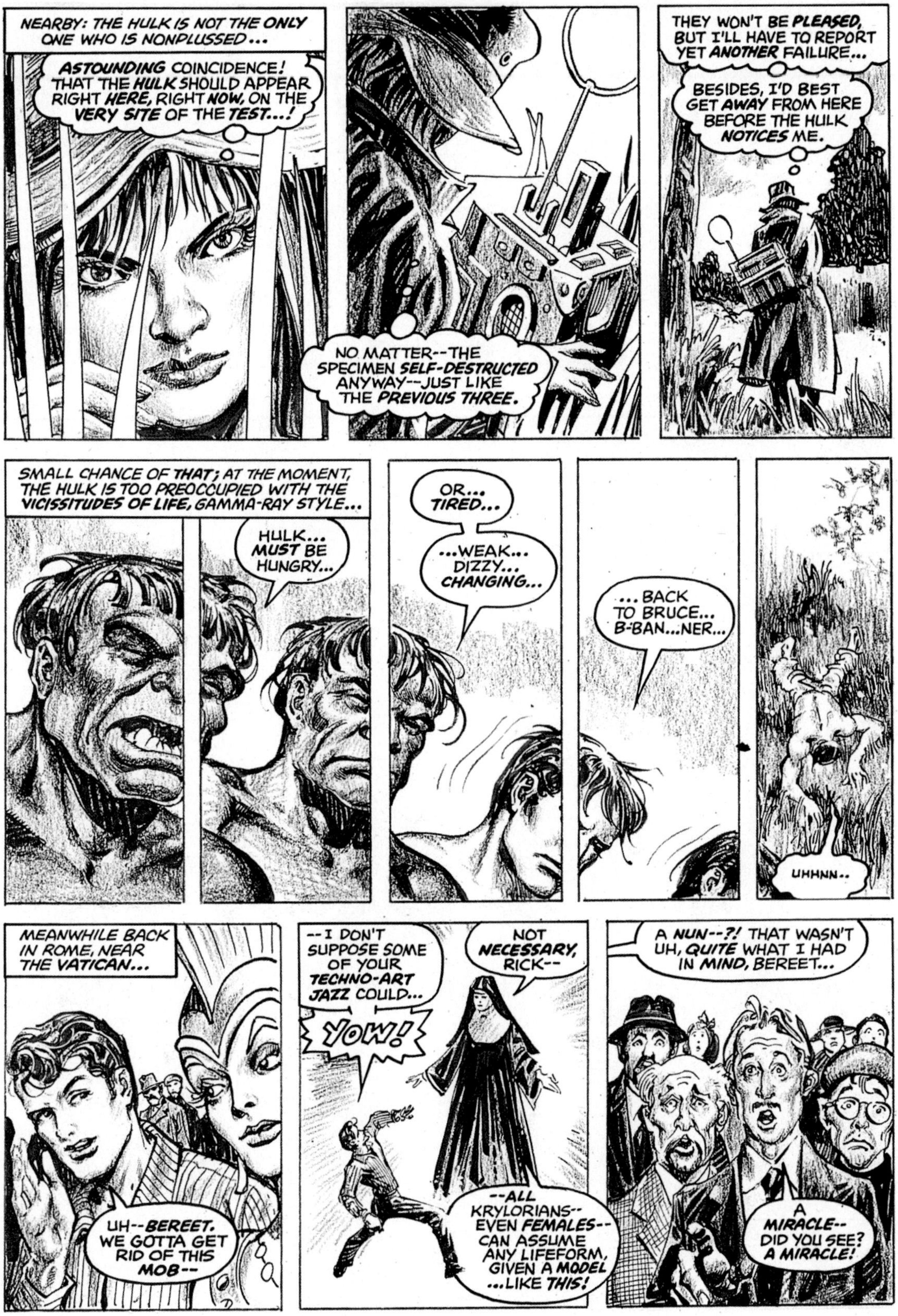
NEARBY: THE HULK IS NOT THE ONLY ONE WHO IS NONPLUSSED...
ASTOUNDING COINCIDENCE! THAT THE HULK SHOULD APPEAR RIGHT HERE, RIGHT NOW, ON THE VERY SITE OF THE TEST...!
NO MATTER--THE SPECIMEN SELF-DESTRUCTED ANYWAY--JUST LIKE THE PREVIOUS THREE.
THEY WON'T BE PLEASED, BUT I'LL HAVE TO REPORT YET ANOTHER FAILURE...
BESIDES, I'D BEST GET AWAY FROM HERE BEFORE THE HULK NOTICES ME.
SMALL CHANCE OF THAT; AT THE MOMENT, THE HULK IS TOO PREOCCUPIED WITH THE VICISSITUDES OF LIFE, GAMMA-RAY STYLE...
HULK... MUST BE HUNGRY...
OR... TIRED...
...WEAK... DIZZY... CHANGING...
...BACK TO BRUCE... B-BAN...NER...
UHHNN..
MEANWHILE BACK IN ROME, NEAR THE VATICAN...
UH--BEREET. WE GOTTA GET RID OF THIS MOB--
--I DON'T SUPPOSE SOME OF YOUR TECHNO-ART JAZZ COULD...
NOT NECESSARY, RICK--
YOW!
--ALL KRYLORIANS-- EVEN FEMALES-- CAN ASSUME ANY LIFEFORM, GIVEN A MODEL ...LIKE THIS!
A NUN--?! THAT WASN'T UH, QUITE WHAT I HAD IN MIND, BEREET...
A MIRACLE-- DID YOU SEE? A MIRACLE!

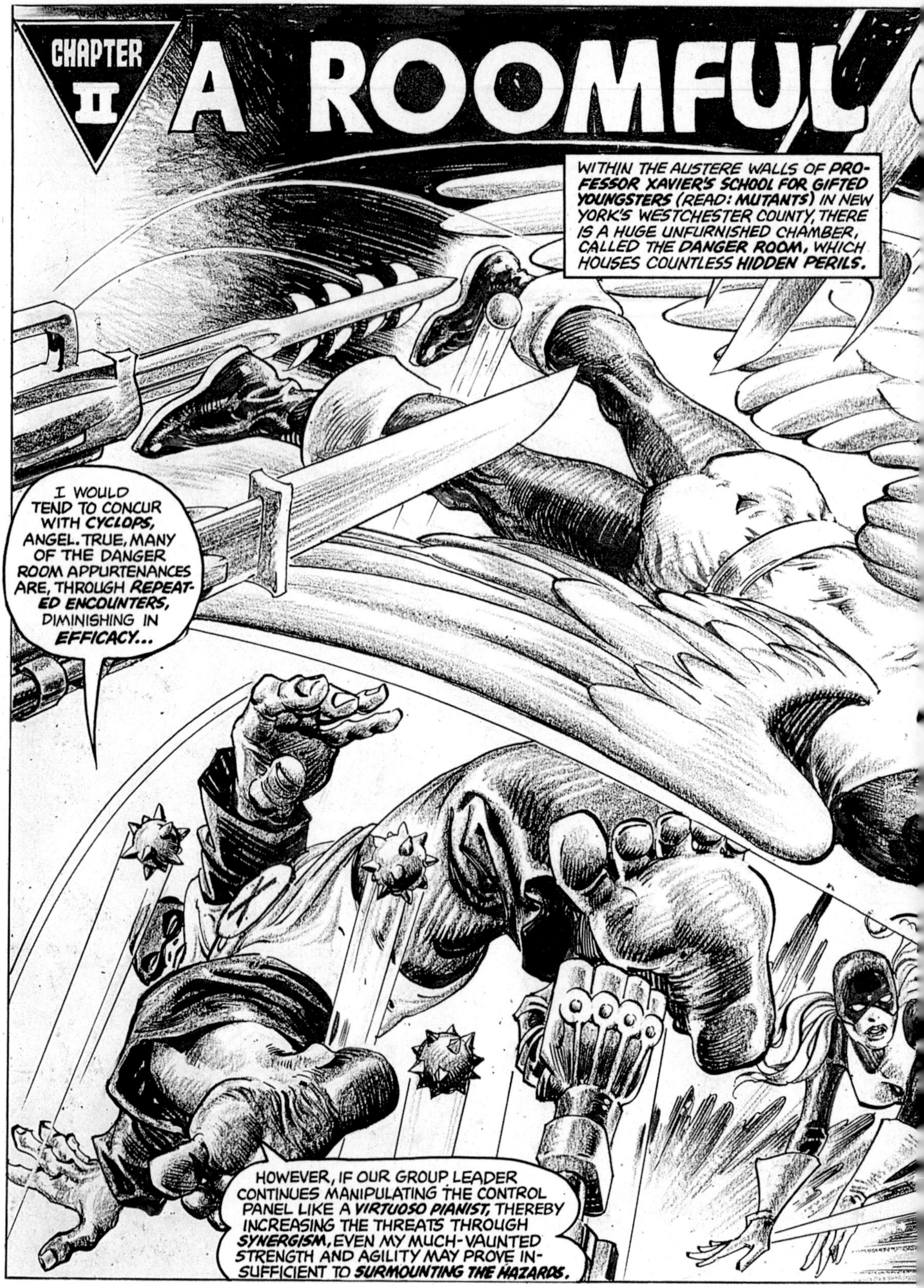
CHAPTER II
A ROOMFUL
WITHIN THE AUSTERE WALLS OF PROFESSOR XAVIER'S SCHOOL FOR GIFTED YOUNGSTERS (READ: MUTANTS) IN NEW YORK'S WESTCHESTER COUNTY, THERE IS A HUGE UNFURNISHED CHAMBER, CALLED THE DANGER ROOM, WHICH HOUSES COUNTLESS HIDDEN PERILS.
I WOULD TEND TO CONCUR WITH CYCLOPS, ANGEL. TRUE, MANY OF THE DANGER ROOM APPURTENANCES ARE, THROUGH REPEATED ENCOUNTERS, DIMINISHING IN EFFICACY...
HOWEVER, IF OUR GROUP LEADER CONTINUES MANIPULATING THE CONTROL PANEL LIKE A VIRTUOSO PIANIST, THEREBY INCREASING THE THREATS THROUGH SYNERGISM, EVEN MY MUCH-VAUNTED STRENGTH AND AGILITY MAY PROVE INSUFFICIENT TO SURMOUNTING THE HAZARDS.

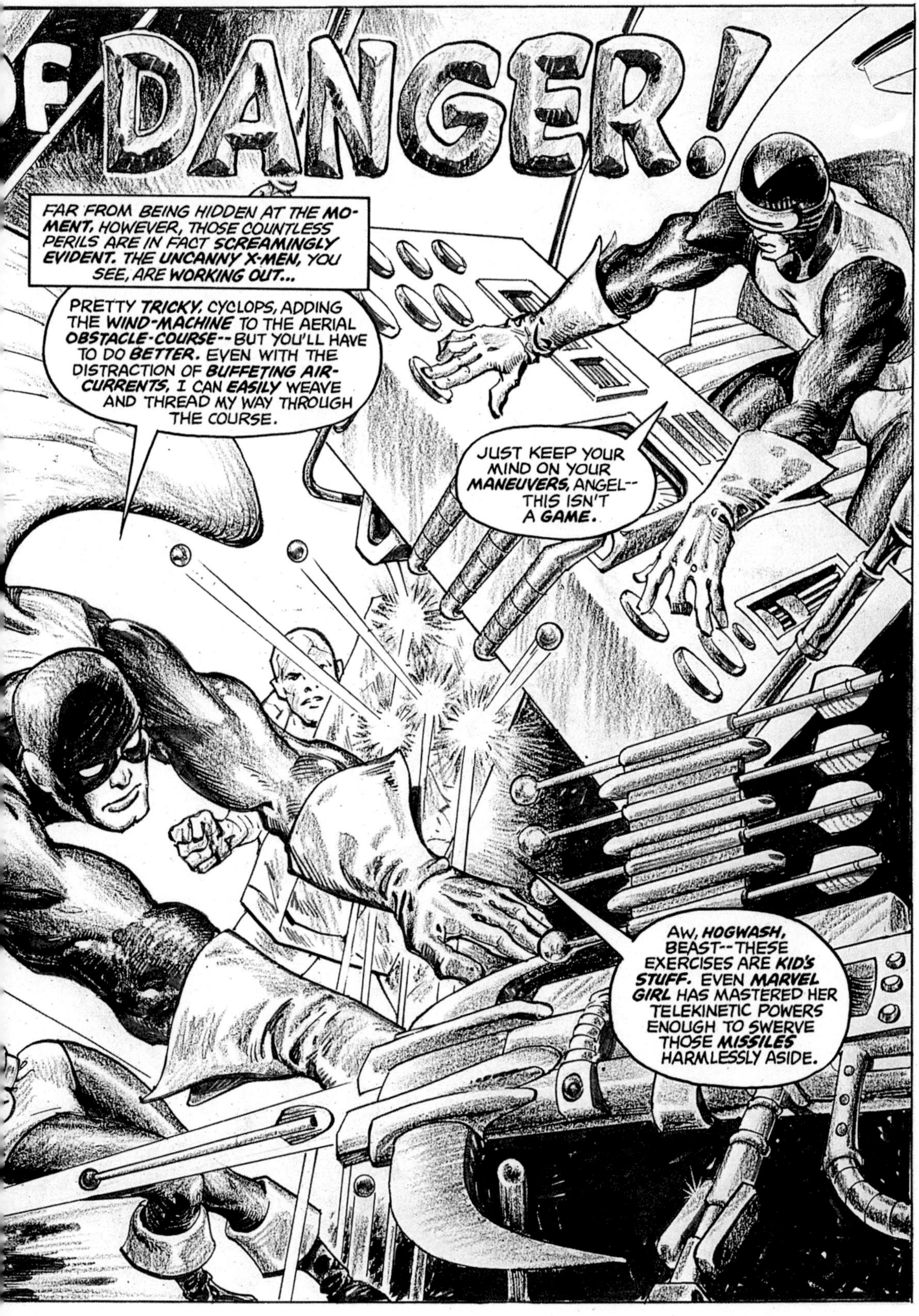
...OF DANGER!
FAR FROM BEING HIDDEN AT THE MOMENT, HOWEVER, THOSE COUNTLESS PERILS ARE IN FACT SCREAMINGLY EVIDENT. THE UNCANNY X-MEN, YOU SEE, ARE WORKING OUT...
PRETTY TRICKY, CYCLOPS, ADDING THE WIND-MACHINE TO THE AERIAL OBSTACLE-COURSE-- BUT YOU'LL HAVE TO DO BETTER. EVEN WITH THE DISTRACTION OF BUFFETING AIR-CURRENTS, I CAN EASILY WEAVE AND THREAD MY WAY THROUGH THE COURSE.
JUST KEEP YOUR MIND ON YOUR MANEUVERS, ANGEL-- THIS ISN'T A GAME.
AW, HOGWASH, BEAST--THESE EXERCISES ARE KID'S STUFF. EVEN MARVEL GIRL HAS MASTERED HER TELEKINETIC POWERS ENOUGH TO SWERVE THOSE MISSILES HARMLESSLY ASIDE.

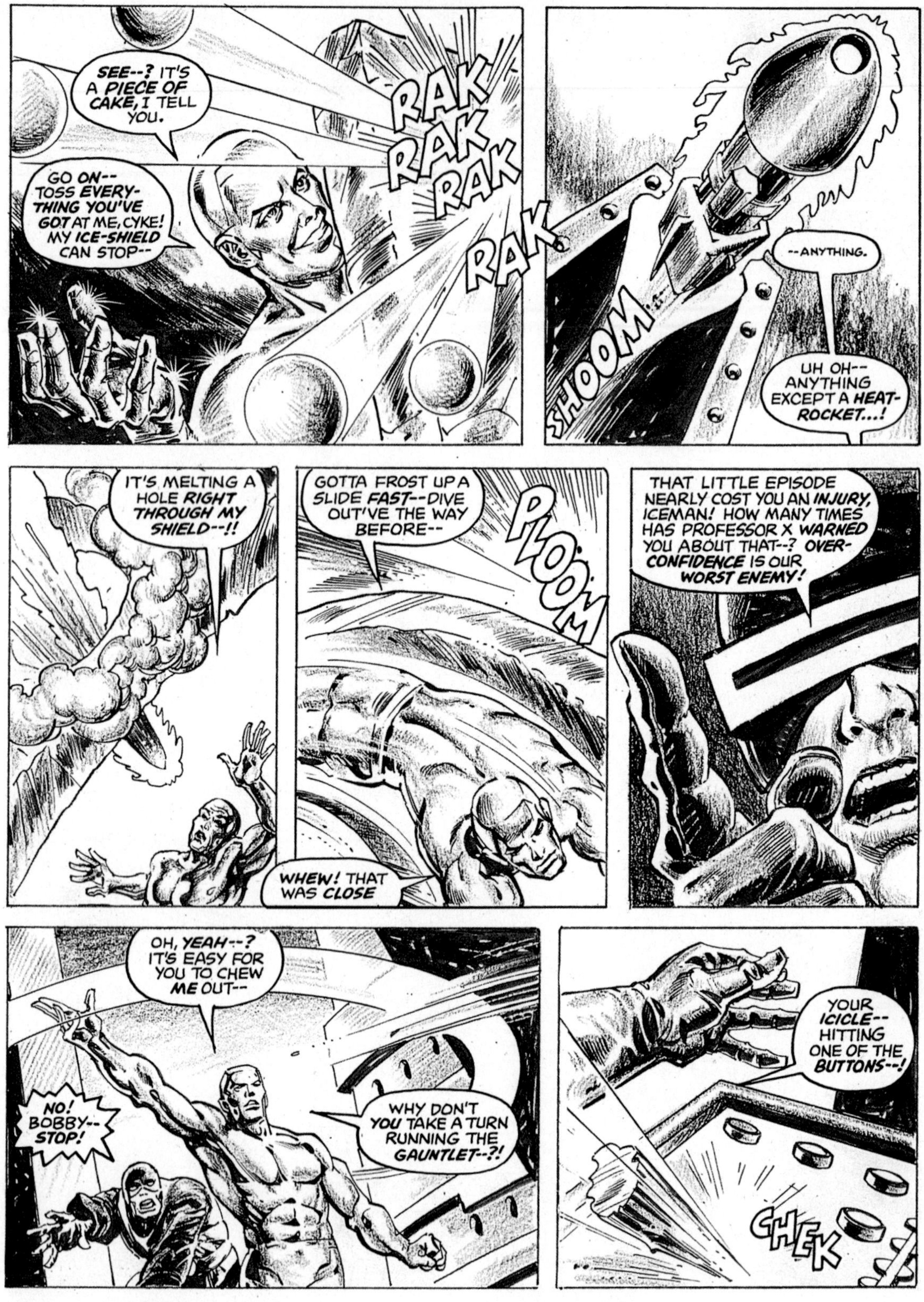
SEE--? IT'S A PIECE OF CAKE, I TELL YOU.
GO ON-- TOSS EVERYTHING YOU'VE GOT AT ME, CYKE! MY ICE-SHIELD CAN STOP--
RAK RAK RAK RAK
--ANYTHING.
SHOOM
UH OH-- ANYTHING EXCEPT A HEAT-ROCKET...!
IT'S MELTING A HOLE RIGHT THROUGH MY SHIELD--!!
GOTTA FROST UP A SLIDE FAST--DIVE OUT'VE THE WAY BEFORE--
PLOOOM
WHEW! THAT WAS CLOSE
THAT LITTLE EPISODE NEARLY COST YOU AN INJURY, ICEMAN! HOW MANY TIMES HAS PROFESSOR X WARNED YOU ABOUT THAT--? OVER-CONFIDENCE IS OUR WORST ENEMY!
OH, YEAH--? IT'S EASY FOR YOU TO CHEW ME OUT--
WHY DON'T YOU TAKE A TURN RUNNING THE GAUNTLET--?!
NO! BOBBY-- STOP!
YOUR ICICLE-- HITTING ONE OF THE BUTTONS--!
CHEK

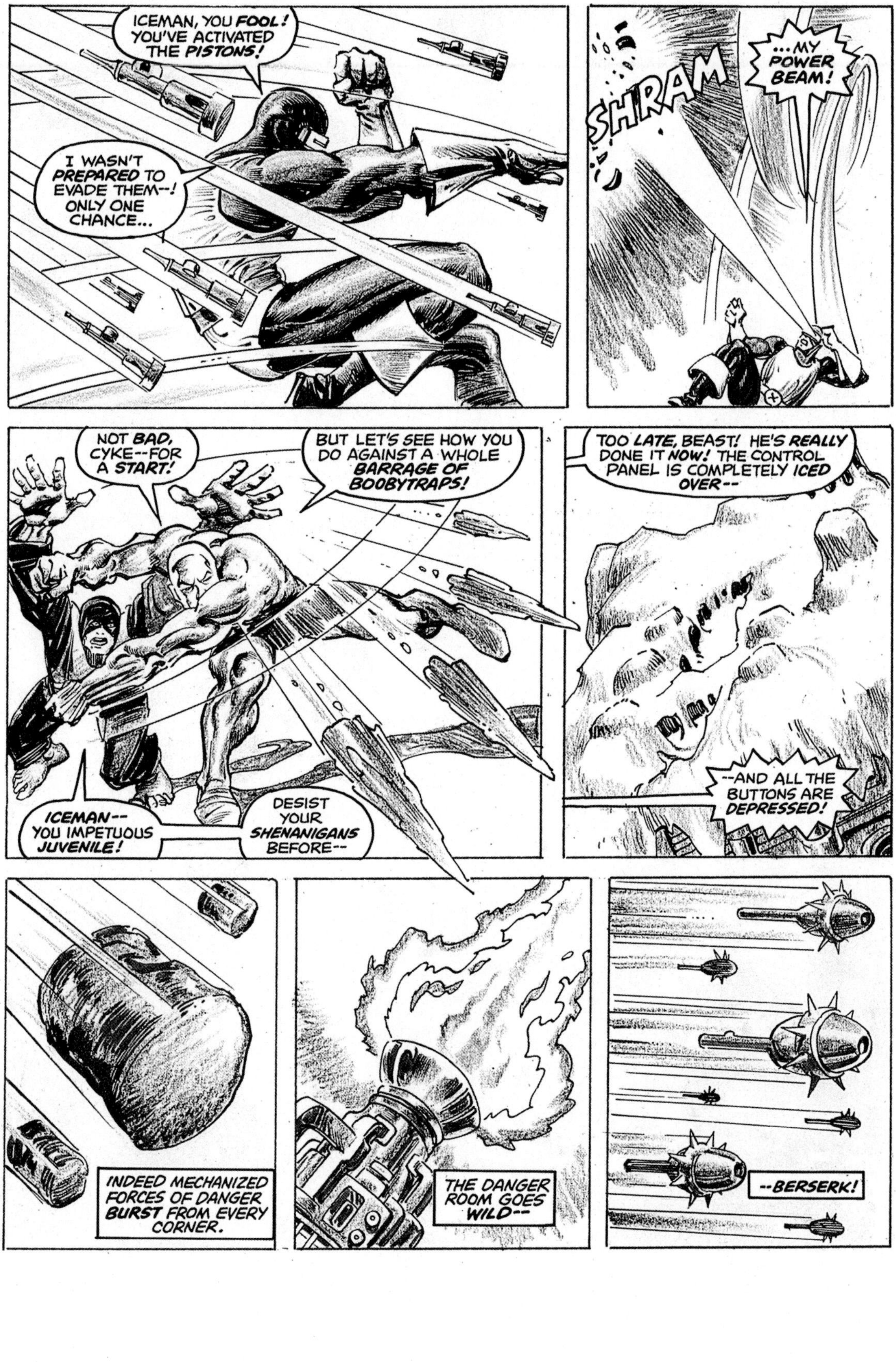
ICEMAN, YOU FOOL! YOU'VE ACTIVATED THE PISTONS!
I WASN'T PREPARED TO EVADE THEM--! ONLY ONE CHANCE...
SHRAM
...MY POWER BEAM!
NOT BAD, CYKE--FOR A START!
BUT LET'S SEE HOW YOU DO AGAINST A WHOLE BARRAGE OF BOOBYTRAPS!
ICEMAN-- YOU IMPETUOUS JUVENILE!
DESIST YOUR SHENANIGANS BEFORE--
TOO LATE, BEAST! HE'S REALLY DONE IT NOW! THE CONTROL PANEL IS COMPLETELY ICED OVER--
--AND ALL THE BUTTONS ARE DEPRESSED!
INDEED MECHANIZED FORCES OF DANGER BURST FROM EVERY CORNER.
THE DANGER ROOM GOES WILD--
--BERSERK!

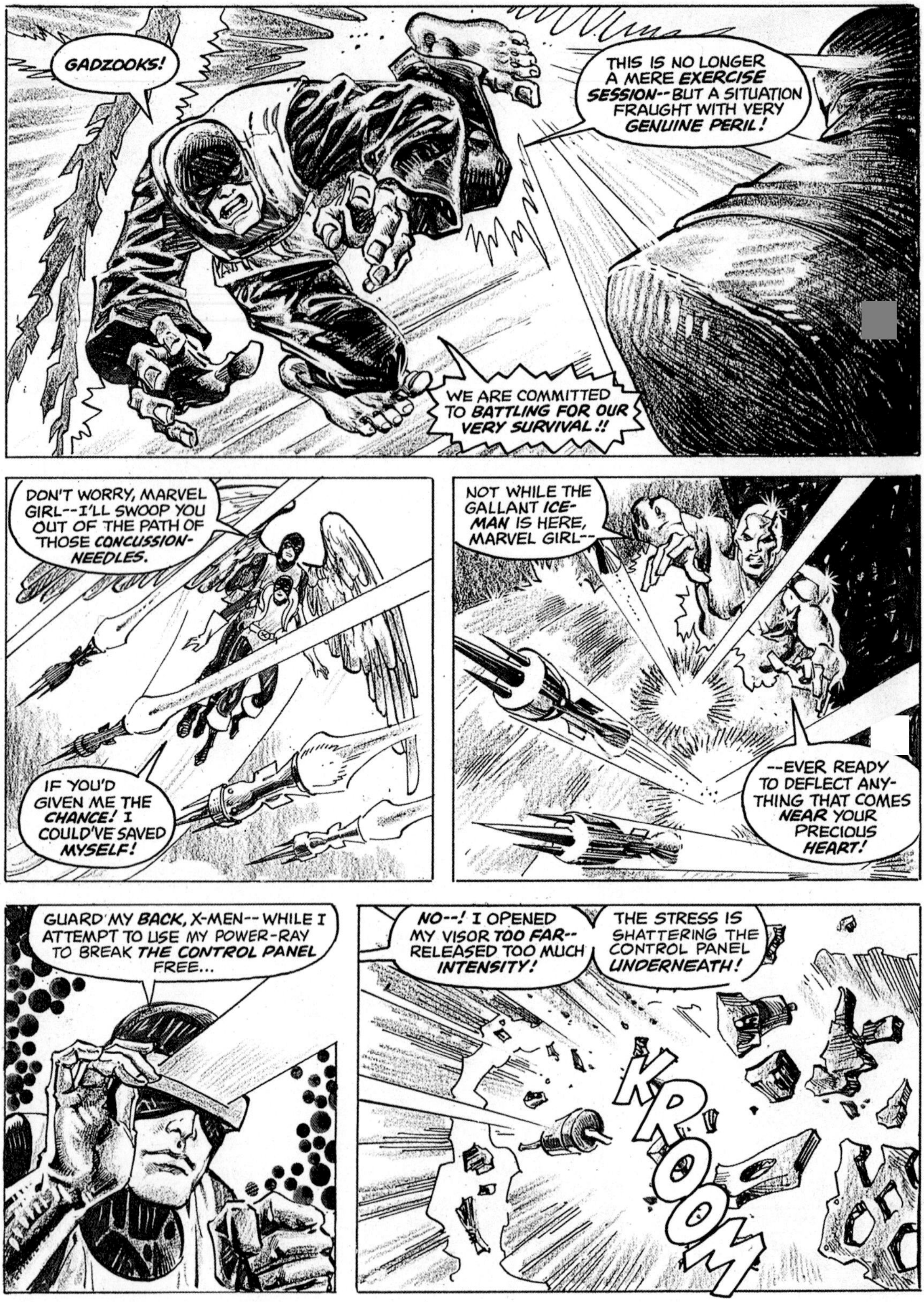
GADZOOKS!
THIS IS NO LONGER A MERE EXERCISE SESSION--BUT A SITUATION FRAUGHT WITH VERY GENUINE PERIL!
WE ARE COMMITTED TO BATTLING FOR OUR VERY SURVIVAL!!
DON'T WORRY, MARVEL GIRL--I'LL SWOOP YOU OUT OF THE PATH OF THOSE CONCUSSION-NEEDLES.
IF YOU'D GIVEN ME THE CHANCE! I COULD'VE SAVED MYSELF!
NOT WHILE THE GALLANT ICE-MAN IS HERE, MARVEL GIRL--
--EVER READY TO DEFLECT ANYTHING THAT COMES NEAR YOUR PRECIOUS HEART!
GUARD MY BACK, X-MEN--WHILE I ATTEMPT TO USE MY POWER-RAY TO BREAK THE CONTROL PANEL FREE...
NO--! I OPENED MY VISOR TOO FAR--RELEASED TOO MUCH INTENSITY!
THE STRESS IS SHATTERING THE CONTROL PANEL UNDERNEATH!
KROOOM

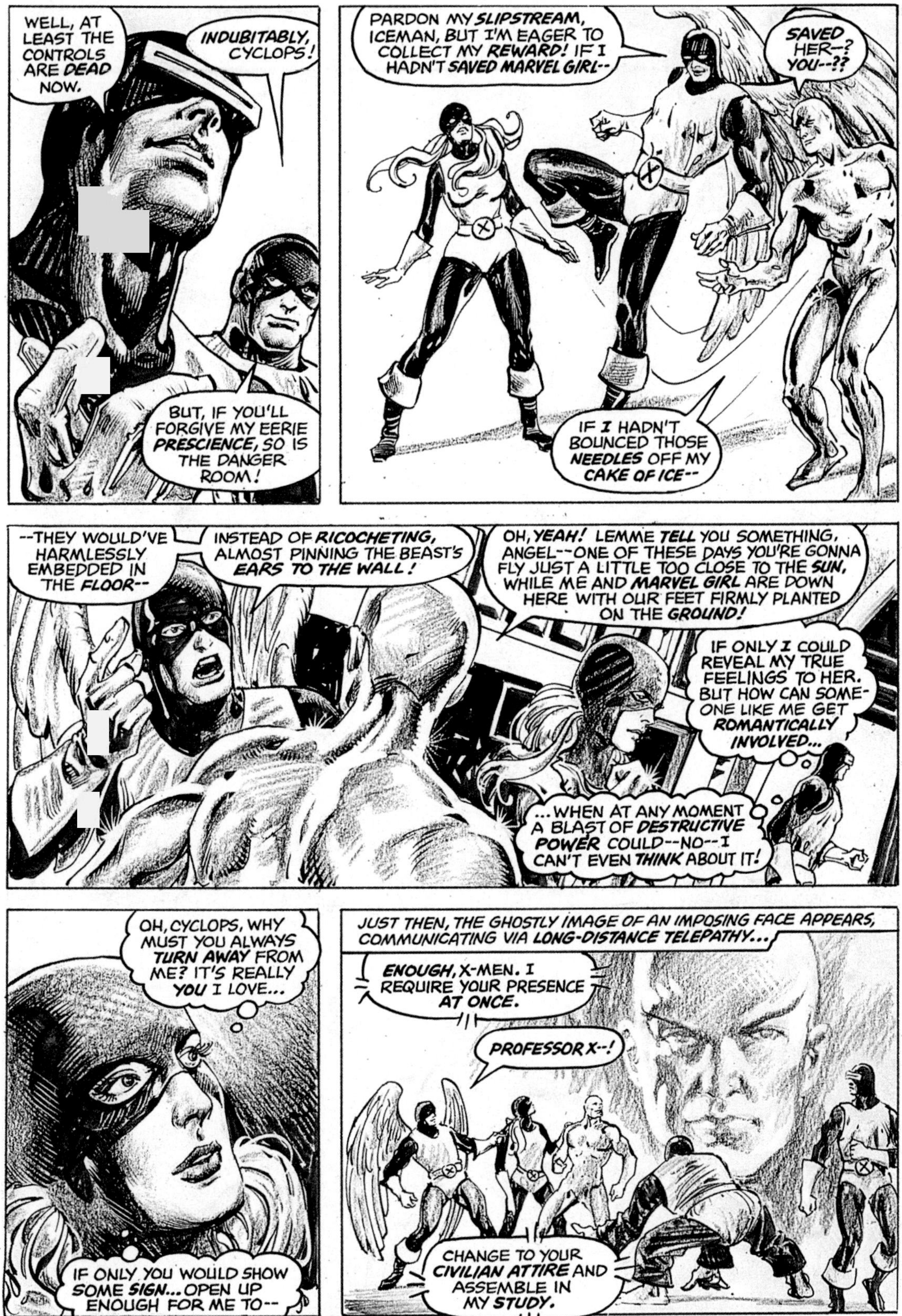
WELL, AT LEAST THE CONTROLS ARE DEAD NOW.
INDUBITABLY, CYCLOPS!
BUT, IF YOU'LL FORGIVE MY EERIE PRESCIENCE, SO IS THE DANGER ROOM!
PARDON MY SLIPSTREAM, ICEMAN, BUT I'M EAGER TO COLLECT MY REWARD! IF I HADN'T SAVED MARVEL GIRL--
SAVED HER--? YOU--??
IF I HADN'T BOUNCED THOSE NEEDLES OFF MY CAKE OF ICE--
--THEY WOULD'VE HARMLESSLY EMBEDDED IN THE FLOOR--
INSTEAD OF RICOCHETING, ALMOST PINNING THE BEAST'S EARS TO THE WALL!
OH, YEAH! LEMME TELL YOU SOMETHING, ANGEL--ONE OF THESE DAYS YOU'RE GONNA FLY JUST A LITTLE TOO CLOSE TO THE SUN, WHILE ME AND MARVEL GIRL ARE DOWN HERE WITH OUR FEET FIRMLY PLANTED ON THE GROUND!
IF ONLY I COULD REVEAL MY TRUE FEELINGS TO HER. BUT HOW CAN SOME-ONE LIKE ME GET ROMANTICALLY INVOLVED...
...WHEN AT ANY MOMENT A BLAST OF DESTRUCTIVE POWER COULD--NO--I CAN'T EVEN THINK ABOUT IT!
OH, CYCLOPS, WHY MUST YOU ALWAYS TURN AWAY FROM ME? IT'S REALLY YOU I LOVE...
IF ONLY YOU WOULD SHOW SOME SIGN...OPEN UP ENOUGH FOR ME TO--
JUST THEN, THE GHOSTLY IMAGE OF AN IMPOSING FACE APPEARS, COMMUNICATING VIA LONG-DISTANCE TELEPATHY...
ENOUGH, X-MEN. I REQUIRE YOUR PRESENCE AT ONCE.
PROFESSOR X--!
CHANGE TO YOUR CIVILIAN ATTIRE AND ASSEMBLE IN MY STUDY.

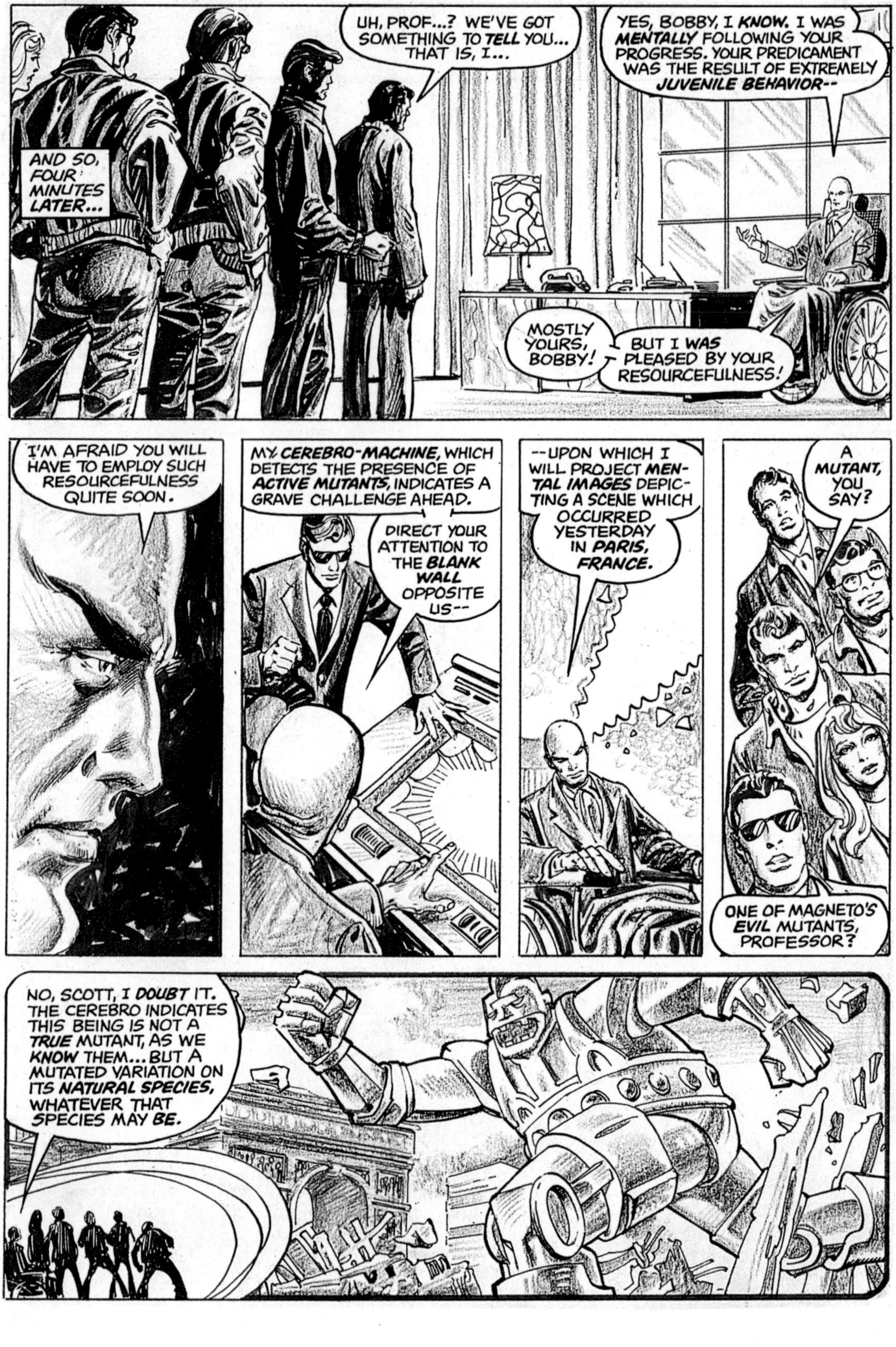
AND SO, FOUR MINUTES LATER...
UH, PROF...? WE'VE GOT SOMETHING TO TELL YOU... THAT IS, I...
YES, BOBBY, I KNOW. I WAS MENTALLY FOLLOWING YOUR PROGRESS. YOUR PREDICAMENT WAS THE RESULT OF EXTREMELY JUVENILE BEHAVIOR--
MOSTLY YOURS, BOBBY!
BUT I WAS PLEASED BY YOUR RESOURCEFULNESS!
I'M AFRAID YOU WILL HAVE TO EMPLOY SUCH RESOURCEFULNESS QUITE SOON.
MY CEREBRO-MACHINE, WHICH DETECTS THE PRESENCE OF ACTIVE MUTANTS, INDICATES A GRAVE CHALLENGE AHEAD.
DIRECT YOUR ATTENTION TO THE BLANK WALL OPPOSITE US--
--UPON WHICH I WILL PROJECT MENTAL IMAGES DEPICTING A SCENE WHICH OCCURRED YESTERDAY IN PARIS, FRANCE.
A MUTANT, YOU SAY?
ONE OF MAGNETO'S EVIL MUTANTS, PROFESSOR?
NO, SCOTT, I DOUBT IT. THE CEREBRO INDICATES THIS BEING IS NOT A TRUE MUTANT, AS WE KNOW THEM... BUT A MUTATED VARIATION ON ITS NATURAL SPECIES, WHATEVER THAT SPECIES MAY BE.

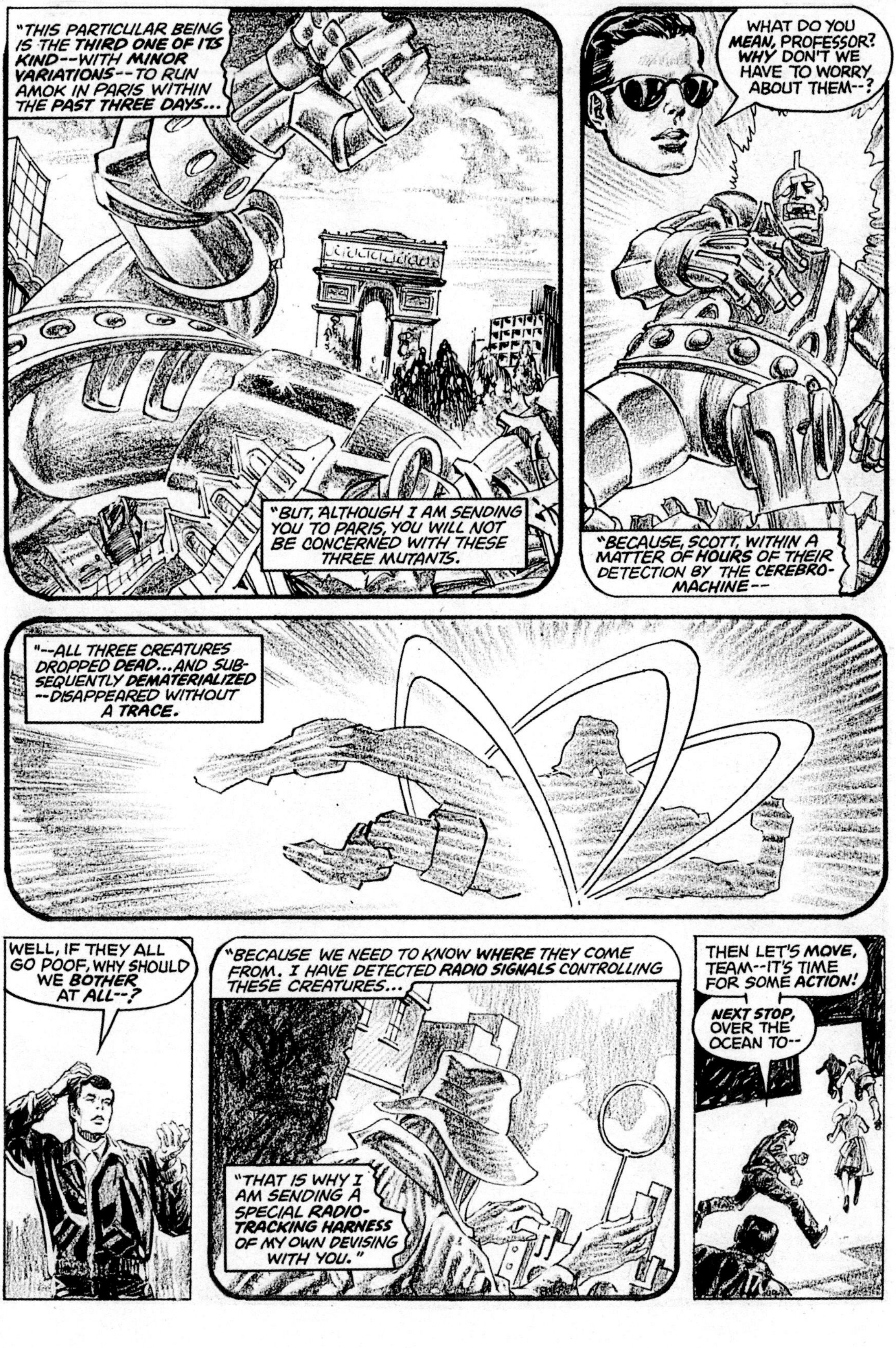
"THIS PARTICULAR BEING IS THE THIRD ONE OF ITS KIND--WITH MINOR VARIATIONS--TO RUN AMOK IN PARIS WITHIN THE PAST THREE DAYS...
"BUT, ALTHOUGH I AM SENDING YOU TO PARIS, YOU WILL NOT BE CONCERNED WITH THESE THREE MUTANTS.
WHAT DO YOU MEAN, PROFESSOR? WHY DON'T WE HAVE TO WORRY ABOUT THEM--?
"BECAUSE, SCOTT, WITHIN A MATTER OF HOURS OF THEIR DETECTION BY THE CEREBRO-MACHINE--
"--ALL THREE CREATURES DROPPED DEAD...AND SUBSEQUENTLY DEMATERIALIZED --DISAPPEARED WITHOUT A TRACE.
WELL, IF THEY ALL GO POOF, WHY SHOULD WE BOTHER AT ALL--?
"BECAUSE WE NEED TO KNOW WHERE THEY COME FROM. I HAVE DETECTED RADIO SIGNALS CONTROLLING THESE CREATURES...
"THAT IS WHY I AM SENDING A SPECIAL RADIO-TRACKING HARNESS OF MY OWN DEVISING WITH YOU."
THEN LET'S MOVE, TEAM--IT'S TIME FOR SOME ACTION!
NEXT STOP, OVER THE OCEAN TO--

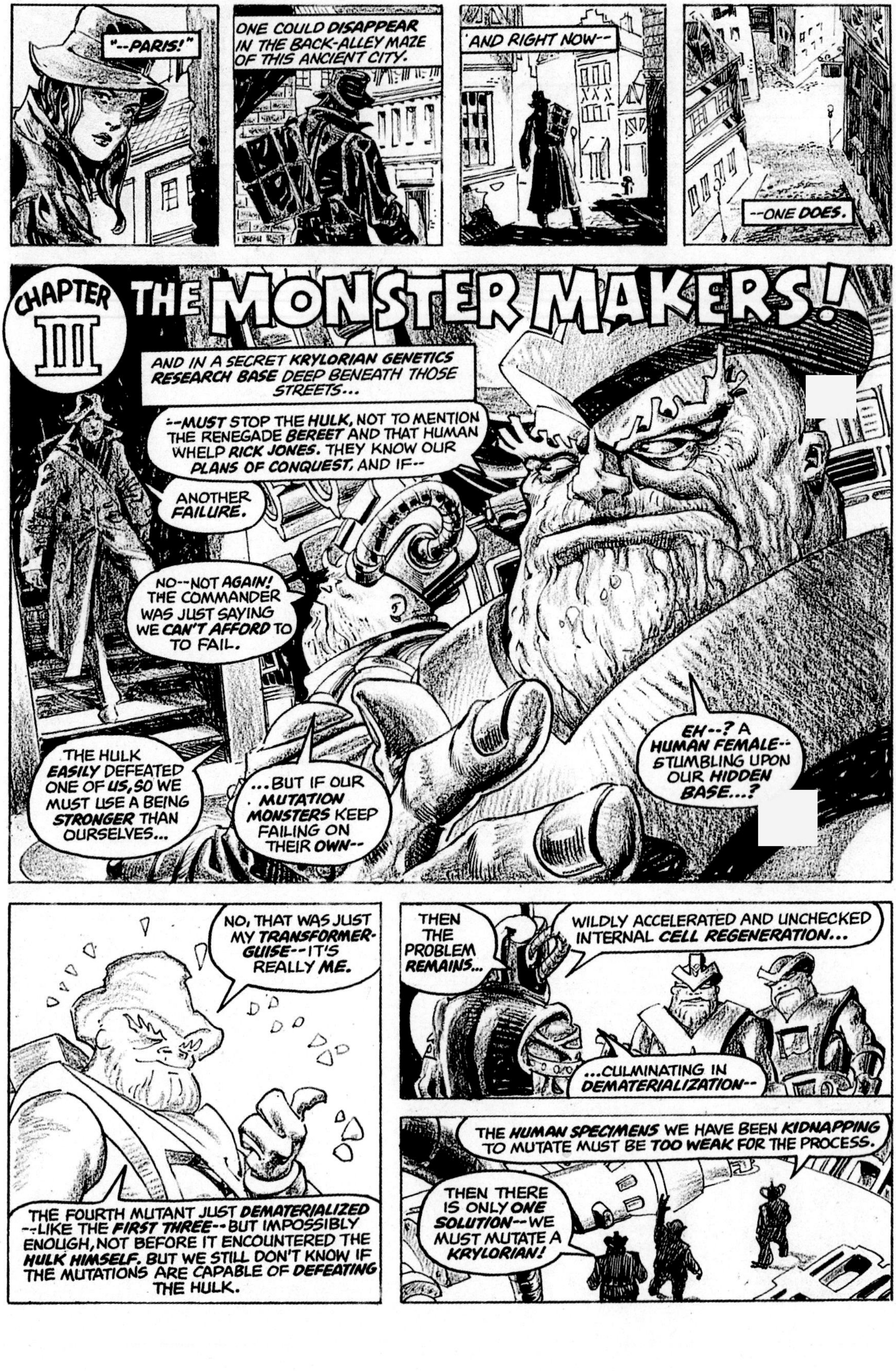
"--PARIS!"
ONE COULD DISAPPEAR IN THE BACK-ALLEY MAZE OF THIS ANCIENT CITY.
AND RIGHT NOW--
--ONE DOES.
CHAPTER III
THE MONSTER MAKERS!
AND IN A SECRET KRYLORIAN GENETICS RESEARCH BASE DEEP BENEATH THOSE STREETS...
--MUST STOP THE HULK, NOT TO MENTION THE RENEGADE BEREET AND THAT HUMAN WHELP RICK JONES. THEY KNOW OUR PLANS OF CONQUEST, AND IF--
ANOTHER FAILURE.
NO--NOT AGAIN! THE COMMANDER WAS JUST SAYING WE CAN'T AFFORD TO TO FAIL.
THE HULK EASILY DEFEATED ONE OF US, SO WE MUST USE A BEING STRONGER THAN OURSELVES...
...BUT IF OUR MUTATION MONSTERS KEEP FAILING ON THEIR OWN--
EH--? A HUMAN FEMALE--STUMBLING UPON OUR HIDDEN BASE...?
NO, THAT WAS JUST MY TRANSFORMER-GUISE--IT'S REALLY ME.
THE FOURTH MUTANT JUST DEMATERIALIZED--LIKE THE FIRST THREE--BUT IMPOSSIBLY ENOUGH, NOT BEFORE IT ENCOUNTERED THE HULK HIMSELF. BUT WE STILL DON'T KNOW IF THE MUTATIONS ARE CAPABLE OF DEFEATING THE HULK.
THEN THE PROBLEM REMAINS...
WILDLY ACCELERATED AND UNCHECKED INTERNAL CELL REGENERATION...
...CULMINATING IN DEMATERIALIZATION--
THE HUMAN SPECIMENS WE HAVE BEEN KIDNAPPING TO MUTATE MUST BE TOO WEAK FOR THE PROCESS.
THEN THERE IS ONLY ONE SOLUTION--WE MUST MUTATE A KRYLORIAN!

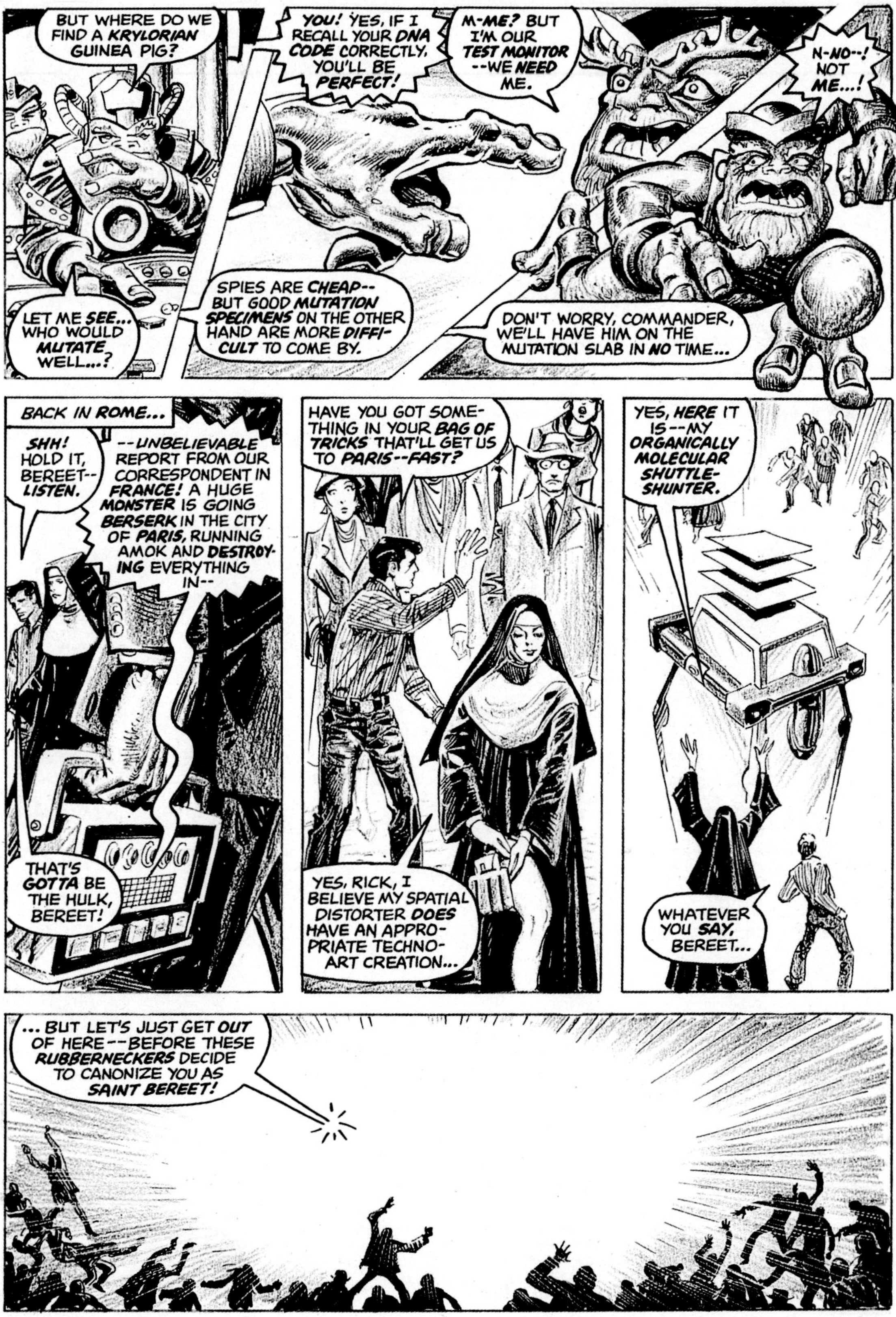
BUT WHERE DO WE FIND A KRYLORIAN GUINEA PIG?
LET ME SEE... WHO WOULD MUTATE WELL...?
YOU! YES, IF I RECALL YOUR DNA CODE CORRECTLY, YOU'LL BE PERFECT!
SPIES ARE CHEAP-- BUT GOOD MUTATION SPECIMENS ON THE OTHER HAND ARE MORE DIFFICULT TO COME BY.
M-ME? BUT I'M OUR TEST MONITOR --WE NEED ME.
N-NO--! NOT ME...!
DON'T WORRY, COMMANDER, WE'LL HAVE HIM ON THE MUTATION SLAB IN NO TIME...
BACK IN ROME...
SHH! HOLD IT, BEREET-- LISTEN.
--UNBELIEVABLE REPORT FROM OUR CORRESPONDENT IN FRANCE! A HUGE MONSTER IS GOING BERSERK IN THE CITY OF PARIS, RUNNING AMOK AND DESTROYING EVERYTHING IN--
THAT'S GOTTA BE THE HULK, BEREET!
HAVE YOU GOT SOMETHING IN YOUR BAG OF TRICKS THAT'LL GET US TO PARIS--FAST?
YES, RICK, I BELIEVE MY SPATIAL DISTORTER DOES HAVE AN APPROPRIATE TECHNO-ART CREATION...
YES, HERE IT IS--MY ORGANICALLY MOLECULAR SHUTTLE-SHUNTER.
WHATEVER YOU SAY, BEREET...
... BUT LET'S JUST GET OUT OF HERE--BEFORE THESE RUBBERNECKERS DECIDE TO CANONIZE YOU AS SAINT BEREET!

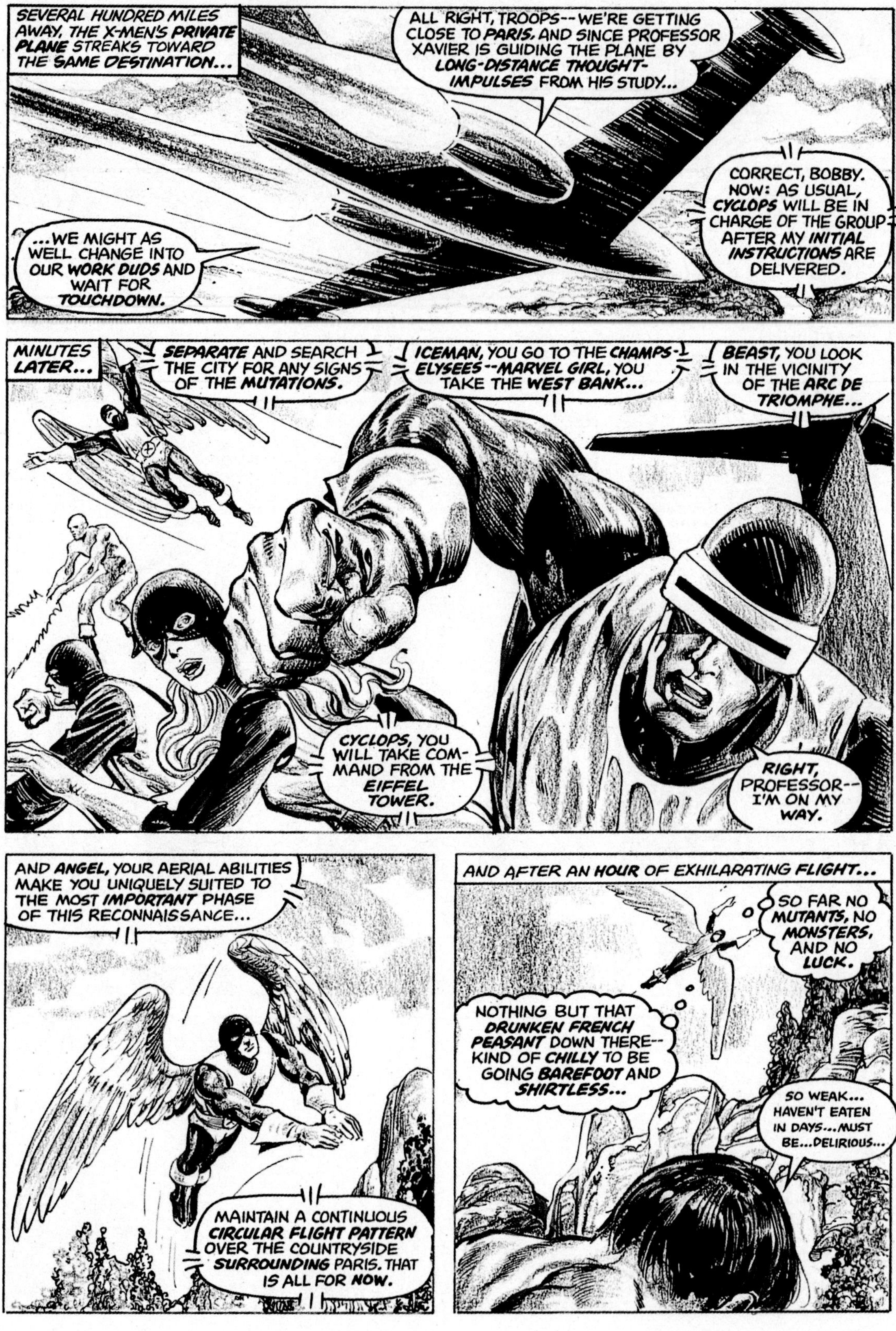
SEVERAL HUNDRED MILES AWAY, THE X-MEN'S PRIVATE PLANE STREAKS TOWARD THE SAME DESTINATION...
ALL RIGHT, TROOPS--WE'RE GETTING CLOSE TO PARIS. AND SINCE PROFESSOR XAVIER IS GUIDING THE PLANE BY LONG-DISTANCE THOUGHT-IMPULSES FROM HIS STUDY...
...WE MIGHT AS WELL CHANGE INTO OUR WORK DUDS AND WAIT FOR TOUCHDOWN.
CORRECT, BOBBY. NOW: AS USUAL, CYCLOPS WILL BE IN CHARGE OF THE GROUP AFTER MY INITIAL INSTRUCTIONS ARE DELIVERED.
MINUTES LATER...
SEPARATE AND SEARCH THE CITY FOR ANY SIGNS OF THE MUTATIONS.
ICEMAN, YOU GO TO THE CHAMPS-ELYSEES--MARVEL GIRL, YOU TAKE THE WEST BANK...
BEAST, YOU LOOK IN THE VICINITY OF THE ARC DE TRIOMPHE...
CYCLOPS, YOU WILL TAKE COMMAND FROM THE EIFFEL TOWER.
RIGHT, PROFESSOR--I'M ON MY WAY.
AND ANGEL, YOUR AERIAL ABILITIES MAKE YOU UNIQUELY SUITED TO THE MOST IMPORTANT PHASE OF THIS RECONNAISSANCE...
MAINTAIN A CONTINUOUS CIRCULAR FLIGHT PATTERN OVER THE COUNTRYSIDE SURROUNDING PARIS. THAT IS ALL FOR NOW.
AND AFTER AN HOUR OF EXHILARATING FLIGHT...
SO FAR NO MUTANTS, NO MONSTERS, AND NO LUCK.
NOTHING BUT THAT DRUNKEN FRENCH PEASANT DOWN THERE--KIND OF CHILLY TO BE GOING BAREFOOT AND SHIRTLESS...
SO WEAK... HAVEN'T EATEN IN DAYS...MUST BE...DELIRIOUS...

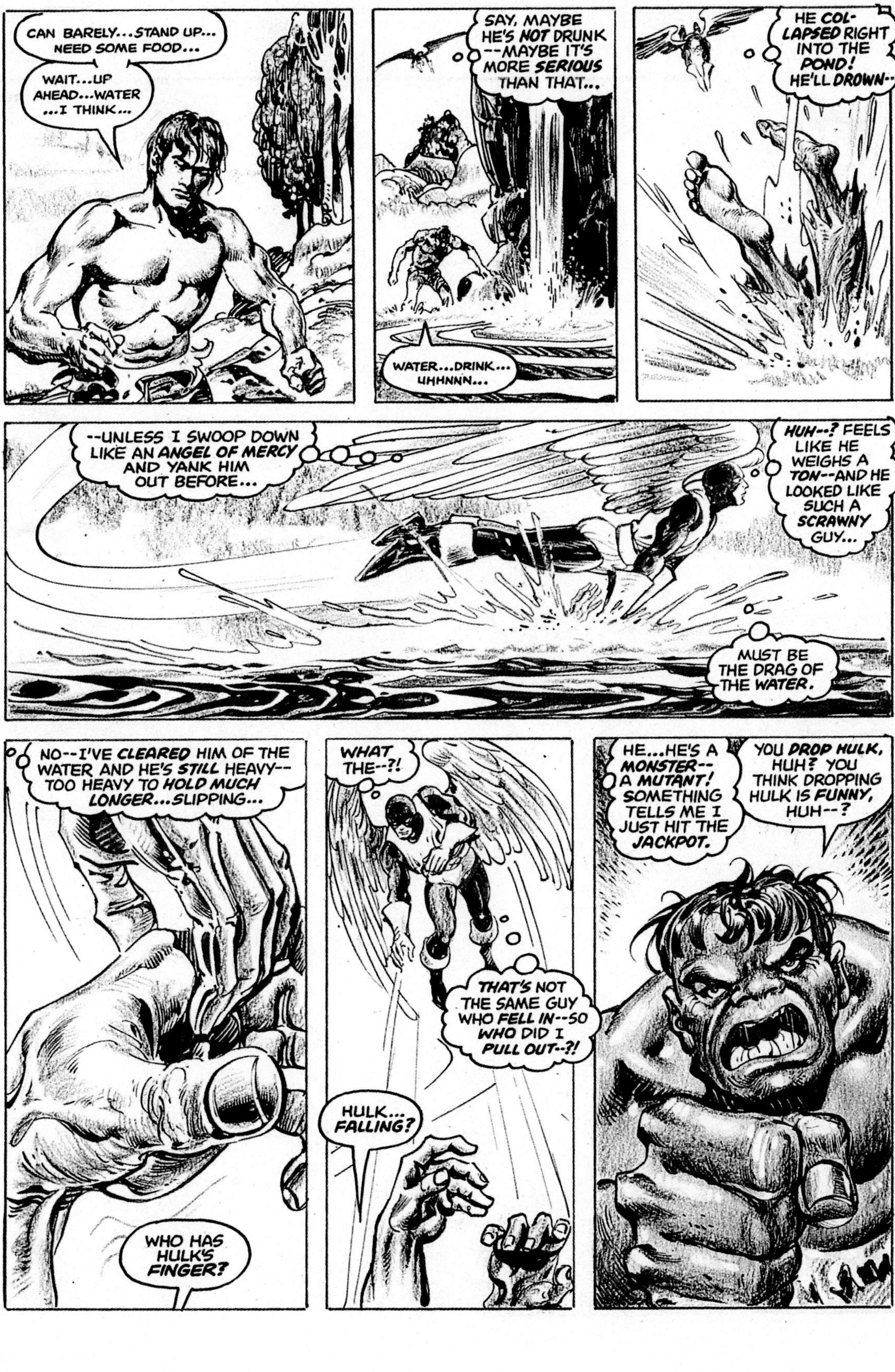
CAN BARELY...STAND UP... NEED SOME FOOD...
WAIT...UP AHEAD...WATER ...I THINK...
SAY, MAYBE HE'S NOT DRUNK --MAYBE IT'S MORE SERIOUS THAN THAT...
WATER...DRINK... UHHNNN...
HE COL-LAPSED RIGHT INTO THE POND! HE'LL DROWN--
--UNLESS I SWOOP DOWN LIKE AN ANGEL OF MERCY AND YANK HIM OUT BEFORE...
HUH--? FEELS LIKE HE WEIGHS A TON--AND HE LOOKED LIKE SUCH A SCRAWNY GUY...
MUST BE THE DRAG OF THE WATER.
NO--I'VE CLEARED HIM OF THE WATER AND HE'S STILL HEAVY-- TOO HEAVY TO HOLD MUCH LONGER...SLIPPING...
WHO HAS HULK'S FINGER?
WHAT THE--?!
THAT'S NOT THE SAME GUY WHO FELL IN--SO WHO DID I PULL OUT--?!
HULK... FALLING?
HE...HE'S A MONSTER-- A MUTANT! SOMETHING TELLS ME I JUST HIT THE JACKPOT.
YOU DROP HULK, HUH? YOU THINK DROPPING HULK IS FUNNY, HUH--?

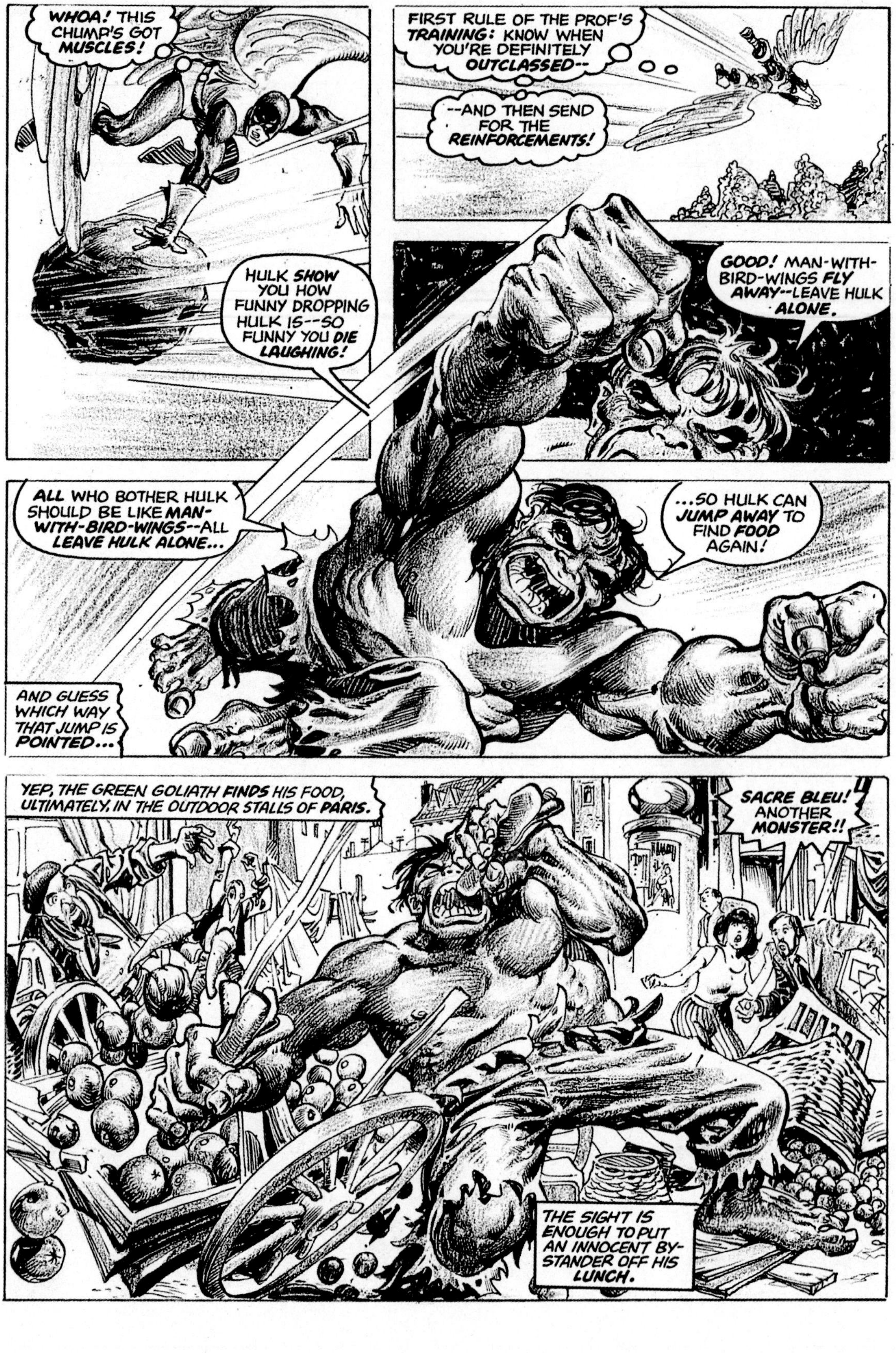
WHOA! THIS CHUMP'S GOT MUSCLES!
FIRST RULE OF THE PROF'S TRAINING: KNOW WHEN YOU'RE DEFINITELY OUTCLASSED--
--AND THEN SEND FOR THE REINFORCEMENTS!
HULK SHOW YOU HOW FUNNY DROPPING HULK IS--SO FUNNY YOU DIE LAUGHING!
GOOD! MAN-WITH-BIRD-WINGS FLY AWAY--LEAVE HULK ALONE.
ALL WHO BOTHER HULK SHOULD BE LIKE MAN-WITH-BIRD-WINGS--ALL LEAVE HULK ALONE...
...SO HULK CAN JUMP AWAY TO FIND FOOD AGAIN!
AND GUESS WHICH WAY THAT JUMP IS POINTED...
YEP, THE GREEN GOLIATH FINDS HIS FOOD, ULTIMATELY, IN THE OUTDOOR STALLS OF PARIS.
SACRE BLEU! ANOTHER MONSTER!!
THE SIGHT IS ENOUGH TO PUT AN INNOCENT BY-STANDER OFF HIS LUNCH.

CYCLOPS--YOU'LL NEVER *BELIEVE* WHAT I JUST--

WE ALREADY *KNOW*, ANGEL.

PROFESSOR X TOLD US ALL TO GATHER *HERE*. HE'S NOT CERTAIN THE BEING IS A *MUTANT*, ANGEL, BUT IT *IS DANGEROUS* --AND SEEMS TO BE HEADING RIGHT THIS WAY TOWARD THE *EIFFEL TOWER*.

BRACE YOURSELVES, X-MEN-- BEAR IN MIND EVERYTHING YOU'VE LEARNED ABOUT *TEAMWORK*.

AND *REMEMBER*, CYCLOPS, I'M COUNT-ING ON YOU TO SEE THAT NO ONE IS *INJURED*.

FOUR BLOCKS AWAY...

MORDIEU! A *MIRACLE*--!

OR ANOTHER *MONSTER*.

DO YOU *SEE*, HIM, RICK?

NOPE. NOT *HERE*, BEREET.

WE MUST'VE CHECKED A *HUNDRED DIFFERENT CORNERS* OF PARIS BY NOW--

--BUT I GUESS WE'VE JUST GOTTA *KEEP LOOKING.*

HULK CAN'T EAT WITH SO MANY *SCREAMING AROUND FOOD!*

HULK *CHASE SCREAMERS* AWAY--EAT IN *PEACE*-- *ALONE.*

THEN IT WAS *NOT* INSURANCE FRAUD! THERE REALLY IS A MONSTER RUNNING AROUND *DESTROYING AUTOMOBILES!*

AND AS THE GLOOM OF TWILIGHT CLOSES IN, THE *RAMPAGING HULK SWIFTLY APPROACHES A FATEFUL STREETCORNER...*

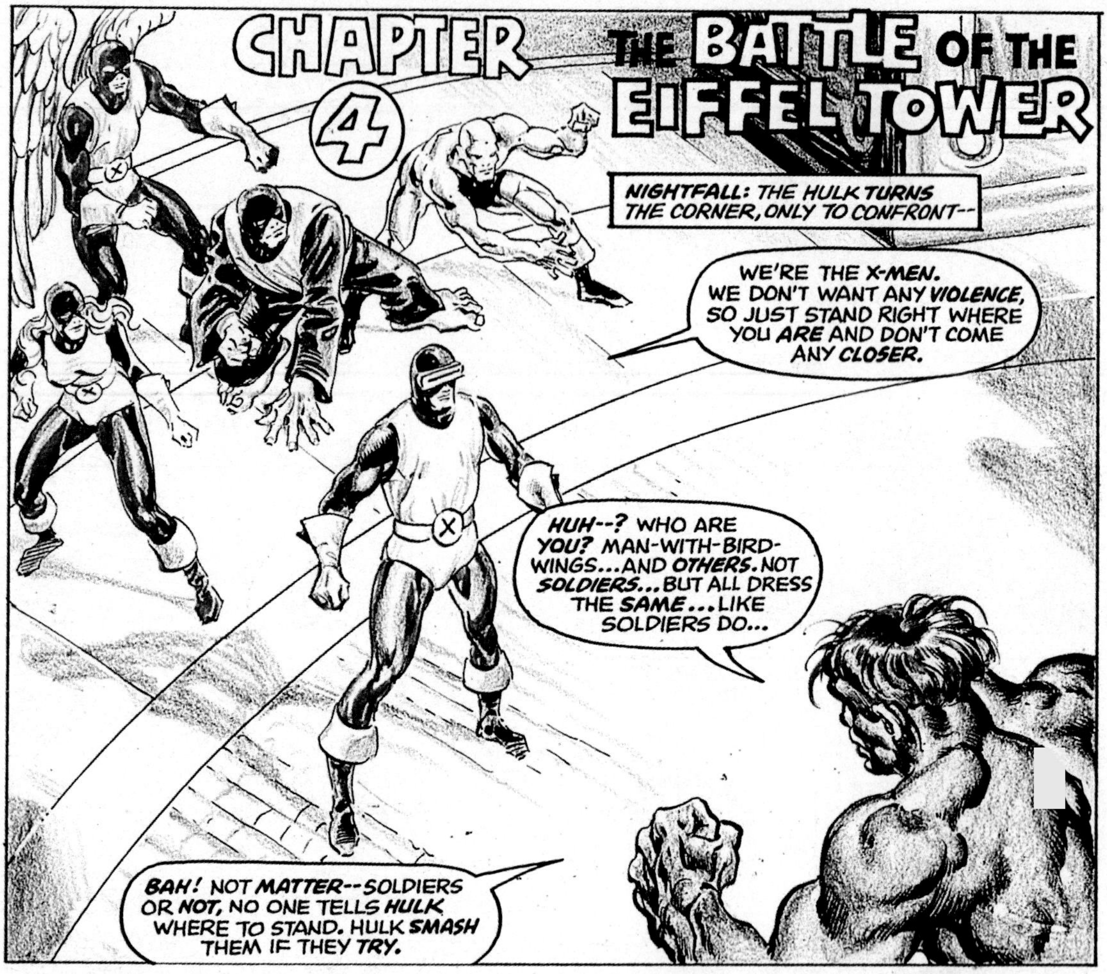
CHAPTER 4
THE BATTLE OF THE EIFFEL TOWER
NIGHTFALL: THE HULK TURNS THE CORNER, ONLY TO CONFRONT--
WE'RE THE X-MEN. WE DON'T WANT ANY VIOLENCE, SO JUST STAND RIGHT WHERE YOU ARE AND DON'T COME ANY CLOSER.
HUH--? WHO ARE YOU? MAN-WITH-BIRD-WINGS...AND OTHERS. NOT SOLDIERS...BUT ALL DRESS THE SAME...LIKE SOLDIERS DO...
BAH! NOT MATTER--SOLDIERS OR NOT, NO ONE TELLS HULK WHERE TO STAND. HULK SMASH THEM IF THEY TRY.

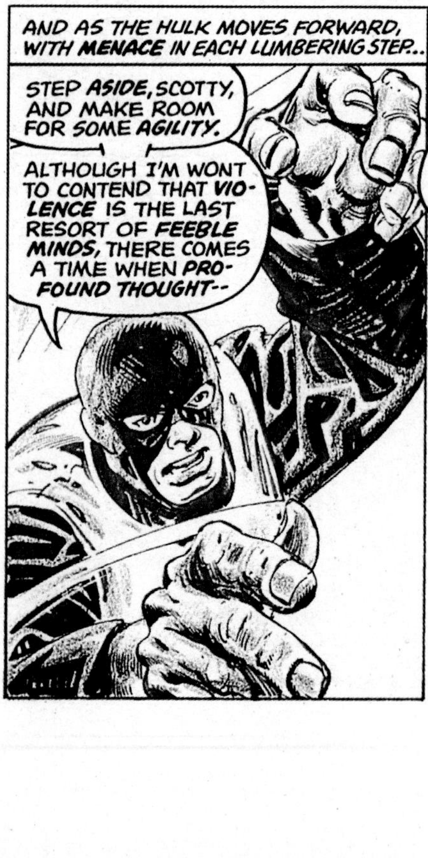
AND AS THE HULK MOVES FORWARD, WITH MENACE IN EACH LUMBERING STEP...
STEP ASIDE, SCOTTY, AND MAKE ROOM FOR SOME AGILITY.
ALTHOUGH I'M WONT TO CONTEND THAT VIOLENCE IS THE LAST RESORT OF FEEBLE MINDS, THERE COMES A TIME WHEN PROFOUND THOUGHT--

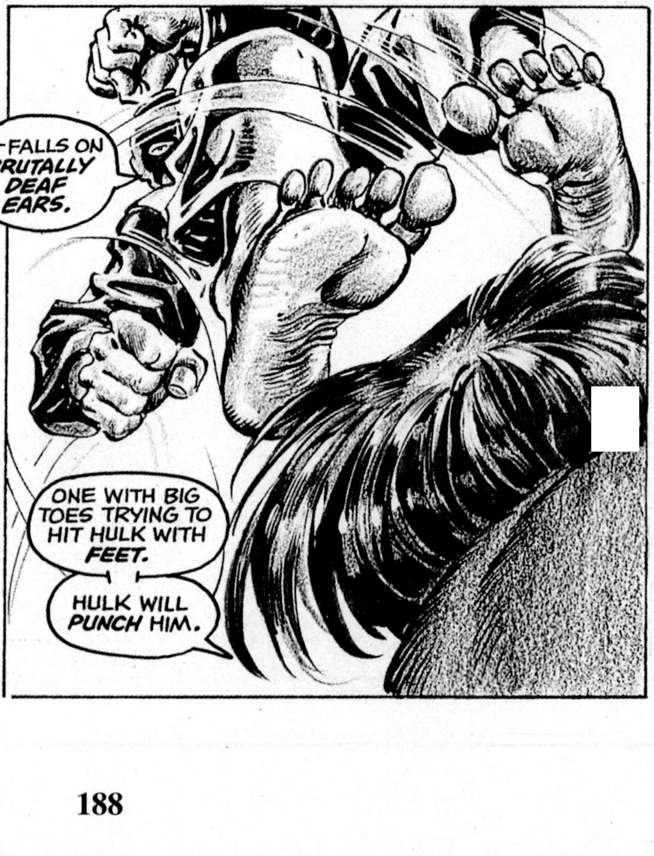
--FALLS ON BRUTALLY DEAF EARS.
ONE WITH BIG TOES TRYING TO HIT HULK WITH FEET.
HULK WILL PUNCH HIM.

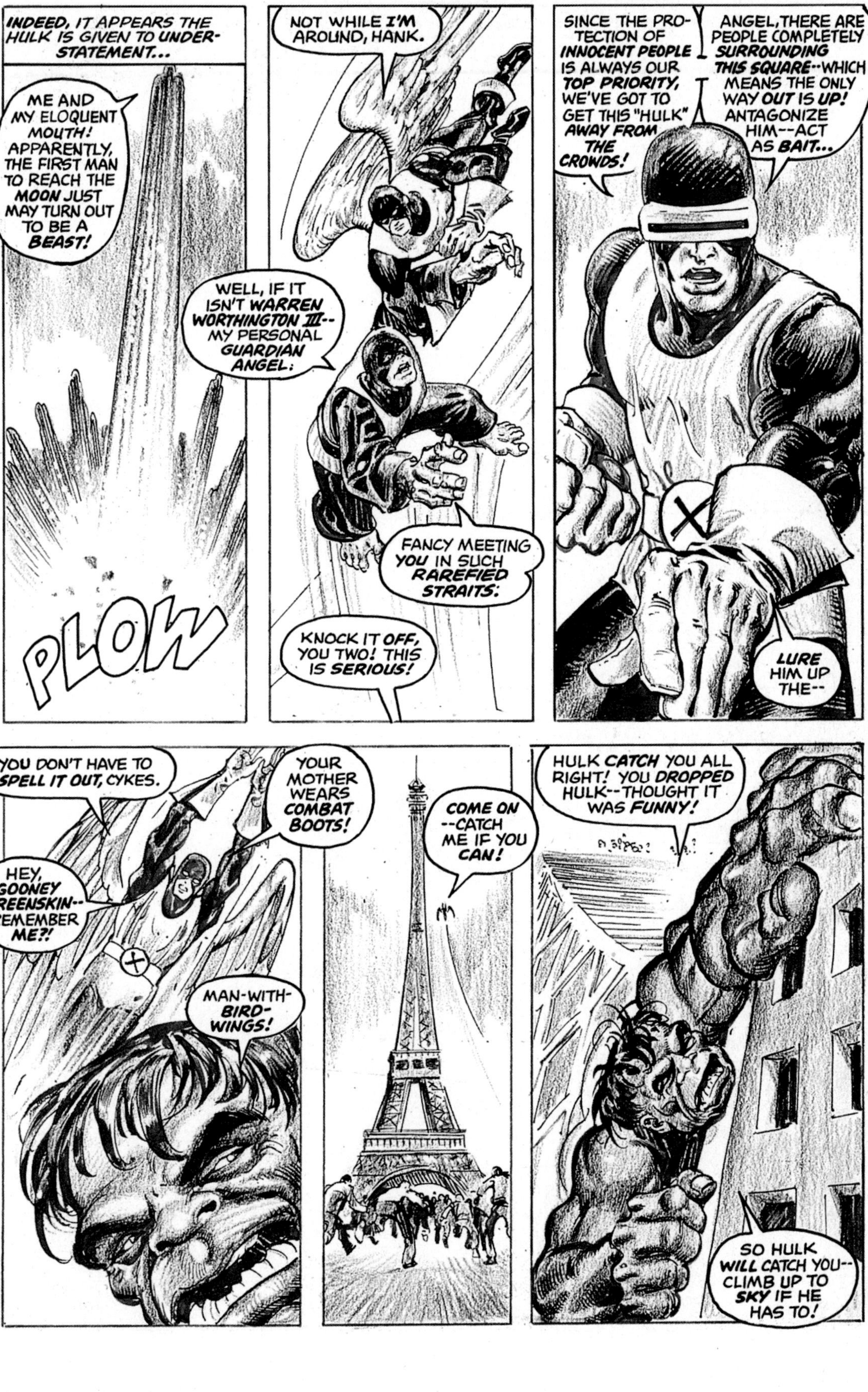
INDEED, IT APPEARS THE HULK IS GIVEN TO UNDER-STATEMENT...
ME AND MY ELOQUENT MOUTH! APPARENTLY, THE FIRST MAN TO REACH THE MOON JUST MAY TURN OUT TO BE A BEAST!
PLOW
NOT WHILE I'M AROUND, HANK.
WELL, IF IT ISN'T WARREN WORTHINGTON III-- MY PERSONAL GUARDIAN ANGEL:
FANCY MEETING YOU IN SUCH RAREFIED STRAITS:
KNOCK IT OFF, YOU TWO! THIS IS SERIOUS!
SINCE THE PRO-TECTION OF INNOCENT PEOPLE IS ALWAYS OUR TOP PRIORITY, WE'VE GOT TO GET THIS "HULK" AWAY FROM THE CROWDS!
ANGEL, THERE ARE PEOPLE COMPLETELY SURROUNDING THIS SQUARE--WHICH MEANS THE ONLY WAY OUT IS UP! ANTAGONIZE HIM--ACT AS BAIT...
LURE HIM UP THE--
YOU DON'T HAVE TO SPELL IT OUT, CYKES.
YOUR MOTHER WEARS COMBAT BOOTS!
HEY, GOONEY GREENSKIN-- REMEMBER ME?!
MAN-WITH-BIRD-WINGS!
COME ON --CATCH ME IF YOU CAN!
HULK CATCH YOU ALL RIGHT! YOU DROPPED HULK--THOUGHT IT WAS FUNNY!
SO HULK WILL CATCH YOU-- CLIMB UP TO SKY IF HE HAS TO!

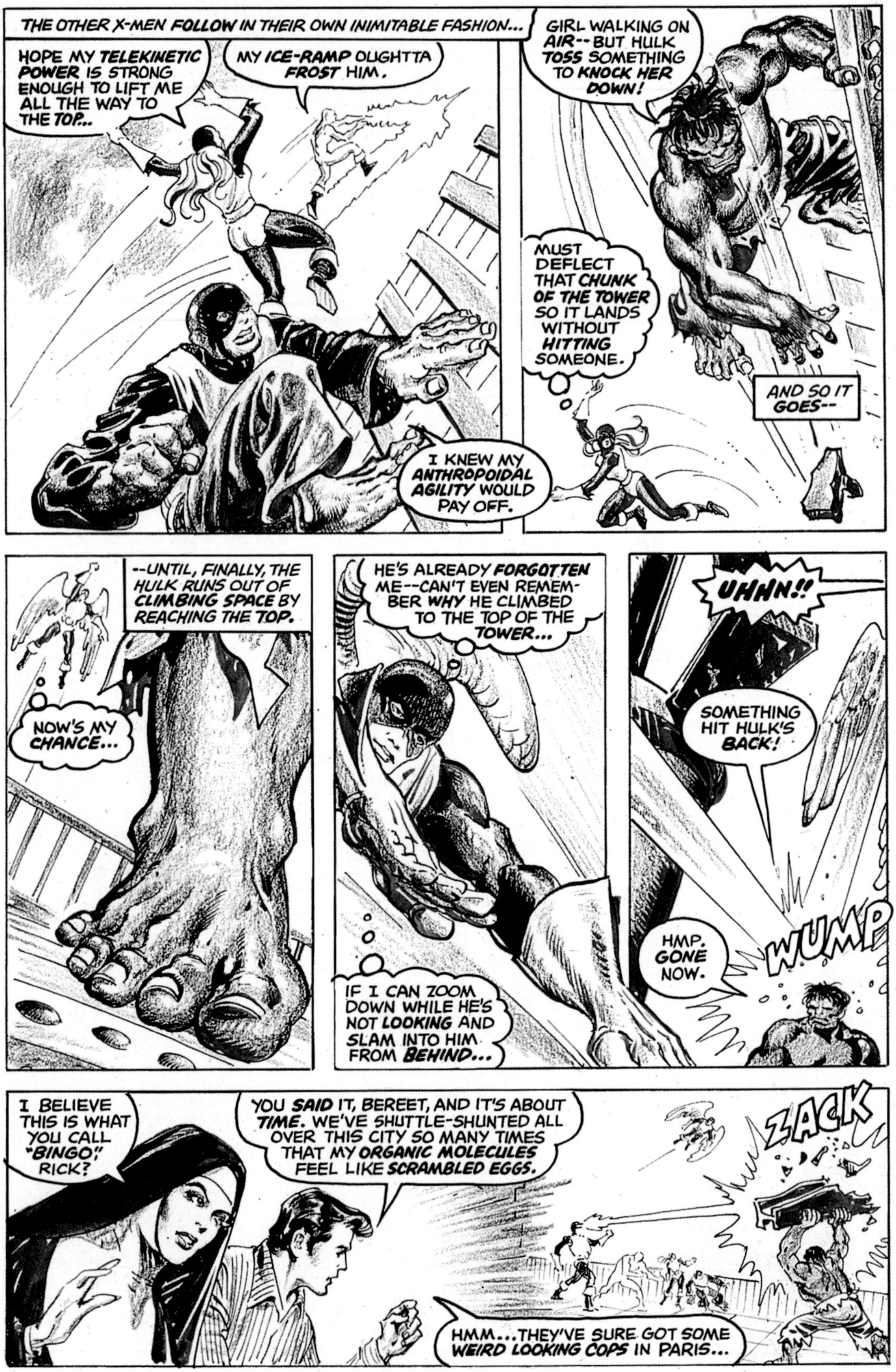
THE OTHER X-MEN FOLLOW IN THEIR OWN INIMITABLE FASHION...
HOPE MY TELEKINETIC POWER IS STRONG ENOUGH TO LIFT ME ALL THE WAY TO THE TOP..
MY ICE-RAMP OUGHTTA FROST HIM.
I KNEW MY ANTHROPOIDAL AGILITY WOULD PAY OFF.
GIRL WALKING ON AIR--BUT HULK TOSS SOMETHING TO KNOCK HER DOWN!
MUST DEFLECT THAT CHUNK OF THE TOWER SO IT LANDS WITHOUT HITTING SOMEONE.
AND SO IT GOES--
--UNTIL, FINALLY, THE HULK RUNS OUT OF CLIMBING SPACE BY REACHING THE TOP.
NOW'S MY CHANCE...
HE'S ALREADY FORGOTTEN ME--CAN'T EVEN REMEMBER WHY HE CLIMBED TO THE TOP OF THE TOWER...
IF I CAN ZOOM DOWN WHILE HE'S NOT LOOKING AND SLAM INTO HIM FROM BEHIND...
UHHN!!
SOMETHING HIT HULK'S BACK!
WUMP
HMP. GONE NOW.
I BELIEVE THIS IS WHAT YOU CALL "BINGO," RICK?
YOU SAID IT, BEREET, AND IT'S ABOUT TIME. WE'VE SHUTTLE-SHUNTED ALL OVER THIS CITY SO MANY TIMES THAT MY ORGANIC MOLECULES FEEL LIKE SCRAMBLED EGGS.
ZACK
HMM...THEY'VE SURE GOT SOME WEIRD LOOKING COPS IN PARIS...

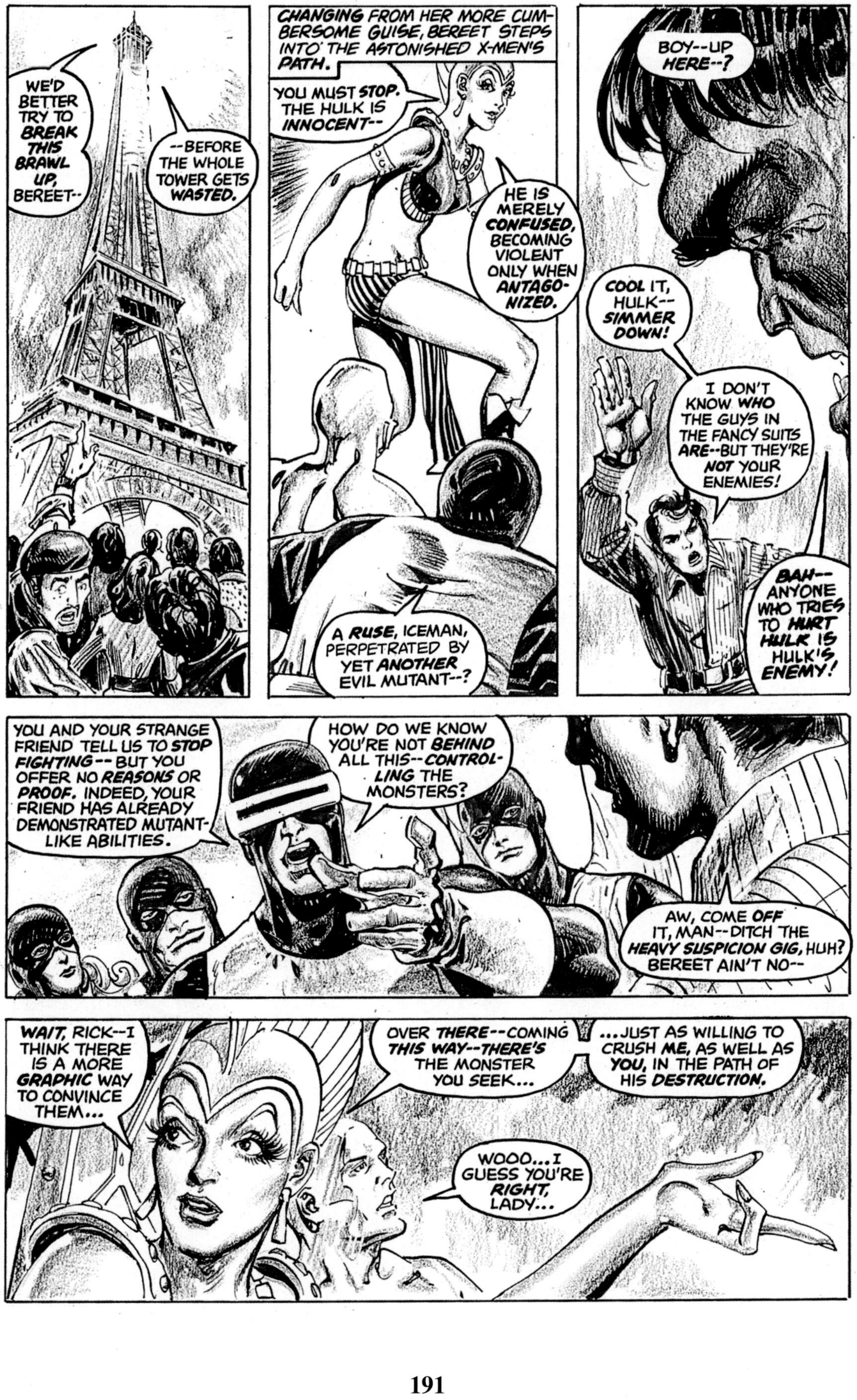
WE'D BETTER TRY TO BREAK THIS BRAWL UP, BEREET--
--BEFORE THE WHOLE TOWER GETS WASTED.
CHANGING FROM HER MORE CUMBERSOME GUISE, BEREET STEPS INTO THE ASTONISHED X-MEN'S PATH.
YOU MUST STOP. THE HULK IS INNOCENT--
HE IS MERELY CONFUSED, BECOMING VIOLENT ONLY WHEN ANTAGONIZED.
A RUSE, ICEMAN, PERPETRATED BY YET ANOTHER EVIL MUTANT--?
BOY--UP HERE--?
COOL IT, HULK--SIMMER DOWN!
I DON'T KNOW WHO THE GUYS IN THE FANCY SUITS ARE--BUT THEY'RE NOT YOUR ENEMIES!
BAH--ANYONE WHO TRIES TO HURT HULK IS HULK'S ENEMY!
YOU AND YOUR STRANGE FRIEND TELL US TO STOP FIGHTING--BUT YOU OFFER NO REASONS OR PROOF. INDEED, YOUR FRIEND HAS ALREADY DEMONSTRATED MUTANT-LIKE ABILITIES.
HOW DO WE KNOW YOU'RE NOT BEHIND ALL THIS--CONTROLLING THE MONSTERS?
AW, COME OFF IT, MAN--DITCH THE HEAVY SUSPICION GIG, HUH? BEREET AIN'T NO--
WAIT, RICK--I THINK THERE IS A MORE GRAPHIC WAY TO CONVINCE THEM...
OVER THERE--COMING THIS WAY--THERE'S THE MONSTER YOU SEEK...
...JUST AS WILLING TO CRUSH ME, AS WELL AS YOU, IN THE PATH OF HIS DESTRUCTION.
WOOO...I GUESS YOU'RE RIGHT, LADY...

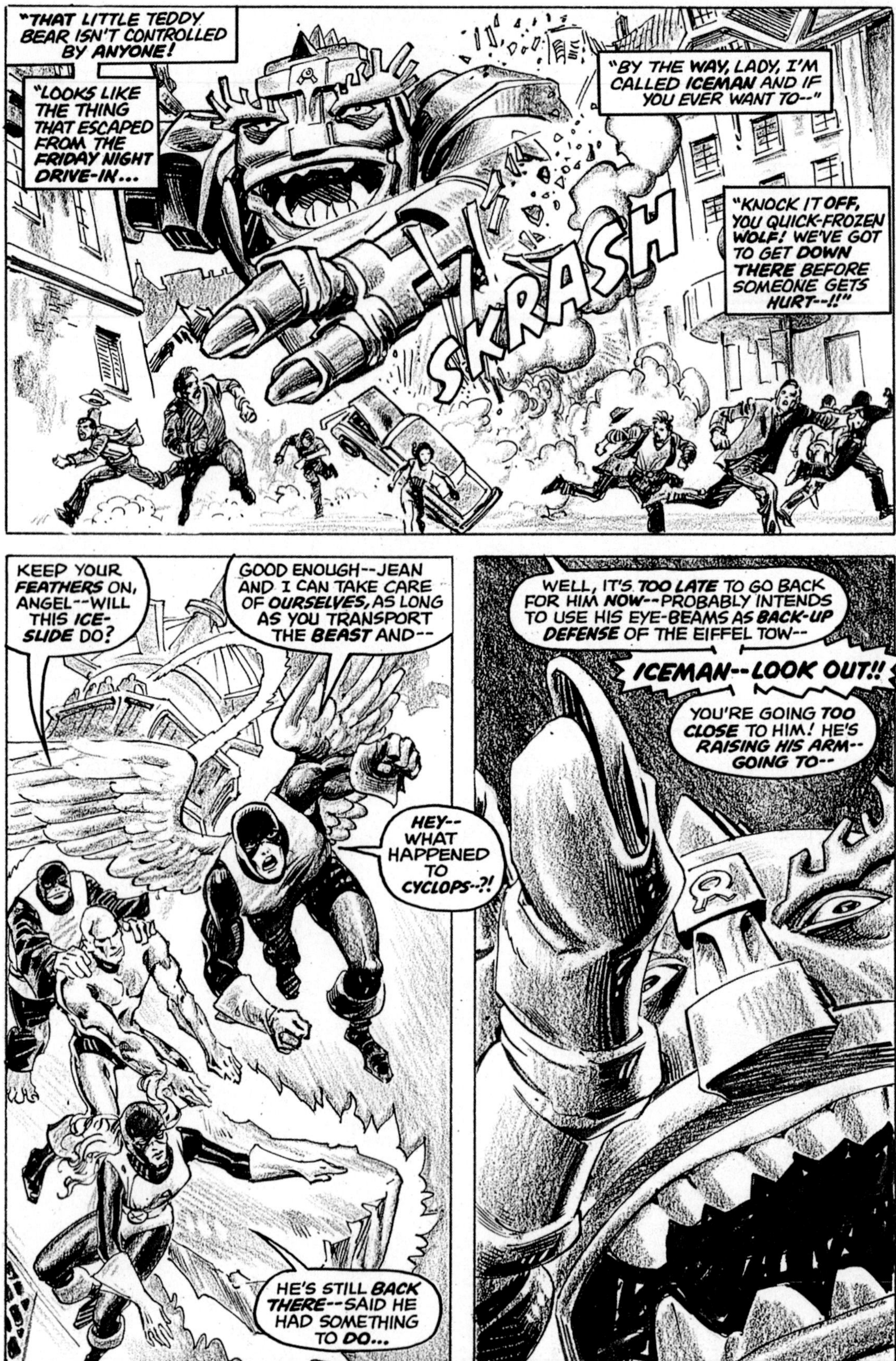
"THAT LITTLE TEDDY BEAR ISN'T CONTROLLED BY ANYONE!
"LOOKS LIKE THE THING THAT ESCAPED FROM THE FRIDAY NIGHT DRIVE-IN...
"BY THE WAY, LADY, I'M CALLED ICEMAN AND IF YOU EVER WANT TO--"
SKRASH
"KNOCK IT OFF, YOU QUICK-FROZEN WOLF! WE'VE GOT TO GET DOWN THERE BEFORE SOMEONE GETS HURT--!!"
KEEP YOUR FEATHERS ON, ANGEL--WILL THIS ICE-SLIDE DO?
GOOD ENOUGH--JEAN AND I CAN TAKE CARE OF OURSELVES, AS LONG AS YOU TRANSPORT THE BEAST AND--
HEY--WHAT HAPPENED TO CYCLOPS--?!
HE'S STILL BACK THERE--SAID HE HAD SOMETHING TO DO...
WELL, IT'S TOO LATE TO GO BACK FOR HIM NOW--PROBABLY INTENDS TO USE HIS EYE-BEAMS AS BACK-UP DEFENSE OF THE EIFFEL TOW--
ICEMAN--LOOK OUT!!
YOU'RE GOING TOO CLOSE TO HIM! HE'S RAISING HIS ARM--GOING TO--

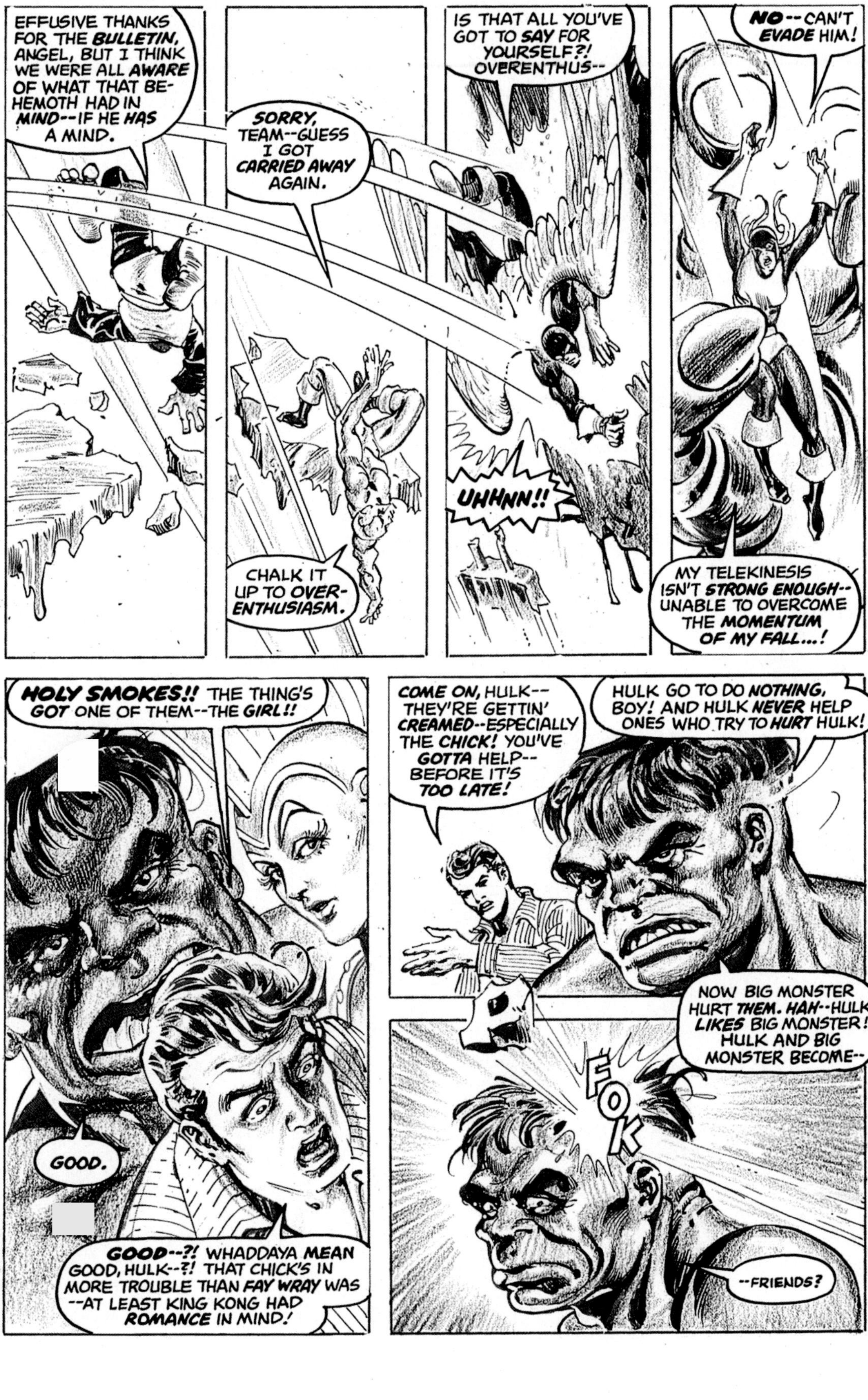

EFFUSIVE THANKS FOR THE BULLETIN, ANGEL, BUT I THINK WE WERE ALL AWARE OF WHAT THAT BE-HEMOTH HAD IN MIND--IF HE HAS A MIND.
SORRY, TEAM--GUESS I GOT CARRIED AWAY AGAIN.
CHALK IT UP TO OVER-ENTHUSIASM.
IS THAT ALL YOU'VE GOT TO SAY FOR YOURSELF?! OVERENTHUS--
UHHNN!!
NO--CAN'T EVADE HIM!
MY TELEKINESIS ISN'T STRONG ENOUGH--UNABLE TO OVERCOME THE MOMENTUM OF MY FALL...!
HOLY SMOKES!! THE THING'S GOT ONE OF THEM--THE GIRL!!
GOOD.
GOOD--?! WHADDAYA MEAN GOOD, HULK--?! THAT CHICK'S IN MORE TROUBLE THAN FAY WRAY WAS --AT LEAST KING KONG HAD ROMANCE IN MIND!
COME ON, HULK--THEY'RE GETTIN' CREAMED--ESPECIALLY THE CHICK! YOU'VE GOTTA HELP--BEFORE IT'S TOO LATE!
HULK GO TO DO NOTHING, BOY! AND HULK NEVER HELP ONES WHO TRY TO HURT HULK!
NOW BIG MONSTER HURT THEM. HAH--HULK LIKES BIG MONSTER! HULK AND BIG MONSTER BECOME--
FOK
--FRIENDS?

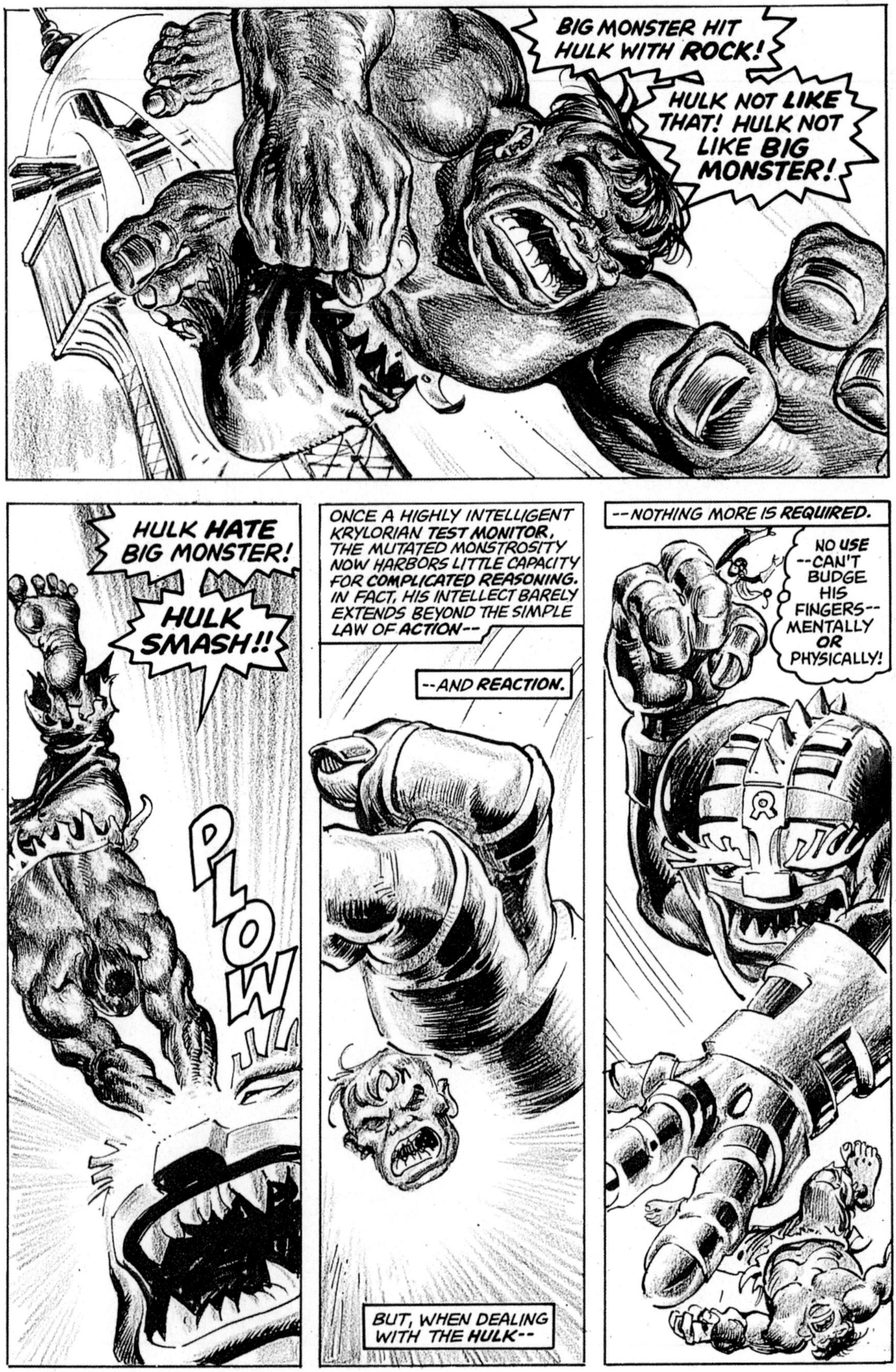
BIG MONSTER HIT HULK WITH ROCK!
HULK NOT LIKE THAT! HULK NOT LIKE BIG MONSTER!
HULK HATE BIG MONSTER!
HULK SMASH!!
PLOW
ONCE A HIGHLY INTELLIGENT KRYLORIAN TEST MONITOR, THE MUTATED MONSTROSITY NOW HARBORS LITTLE CAPACITY FOR COMPLICATED REASONING. IN FACT, HIS INTELLECT BARELY EXTENDS BEYOND THE SIMPLE LAW OF ACTION--
--AND REACTION.
BUT, WHEN DEALING WITH THE HULK--
--NOTHING MORE IS REQUIRED.
NO USE --CAN'T BUDGE HIS FINGERS-- MENTALLY OR PHYSICALLY!

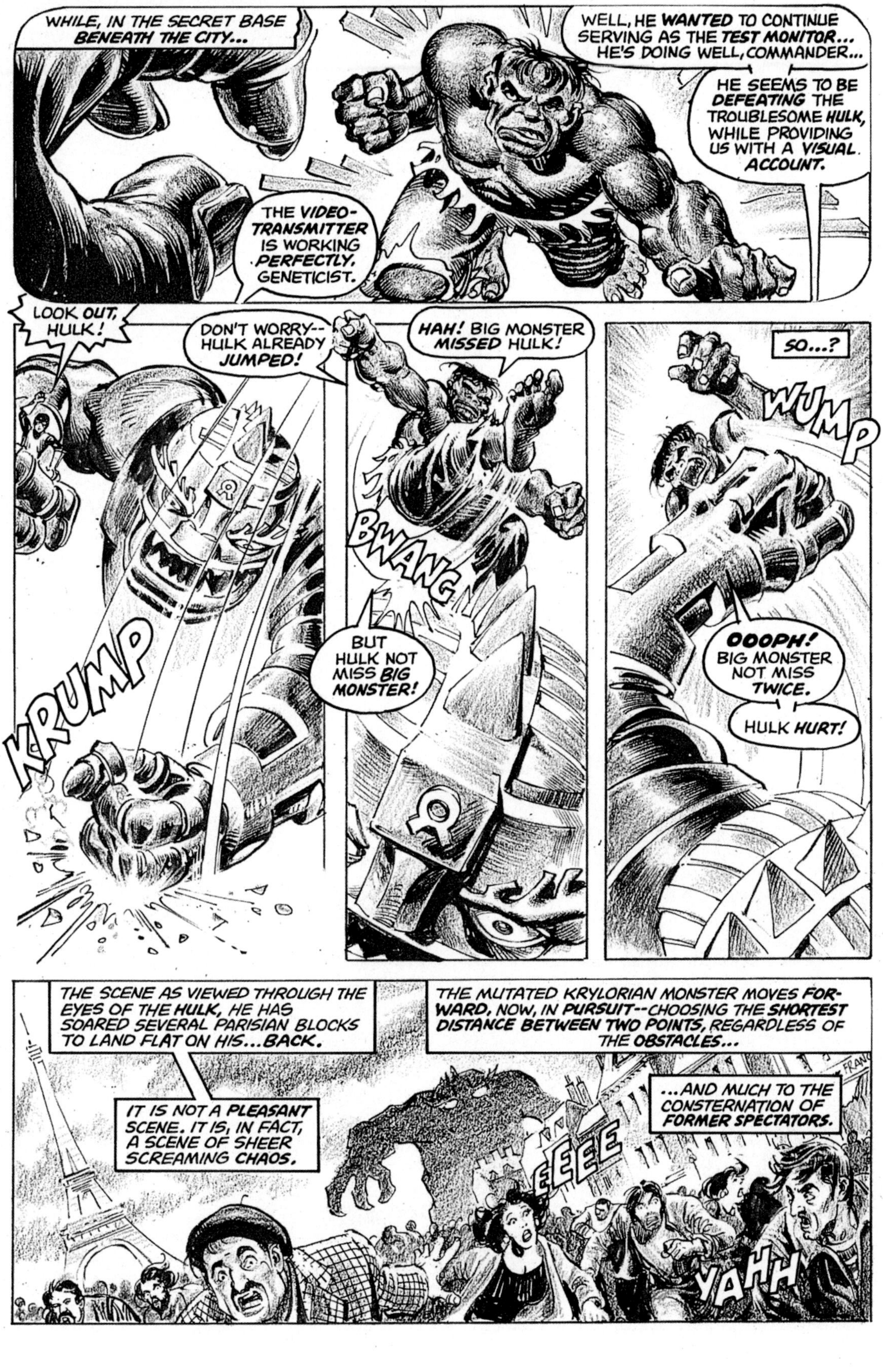
WHILE, IN THE SECRET BASE BENEATH THE CITY...
WELL, HE WANTED TO CONTINUE SERVING AS THE TEST MONITOR... HE'S DOING WELL, COMMANDER...
HE SEEMS TO BE DEFEATING THE TROUBLESOME HULK, WHILE PROVIDING US WITH A VISUAL ACCOUNT.
THE VIDEO-TRANSMITTER IS WORKING PERFECTLY, GENETICIST.
LOOK OUT, HULK!
DON'T WORRY-- HULK ALREADY JUMPED!
KRUMP
HAH! BIG MONSTER MISSED HULK!
BWANG
BUT HULK NOT MISS BIG MONSTER!
SO...?
WUMP
OOOPH! BIG MONSTER NOT MISS TWICE.
HULK HURT!
THE SCENE AS VIEWED THROUGH THE EYES OF THE HULK, HE HAS SOARED SEVERAL PARISIAN BLOCKS TO LAND FLAT ON HIS... BACK.
THE MUTATED KRYLORIAN MONSTER MOVES FORWARD, NOW, IN PURSUIT--CHOOSING THE SHORTEST DISTANCE BETWEEN TWO POINTS, REGARDLESS OF THE OBSTACLES...
IT IS NOT A PLEASANT SCENE. IT IS, IN FACT, A SCENE OF SHEER SCREAMING CHAOS.
...AND MUCH TO THE CONSTERNATION OF FORMER SPECTATORS.
EEEE
YAHH

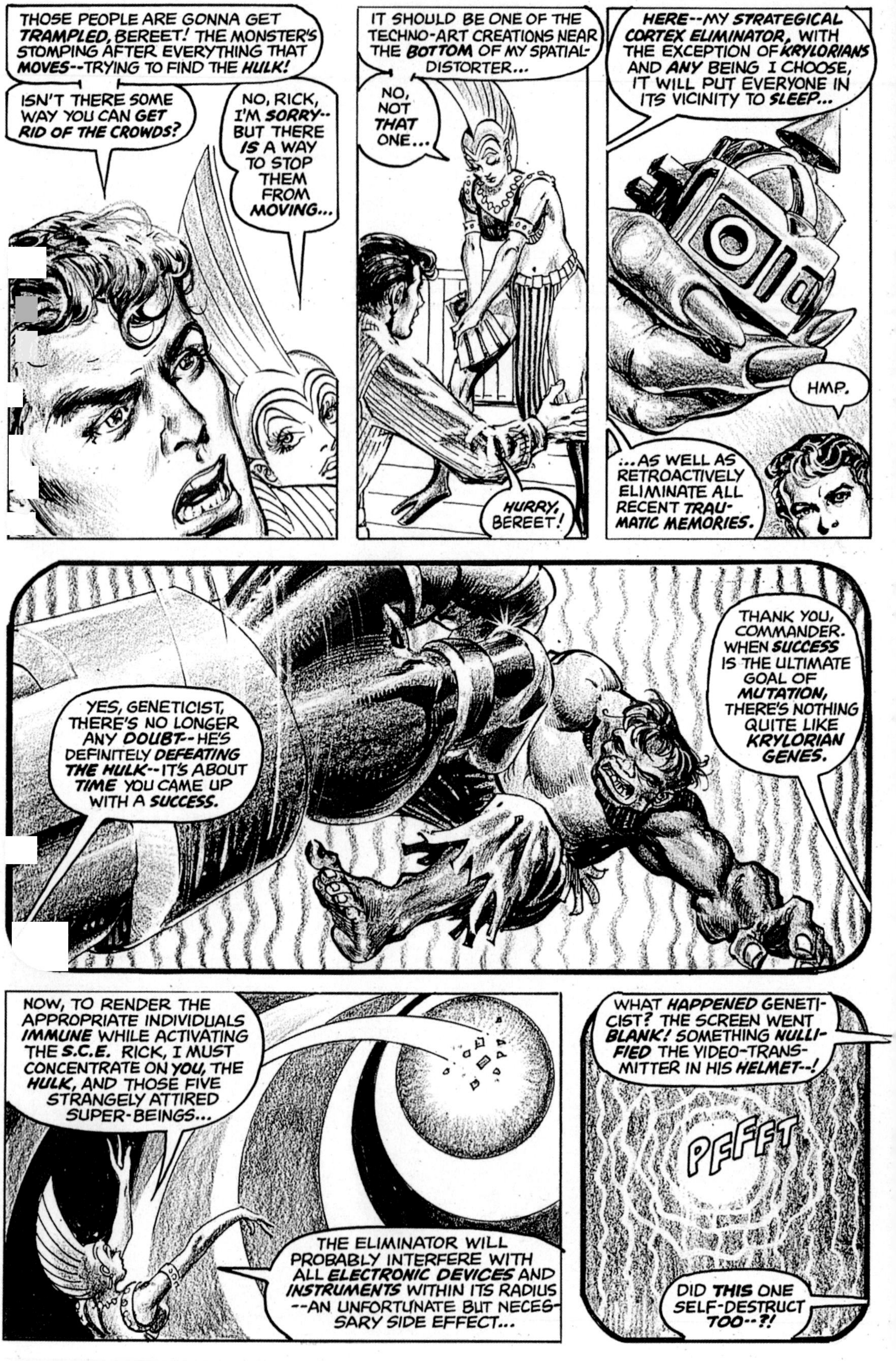
THOSE PEOPLE ARE GONNA GET TRAMPLED, BEREET! THE MONSTER'S STOMPING AFTER EVERYTHING THAT MOVES--TRYING TO FIND THE HULK!
ISN'T THERE SOME WAY YOU CAN GET RID OF THE CROWDS?
NO, RICK, I'M SORRY-- BUT THERE IS A WAY TO STOP THEM FROM MOVING...
IT SHOULD BE ONE OF THE TECHNO-ART CREATIONS NEAR THE BOTTOM OF MY SPATIAL-DISTORTER...
NO, NOT THAT ONE...
HURRY, BEREET!
HERE--MY STRATEGICAL CORTEX ELIMINATOR, WITH THE EXCEPTION OF KRYLORIANS AND ANY BEING I CHOOSE, IT WILL PUT EVERYONE IN ITS VICINITY TO SLEEP...
HMP.
...AS WELL AS RETROACTIVELY ELIMINATE ALL RECENT TRAUMATIC MEMORIES.
YES, GENETICIST, THERE'S NO LONGER ANY DOUBT--HE'S DEFINITELY DEFEATING THE HULK--IT'S ABOUT TIME YOU CAME UP WITH A SUCCESS.
THANK YOU, COMMANDER. WHEN SUCCESS IS THE ULTIMATE GOAL OF MUTATION, THERE'S NOTHING QUITE LIKE KRYLORIAN GENES.
NOW, TO RENDER THE APPROPRIATE INDIVIDUALS IMMUNE WHILE ACTIVATING THE S.C.E. RICK, I MUST CONCENTRATE ON YOU, THE HULK, AND THOSE FIVE STRANGELY ATTIRED SUPER-BEINGS...
THE ELIMINATOR WILL PROBABLY INTERFERE WITH ALL ELECTRONIC DEVICES AND INSTRUMENTS WITHIN ITS RADIUS --AN UNFORTUNATE BUT NECESSARY SIDE EFFECT...
WHAT HAPPENED GENETICIST? THE SCREEN WENT BLANK! SOMETHING NULLIFIED THE VIDEO-TRANSMITTER IN HIS HELMET--!
PFFFT
DID THIS ONE SELF-DESTRUCT TOO--?!

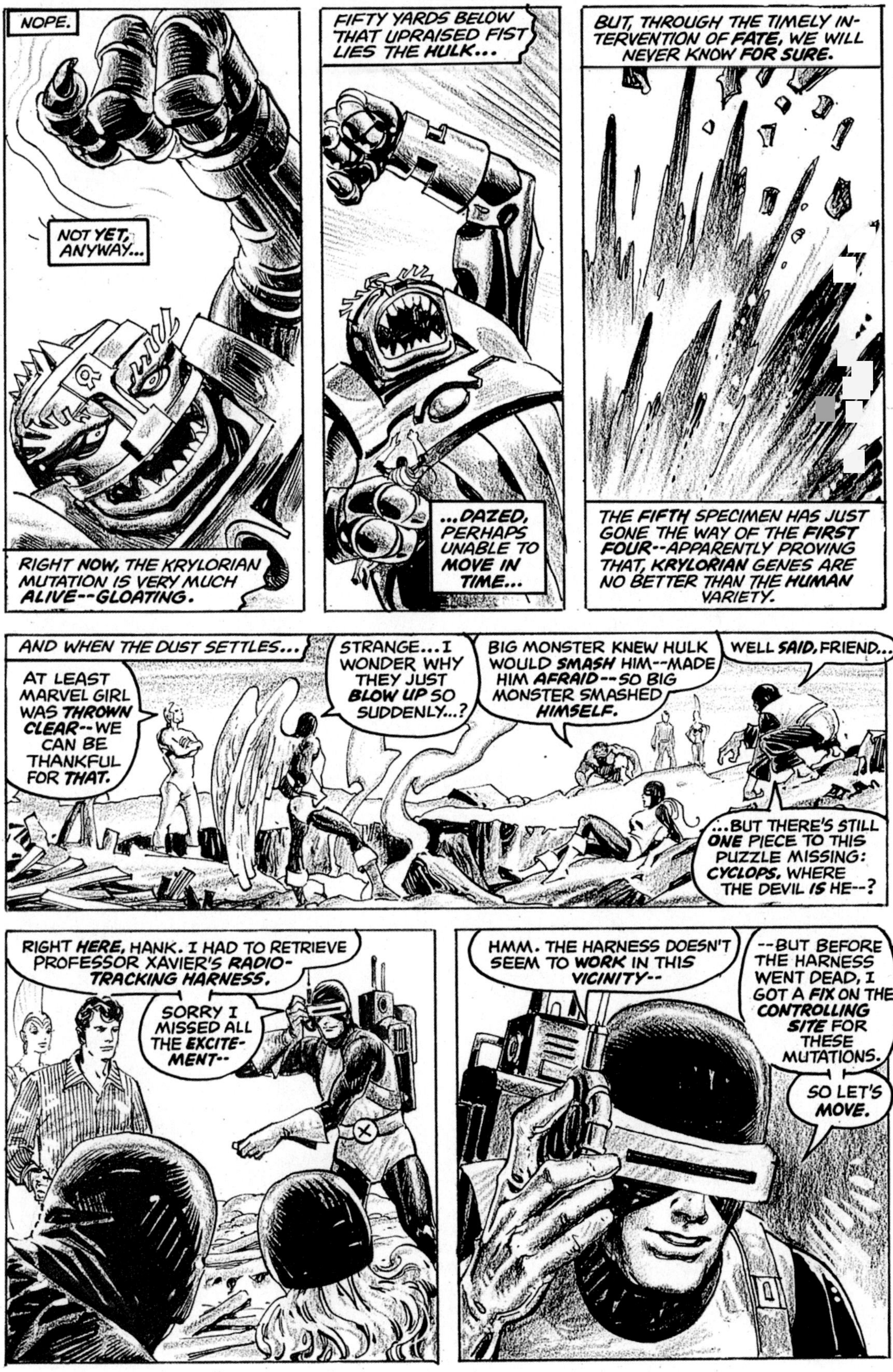
NOPE.
NOT YET, ANYWAY...
RIGHT NOW, THE KRYLORIAN MUTATION IS VERY MUCH ALIVE--GLOATING.
FIFTY YARDS BELOW THAT UPRAISED FIST LIES THE HULK...
...DAZED, PERHAPS UNABLE TO MOVE IN TIME...
BUT, THROUGH THE TIMELY INTERVENTION OF FATE, WE WILL NEVER KNOW FOR SURE.
THE FIFTH SPECIMEN HAS JUST GONE THE WAY OF THE FIRST FOUR--APPARENTLY PROVING THAT, KRYLORIAN GENES ARE NO BETTER THAN THE HUMAN VARIETY.
AND WHEN THE DUST SETTLES...
AT LEAST MARVEL GIRL WAS THROWN CLEAR--WE CAN BE THANKFUL FOR THAT.
STRANGE...I WONDER WHY THEY JUST BLOW UP SO SUDDENLY...?
BIG MONSTER KNEW HULK WOULD SMASH HIM--MADE HIM AFRAID--SO BIG MONSTER SMASHED HIMSELF.
WELL SAID, FRIEND...
...BUT THERE'S STILL ONE PIECE TO THIS PUZZLE MISSING: CYCLOPS. WHERE THE DEVIL IS HE--?
RIGHT HERE, HANK. I HAD TO RETRIEVE PROFESSOR XAVIER'S RADIO-TRACKING HARNESS.
SORRY I MISSED ALL THE EXCITE-MENT--
HMM. THE HARNESS DOESN'T SEEM TO WORK IN THIS VICINITY--
--BUT BEFORE THE HARNESS WENT DEAD, I GOT A FIX ON THE CONTROLLING SITE FOR THESE MUTATIONS.
SO LET'S MOVE.

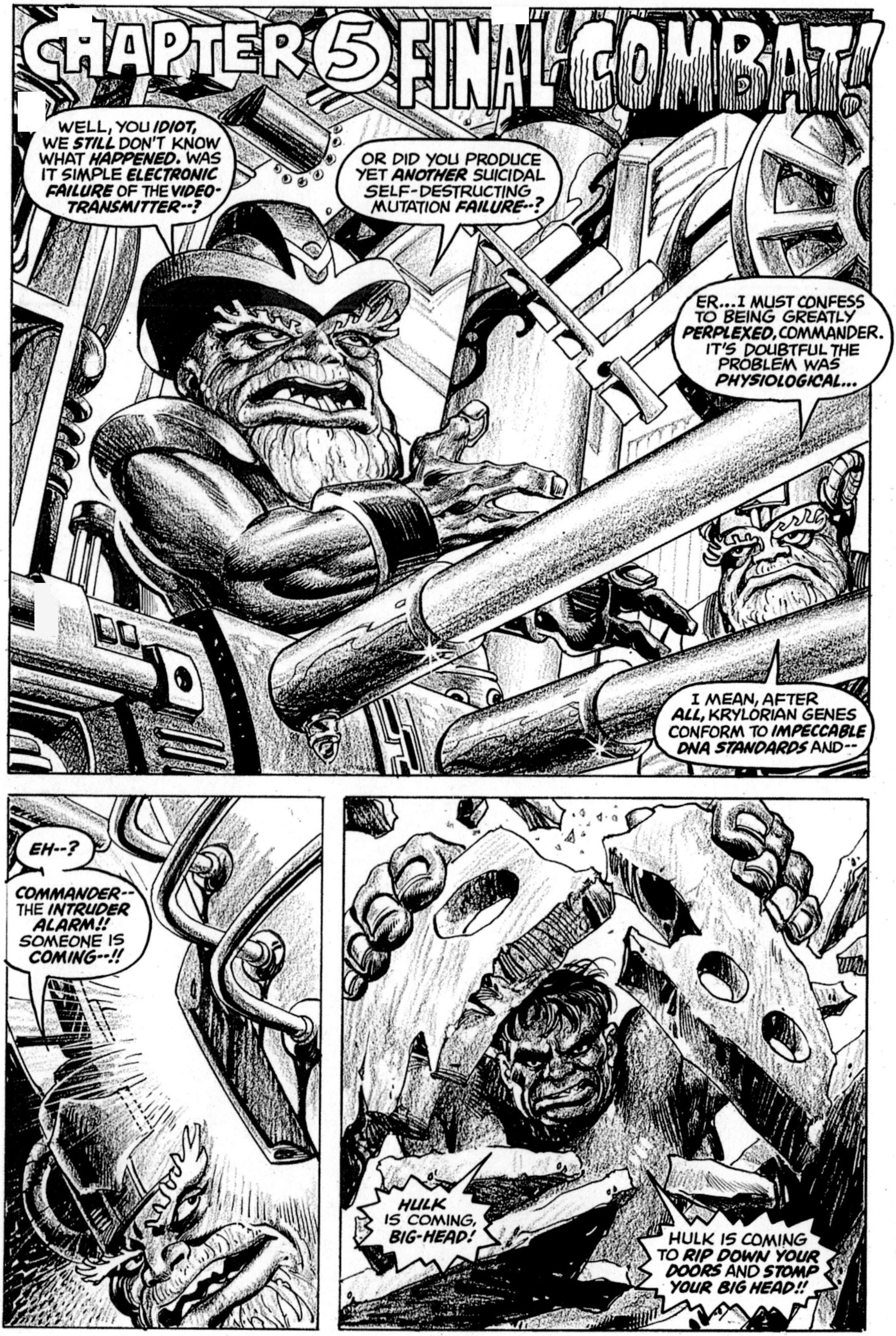
CHAPTER 5 FINAL COMBAT!
WELL, YOU IDIOT, WE STILL DON'T KNOW WHAT HAPPENED. WAS IT SIMPLE ELECTRONIC FAILURE OF THE VIDEO-TRANSMITTER--?
OR DID YOU PRODUCE YET ANOTHER SUICIDAL SELF-DESTRUCTING MUTATION FAILURE--?
ER...I MUST CONFESS TO BEING GREATLY PERPLEXED, COMMANDER. IT'S DOUBTFUL THE PROBLEM WAS PHYSIOLOGICAL...
I MEAN, AFTER ALL, KRYLORIAN GENES CONFORM TO IMPECCABLE DNA STANDARDS AND--
EH--?
COMMANDER-- THE INTRUDER ALARM!! SOMEONE IS COMING--!!
HULK IS COMING, BIG-HEAD!
HULK IS COMING TO RIP DOWN YOUR DOORS AND STOMP YOUR BIG HEAD!!

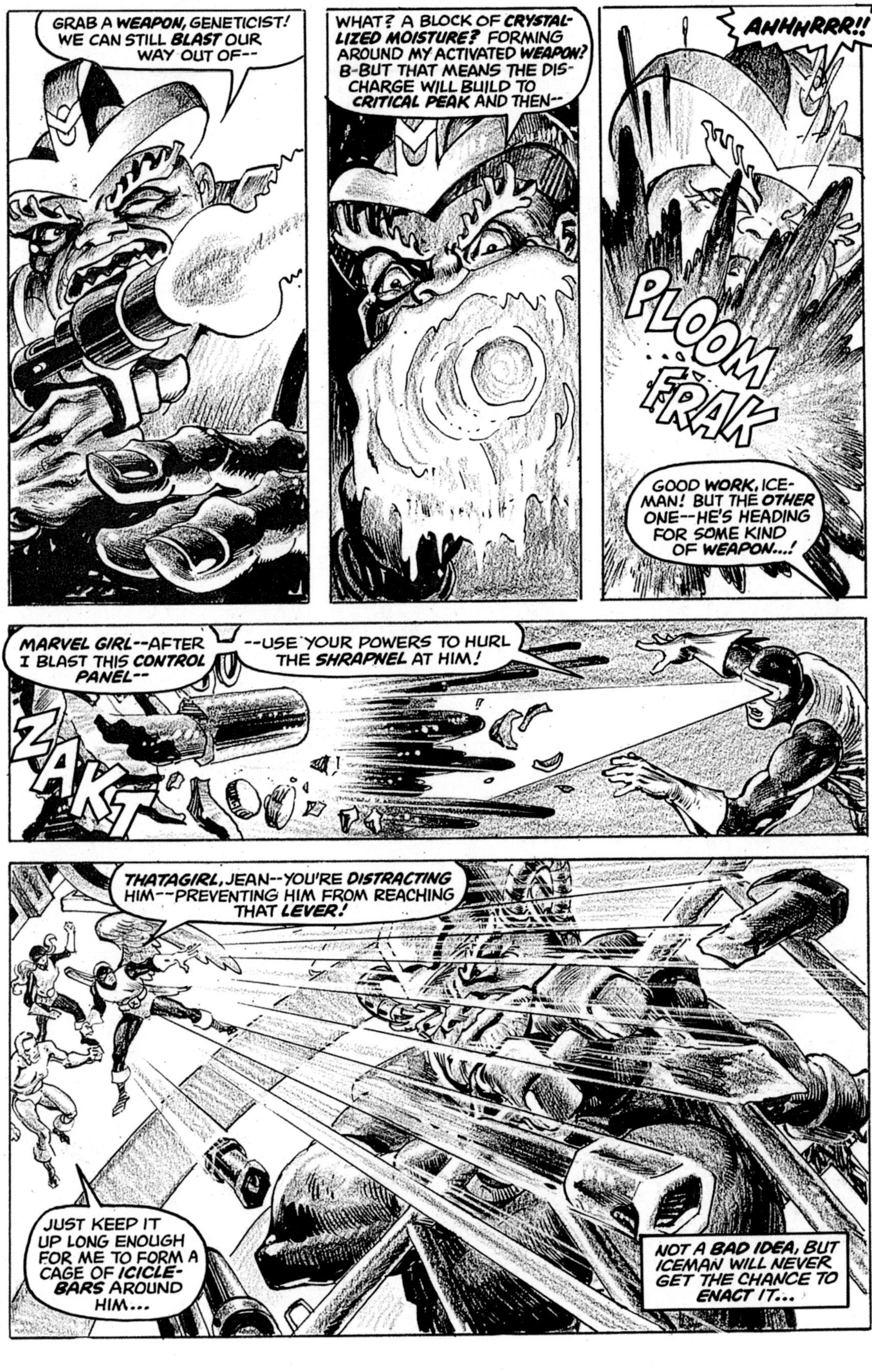

GRAB A WEAPON, GENETICIST! WE CAN STILL BLAST OUR WAY OUT OF--
WHAT? A BLOCK OF CRYSTALLIZED MOISTURE? FORMING AROUND MY ACTIVATED WEAPON? B-BUT THAT MEANS THE DISCHARGE WILL BUILD TO CRITICAL PEAK AND THEN--
AHHHRRR!!
PLOOM
FRAK
GOOD WORK, ICEMAN! BUT THE OTHER ONE--HE'S HEADING FOR SOME KIND OF WEAPON...!
MARVEL GIRL--AFTER I BLAST THIS CONTROL PANEL--
--USE YOUR POWERS TO HURL THE SHRAPNEL AT HIM!
ZAKT
THATAGIRL, JEAN--YOU'RE DISTRACTING HIM--PREVENTING HIM FROM REACHING THAT LEVER!
JUST KEEP IT UP LONG ENOUGH FOR ME TO FORM A CAGE OF ICICLE-BARS AROUND HIM...
NOT A BAD IDEA, BUT ICEMAN WILL NEVER GET THE CHANCE TO ENACT IT...

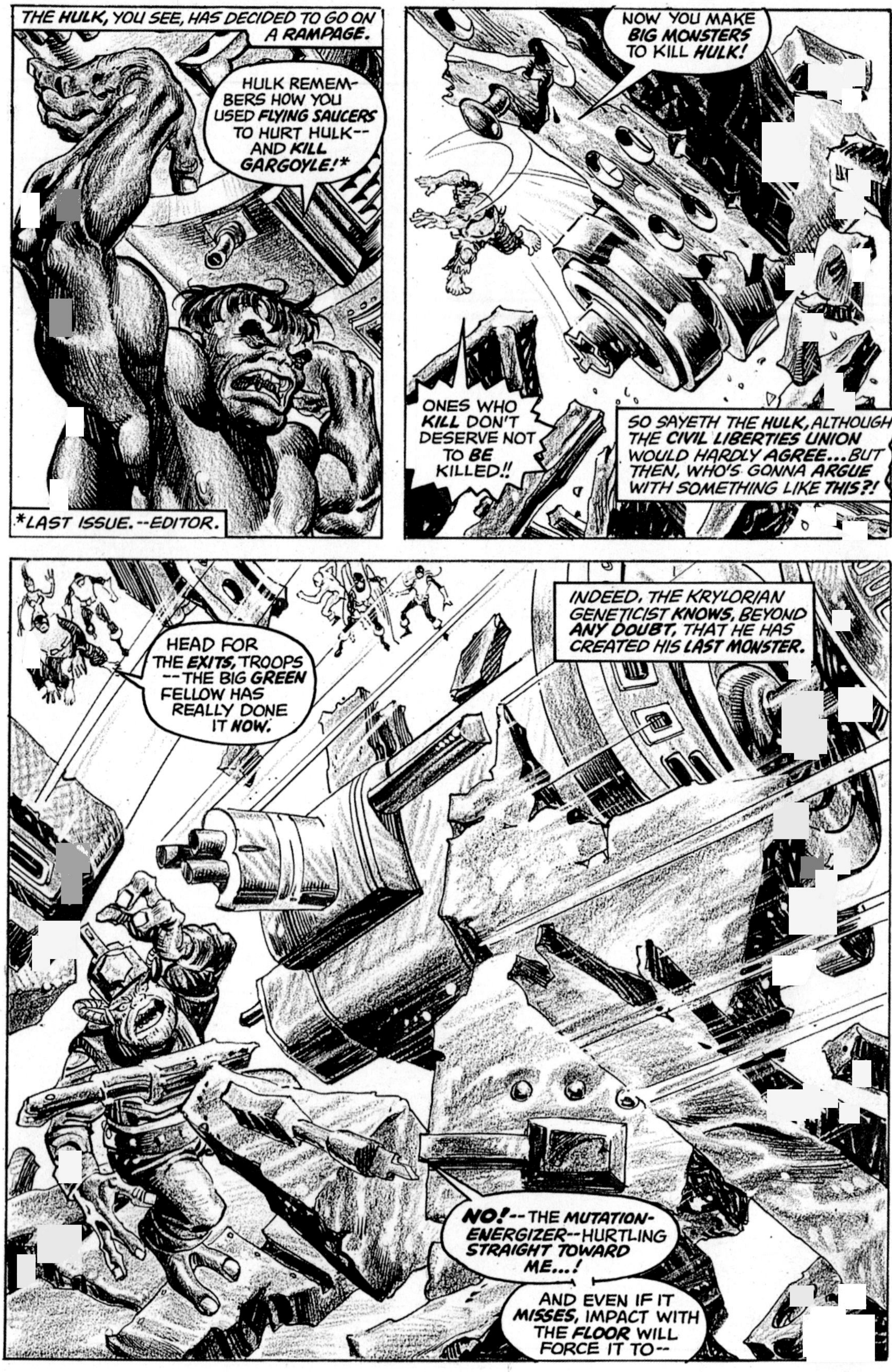

THE HULK, YOU SEE, HAS DECIDED TO GO ON A RAMPAGE.
HULK REMEMBERS HOW YOU USED FLYING SAUCERS TO HURT HULK-- AND KILL GARGOYLE!*
*LAST ISSUE. --EDITOR.
NOW YOU MAKE BIG MONSTERS TO KILL HULK!
ONES WHO KILL DON'T DESERVE NOT TO BE KILLED!!
SO SAYETH THE HULK, ALTHOUGH THE CIVIL LIBERTIES UNION WOULD HARDLY AGREE... BUT THEN, WHO'S GONNA ARGUE WITH SOMETHING LIKE THIS?!
HEAD FOR THE EXITS, TROOPS --THE BIG GREEN FELLOW HAS REALLY DONE IT NOW.
INDEED, THE KRYLORIAN GENETICIST KNOWS, BEYOND ANY DOUBT, THAT HE HAS CREATED HIS LAST MONSTER.
NO!--THE MUTATION-ENERGIZER--HURTLING STRAIGHT TOWARD ME...!
AND EVEN IF IT MISSES, IMPACT WITH THE FLOOR WILL FORCE IT TO--

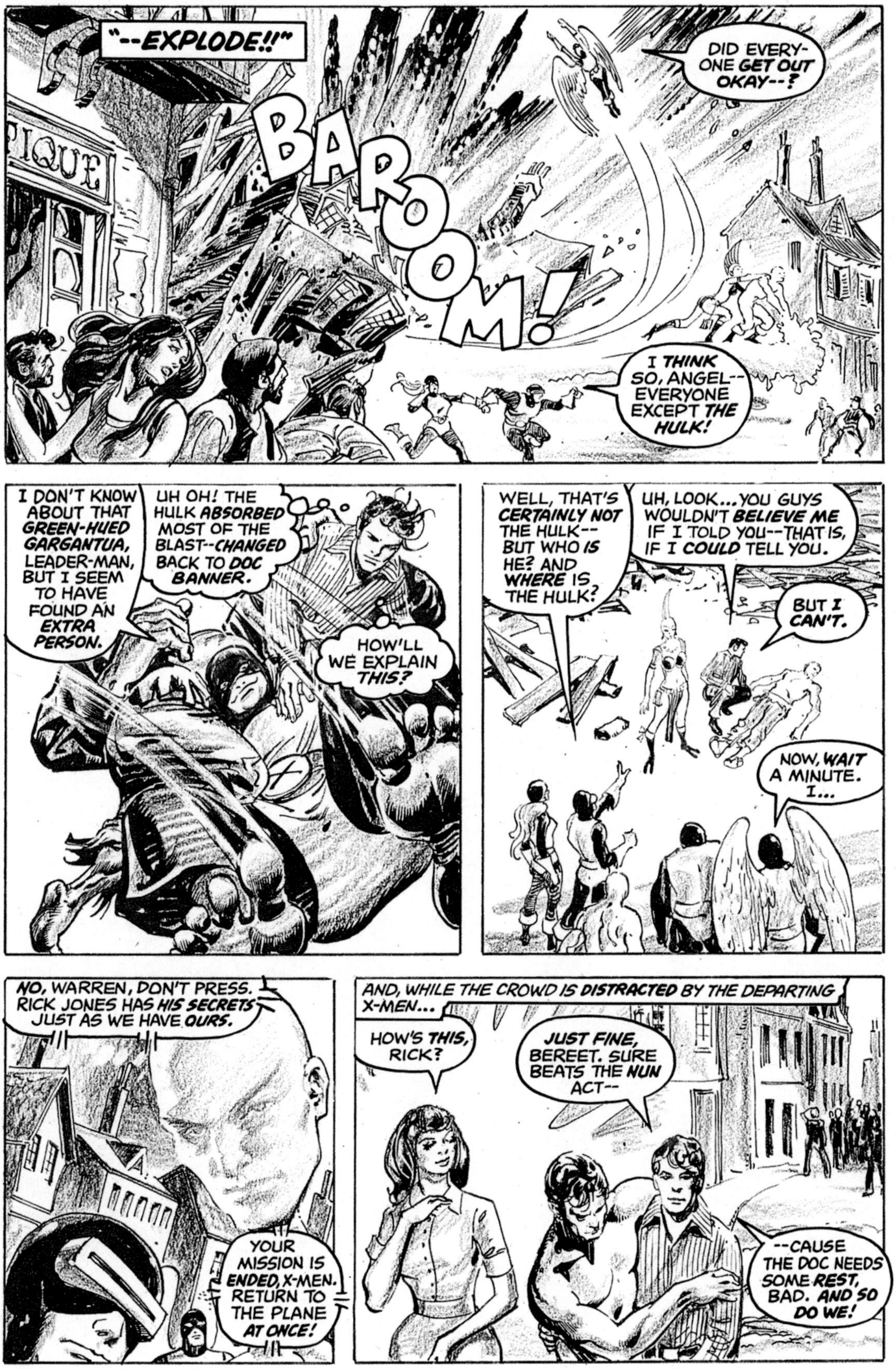
"--EXPLODE!!"
BAROOM!
DID EVERY-ONE GET OUT OKAY--?
I THINK SO, ANGEL-- EVERYONE EXCEPT THE HULK!
I DON'T KNOW ABOUT THAT GREEN-HUED GARGANTUA, LEADER-MAN, BUT I SEEM TO HAVE FOUND AN EXTRA PERSON.
UH OH! THE HULK ABSORBED MOST OF THE BLAST--CHANGED BACK TO DOC BANNER.
HOW'LL WE EXPLAIN THIS?
WELL, THAT'S CERTAINLY NOT THE HULK-- BUT WHO IS HE? AND WHERE IS THE HULK?
UH, LOOK... YOU GUYS WOULDN'T BELIEVE ME IF I TOLD YOU--THAT IS, IF I COULD TELL YOU.
BUT I CAN'T.
NOW, WAIT A MINUTE. I...
NO, WARREN, DON'T PRESS. RICK JONES HAS HIS SECRETS JUST AS WE HAVE OURS.
YOUR MISSION IS ENDED, X-MEN. RETURN TO THE PLANE AT ONCE!
AND, WHILE THE CROWD IS DISTRACTED BY THE DEPARTING X-MEN...
HOW'S THIS, RICK?
JUST FINE, BEREET. SURE BEATS THE NUN ACT--
--CAUSE THE DOC NEEDS SOME REST, BAD. AND SO DO WE!

X-MEN X-POSÉ

By Ralph Macchio

"THE STRANGEST SUPER-HEROES OF ALL!" That's how they were billed over the logo "X-MEN," on the cover of their first issue (published midway through 1963) lo those thirteen years ago. And that singular pronouncement introduced a team of radically different super-doers, both in terms of personalities and powers. And that's no hype.

After all, when was the last time you heard of a bunch of characters who'd banded together as much for their *own* protection as for the purposes of saving the world. Whereas the Avengers and the Fantastic Four were (for the most part) adored by the general public and given special clearances with Uncle Sam, the X-Men were at the bottom of the super-group totem pole. In fact, Professor Xavier had to report

to an agent of the F.B.I. every few months to placate the government's uneasiness over mutants. What's worse, the X-Men were not only shunned by an uncomprehending humanity, they were actively hunted and pursued by members of their own mutant ilk. That's right, Magneto and his Brotherhood of Evil Mutants. Let's face it, the life of Riley it wasn't for these poor guys. Professor X (as he's affectionately known) had chosen a formidable task for himself and his new charges at his "School for Gifted Youngsters" in Westchester County, New York. When the F.F. or the Avengers battled for the fate of humanity, trumpets of triumph blared at their illustrious return. But the X-Men were lucky they weren't skinned alive just for venturing beyond the grounds of their spacious sanctuary. And all this be-

lievers, all this because they'd committed the unpardonable sin of being different. Different.

But, before we delve any further into our fascinating little subject, what say we take a bit of a breather and lay a little of the vital statistics about our sextet of super-stars on you. And awaaaaay we go:

Professor Xavier: The prof. is a mutant whose powers reside in the area of mental phenomena. In terms of simple intellect, he's unrivalled in all the world. As he was growing up, Xavier began to experience the first stirrings of his evolving powers. He began to anticipate events in advance and the reading of his teachers' minds became commonplace. Although an accident had

placed him in a wheelchair for life, he was still able to send out his consciousness in the form of an invisible thought-projection completely around the world. It was while noting the growing fear humanity had developed towards mutants in the early sixties that Professor Xavier decided to come forth from his secluded mansion and form a group which in the long-run would act in the best interest of mankind as a whole. That group came to be known as the X-Men.

Cyclops (Scott Summers): the first mutant to join the professor's new team. Orphan Scott was being used as a pawn by an evil mutant to gain wealth, until Xavier, searching out mutants, entered the picture. He and the professor defeat the menace and Xavier asks Scott to become the first of those he will ask to begin a new era for mutant-kind. With little trepidation, Scott accepts.

Powers: Cyclops' force beam can be used in varying degrees to repel objects or, at a higher intensity, to blast them apart. His eyes act as solar batteries which absorb energy from the sun and release it in the form of deadly rays of destruction. The only known substance able to contain this energy is ruby quartz, from which Cyclops' visor and non-costume glasses are made.

Iceman *(Bobby Drake): The second individual to join the team. Bobby is from a small town in Nassau County (Long Island). Arrested for displaying his snow creating powers, he was freed from jail by Cyclops (whom he then battles, briefly) and finally joins up with Professor X.*

Powers: Bobby's body chemistry allows him to concentrate and freeze moisture around him with mental commands, thus permitting him to form a variety of frosty objects, such as ladders, ice slides, etc.– not to mention the ability to send sheets of ice or snow streaming from his body. Depending on the degree of concentration, Bobby can turn atmospheric moisture in his immediate vicinity into either snow or ice.

Beast *(Hank McCoy): The Beast's father was a worker in an atomic energy plant where, during an emergency, he was exposed to harmful radioactivity. Later, when Hank was born, it was learned he'd been affected by his father's exposure. At an early age he developed enlarged hand and foot extremities as well as a loping ape-like stature.*

Powers: The Beast (today more true to his namesake than he was in the sixties) has developed much of the coordination and dexterity of the most agile of anthropoids. His feet function as adroitly as an extra pair of hands and his physical strength is well above that of a normal man's.

Angel *(Warren Worthington III): While attending private school in his mid-teens,*

(Continued on page 62)

BAMF

R.I.P.
NDERBIRD

DAVE COCKRUM '76

(Continued from page 41)

Warren was shocked to notice wings sprouting from his shoulder blades over a period of weeks. When the wings had further developed he became the Avenging Angel for a short period of time. He was the only X-Man to have had a costume and heroic identity before joining the group. Warren was the most truculent of those asked to join the team and was rather hard to convince. Eventually, he relented and accepted the offer, though he maintained a highly individualistic attitude through the years.

Powers: The Angel has practiced for years at complex aerial maneuvers which make him among the most elusive of adversaries. When not in use, he keeps his feathery protrusions strapped to his back with the use of a specially designed harness.

Marvel Girl *(Jean Grey):* We know little of Jean's background, though she came to join the team in the first issue. Despite her being the only female member of the X-Men, she worked in admirably, leaving no doubt that she intended to be treated as an equal.

Powers: Jean possesses the power of telekinesis, the ability to move objects with mental commands alone. In addition to this ability, she is telepathic even over vast distances and this power has more than once saved the X-Men's hides. She is also able to mentally invade another's mind and temporarily take control of it, forcing unconsciousness on the victim.

And now back to our regularly scheduled article. The X-Men shared a closeness, a warm camaraderie which did not exist, in fact, could not exist in any other group. In-fighting was kept to a minimum as these carriers of genetically induced traits which had made them rejects, concentrated on developing their powers to the fullest. And they had to. Hooo0 boy, did they ever. Misguided and often dangerous persecution came from all directions. Magneto, the ultimate mutant-villain, believed he was acting out the will of destiny, through the formation of a group of mutants (the aforementioned Brotherhood of Evil Mutants) whose task it was to insure that "homo-superior" eventually ruled the world. Of course, our ever-anxious-for-punishment X-Men were committed by principle to oppose such shenanigans and they frequently got their lumps battling this architect of evil and his crummy cohorts. As any X-Man fan worth his wings will tell you, the battle between these two groups have been among the most memorable in both their careers. Unfortunately, Magneto's autocratic promulgations were hardly good press for our much maligned mutants; and so even in defeat, Magneto had eroded the sought after goal of trust between man and mutant.

Others were quick to lump all mutants together. One such man was Bolivar Trask and later his son Larry (himself an unsuspected mutant) who created a veritable army of enormous "Sentinels" (your standard, giant-size, bilaterally symmetrical automations) to capture the X-Men and any other mutants they happen to run across for the "good of humanity." Still, through it all, that spirit of friendship and love permeated the lives of the X-Men, who came to accept the condition into which fate had thrown them. And in the best tradition of "chin up" they held as a team and prospered as a magazine title. As with so many of the early Marvel creations, readers could feel a depth of sympathy and compassion for these starcrossed freaks. And they came to realize that the acquisition of super-powers was not always a blessing in disguise.

Now that we know a bit about our ebullient X-Men, the mind must inevitably wander onto the subject of the men who created these costumed cavorters and the boundless fields of imagination from which the X-Men were culled. To discover it, one need only look in the direction of messers. Stan Lee and Jack Kirby, the creative combo that has made a habit out of translating ideas into overnight commercial successes. It seems that Stan had been searching for a new approach to the manner in which characters are given their distinguishing super powers. The answer to gamma ray bombardment and radioactive spiders was to have heroes (and villains, natch) *born* with their exceptional abilities. Not only did the concept of genetic mutations allow for maximum latitude in the sculpting of new characters (because the possible variations on human development are virtually limitless) it was also scientifically sound. At this point, Stan and Jack introduced a concept and a number of members for this potential group of mutants. But what does one call a group of mutants? Well, "The Mutants" seems an obvious choice and *was* actually considered at the time, though for a variety of reasons it was rejected. There had to be something with more life, more mystery, more pizzazz. There was. Mutants have something exceptional about them, something · extraordinary, some extreme characteristic. Hmmmm, there seem to be a lot of "x's" in there for some reason. The next step was to take their x-factor and turn it into the title of the mag. The name fit like a glove: the X-Men.

Professor Xavièr was (and still is) the leader of our Merry Marvel Misfits. During their period of tutelage under him, the original X-Men spent much time learning the ropes of the evil-battling biz in their designated "Danger Room" (and if you don't know what that is, take a peek at the indescribable double-page spread Wondrous Walt and Ambitious Alfredo have drawn for your pleasurable edification elsewhere in this issue. End of interpolation.) By issue #7, the professor apparently felt his new team had passed through its initial baptism of fire and he graduated them with x-honors. This hardly signalled the end of their development as super-powered beings, as each in his or her own way continued to hone their talents to a razor's edge. For example, in issue #8, Iceman had developed the ability to turn his somewhat snowy body into hard ice crystals, which represented a major step forward in the control of his abilities. And the same was true for each of the X-Men. The Beast became ever more dexterous with his pedal extremities while Cyclops developed greater command of the terrible forces he could unleash. And so it went. In issue #39, the X-Men were given more distinctive costumes, which were designed to highlight the fact that each of them was an individual and not strictly a group fixture.

With issue #42, the first really major change overtook the lives of the X-Men. Up until then, there had been little if any changes made in the membership or individual status of any one X-Man. But the mind-wrenching events of that issue (#42) were to change their lives directly and tragically. While battling the sub-human being known as Grotesk, Professor Xavier was caught in a massive explosion and killed. Suddenly, the lives of these young teenagers were thrown into a grief-stricken tumult. Although Cyclops (deputy leader) desperately attempted to keep the team together, the purpose for the X-Men's existence seemed to have died with Professor X. Thus, in issue #46, after defeating one of their deadliest foes, the Juggernaut, the X-Men split up. Iceman and the Beast went off together to California, Cyclops and Marvel Girl left for the wilds of Manhattan and the Angel went off on his own as a roving agent. This lasted for several issues until the newly awakened horror of Magneto reunited the splintered team as of issue #49. Aside from bringing the X-Men back as a group, this new struggle with Magneto introduced a new character who was to play a major role in their lives in the coming months. Her name was Lorna Dane and she was allegedly the deadly daughter of Magneto. Her own mastery of magnetism seemed to bear this out, but later it was learned she was merely another mutant, one that Magneto had brainwashed into believing was his daughter to further his devilish ends.

Now the extraordinary X-Men were back together as a team and things began to move into high gear. In issue #54, Alex Summers, brother of the tragic Cyclops made the scene; and in future issues it was revealed that he too was a mutant. And Alex had an even more deadly power than his power-beaming-sibling. Alex had been born with the awesome ability to channel the cosmic rays which traverse the universe through his body and outward in concentrated blasts of explosive fury. Later he was given a costume to help focus these incredible forces. And Alex Summers became the man called Havoc. Nifty name, no? Although not a true member of the group, Alex remained for quite a spell before splitting for the southwestern part of the country to ponder the powers given him.

With the addition of Lorna Dane and Havoc, the X-Men proceeded to have return engagements with both Magneto and the Sentinels before being subjected to an extraordinary shock in issue #65. That wholly

(Continued on page 64)

(*Continued from page* 62)

unexpected shock was none other than the reappearance of the supposedly dead Professor Xavier. It seems that the good prof. had brought in a look-alike replacement called the Changling to take his place, while he worked in a sub-basement of the Westchester mansion, trying to prepare for an interplanetary invasion his exceptional senses had made him aware of. Needless to say, the death of Professor X's doppleganger was wholly unexpected, though even this could not force him from the concentrated seclusion he had enwrapped himself in. But enough of the bad news. The X-Men were a full family once again, though their grateful audience had little time to revel in their good fortune. As of the next issue of X-MEN, #66, the magazine was discontinued (January of 1970).

But weep not for our tenacious playmates. In the world of Munificent Marvel, even when a character or group has had his/their title axed, life for them still goes on. The X-Men were no exception. The first to be granted a new lease on publication life was Hank McCoy, the blushing Beast, whose oversized extremities and voluminous vocabulary had made him a popular member of the team. Hank left the X-Men to seek employment as a genetics researcher with the Brand Corporation. (These events are chronicled in AMAZING ADVENTURES #11 through #17). Hank discovers a serum which he believes holds the key to the nature of genetic mutation. He foolishly takes a bit of the serum which reacts on his mutant genes and transforms him into a literal Beast, complete with the obligatory fur and fangs. Cute he wasn't. Although the change was supposed to have been temporary, the flying fickle finger of fate had thrown yet another curve to this encyclopedic lad. The change was *permanent*. And along with his new physical appearance, Hank dropped his tendency towards circumlocution and became a truly absurd wisecrack specialist, able to trade quips with the best of them. Soon after the suspension of the Beast's series, he went into a short, self-imposed exile, until he'd heard the Avengers were looking for new members. Apparently super-doing with a group is infectuous, because Hank signed up immediately in AVENGERS #137 and has been with the Assemblers ever since.

While Hank McCoy had gone to seek his fame and fortune alone, the rest of the X-Men were anything but idle. They played peripheral roles in a few issues of the AVENGERS and also became intertwined with the Secret Empire plotline in CAPTAIN AMERICA. And then they returned to apparent seclusion in Westchester.

That was in 1974.

A bit more than half a year passed, during which Marvel reprinted some of the X-Men's earlier forays (numbering the issues consecutively from #67 onward, for you footnote fetishists). Mail reaction was good and so were sales. Not being ones to sit on their laurels, Marvel's many minions set about plans to return the merry mutants in

all-new adventures under the old familiar title. But there was one catch. In addition to all-new storylines, the characters would be all-new as well. Doubtless a number of old X-Men fans stifled a heartfelt groan when they learned of these pandemonious developments, but most took little time in finding themselves endeared to the *new* line-up of X-People.

Break time. Relax for a moment while we pause from the preceding paragraphs of deathless commentary and once again, list the ladies and gents who fill the ranks of X-Men members. Only now it's 1975, folks.

Nightcrawler *(Curt Wagner): He was the first mutant to be sought out by Professor X. Curt was a circus side-show freak in Germany who quit the carnival life only to be hounded by the rest of mankind. He was about to have a stake driven through his heart by an angry mob when the professor appeared and thus it took little persuasion to convince him to join.*

Powers: Nightcrawler possesses several insect attributes including the ability to scale walls and the like. Aside from great speed, agility and strength, Nightcrawler has the unique talent of being able to instantly teleport himself to a desired location (even through walls) by attuning his body to the magnetic flow lines which cross the Earth.

Wolverine *(Logan): He was originally a "living weapon" utilized by the Canadian Government to battle the Hulk (HULK #181) and was since enlisted by the professor over the protest of the Canadians to help in forming the new team.*

Powers: Wolverine possesses a ferocious killer instinct, which coupled with his agility and adamantium claws that retract right into his wrist make him a formidable foe. He unquestionably lives up to his deadly namesake.

Storm *(Ororo): She was considered a goddess by those who worshipped her in her African home, though she gave up godhood to serve her fellow mutants and has since become a member of the X-Men.*

Powers: Storm's powers stem from her innate ability to control those turbulent conditions we call weather. At her most awesome, Storm can actually focus the entire force of a raging hurricane over a small area of some few city blocks.

Sunfire *(Shiro Yoshida): He was a young, Japanese nationalist, who allowed a misguided fervor to bring him to conflict with the X-Men in issue #64. However, fences were temporarily mended and he joined the new X-Men in their search for the old. After the initial adventure, he left the group.*

Powers: Sunfire, as his name implies has the ability to fire concentrated bursts of sunlight from his body in rays of great power. He also

is able to fly.

Colossus *(Peter Rasputin): Was a manual laborer on one of Russia's many farm collectives until he was summoned by Professor X to serve a greater cause than the state.*

Powers: Colossus is the brute power backbone of the new X-Men. Although under normal circumstances he appears entirely human, once he is excited his bodily structure changes to a steel-like substance which is also impenetrable. Accompanying the bodily change is a drastic increase in strength.

Thunderbird *(John Proudstar): He was an embittered American Indian whose mutant powers seemed to matter little to him in the face of his people's despair. After much persuasion, he was convinced of the necessity of joining the new X-Men. Tragically, after but the briefest of stays, he was killed in X-Men #95.*

Powers: Thunderbird had the twin abilities of prodigious strength and awesome speed, as well as a mind sharpened from years of hunting on the prairies.

Banshee *(Sean Cassidy): He was originally a powerful foe of the X-Men who first appeared in issue #28. Despite his animosity towards the X-Men he was persuaded by Professor X to tread the straight and narrow path for a change. He has apparently liked being a member of the team, for he remains a valued component of the X-Men.*

Powers: The Banshee can emit sonic vibrations of varying frequencies due to his mutant molecules. They can be directed at objects with the possible destruction of them depending on the frequency level. The Banshee is also able to vibrate his own body at incredible speeds allowing him to fly.

Quite a fascinating bunch of stalwarts wouldn't you say? Well Marvel thought enough of them to make their premiere appearance a giant-sized special, featuring some 36 new pages of story and art, detailing the transition from old to new. And a brief summary of that pivotal pilot seems in order at this moment.

It seems that most of the X-MEN except for Scott Summers had been captured (or worse) on a mission to a strange island. Cyclops and the professor scour the globe for new mutants to help in the search for the missing X-Men. One by one, from every corner of the globe they were chosen for this mission and once it had been completed and the original X-Men had been rescued, unhurt — we had thirteen mutants on hand altogether. Sheesh, it was getting so bad, even Professor Xavier needed a program to tell the players apart. Things didn't remain like that for long. No way. With the second issue of the all-new X-Men, (which adapted to the more conventional sized comic of today and began the numbering with #94) Sunfire left, as did Havoc, Lorna Dane.

Angel, Iceman, and Marvel Girl. And then in #95, tragedy struck this now truly international brotherhood of mutants: Thunderbird was killed. And that, long-suffering ones, is where their membership roster stands now. With one small addition. Jean Grey, who you all remember as Marvel Girl, has just recently undergone a massive transformation into the woman known only as Phoenix. (For more info on her and the other new X-Men, you'll just have to pick up current issues of X-MEN. End of hard sell.) But wait, don't grab your hat yet. It's a well-known axiom that births and deaths precipitate *other* births and deaths. Case in point: the ex-X-Men, Iceman and Angel, for whom things have begun all over again with the formation of a new super-group: The Champions.

After leaving the X-Men roughly a year ago, Bobby Drake and Warren Worthington relocated to the West Coast, where for a short time they attended U.C.L.A. Soon after their arrival, a war of the gods erupted with the focal point being right on campus. And when something like that happens, you can bet the protests of the sixties look like fizzled out firecrackers by comparison. Not being fellows to miss out on action, Bobby and Warren quickly ditched their civvies and went into costume. Others, who were on the campus at the same time were drawn into the conflict — notably, Ghost Rider, Hercules, and the Black Widow. When the war had finally been concluded, the above mentioned crew of supposedly dissimilar doers of derring-do discovered themselves strangely linked as individuals and decided to make a go of it as a team. The Angel, who luckily enough comes from a rather wealthy family, is even now using the considerable fiscal resources (which are his by inheritance) to make the Champs into more than a simple crime fighting group. And step one began with the formal organization of this unlikely menagerie which has been covered in recent issues of THE CHAMPIONS. And what may lie ahead for them neither mortal nor demi-god may surmise.

Well, as is very obvious from the preceding pages, the winds of change have blown stiffly through the lives of the X-Men, regardless of *who* fought under that mysterious banner. There've been good times mixed with bad, the victories simmering with the defeats. And behind all those flashy costumes, startling super-powers, and the ever present lure of adventure, lies the gnawing specter of alienation and loneliness. But take heart. Although no supergroup in all of comics has ever had to contend with the unique kind of burdens the X-Men have, they've had thirteen years worth of practice and show no signs of letting up now. In tribute to perhaps the most noble team effort the world has ever seen we say: All hail the X-Men, they shall overcome!

DAVE COCKRUM 76

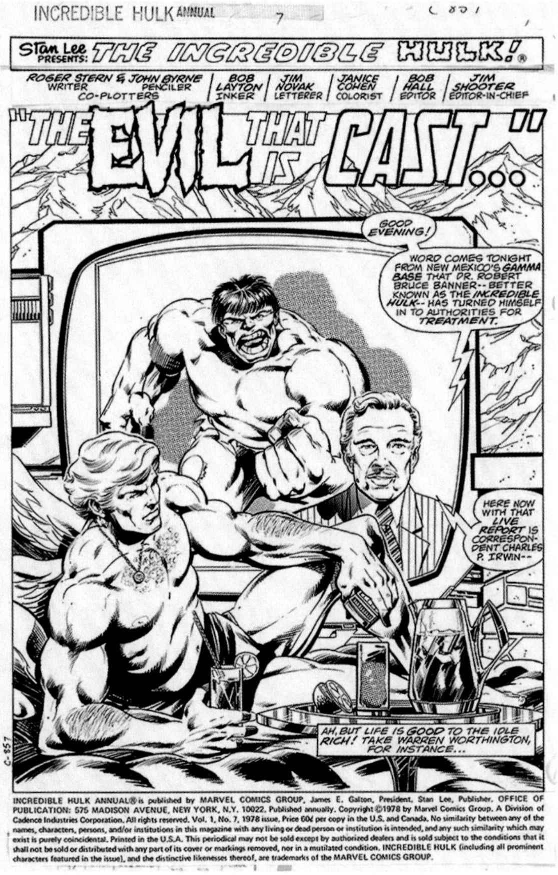
INCREDIBLE HULK ANNUAL 7
Stan Lee PRESENTS: THE INCREDIBLE HULK!®
ROGER STERN & JOHN BYRNE WRITER PENCILER CO-PLOTTERS
BOB LAYTON INKER
JIM NOVAK LETTERER
JANICE COHEN COLORIST
BOB HALL EDITOR
JIM SHOOTER EDITOR-IN-CHIEF
"THE EVIL THAT IS CAST..."
GOOD EVENING!
WORD COMES TONIGHT FROM NEW MEXICO'S GAMMA BASE THAT DR. ROBERT BRUCE BANNER-- BETTER KNOWN AS THE INCREDIBLE HULK-- HAS TURNED HIMSELF IN TO AUTHORITIES FOR TREATMENT.
HERE NOW WITH THAT LIVE REPORT IS CORRESPONDENT CHARLES P. IRWIN--
AH, BUT LIFE IS GOOD TO THE IDLE RICH! TAKE WARREN WORTHINGTON, FOR INSTANCE...
C-857
INCREDIBLE HULK ANNUAL® is published by MARVEL COMICS GROUP, James E. Galton, President, Stan Lee, Publisher. OFFICE OF PUBLICATION: 575 MADISON AVENUE, NEW YORK, N.Y. 10022. Published annually. Copyright ©1978 by Marvel Comics Group. A Division of Cadence Industries Corporation. All rights reserved. Vol. 1, No. 7, 1978 issue, Price 60¢ per copy in the U.S. and Canada. No similarity between any of the names, characters, persons, and/or institutions in this magazine with any living or dead person or institution is intended, and any such similarity which may exist is purely coincidental. Printed in the U.S.A. This periodical may not be sold except by authorized dealers and is sold subject to the conditions that it shall not be sold or distributed with any part of its cover or markings removed, nor in a mutilated condition. INCREDIBLE HULK (including all prominent characters featured in the issue), and the distinctive likenesses thereof, are trademarks of the MARVEL COMICS GROUP.

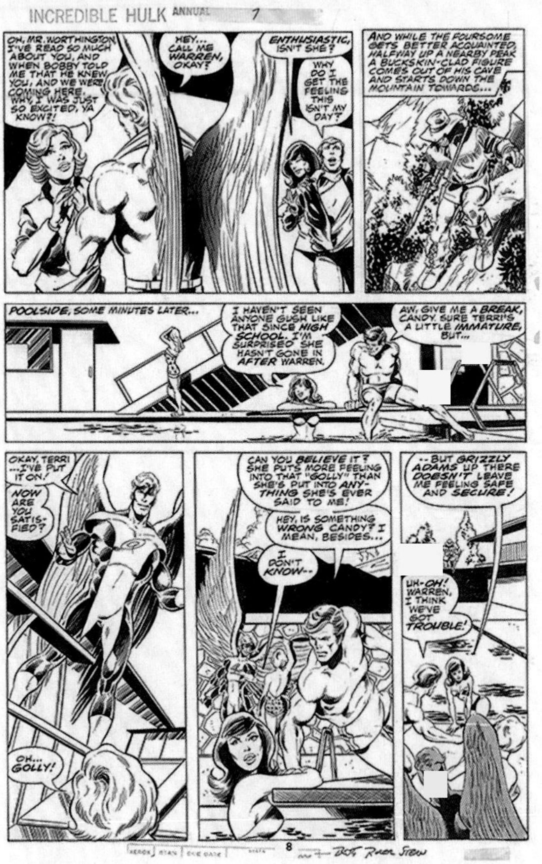
INCREDIBLE HULK ANNUAL 7
OH, MR. WORTHINGTON I'VE READ SO MUCH ABOUT YOU, AND WHEN BOBBY TOLD ME THAT HE KNEW YOU, AND WE WERE COMING HERE, WHY, I WAS JUST SO EXCITED, YA KNOW?!
HEY... CALL ME WARREN, OKAY?
ENTHUSIASTIC, ISN'T SHE?
WHY DO I GET THE FEELING THIS ISN'T MY DAY?
AND WHILE THE FOURSOME GETS BETTER ACQUAINTED, HALFWAY UP A NEARBY PEAK A BUCKSKIN-CLAD FIGURE COMES OUT OF HIS CAVE AND STARTS DOWN THE MOUNTAIN TOWARDS...
POOLSIDE, SOME MINUTES LATER...
I HAVEN'T SEEN ANYONE GUSH LIKE THAT SINCE HIGH SCHOOL. I'M SURPRISED SHE HASN'T GONE IN AFTER WARREN.
AW, GIVE ME A BREAK, CANDY. SURE TERRI'S A LITTLE IMMATURE, BUT...
OKAY, TERRI ...I'VE PUT IT ON!
NOW ARE YOU SATISFIED?
OH... GOLLY!
CAN YOU BELIEVE IT? SHE PUTS MORE FEELING INTO THAT "GOLLY" THAN SHE'S PUT INTO ANYTHING SHE'S EVER SAID TO ME!
HEY, IS SOMETHING WRONG CANDY? I MEAN, BESIDES...
I DON'T KNOW--
--BUT GRIZZLY ADAMS UP THERE DOESN'T LEAVE ME FEELING SAFE AND SECURE!
UH-OH! WARREN, I THINK WE'VE GOT TROUBLE!
8

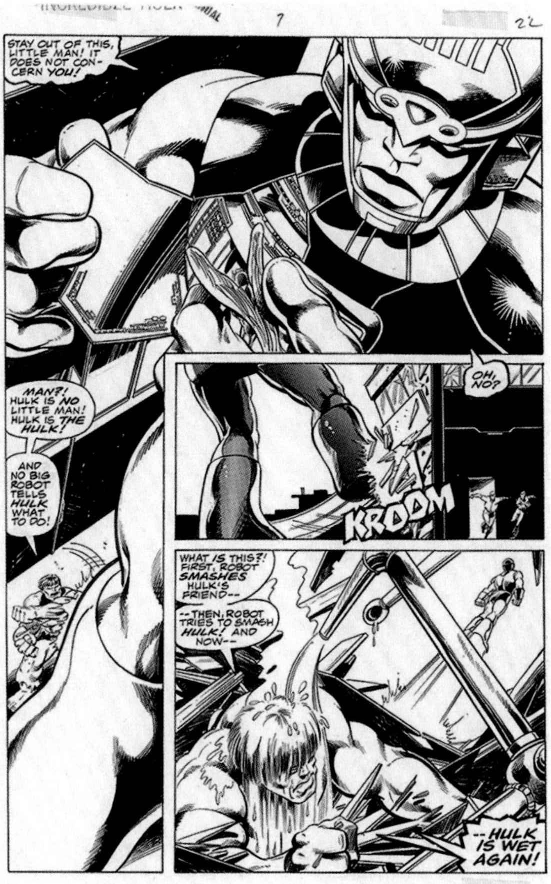
7
22
STAY OUT OF THIS, LITTLE MAN! IT DOES NOT CONCERN YOU!
MAN?! HULK IS NO LITTLE MAN! HULK IS THE HULK!
AND NO BIG ROBOT TELLS HULK WHAT TO DO!
OH, NO?
KROOM
WHAT IS THIS?! FIRST, ROBOT SMASHES HULK'S FRIEND--
--THEN, ROBOT TRIES TO SMASH HULK! AND NOW--
--HULK IS WET AGAIN!

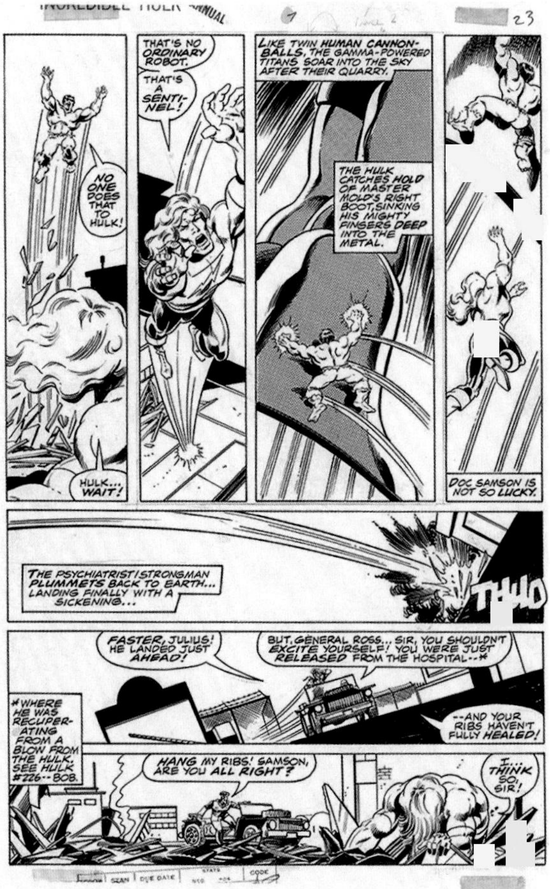
7
23
NO ONE DOES THAT TO HULK!
HULK... WAIT!
THAT'S NO ORDINARY ROBOT.
THAT'S A SENTINEL!
LIKE TWIN HUMAN CANNONBALLS, THE GAMMA-POWERED TITANS SOAR INTO THE SKY AFTER THEIR QUARRY.
THE HULK CATCHES HOLD OF MASTER MOLD'S RIGHT BOOT, SINKING HIS MIGHTY FINGERS DEEP INTO THE METAL.
DOC SAMSON IS NOT SO LUCKY.
THE PSYCHIATRIST/STRONGMAN PLUMMETS BACK TO EARTH... LANDING FINALLY WITH A SICKENING...
THUD
FASTER, JULIUS! HE LANDED JUST AHEAD!
BUT, GENERAL ROSS... SIR, YOU SHOULDN'T EXCITE YOURSELF! YOU WERE JUST RELEASED FROM THE HOSPITAL--*
*WHERE HE WAS RECUPERATING FROM A BLOW FROM THE HULK. SEE HULK #226--BOB.
--AND YOUR RIBS HAVEN'T FULLY HEALED!
HANG MY RIBS! SAMSON, ARE YOU ALL RIGHT?
I... THINK SO, SIR!

INCREDIBLE HULK ANNUAL #7, PAGES 1, 6, 16 & 17 ART BY JOHN BYRNE & BOB LAYTON

RAMPAGING HULK #2 ART BY WALTER SIMONSON & ALFREDO ALCALA

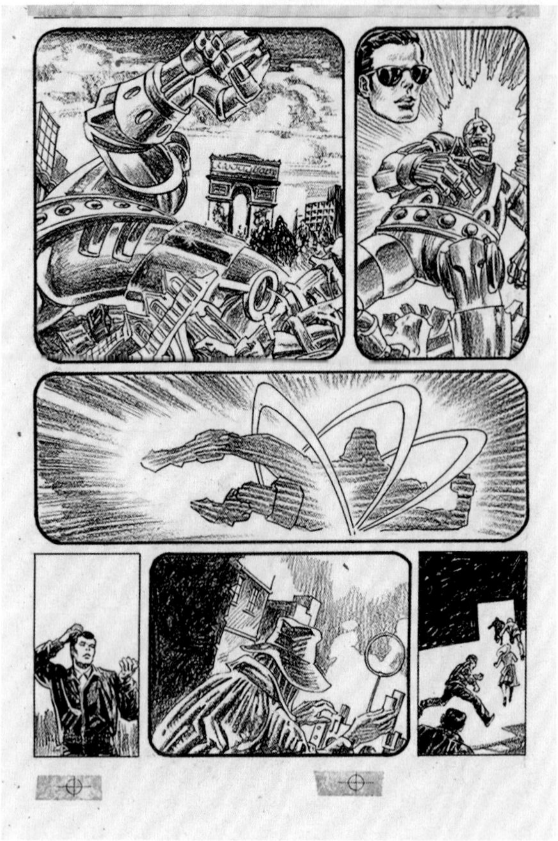

PAGE 13 ART

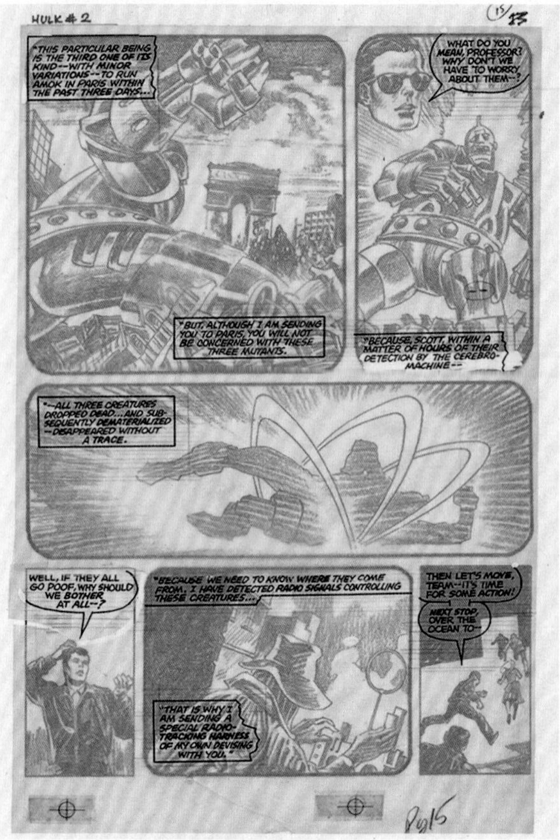
HULK #2
"THIS PARTICULAR BEING IS THE THIRD ONE OF ITS KIND--WITH MINOR VARIATIONS--TO RUN AMOK IN PARIS WITHIN THE PAST THREE DAYS...
WHAT DO YOU MEAN, PROFESSOR? WHY DON'T WE HAVE TO WORRY ABOUT THEM--?
"BUT, ALTHOUGH I AM SENDING YOU TO PARIS, YOU WILL NOT BE CONCERNED WITH THESE THREE MUTANTS.
"BECAUSE, SCOTT, WITHIN A MATTER OF HOURS OF THEIR DETECTION BY THE CEREBRO-MACHINE--
"--ALL THREE CREATURES DROPPED DEAD... AND SUBSEQUENTLY DEMATERIALIZED --DISAPPEARED WITHOUT A TRACE.
WELL, IF THEY ALL GO POOF, WHY SHOULD WE BOTHER AT ALL--?
"BECAUSE WE NEED TO KNOW WHERE THEY COME FROM. I HAVE DETECTED RADIO SIGNALS CONTROLLING THESE CREATURES...
"THAT IS WHY I AM SENDING A SPECIAL RADIO-TRACKING HARNESS OF MY OWN DEVISING WITH YOU."
THEN LET'S MOVE, TEAM--IT'S TIME FOR SOME ACTION!
NEXT STOP, OVER THE OCEAN TO--
Pg15

PAGE 13 WITH LETTERING OVERLAY

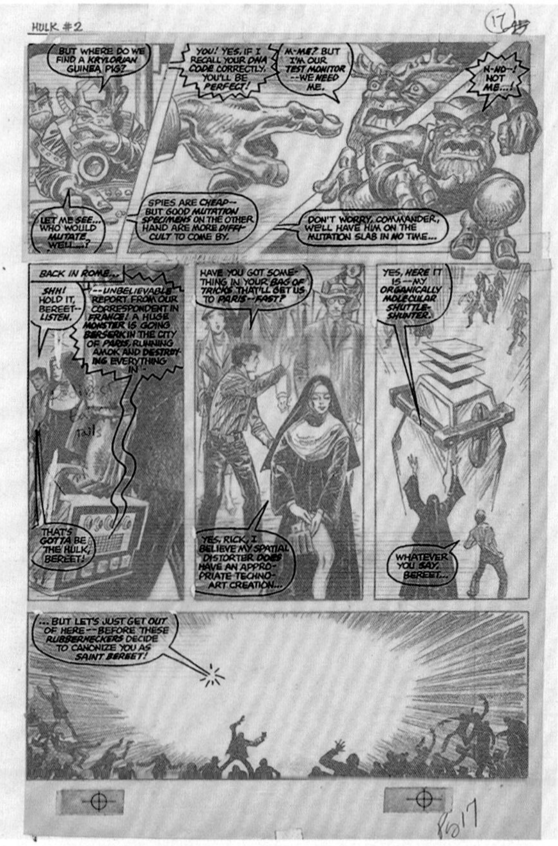
HULK #2
BUT WHERE DO WE FIND A KRYLORIAN GUINEA PIG?
YOU! YES, IF I RECALL YOUR DNA CODE CORRECTLY, YOU'LL BE PERFECT!
M-ME? BUT I'M OUR TEST MONITOR --WE NEED ME.
N-NO--! NOT ME...!
LET ME SEE... WHO WOULD MUTATE WELL...?
SPIES ARE CHEAP-- BUT GOOD MUTATION SPECIMENS ON THE OTHER HAND ARE MORE DIFFICULT TO COME BY.
DON'T WORRY, COMMANDER, WE'LL HAVE HIM ON THE MUTATION SLAB IN NO TIME...
BACK IN ROME...
SHH! HOLD IT, BEREET-- LISTEN.
--UNBELIEVABLE REPORT FROM OUR CORRESPONDENT IN FRANCE! A HUGE MONSTER IS GOING BERSERK IN THE CITY OF PARIS, RUNNING AMOK AND DESTROYING EVERYTHING IN--
THAT'S GOTTA BE THE HULK, BEREET!
HAVE YOU GOT SOMETHING IN YOUR BAG OF TRICKS THAT'LL GET US TO PARIS--FAST?
YES, RICK, I BELIEVE MY SPATIAL DISTORTER DOES HAVE AN APPROPRIATE TECHNO-ART CREATION...
YES, HERE IT IS--MY ORGANICALLY MOLECULAR SHUTTLE-SHUNTER.
WHATEVER YOU SAY, BEREET...
...BUT LET'S JUST GET OUT OF HERE--BEFORE THESE RUBBERNECKERS DECIDE TO CANONIZE YOU AS SAINT BEREET!

PAGE 15 WITH LETTERING OVERLAY